Words in Time

THE LANGUAGE LIBRARY

EDITED BY DAVID CRYSTAL

The Articulate Computer	*Michael McTear*
The Artificial Language Movement	*Andrew Large*
Australian Aboriginal Languages	*Colin Yallop*
Children's Writing and Reading	*Katharine Perera*
A Child's Learning of English	*Paul Fletcher*
A Companion to Old and Middle English Studies	*A. C. Partridge*
A Dictionary of Literary Terms (revised)	*J. A. Cuddon*
Early English (revised)	*J. W. Clark*
Early Modern English	*Charles Barber*
English Dialects (revised)	*G. L. Brook*
A Dictionary of Linguistics and Phonetics (second edition)	*David Crystal*
The Foreign-Language Barrier	*J. A. Large*
A History of the English Language	*G. L. Brook*
A History of Foreign-Language Dictionaries	*R. L. Collison*
How Conversation Works	*Ronald Wardhaugh*
An Informal History of the German Language	*W. B. Lockwood*
John Donne: Language and Style	*A. C. Partridge*
Language and Class in Victorian England	*K. C. Phillipps*
The Language of 1984	*W. F. Bolton*
The Language of Walter Scott	*Graham Tulloch*
Language, Society and Identity	*John Edwards*
Languages of the British Isles: Past and Present	*W. B. Lockwood*
Languages in Competition	*Ronald Wardhaugh*
Modern Englishes: Pidgins and Creoles	*Loreto Todd*
Non-standard Language in English Literature	*N. F. Blake*
Puns	*Walter Redfern*
Scientific and Technical Translation	*Isadore Pinchuck*
Sense and Sense Development (revised)	*R. A. Waldron*
Speaking of Chinese	*R. Chang & M. Scrogin Chang*
The Study of Dialect	*K. M. Petyt*
A Survey of Structural Linguistics	*G. L. Lepschy*
Thomas Hardy's English	*Ralph W. V. Elliott*
The Treatment of Sounds in Language and Literature	*Raymond Chapman*

WORDS IN TIME

A Social History of the English Vocabulary

Geoffrey Hughes

Basil Blackwell

First published 1988
Reprinted 1988

Basil Blackwell Ltd
108 Cowley Road, Oxford OX4 1JF, UK

Basil Blackwell Inc.
432 Park Avenue South, Suite 1503
New York, NY 10016, USA

British Library Cataloguing in Publication Data
Hughes, Geoffrey
Words in time: a social history of the English vocabulary – (Language library).
1. English language – Etymology
I. Title II. Series
422 PE1574
ISBN 0-631-15832-4

Library of Congress Cataloging in Publication Data
Hughes, Geoffrey, 1939 –
Words in time.
Bibliography:p.
Includes index.
1. English language – Lexicology. 2. English language – Etymology. 3. English language – Social aspects. 4. English language – History. I. Title.
PE1571.H84 1988 423'.028 87-35784
ISBN 0-631-15832-4

Typeset in 10½ on 12½pt Ehrhardt
by Joshua Associates Limited, Oxford
Printed in Great Britain by
TJ Press, Padstow

Contents

To
all workers
at the alveary

Preface

DR JOHNSON complained that when he undertook the first survey for his monumental dictionary, he found the language 'copious without order and energetick without rules'. Would he perhaps now find it 'copious without order and flaccid without rules'? It is, assuredly, the perennial condition of effervescence and decay, of growth and confusion, which provides the motive for any book on the English language. Semantic change over the past millenium is not a small field. In some cases it is so randomly peculiar that it resembles a protracted game of consequences. In others, which form the ambit of this study, words have shifted their meanings in concert with societal changes so that they become the silent witnesses and chronicles of those altered states.

In exploring this fertile field I have been fortunate in having the support and encouragement of various institutions and scholars. I am, accordingly, pleased to record my gratitude to the President and Fellows of Harvard College for the opportunity of being a Research Associate in the Department of English for the academic year 1974–5; to the Human Sciences Research Council, the Hamilton Bequest and the Anderson-Capelli Fund for their respective grants; to the late Professor Morton Bloomfield for his scholarly encouragement and mentorship, especially while I was at Harvard; to Professor Ridley Beeton for his support and patient supervision of a lengthy doctoral thesis, portions of which the University of South Africa has kindly allowed me to use in this study; and to Dr Robert Burchfield for his genial co-operation in allowing me access to the files of the *OED Supplement* during the winters of 1978 and 1983.

The brunt of the typing was cheerfully borne by Amanda Daly and Margaret Knee. This made both the 'weariness of copying' and 'the vexation of expunging' a great deal simpler. The punctilious editing of Veronica Ions improved the typescript enormously, and Sue Vice of Blackwell indefatigably incorporated gobbets of 'final' supplementary material with generous stoicism.

G.H.

Pineslopes, Transvaal

Acknowledgements

THE author and publishers are grateful to the following for permission to reproduce previously published material: Marion Boyars Publishers Ltd for excerpts from Paul Hoch, *The Newspaper Game*; Sage Publications Inc. for excerpts from Colin Seymour-Ure, *The Political Impact of Mass Media*; the *Mail on Sunday* London for the front page of the *Mail on Sunday*, the Mirror Group, London for the front page of *The People*; *News of the World*, *Today*, and *Sunday Telegraph* all for their front pages 1 March 1987; Harcourt Brace Jovanovich Inc. for excerpts from George Orwell, 'Politics and the English Language', in *Shooting an Elephant and Other Essays*, copyright © 1946, 1974 Sonia Orwell; George Steiner for excerpts from *The Death of Tragedy*, copyright © George Steiner 1961.

Sources and Abbreviations

THIS study is, of necessity, heavily dependent on the master-work on semantic change in English, the *Oxford English Dictionary* (*OED*). For economy of reference, a raised 'O' is used (e.g. 1934°) to refer to the main *Dictionary* (1883–1928), which was the collaboration of Murray (pre-eminently), Bradley, Craigie, Onions and Furnivall, 'with the assistance of many scholars and men of science'. A raised 'S' refers to the *OED Supplement* (1972–86), produced by Dr Robert Burchfield and his research team at Oxford. The fourth and last volume, published in 1986, completes what is clearly a worthy sequel to its predecessor, so aptly described by Otto Jespersen as 'that splendid monument of English scholarship'. This acknowledgement of logophiliac dependence is in no way intended to implicate any Oxford lexicographer in the inferences and conclusions which follow.

Other abbreviations used are:

OE	Old English
A-S	Anglo-Saxon
ME	Middle English
Mn.E	Modern English
ON	Old Norse
OF	Old French
EETS	*Early English Text Society*
THES	*Times Higher Education Supplement*
COD	*Concise Oxford Dictionary*
ODQ	*Oxford Dictionary of Quotations*

I

Introduction: Words and Social Change

> . . . until a few years ago – within the memory of men still living – very little use had been made of language itself, that is to say, of the historical forms and meanings of words as interpreters both of the past and of the workings of men's minds. It has only just begun to dawn on us that in our own language alone, not to speak of its many companions, the past history of humanity is spread out in an imperishable map, just as the history of the mineral earth lies embedded in the layers of its outer crust. But there is this difference between the record of the rocks and the secrets which are hidden in language: whereas the former can only give us a knowledge of outward, dead things – such as forgotten seas and bodily shapes of prehistoric animals and primitive men – language has preserved for us the inner, living history of man's soul. It reveals the evolution of consciousness.
>
> Owen Barfield

> History, in the human sense, is a language net cast backwards.
>
> George Steiner

LANGUAGE is one of the primary defining qualities of man, both individually and collectively. It surrounds us, moulding our ways of thinking and feeling, from the infant's cry to the obituary notice. People deprived of language in some way, be they deaf, dumb, illiterate or inarticulate, are essentially handicapped. All kinds of social control, all manner of manipulation, from the 'hypnotic mendacities of the mass media' – as George Steiner has memorably called them (1969, p. 261) – to the most potent subliminal propaganda, are achieved through it. People who are normally shrewd will be persuaded by banal advertising copy; those who are normally politically inert or pacifist can be mobilized to die for a slogan. The vehemence of people's attachment to their language is very apparent in contemporary Belgium, while the violent rejection of

Afrikaans as the language of oppression was made manifest by the schoolchildren of Soweto in 1976.

In all cultures the pre-eminently articulate use of language is praised and honoured. Poets, traditionally the guardians and exhibitors of the word-hoard in its most highly charged form, are invested (even today) with a certain mystique. In 'primitive' societies, those in high office employ praise poets, while their equivalents in allegedly more advanced societies employ speech-writers to put on a style which is befitting the leader's status. In virtually all cultures there is a profound desire to conform to established linguistic usage, and concern over the abuse of language. It is probably not an overstatement to say that in the West the dictionary is consulted more than the Bible or equivalent sacred text.

In this century we live, not simply amidst change, but in the expectation of change. Perhaps, realizing this expectation mentally, we are inclined to realize it in fact. Yet linguistic change has been the norm in English for at least a thousand years: all major commentators on the state of the language have been impressed – usually depressed – by its transience in spelling, in grammar, in syntax and in semantics, aspects which, generally speaking, have been studied in that order.

The past millennium of English history has witnessed huge changes in the social, economic and political structures, as well as in the make-up of the English-speaking peoples. This book is an attempt to correlate the main social and semantic shifts. By taking a panoramic perspective, subtle alterations in the social fabric and in the language, which may be matters of nuance in an individual's life-span, become arresting and illuminating in their magnitude. Today, for example, *cell*, *office*, *propaganda* and *sanction* are common secular words with clearly developed scientific, commercial and political denotations or prime meanings. Yet they all have common ecclesiatical origins, *cell* deriving from the monastic tradition, *office* from the liturgy, *sanction* from the imposition of penance and *propaganda* from the Counter-Reformation. Similarly, there is the phonetic erosion of the name of God (reflecting semantic change) in such forms as *goodbye* ('God be with you'), *gospel* ('God's message') and *gossip* ('relation in God'). These and many others reflect in the secularization of their meanings the eclipse of the influence of the Church.

Semantic change is widespread and astonishing in its extent. Even the most intellectually incurious must be prompted to ask how it comes about that *lobster* and *locust* are doublets (in origin the same word), as are *glamour* and *grammar*, *cretin* and *Christian*, *zero* and *cypher*, how *school* has its conceptual roots in 'leisure' or how *silly* once meant 'blessed'.

One easily becomes overwhelmed in the fascinating diversity of the avalanche of verbal evidence which confronts one upon venturing into a large dictionary. Sometimes obscure, tantalizing connections emerge, such as the etymological roots binding *giddy* to *god*, *whore* to *caritas*, *custom* and *habit* to the concept of clothes. Alternatively, a central root term may ramify and mutate to the point that its descendants no longer resemble the parent. The roots of *salt* (once a valuable commodity, as is evidenced in the phrases 'the salt of the earth', to be 'worth one's salt' and so on) have spread and grown into the diverse forms of *salary*, *salad*, *sauce*, *saucer*, *sausage*, *silt* and the verb to *souse.* Here the root sense of 'salt' has virtually disappeared, together with its previous sense of value. In cases like this, it is easy to understand the scepticism behind Voltaire's witty observation that in etymology the consonants count for little and the vowels count for nothing.

The great storehouse of semantic change in English is the *OED*, originally the *New English Dictionary on Historical Principles* (1883–1928). This revealed the existence and traced the development of 414,825 words. To this total the *Supplement* (1972–86) added approximately 63,000 words. Of this vast number, only a minute proportion are shown to have a single sense which has remained stable throughout the word's history. In fact, the more common the word, the wider its range of uses, an axiom which G. K. Zipf has corroborated with the alarming statistic that, except for a few core words, 'different meanings of a word will tend to be equal to the square root of its relative frequency' (1945, p. 255).

If English had remained a homogeneous language, in the sense that it might be said that German has, the study of semantic change would be a relatively simple affair, since one would be dealing with the same basic word-stock, and analysing the ways in which it has accommodated the various social, political and technical changes which have occurred. The essential semantic trend, one surmises, would be that of **generalization**, or widening of meaning, as the vocabulary took on more and more shades of meaning. However, such a simple scheme does not obtain, for the vocabulary of English is richly heterogeneous, luxuriant in its profuseness and quirkish in its changes of meaning. Yet it reflects the main social developments of the past thousand years in profound, uncanny and fascinating ways. If all the main historical sources of the early period (for example, 900 to 1300) had been lost, the word-stock itself would remain a remarkably accurate record of those times. In it can be traced the differing linguistic legacies left by a conquering Norman elite, a decimated Celtic minority, a partially successful invasion of Norse rivals, and a series of four major Latin influxes which can be respectively characterized (in terms of historical period) as basic, religious, bookish and scientific. In the format of linguistic archaeology, the different strata of the Latin borrowings (often ultimately derivable from Greek) could be represented in this fashion:

Scientific: (17th–18th centuries)	*nucleus, formula, vertebra, corpuscle, atomic, carnivorous, incubate, aqueous, molecule*
Literary: (Renaissance)	*democratic, juvenile, sophisticated, aberration, enthusiasm, pernicious, imaginary, allusion, anachronism, dexterity*
Religious: (6th–7th centuries)	*mass, monk, nun, bishop, abbot, minster, apostle, pope, altar, hymn, angel, devil*
Basic: (Continental borrowings)	*street, mile, butter, cheese, wine, inch, ounce, pound, kitchen, plum, cup, dish, mint* (both senses)

While most standard histories of the language distinguish these four stages of classical borrowing, the enormous influx of technical terminology in the nineteenth and twentieth centuries in effect constitutes a Fifth Borrowing. Examples would be *allopathic*, *floccilation*, *otorhinolaryngology*, *chthononosology*, *sphygmomanometer* and *zomotherapy*. These forms, unlike the early Latin and Greek borrowings, maintain their native inflections and spelling conventions to the point that they appear quite alien to English speakers. They also have a propensity to agglutination, as in the (admittedly factitious) word *pneumonoultramicroscopicsilicovulcanoconiosis*.

As one goes back to the 'deep strata' of the early Roman and Christian borrowings, so a phonetic assimilation is evident: *inch*, *devil* and *bishop* have the sound and the appearance of English words, since their distinctive Classical inflections (in Latin *uncia*, Greek *diabolos* and *episkopos*) have been eroded or distorted; this is not true of the later borrowings *nucleus* and *pernicious*. Some of these ancient invaders have worked their way right to the core of the language: *they are ill* is, etymologically speaking, pure Norse. Others have been halted on, or ousted to, the outer perimeters of obscurity and nicety.

Of the original Anglo-Saxon word-hoard which has survived – about one-third of the vocabulary, it is estimated by Herbert Koziol (1937, p. 8) – many central terms have been supplanted or changed out of recognition. It seems extraordinary, for example, that the Old English words for uncle, nephew, body, skin, face, take, breakfast, vegetables, fruit, money, number, war, touch, window and furniture should have been ousted from the vocabulary entirely, or survive only in remote, recondite caches. (For example, OE *niman* 'to take' became underworld slang before becoming obsolete, now surviving only in *nimble* and *numb*, while Dr Johnson tells us that *eame* ('uncle') was 'still used in the wilder parts of Staffordshire'.) Similarly, the updating of the forms and meanings of major terms from Anglo-Saxon heroic poetry produces some strange results: by such means it might be said that Beowulf took *lust* (A-S *lust*, 'pleasure', 'joy') in *dreary* (A-S *dreorig*, 'bloodstained') battle, was *moody* (A-S *modig*, 'brave', 'spirited'), rode a *mare* (A-S *mearh*, 'a steed'), *yelped* (A-S *gielpan*, 'to boast or challenge'), *fazed* his enemies (A-S *fesian*, 'to put to flight'), fought a *worm* (A-S *wyrm*, 'a dragon') and then *cringed* (A-S *cringan*, 'to die, fall in battle'). The once-proud words of his poet now present a sorry figure. On a more mundane level are the semantic changes of A-S *deor* from 'animal' to 'deer', *fugol* from 'bird' to 'fowl', *wambe* from 'stomach' to 'womb', *steorfan* from 'die' to 'starve', *mete* from 'food' to 'meat', *spillan* from 'destroy' to 'spill', *sellan* from 'give' to 'sell' and *stol* from lofty 'throne' to humble, fundamental 'stool'. Here one notices that in each case the broad, general sense has been lost, for a loan-word has usually insinuated itself as the central term of the word-field. The native term has consequently become narrower in meaning and frequently lost status, as the *Beowulf* sample indicates.

By contrast, Norman terms, reflecting the prestige of their speakers, became the vocabulary of the upper echelons of society: *crown*, *court*, *parliament*, *army*, *castle*, *mansion*, *costume*, *gown*, *ermine*, *beauty*, *banquet*, *feast*, *art* and a host of technical terms (discussed in chapter 2) all attest to their sophistication and stylishness. A telling sociolinguistic example resides in the nomenclature of meat: the animal on the hoof, supervised by the Saxon shepherd, hireling or hand, carries the Saxon term of *calf*, *cow*, *sheep*, *deer*, *boar* and *pig*, until served up at the Norman lord's table, culinarily transformed to Norman *veal*, *beef*, *mutton*, *venison*, *brawn*, *pork*, *ham* and *gammon*. They are cooked, furthermore, in the Norman terms of *roast*, *boil*, *broil* or *fry*.[1]

There emerges a clear sociolinguistic connection between the social status or function of a speech-community and the register or tone of the verbal legacy left by it. It is also clear that English has not been a pure language for over a thousand years: it was, even in the Middle Ages, what Daniel Defoe satirically styled in *The True-Born Englishman* (1701): 'Your Roman-Saxon-Danish-Norman English' (l. 139).

SEMANTIC CHANGE AND SOCIAL CHANGE

Of the many changed assumptions, the many altered forms of society which separate us from the traditional pattern of medieval life, the erosion of feudalism, and its assumptions of inherited hierarchy and unequal birthright, is obviously the most important. In this process capitalism clearly played a significant role, for money was initially used to commute feudal debts of labour and then developed into what we call the credit system, liberating free enterprise, whereby individual initiative was encouraged. The Church, though meritocratic in some of its practices, was a generally conservative and repressive institution. As society became secularized, so the notion of equality developed into a general assumption and then a right. In related developments, democracy and freedom of thought gained slow acceptance. In addition, print and the electronic media gave rise to the possibilities of mass propaganda and dissent, education and advertising.

These developments were gradual, related, and had one thing in common: they encouraged mobility and freedom, in thought, in people, in money and, above all, in words. The mobility of key concepts and their semantic correlatives is everywhere apparent. The rational discourse of science, for example, in which the mind can go wherever logical proof and empirical data take it, replaced the older mode of received lore, bound by tradition, authority, dogma and taboo. Consequently the word *science* itself changes from its medieval sense of 'learning', denoting a traditional body of knowledge known by rote, to its modern sense of a method of exploration, a technique for discovery and discrimination. Since the Renaissance there has been an enormous proliferation of what are called 'the sciences', particularly the natural sciences. These are now generally referred to as 'the exact sciences', to distinguish them from the more recent and more theoretical or hypothetical disciplines of political science, sociology and psychology.

The liberating capacity of money to commute feudal obligations and its use as a mode of legitimate acquisition is reflected in the semantic shifts of key terms, such as *purchase*, *finance* and *fortune*, discussed in chapter 3. The earliest senses of *purchase* involve taking by force; the emergence of our modern sense of 'acquisition by payment' took place only about four centuries ago. *Finance* has moved from its plain etymological sense of 'end' or 'ending' and 'settlement of a debt' (still evident in *fine*) to the modern, entrepreneurial meaning of 'borrowing money at interest', with quite different associations of *initiating* a transaction. Perhaps the most striking evidence of the liberating effect of the power of money is to be found in the word *fortune*. Its earlier conception was of a force which dominated human life, familiar in the great medieval symbol of the Wheel of Fortune; around 1600 emerges the sense of 'an amount of wealth' which, being made by shrewdness or sagacity, allows man to control his own life. In a related development, security from the ordinary vicissitudes of human existence, by means of securities and insurance policies, has been one of the promotions of capitalism. However *security*, now signifying not only a good, but a virtual right in advanced Western capitalist society, was originally a 'bad' word meaning 'a culpable absence of anxiety, carelessness'[O].

The capitalist ethos of conspicuous consumption has likewise had its semantic correlatives. Prominent amongst these is *luxury*, which has as its earliest dominant sense (from the fourteenth century) that of 'lust, lasciviousness or generally sinful self-indulgence'. Though it has not yet lost all its pejorative associations, *luxury* has ameliorated as the concept of 'the good life' has changed from the ascetic model of the Middle Ages to the hedonistic imperatives of modern times.

As democracy has replaced the older notion of hierarchy (literally, 'a sacred order'), so related key terms have shifted. *Democracy* itself and *politician*, both originally very unfavourable terms, have since achieved differing degrees of acceptability. Contrariwise, *aristocracy* had as its original, etymological sense 'rule by the best', a meaning which would hardly be popular now. As elites have become viewed with suspicion and envy, so *elite* itself has deteriorated.

Put simply, the alternative to the medieval model of hierarchy is that of competition. Though such competition (vividly described by Hobbes)[2] does away with previously entrenched privilege, the resulting meritocracy is likely to reflect inequalities of ability or resources, thereby ultimately producing oligarchies. This study is therefore also concerned with the various establishments, institutions and oligarchies which have grown up in the post-medieval world, and their semantic effects. For all of these developments have linguistic consequences, some more direct than others.

While central value-terms have shifted in concert with the ethics of society, the developing media have also had widespread effects on the language. The development of printing initially provided a measure of stability for the language, but this was largely confined to the formal aspects, for print emphasized the regional and individual anomalies of manuscript spelling, accelerating their removal. Since most of the early presses were in the South-East, which was also an area of financial and cultural dominance, so the East Midland, later the London, dialect became predominant. However, printing fundamentally and irreversibly altered the balance of power which had hitherto existed between hearers and speakers, or readers and writers. In an oral situation the hearer may intervene to concur, elucidate, protest or refute what is being said. The meanings of words, though not necessarily precise, cannot with impunity be juggled with since the potentially censorious presence of the hearer is immediate. The balance of power between what G. K. Zipf (1949, pp. 19–20) has termed 'the auditor's economy' and 'the speaker's economy' is thus preserved by the dynamic of the situation.[3] There is, in consequence, an organic link between 'meaning' and speech-community, so long as the language is oral. This link, weakened by writing, is broken entirely by the invention of printing, which enables all sorts of liberties to be taken with the meanings of words by those in control of the press. And it is only through access to the press – not always a viable possibility – that these agreed meanings can be restored.

As power has been extended to a variety of interests, first through capitalism, and then through democracy, so oligarchies – both political and economic – have been able to manipulate words in their favour. In totalitarian regimes they have virtually absolute control over the semantic description of society and individuals. In democratic societies the result may be called *logomachy*, or the 'war of words'.[4] This is the natural semantic consequence of dispute over such 'essentially contested concepts' as democracy, freedom, justice, equality and so on (Gallie, 1964, p. 157). It also derives from the competition for some market or spending-power, the semantic result being linguistic capitalism, or the appropriation of words as brand-names or boosters in the verbal selling package of advertising copy. As the fourth chapter of this study will attempt to elucidate, there is an impressive promptitude with which the press in England and on the Continent was harnessed to the requirements of authoritarian propaganda, religious controversy and commercial advertising.

Consequently, in terms of the conflict of speech economies, the alternatives are either the controlled semantic market of totalitarianism, or the free market, with all its inevitable fluctuations and instability. Here various oligarchical sublanguages, such as the jargons of tabloidese, adspeak, computerese, newspeak and doubletalk all compete in a state of general linguistic anarchy.

By and large, the right of politicians, businessmen, journalists and copywriters to appropriate or manipulate language (the communal product and possession of the speech-community) is not now seriously questioned. It is tacitly assumed, in fact, that the language of advertising and politics need not have the same standards of responsibility, honesty and literalness as would be expected to apply to statements between individuals. These altered assumptions have been subsumed into what Lord Acton called so memorably 'the atmosphere of accredited mendacity' (1973, p. 20).

There has developed in recent times an awareness that language contains assumed ideologies or 'compacted doctrines', as William Empson has called them (1977, p. 21). Some, like *conspicuous consumption* or *civil disobedience*, are the illuminating coinages of individuals (in these instances, Veblen in 1899 and Thoreau in 1866). Others, like *free enterprise*, *capitalism*, *profit*, *democracy* and *exploitation*, evolve slowly through the state of communal flux before acquiring a political tone which has become first emotive and then militant.

The awareness of the ideological content or assumptions in such language has made the definition of certain semantic areas concerning race and politics a very sensitive issue. In consequence, some pressure has been brought to bear on dictionaries to restrict the currency given to opprobrious racial terminology. As chapter 8 seeks to show, xenophobia is a deeply embedded linguistic feature. Its long, ugly history suggests, in fact, that it is an ingrained sociolinguistic habit of prejudice which is more likely to be eradicated by rational exposure than by attempted suppression.[5]

KINDS OF SEMANTIC CHANGE

At this point some definition is needed of what is meant by 'semantic change' in this study. The concept covers three basic aspects. First, and most obviously, it concerns a change of meaning undergone by an individual word in the course of time. Secondly, it involves **lexical** change, meaning the addition of new words (via invasion, borrowing or technical innovation) or the obsolescence of archaisms in a given word-field. Thirdly it involves **register**, a fairly recent term denoting the special word-choice appropriate to a given social situation or literary context.

Semantic changes are seldom simple and abrupt. Typically they are slow elisions between senses which are established and those which are coming into being. Sometimes they involve erosions of the phonetic form of the word as well, as in the case of the interesting word *silly*, illustrated in figure 1.1.

Of the first category of semantic change there are many varieties.[6] Words may undergo **generalization**, that is, take on a broader range of meanings. *Box* in Anglo-Saxon times referred to a container made of

FIGURE 1.1 The semantic development of *silly*

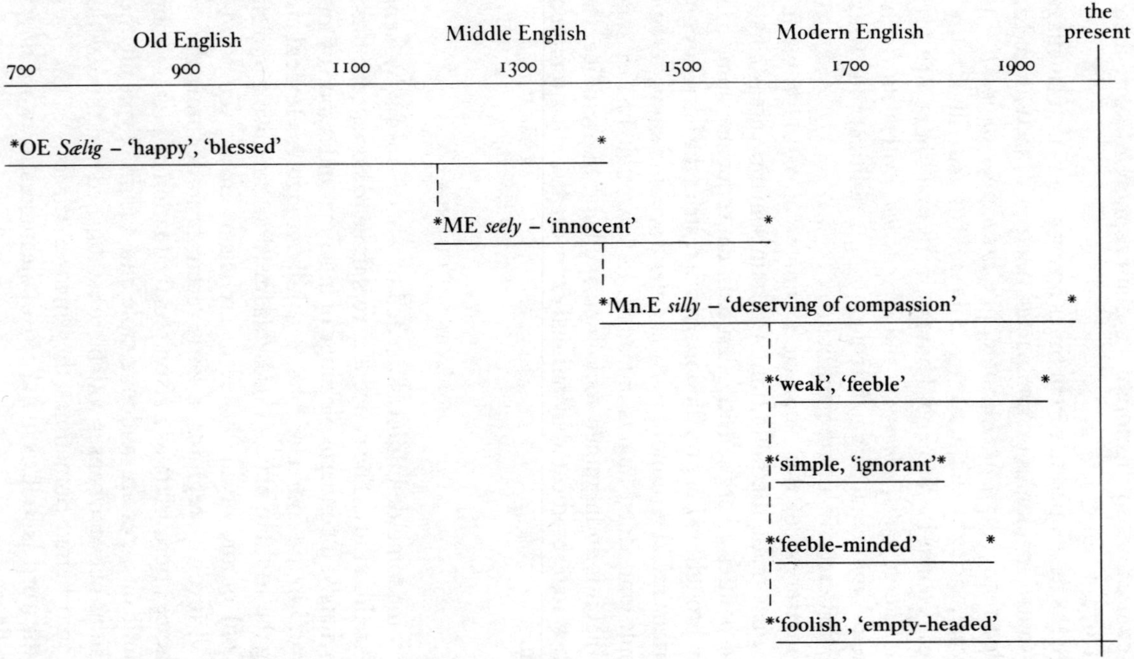

Note: Asterisks indicate the historical extent of a particular meaning
Summary: *Silly* has undergone **deterioration**, particularly since *c.* 1600

box-wood, normally for the safe-keeping of something precious, such as ointment or jewelry. (A *box at the opera* is a facetious extension of this notion.) Technological change – a frequent catalyst of semantic change – has evolved multifarious boxes, no longer even commonly made of wood, and seldom containing anything precious: that role has been assumed by *casket* or *chest*. Metaphorical extension, shown in the generalization of *pilot* and *ship* from contexts of sea, via air to space, is a frequent reflection of technical change. Metaphors, once no longer recognized as figurative, become 'dead', as in flower-*bed*, *blind* corner and *dead* metaphor itself. The language is full of these imaginative extensions of meaning. Contrariwise, *engine* has undergone the opposite shift of **specialization** or narrowing, from its broad medieval sense of 'mechanical contrivance' (often of war and torture but still surviving in its old general sense in cotton *gin*) to the modern meaning of 'a mechanical source of power', a specialization occasioned by Watt's invention of the steam engine. (The whole technology of steam has given rise to many terms and idioms, some of which still thrive.) Reluctance to accept metaphorical change and unwillingness to cut loose from etymology can be important factors in the acceptance of semantic change. When Freud was doing the research for his *Studies in Hysteria* he had to overcome considerable resistance from his clinical colleagues, who were firmly inclined to the belief that, since *hysteria* was derived from the Greek word for a womb, male hysteria was as much a contradiction in terms as a male hysterectomy.

Certain areas of the vocabulary perennially generate specialization. As the explicit terms for sexual activity became unacceptable and then taboo, numerous general latinized words were drawn into the 'semantic vacuum'. Among them were *rape* (1482), *consummation* (1530), *seduce* (1560), *erection* (1594), *copulation* (1632), *intimacy* (1676), *orgasm* (1684), *intercourse* (1798), *climax* (1918), *ejaculation* (1927) and *interfere* (1948)^{O}. (*Seduce* was originally a feudal term, meaning to 'poach' labour from another man's service, while *interfere* is in origin an equine term for a horse's front legs striking against each other.) However, the oldest sense of *provocative* is 'sexually enticing' (as in 'she wore a provocative, body-hugging dress'). Hoccleve (a contemporary and imitator of Chaucer) has an interesting passage from *c.* 1412: 'Ðei receyuen eeke prouocatyues Tengendre hem luste' ('They also consume aphrodisiacs to induce lust').

Some terms, having become too explicit, are avoided and replaced. *Occupy* acquired a sexual sense from the fifteenth century, recorded in this amusing passage from the universal historian, Ranulf Higden: 'Men of Lacedemonia . . . fatigate and wery thro the compleyntes of their wifes beenge at home, made a decre and ordinaunce that thei scholde occupye mony men, thenkenge the nowmbre to be encreasede by that.' The last quotation is from 1660, and the *OED* comments: 'The disuse of this verb in the 17th and most of the 18th c. is notable. . . . This avoidance seems to be due to its vulgar employment in sense 8 [under discussion]; cf. 1597 SHAKS. *2 Henry IV*, II iv 161: "Gods light these villaines wil make the word as odious as the word occupy, which was an excellent good worde before it was il sorted."' *Conversation* took on its sexual specialization from *c.* 1511, and the set phrase for adultery, *criminal conversation*, often abbreviated to *crim. con.*, is recorded from *c.* 1770. The offence was abolished in 1857. *Intrigue* soon took on the sense of 'amorous liaison'; there is a topical reference from 1668^{0}. The equally Gallic origins of *liaison* itself (initially a cookery term for the thickening of sauces) no doubt helped it follow suit after a most apposite first reference in Byron to 'a chaste *liaison*' in 1821. *Affair* has always maintained a discreet vagueness.

Amelioration, whereby a word takes on favourable connotations, and **deterioration** whereby it takes on pejorative associations, are often telling indications of social change. There is a particularly pregnant category ably defined by C. S. Lewis as 'the moralization of status words' (1960, pp. 21–3), discussed fully in chapter 2. By this process terms originally denoting status and class slowly acquired moral connotations, favourable and otherwise, evaluative of the moral conduct commonly attributed to that class. Hence *villein*, a medieval serf, and Anglo-Saxon *ceorl*, still lower in the hierarchy, deteriorated to *villain* and *churlish*, while *noble* and *gentle*, predictably, rose in moral connotation. In more recent times, the steady amelioration of *ambitious* and *aggressive* reveals a change in attitude towards those who seek advancement or 'success' in a highly competitive fashion.

Value-terms and ethos-terms reflect social acceptability or stricture, with consequent amelioration or deterioration. The amelioration of *luxury* and *democracy*, and deterioration of *aristocracy*, have already been mentioned. *Propaganda* was acceptable as an institution for the buttressing of faith during the Counter-Reformation; the term deteriorated once the cynical abuse of credibility was applied in the service of the modern state. With the spread of education, literacy and learning acquired greater value; consequently terms like *lewd* (Anglo-Saxon *læwed*, meaning 'of the laity, uneducated') deteriorated sharply, a process seen in our times in the strongly stigmatic associations of 'illiterate' and 'uneducated'.

These social determinants of semantic change refute a prevailing generalization most strongly put by Barber: 'Human nature being what it is, deterioration is commoner than amelioration: we are only too prone to believe the worst of anybody, and this is reflected in the way our words change' (1964, p. 251). This 'doctrine of deterioration' (to which Margaret Schlauch, Stephen Ullmann and Anthony Burgess all subscribe in varying degrees), has a dubious psycholinguistic basis, in that it does not explain how the deteriorated words acquired 'good' senses in the first place. Furthermore, it takes the form of a circular argument, being an explanation for an assumed psychological process for which the only evidence is the fact to be explained.

One of the few genuinely psycholinguistic changes would seem to be the 'law of procrastination', whereby words that used to mean 'immediately' (such as A-S *sona*, now *soon*, A-S *anon* and Elizabethan English *presently*) have all come in time to mean 'in a little while'. Of a different order, but possibly revealing, are the dishonest senses which have accumulated around *forge*, *counterfeit*, *shred* (documents) and *bug* (listen in to covertly – which has yielded a new sense to *bugger*). These all suggest that criminal propensity is not slow to take advantage of technical innovation.

Other kinds of semantic change are less obviously related to societal developments. There is, for instance, the trend of **emotive intensification**, whereby formidable, classically derived words such as *phenomenal*, *categorical*, *sensational* and *diametrical* are used in emotive, emphatic ways. (Dr Johnson, clearly aware of this process, used the condemning adjective 'ludicrous' of such affected eighteenth-century uses as *desperately* and *abominably*: of the latter he remarked: 'in low and ludicrous language, it is a term of loose and indeterminate censure'.) Yet 'phenomenal achievements' and 'sensational developments' are still very much the order of the day. Smaller, native terms, such as *little*, *tiny*, *great* and *big* are used in similar emotive fashion, exemplified in 'one of those noisy little men', from Disraeli's *Vivian Gray* (1827).

There are curiosities, such as the **shift to opposite**, evidenced in *wan* (originally in Anglo-Saxon 'dark', now 'pale'), *fast* (originally 'fixed' or 'firmly', now 'rapidly') and *obnoxious* (literally 'prone to harm'), but now commonly 'unpleasant'). *Garble* has become a curious example of its own modern meaning, since in Renaissance times it meant not to confuse, but 'to sift out the *garble* (the refuse of spices) from the spice itself'. *Botch* originally meant 'to repair'. Less severe sources of confusion in phonetic development are *stark*, which in *stark naked* should be *start naked*, literally 'tail naked' and *ye* as a misreading of Anglo-Saxon *þe*, later *the*, now surviving in such pseudo-archaisms as *ye olde tea shoppe*. A stranger instance is *sneeze*, a misreading of Anglo-Saxon *fneosan*, which should have rendered the highly improbable (but phonetically much more exciting) form *fneeze*.

These changes can be assumed to have been gradual evolutions within the speech-community. More serious are the trends of **verbicide** or **weakening** and **distortion**. *Verbicide* was coined in 1858 by Oliver Wendell Holmes, though C. S. Lewis gave the word a recent currency in *Studies in Words* (1960, p. 7). It seems no coincidence that the term should have originated in the period of mass-circulation newspapers with their sensationalist copy and their extravagantly worded advertisements colloquially, but evocatively, called *puffs*. By this process words such as *tremendous*, *monstrous*, *ghastly* and many others are applied indiscriminately, through fashionable affectation, to a variety of trivia. (They have become deflated, while *phenomenal*, *categorical*, etc., have been inflated.) *Terrific* has, in the whirligig of time, become a word of approval. Much verbicide seems to be an upper-class affectation. One cannot imagine coal-miners or crofters or shepherds complaining about 'ghastly weather' or praising a 'divine party'. Within this area of exaggeration Johnson detected a particular syndrome of feminine affectation. These instances he simply condemned as 'women's words'. *Frightful*, he noted, was 'a cant word among women for anything unpleasing'; *flirtation* in the sense of a 'quick sprighly motion' is similarly categorized, while *horrid* is designated as 'women's cant' for 'shocking, offensive, unpleasing'. The echoes can still be heard in fashionable suburbs, although the mode can certainly no longer be termed a feminine speciality.[7]

Verbicide may be committed collectively, fashionably or individually. In recent times it has moved beyond harmless personal exaggeration to various forms of organized commercial and political deceit. It is a form of distortion deriving clearly from liberties taken with the prime meanings of words by those in control of some medium. Thus one finds in advertising language such shop-worn examples as 'miracle product', 'dream house', 'magic cleanser' or 'luxury margarine', while political adjectives show a similar combination of emotion and imprecision, as in *fascist*, *democratic*, *bourgeois* and *reactionary*. The problem with verbicide is that words no longer die: having been drained of their vitality, they are sustained by press circulation in a state of suspended animation. Rather than being buried in a 'graveyard of murdered words' (Lewis, 1960, p. 228), they become zombies.

Finally, there is **euphemism**, which, being a linguistic indicator of a variety of taboos, is more revealing of certain cultural and psychological determinants than other trends. Euphemism, reflecting these taboos, is concerned principally with certain socially sensitive areas such as sex, race, illness, financial collapse, poverty, mental incapacity of various sorts, death, excretion and swearing. In the last-mentioned category, one can observe that the 'openness' of medieval religious swearing (so apparent in Chaucer) was curtailed in literary forms by Puritan injunctions against Profanity on the Stage. In time the taboo has relaxed, but left us with the curious mutilations and suppressions of the name of God, such as *zounds* (God's wounds) and *gosh*, a 'mincing pronunciation of GOD', as the *OED* terms it.

As swearing has moved away from a religious focus to that of bodily functions, so there have emerged the suppressed forms of *sherbet* (for *shit*), *blooming* (for *bloody*) and *flaming* (amongst others) for *fucking*. Today these taboos are self-consciously violated by many who wish to assert their independence from or rejection of 'decent' bourgeois society. This rejection of the taboo was a feature of the American Flower Children of the 1960s and the Skinheads of contemporary Britain.

Within the same broad cultural group there can be different taboos. For instance, *mother-fucker*, virtually unheard of in the UK, is a common demotic usage in the US, particularly in the street argot of blacks, among whom it can be used with the familiar, friendly tone of Australian *bastard.* Yet *cock*, which is commonly heard in all classes of speech in the UK, has traditionally been edited out, studiously (or unconsciously), from much American parlance. Consequently *cockroach* emerges in the emasculated form *roach*, *faucet* displaces *cock* in all senses of *tap*, and *rooster* does service for *cockerel*, although the associations of 'penis' have been well established at least as far back as the late fourteenth century lyric 'I have a gentle cock'.[8] However, with the recent liberation from taboos on swearing, *cock-teaser*, a common American student usage for a flirtatious but ultimately 'unbeddable' woman, and *cock-sucker*, a damning fellatious term for a toadying, servile underling, have gained considerable currency.

Euphemisms can also be contrived by vested interests for public consumption. Some of the more recent socially conditioned euphemisms are *industrial action* for 'strike', *recession* for 'depression', and – in the fruitful area of the semantic disguise of violence and war – *explosive device* for 'bomb', *operation* for 'campaign', *liquidation* for 'murder', *strategic weapon* for 'nuclear missile' and *incident* for any unpleasant occurrence, social, political or military.

Taboo areas of discourse can, paradoxically, attract the opposite mode, which is the less well known process of **dysphemism**. Here meaning is directly, even crudely, conveyed with a shocking lack of nicety which deliberately violates the taboo. In the semantics of dying, *to pass away*, *to pass on* and the many variations of a journey to the great unknown comprise the standard euphemisms, while *to push up daisies* is a dysphemism. Both varieties proliferate in underground argots.

Older meanings are frequently preserved in phrases by impacted fossilization: 'by *virtue* [strength] of the fact', 'fondly [foolishly] imagine', 'one man's *meat* [food] is another man's poison' and 'God speed [give you success]' are examples.

The second category of semantic change involves **lexical change**, more simply, the obsolescence of old words and the introduction of new words, via borrowing or invention. Recent acquisitions are *ombudsman* (1911[S]), very current from the mid 1960s, *anti-missile missile* (1956[S]), *video* (1958[S]), *video nasty* (1983[S]) and *laser* (1960[S]). Such terms, often a direct reflection of some technical advance, have been categorized as 'witness words' by Georges Matoré. Sometimes words are borrowed twice. For example *satellite* dates originally from *c.*1548 as 'an attendant on an important person'[O], but remained a rarity (unincluded in Johnson's *Dictionary* of 1755) until the launching of the Russian *sputnik* in 1957.

Obviously, not all technical words are reliable witnesses: *railway* is first recorded in 1776 (Act 16 of George III), but the first railway (Stockton to Darlington) was opened nearly fifty years later (1825). Clearly, the first recorded use of *contraception* (1886[O]) did not herald the start of a practice to which there are oblique references as far back as the *Ancrene Riwle* [*The Rule for Nuns*] in the twelfth century. The same time-lag may be assumed to apply in the cases of *sadism* (1880[O]), *masochism* (1893[O]) and *security blanket* (1956[S]). Forms like *WASP* (1964[S]), *blue-collar* (1950[S]) and *yuppie* (1984[S]) are sociological formulations rather than reflections of social change. Words can, of course, refer to mythical entities, as in *unicorn* and, more bizarrely, *sooterkin*: 'an imaginary kind of afterbirth formerly attributed to Dutch women.'[O] It would be naive to attribute *democracy* in even the vaguest modern sense to ancient Greece, on the semantic evidence alone, since women and slaves did not have the vote. This error is not very different from supposing that baseball must have been a highly developed skill at Northanger Abbey because the word occurs in chapter 1 of Jane Austen's novel of that name. Some words become obsolete for clear social or technical reasons, for example, *vambrace*, *rerebrace*, *crinet* and *peytral*, medieval terms for armour. Others pass out of usage for no obvious reason. Examples are *wittol*, 'a contented or conniving cuckold', *swive*, 'to copulate' (fl. *c.*1386–*c.*1884), *gimcrack*, 'showy but worthless', and *cant*, 'sophistic hypocrisy', all of which continue to thrive in fact if not in word.

Thirdly, 'semantic change' involves shifts in social connotation or **register**.[9] These more subtle changes in verbal appropriateness to varying contexts are most apparent, and most illuminatingly discussed, via the relationship of particular words to others in the same field, rather than solely through the relationship of the word to some referent or concept. *Register*, a fairly recent linguistic term recorded only from *c.* 1956[S], refers principally to language variation according to social role or social situation, especially to the degree of formality in the language employed. Eliza Doolittle's cockney ejaculation 'Not bloody likely!' (in Shaw's *Pygmalion*) was a notorious violation of the register (and the accent) appropriate to Edwardian polite society. The excitement of the popular press over Princess Anne's curt suggestion (*c.* 1982) that they should 'Naff off!' derives from the same breach of linguistic etiquette. By contrast, Queen Victoria's staid response, 'We are not amused', was appropriate to her role and the times, even in a diary entry.

What is remarkable in English is the way that the basic contrast in register between formal and informal usage can be transposed exactly into the historical evolution of the language. Most of the informal usage derives from the Anglo-Saxon and Norse element, while most of the formal usage emanates from the Norman French, Latin and Greek input. Thus, the following piece of enticing copy is pure Saxon: 'Warm, rich and full of golden-goodness, Fido dog food will give your furry friend health, strength and get-up-and-go.' Because Anglo-Saxon forms the core of the language, it is impossible to form, even facetiously, full statements exclusively comprising the other registers, but the following examples (with borrowings from French, Latin and Greek in bold) will serve: 'The **Consul-General** of **France cordially invites** you to **attend** a **reception** in **honour** of . . .'; 'the **patient** is **experiencing** a **potentially fatal haemorrhage situation**' ('the patient is bleeding to death'). Dickens sharply defined one functional difference between registers in his characteristically witty essay 'Saxon-English' in *Household Words* in 1858: 'When a man has anything of his own to say, and is really in earnest that it should be understood, he does not usually make cavalry regiments of his sentences, and seek abroad for sesquipedalian words.'

Although the degree of formality is traditionally the aspect most stressed in discussion of register, this emphasis is essentially limiting. Register can also be demonstrated via numerous alternatives in word-choice: old or new; concrete or abstract; blunt (or sharp) as against polite or refined; direct or vague; literary or recherché as against slang or demotic; provocative or annoying as against humorous or bland.

The familiar characterization (alluded to by Dickens) that high register terms are polysyllabic, while low register terms are commonly short, is essentially true. This is seen most simply in evolutionary terms by ME *physiognomy* becoming *phiz* *c.* 1688, subsequently *fizz*; ME *lunatic* becoming vulgar *loony* *c.* 1872; *fanatic* becoming *fan* (US) *c.* 1889; Renaissance *obstreperous* becoming *stroppy* *c.* 1951 and so on. The process of attrition is continuous, as is evident in *bus*, *taxi*, *bi* (*sexual*), *demo*, *porno* and many others.

Registers can most clearly be understood through **semantic fields** containing those words or meanings which cohere around a particular

FIGURE 1.2 Registers in a semantic field

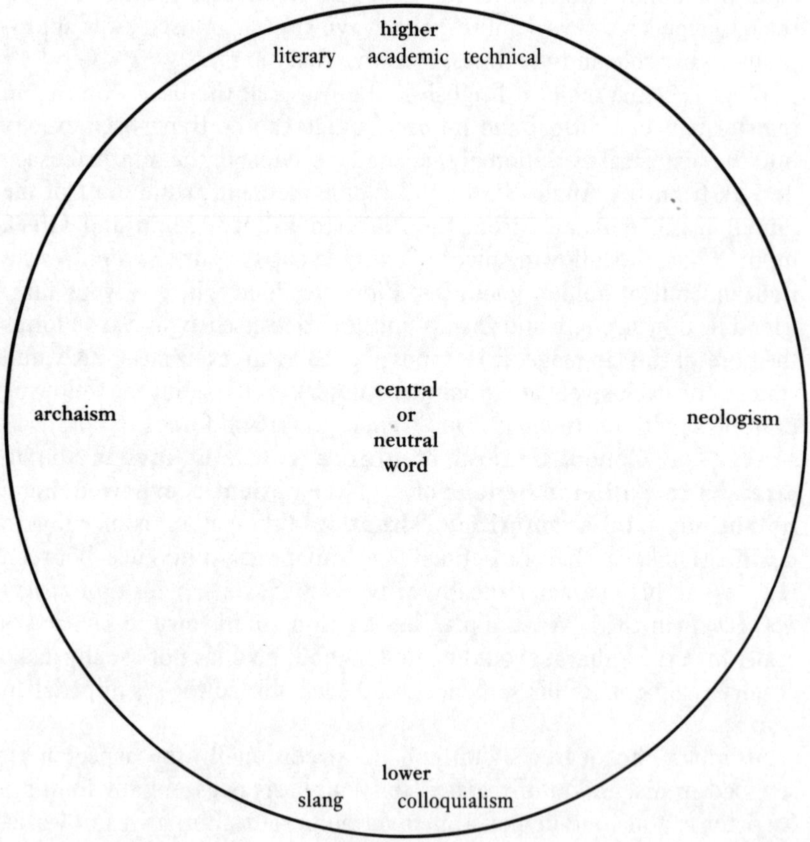

concept, topic or thing. Fields dealing with scientific and technical areas are necessarily specific and specialized. Others may contain no specific terms, being composed entirely of general words with particular nuances which relate to the field in question. For example, *body*, *fruit*, *sugar*, *dry*, *character*, *nose*, *palate*, *noble*, *bouquet* and *finish* seem to be an agglomeration of generalized physical and abstract terms: they have all, however, acquired specific meanings which have combined and evolved to make up the connoisseur's quaint and slightly precious terminology of wine.

A semantic field may be represented diagrammatically, using the disposition of differing registers in the schematic fashion of figure 1.2. Some fields are predominantly 'bottom-heavy', as is that of drunkenness.

FIGURE 1.3 The semantic field of *mad*

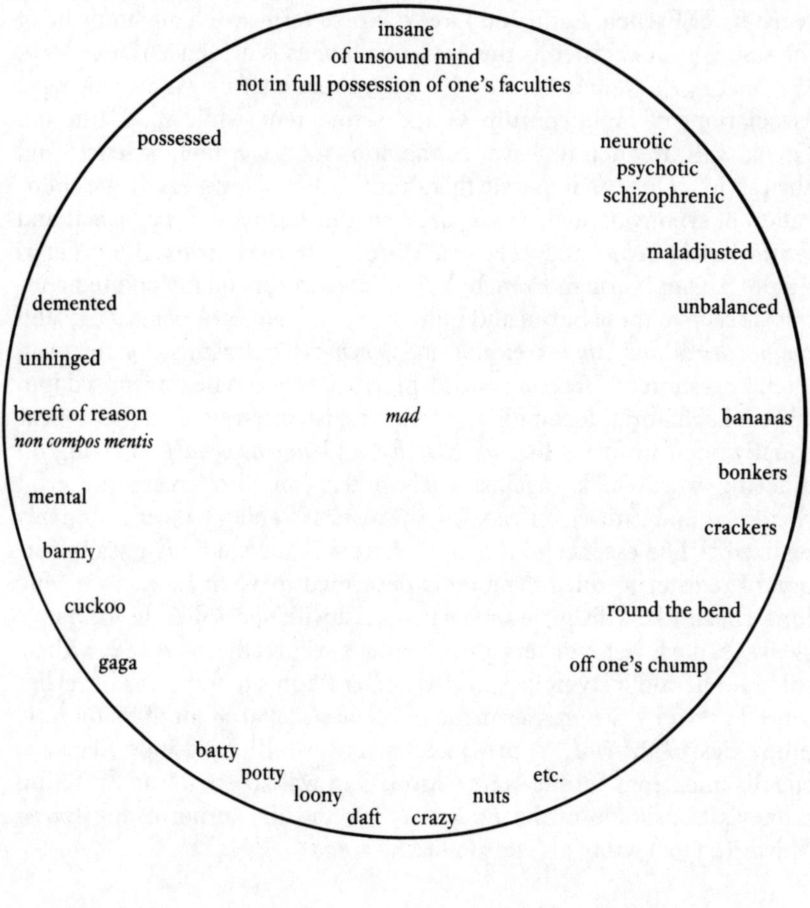

Apart from the elevated terms *inebriated* and *intoxicated*, there are dozens of low register dysphemisms, shown in this brief sample confined to words beginning with the letter 's': *slammed*, *sloshed*, *smashed*, *slewed*, *stewed*, and *screwed*. Other fields are largely 'top-heavy', for instance that to do with poverty, which abounds in such elevated euphemisms as *indigent*, *impecunious*, *destitute*, *distressed*, *financially underprivileged* and *of modest income*. That of synonyms for *mad* (figure 1.3) is nicely balanced.

George Steiner's epigraph to this chapter, 'History . . . is a language net cast backwards', is seminal in various ways. As has been mentioned, word-fields of synonyms in English tend to separate broadly into a hierarchical patterning of registers, one which reflects the historical development of the language to an uncanny degree. Thus, one will usually find that the primary, basic or neutral word (such as *house*, *food* or *clothes*) will be Anglo-Saxon, forming the foundation on which a vast lexical superstructure of refinement and nuance is built, mainly from the registers of French, Latin and Greek. Norse terms will commonly be of the same, basic register as the Anglo-Saxon, as is evidenced in *window*, *sky*, *law*, *cast*, *odd* and *leg*. The Norman French terms will usually have associations of rank, courtliness and refinement, while the Latin and Greek will frequently have connotations of learning, science and abstraction. One can illustrate this stratification of registers by the collocation of synonyms such as *ask*, *question* and *interrogate*; *rise*, *mount* and *ascend*; *leech*, *doctor* and *physician.* (In each of these trios, the order is Anglo-Saxon; Norman French; Latin/Greek.) An equally pointed contrast is seen in these Saxon and Latin pairings: *catty* and *feline*; *doggy* and *canine*; *horsy* and *equine*; *piggish* and *porcine*. Contrasting registers can often be a source of facetious word-play: *skipping* can be transposed into 'bipedal saltatorial locomotion'; native register can be made to appear equally alien in forms like *ungettatable* and *unputdownable*. Playing off differing word-stocks against each other can also create powerful rhetorical and satirical effects, as Shakespeare and Chaucer intuitively realized.[10] The essence of the mock-heroic is the studious misapplication of register to role, memorably described by C. S. Lewis as having Juno speak like a fishwife or having a fishwife speak like Juno. As we shall see, the lower registers are not always secure: the *dandelion*, with its splendid heraldic etymology of *dent de lion* ('lion's tooth'), was in earlier times known by the grosser name of *pissabed*, on account of its diuretic properties. *Turd-bird*, 'a provincial name for Richardson's Skua', is equally uncurrent, for the same reason. *Guts* was acceptable in Sir Philip Sidney's translation of the *Psalms* (1580), and the author of the *Cursor Mundi* (*c.* 1300) wrote of Samson taking a *nap.*

The form of *pissabed* reminds us that over time words can be twisted, telescoped and stretched in shape, with semantic consequences. Some, like *culprit* are 'fortuitous or ignorant running together of forms'[O]. Others are ingenious *portmanteaux*, to use the term coined by the creative Victorian word-lover, Lewis Carroll. In the increasingly quoted chapter on Humpty Dumpty in *Through the Looking Glass* (1872), that entertaining semantic anarchist observes that '*slithy* means "lithe and slimy" . . . You see it's like a portmanteau – there are two meanings packed into one word'. After Carroll's own coinages, the most familiar early term was *brunch*, dating from *c.* 1896[O]. Today the major growth areas of portmanteaux are in technical terms (*hi-fi*, *slo-mo*, *ergonomic*), new developments like *Chunnel* and *Laundromat*, and brand names (*Natwest*, *Monergy*, *Instamatic* and *Xpelair*).

The vocabulary has grown with each wave of invaders, and as the means of recording language have become more efficient. (*Beowulf* is preserved in a unique, charred manuscript; *The Canterbury Tales* survives in about 80, of varying completeness and quality, while there are approximately 50 printed copies of Shakespeare's *First Folio* still in existence.) The original Anglo-Saxon language is estimated to have had 50,000–60,000 words, many exclusively reserved for poetry; the Scandinavian invasions contributed about 2,000, while the influx of the Norman conquerors swelled the hybrid language of Middle English to approximately 100,000–125,000 words. The steady accretion of Latin words resulted in the Renaissance form of the language (Early Modern English) being twice the verbal volume of Middle English. The vocabulary of Modern English is now well in excess of half a million words.[11]

In modern times, the lexicon (while preserving these main divisions of register) has reflected the ages of exploration and colonialism by becoming increasingly polyglot and cosmopolitan. The following everyday words, erstwhile linguistic tourists, now jostle together with the natives as assimilated immigrants: *trek* (Boer Dutch), *anorak* (Eskimo), *cork* (Spanish), *dekko* (Hindustani), *manifesto* (Italian), *molasses* (Portuguese), *yacht* (Dutch), *mumps* (Icelandic), *cravat* (Slavonic), *gimmick* (German), *schmaltz* (Yiddish), *bazaar* (Persian), *pundit* (Sanskrit), *cherubic* (Hebrew), *charismatic* (Greek), *paradise* (Avestic), *nark* (Romany), *sherbet* (Arabic), *kamikaze* (Japanese) and *juggernaut* (Hindi). An interesting record of cultural contact is to be found in the schematic rendering of the historical evolution of food-terms, set out in figure 1.4 as 'A Historical Menu'.

However, these samples should not mislead us. For essential purposes we are still heavily dependent on the Anglo-Saxon core of words, and the ancient assimilated borrowings described by Murray in his Preface to the

FIGURE 1.4 A Historical Menu

	Food	*Drink*
	tacos quiche schwarma	
	pizza osso bucco	
1900	paella tuna goulash	
	hamburger mousse borscht	Coca Cola
	grapefruit éclair chips	soda water
	bouillabaisse mayonnaise	
	ravioli crêpes consommé	riesling
1800	spaghetti soufflé bechamel	tequila
	ice cream	
	kipper chowder	
	sandwich jam	seltzer
	merinque hors d'oeuvre welsh rabbit	whisky
1700	avocado pâté	gin
	muffin	port
	vanilla mincemeat pasta	champagne
	salmagundi	brandy
	yoghurt kedgeree	sherbet
1600	omelette litchi tomato curry chocolate	tea sherry
	banana macaroni caviar pilav	coffee
	anchovy maize	
	potato turkey	
	artichoke scone	sillabub
1500	marchpane (marzipan)	
	whiting offal melon	
	pineapple mushroom	
	salmon partridge	
Middle	venison pheasant	muscatel
English	crisp cream bacon	rhenish (rhine wine)
	biscuit oyster	claret
	toast pastry jelly	
	ham veal mustard	
	beef mutton brawn	
	sauce potage	
	broth herring	
	meat cheese	ale
Old	cucumber mussel	beer
English	butter fish	wine
	bread	water

OED as 'a nucleus or central mass of many thousand words whose "Anglicity" is unquestioned'. Since Anglo-Saxon remained the language of the majority of the common people after the Norman Conquest, it remained the nucleus or skeleton of the surviving Middle English language. It is this Germanic core of basic words, many writers have insisted, which preserves meaning most surely; for them the less familiar areas of Norman and Latin refinement are suspect.[12]

The analysis of linguistic change in more recent times, when English has become an international language and is being used in many manipulable ways, has always seemed to me a matter of urgency inexplicably ignored by major studies. Once printing and the electronic media break the organic link between language and society, words can be created, exterminated, warped and manipulated semantically by a group of vested interests or even a single person.

Furthermore, the distinction between 'legitimate' or 'correct' usage and 'unacceptable' usage has become harder to verify, particularly with the growth of metalanguages, idiolects and major dialects and variants of English, notably American English. The infiltration of American vogue-words, idiom and syntax has been perhaps the most important modern influence on English. Indeed, a discussion of modern English can hardly ignore terms of technical vigour and progress, as well as a whole register of vibrant demotic idiom (comprising, for instance, *cool*, *neat*, *smart*, *mean*, *with it*, *dumb*, *uptight*, *rip-off*, *wild*, *weird* and *out of sight*). Here communication through wide, vague, emotive use is usually gained at the expense of the precision which the words have traditionally maintained. Some are not as new as might be supposed. *Hump* ('a fashionable word for copulation'), *pig* ('a police officer'), *pad* (base), *screw* ('to copulate') and *freak out* are underground words datable to the eighteenth century.[13] Of the last there is a nonce-use in Cleland's *Memoirs of a Woman of Pleasure* (1749): 'She had had her freak out [orgasm]. . . .' Whether the recent trans-atlantic infiltration has been an enriching or an impoverishing influence on English remains a matter of dispute.

THE STUDY OF SEMANTICS

It might be said, sharply but not unfairly, that the study of language has moved from the smallest unit, sound, and progressed to the largest, syntax, with treatments of meaning becoming increasingly obscure. *Semantics* is, consequently, a comparatively new word in the language. Michel Bréal coined it in the title of his pioneering study, *La Sémantique*, in 1895, about 75 years after the revolutionary discoveries by the brothers Grimm, Bopp,

Rask et al. of sound-shifts in the evolution of the Indo-European languages. Bréal sought a word which was scientific, stable and thus suitable for the analysis of 'the science of meaning'. Though Bréal used the word 'law' frequently of language, he was scornful of the proposition that there could be 'tendencies of words': 'Nothing could be more chimerical,' he asserted. 'How should words have tendencies? Nevertheless, we hear of a pejorative tendency, of a tendency to deteriorate, etc.' (1964, p. 99).

Saussure in 1915 was largely in agreement, though from different bases of argument. He insisted on 'the arbitrary nature of the sign', and on the primacy of the 'synchronic' aspect of the language (its continuing system) rather than the 'diachronic' aspect (its historical evolution). Divorcing language from its social roots, he affirmed that it was 'a self-contained whole and a principle of classification' (1966, p. 9). To some extent, Saussure was reacting against the contemporary emphasis on historical studies which searched for language laws and organic patterns of development. Of course, in quoting anything from Saussure's *Course*, one has to concede that the text might be more the synthesis and overstatement of his students Bally and Sechehaye than the transcript of the master's voice. Thus, the final statement, 'The true and unique object of linguistics is language studied in and for itself' (1966, p. 232), which has proved so influential, was an addition of the disciples. Saussure elsewhere concedes that 'Language has an individual side and a social side, and one cannot conceive of one without the other' (Leroy, 1967, p. 55).

Since 'meaning' is essentially a shared, plural or social notion (the alternative being literal *idiocy*, the incapacity to relate or communicate rationally), a more fruitful approach is to relate language to the mores and values of its society. Works by Gustav Stern in 1921 and Hans Sperber in 1922 discussed in Ullmann (1957, pp. 254–5) sought to formulate certain 'laws' of semantic development. Out of this enterprise evolved the study of specific 'lexical fields' or 'semantic fields', a concept which seems to have been introduced in 1924. Jost Trier, 'the chief architect of the field theory', as Ullmann calls him, published his major study into the linguistic field ('*sprachliche Zwischenwelt*') in 1931, an approach followed by Georges Matoré from 1953 into broader 'fields of ideas' ('*champs notionelles*'). Matoré also refined the vocabulary by making a useful (but not absolute) distinction between 'witness words' ('*mots-témoins*') reflecting material progress, and 'key words' ('*mots-clés*') reflecting ethical change (1953, pp. 65–8). The richest study of this kind in English is still Owen Barfield's *History in English Words* of 1926, revised 1954, 1962 and 1985.[14] Other studies delineating word-histories in a social context were C. S. Lewis's *Studies in Words* of 1960, which dealt with a narrower canvas, Raymond Williams's more ideological collection, *Keywords* (1976), monographs on a single word, such as Charles Barber's *The Idea of Honour in English Drama (1590–1700)* (1957), and Susie Tucker's *Enthusiasm* (1972). Normative or prescriptive studies and structural–theoretical analyses have been more numerous, in the UK and the US, respectively. They will be covered in the Conclusion (chapter 9).

The study of language is one of the most testing of disciplines. At one extreme stands the chimerical chessboard or grid of scientific system, exact but inhuman, produced by the lust for order Bacon so percipiently described: 'The human understanding is of its own nature prone to suppose the existence of more order and regularity in the world than it finds' (*Novum Organum*, XLV). At the other extreme stands the distorting mirror of impressionism or solipsism, human but confused: 'The human understanding is moved by those things most which strike and enter the mind simultaneously and suddenly, and so fill the imagination; and then it feigns and supposes all other things to be somehow, though it cannot see how, similar to those things by which it is surrounded' (*Novum Organum*, XLVII).

The mode of approach used in this study is a combination of the atomistic, philological study of individual words, combining their case-histories with those of similar background or meaning, but not losing sight of the social determinants of the language, nor its overall system. The assumed relationship between semantic change and social change is that of a flexible symbiosis. This is not a question-begging formulation, since the problem of cause and effect in semantic matters produces different solutions according to time and field. For example, *computer* and *transistor* are semantic effects of technical change, whereas the terminologies of psychology and politics indicate the causes and also record the effects of change. The symbiotic model thus obviously involves choice on the part of the investigator in both overall shape and detail of his construct, the semantic field. Nor is this choice wrong; for, as Bacon asserted in his own model for scientific enquiry, what is needed is 'not the method of an ant, which merely collects and uses, nor yet that of a spider, which spins cobwebs out of its own substance, but that of a bee, which transforms and digests the material it gathers by a power of its own' (*Novum Organum*, XCV). The problems are considerable. One needs to simplify and schematize, without crudifying, tracing major tides and currents while being aware of eddies and waves. Furthermore, as Geoffrey Leech has observed (1974, p. vii), 'a writer on semantics has to try to play many parts (not only linguist, but philosopher, anthropologist, psychologist, even perhaps social reformer and literary critic).'

The sources of evidence are not uniformly reliable. Language in its spoken forms is so protean, elusive and full of creative and idiomatic quirks that it often evades grammatical analysis and historical placement. For instance, the origins of *to be done in* or *to be done* (cheated, swindled) cannot be positively located in time, while to *do famously* can, fortunately, be traced to an unusual source, Shakespeare's *Coriolanus* (1608). Colloquialisms are hard to pin down precisely, since context commonly governs meaning. The *COD* defines *chuffed* confusingly as 'pleased; displeased', while the exclamation *shit!* can convey anger, pleasure, surprise, disappointment, astonishment and resignation. Consequently, this study is predominantly concerned with dictionary definitions and lexicographical locations in time, even though it must be conceded that the dictionary, as we understand this term, has been in existence for little more than two centuries.

Developing Bacon's metaphor of the bee, it goes without saying that the semantic data should be collected and categorized by the most fastidious, punctilious alveary. Like any other researcher or enthusiast in the field, I have been almost entirely reliant on the labours of Murray, Bradley, Craigie, Onions, Furnivall, their heirs and successors, and their numerous sub-editors, contributors and assistants. Owen Barfield, who has contributed in such an imaginative and illuminating fashion to the study of semantic fields, has paid just tribute to the greatest achievement of English lexicographical scholarship, the *OED*: 'The immense debt which the foregoing pages owe to the *Oxford English Dictionary* is, I hope, too obvious from the text to need further emphasis. Without access to that unrivalled monument of imaginative scholarship, a great deal of this book could never have been even attempted' (1954, p. 216).

To Barfield's acknowledgement must now be added one appropriate to the *Supplement* (1972–86). In the half-century or so which has elapsed since the publication of the main work, there have been major changes in both the lexis and the assumptions underlying lexicography. Technological progress has produced a stupefying proliferation of technical terms. Of greater daily relevance has been the clear diminution of verbal taboos and the growth of the allied assumption that dictionaries should be descriptive, recording all usage, and not simply the polite, literate forms. Dr Robert Burchfield and his editorial team at Oxford have incorporated in the *Supplement* an alarmingly thorough coverage of the new technical language, and – equally important – a judicious record of demotic English, an area which, it must be acknowledged, was not fully treated by their predecessors.

The *Supplement* makes good a deficiency in the main work, one which went further than Burchfield's description as simply 'the absence of two famous four-letter (sexual) words'.[15] Murray, for all his robust individualism, still felt constrained by the practice evident as far back as Caxton (and mentioned in chapter 4), of censoring 'rude' words in print. The stratification of registers, so marked in relation to 'bodily functions', had over the centuries become a set pattern, with the 'low' (commonly, but not exclusively, Anglo-Saxon) word hovering beyond the pale of respectability, but usually being displaced by more 'polite' or euphemistic French or Latin variants, some of them, like *fellatio* and *cunnilingus*, resorting totally to 'the decent obscurity of a learned language'.[16] The broad schematic arrangement of the major terms in figure 1.5, with words of Romance origin in bold type, illustrates the point fairly clearly. It also gives the lie to the popular notion that the 'four-letter-words' are exclusively Anglo-Saxon, and shows that one of the commonest euphemistic formulas, *to sleep with*, was established in the remotest period of the language. The scheme necessarily involves crudification: for instance, *make love*, originally *make love to*, moves through a prolonged 'seduction', so to speak, through the eighteenth and nineteenth centuries, before explicit coitus is

FIGURE 1.5 The semantic field of 'rude' words

Anglo-Saxon	*Middle English*	*Renaissance*	*Augustan*	*Victorian*	*Modern*
shit(n) turd	**ordure**	**excrement**		crap*	**defecation**
	piss(v)	**urinate**	**micturate**[1]	pee	
sleep with	swive	fuck*	**copulate** screw	make love	bonk
	pollution	frig[2]	onanism **digitation** self-abuse **masturbation**		wank
arse	bum* buttocks	**fundament anus**	bottom **posterior(s)**		
	cunt thing[3]	coney **pudendum**	twat* **vagina**	quim*	
weapon[4]	cock yard	tool prick	**penis** (privy) **member**		

Notes: **Bold** type indicates Romance origin
* Origin uncertain
1 'The sense is incorrect as well as the form' (*OED*)
2 *Frig* overlapped with *fuck* in the seventeenth and eighteenth centuries
3 *Thing* has served for both male and female genitalia since Middle English
4 OE *wæpened* ('weaponed' or 'armed') has the basic sense of 'male' in many compounds including gender in children and plants

attained. I have not included the new 'liberated' term, *self-pleasuring*, designed to supplant the old, guilt-suffused, punitive words for masturbation, like *self-abuse* (still used in the *COD*).

Curiously, the taboo was not rigorously observed in the *OED*. Readers could be thoroughly informed on *masturbation* and the extraordinary history of *bugger*, covered in chapter 8. But *fuck* was excluded, though a place was found for *windfucker*, also known as a *fuck-wind*, more politely a *windhover* or *kestrel*. While Hopkins celebrated the *windhover*, George Chapman could use *windfucker* in the Preface to his *Iliad*, without embarrassment. *Cunt* was similarly excluded, though the underground euphemism *coney* (pronounced and often spelt *cunny* in earlier times) was fully revealed and illustrated by jaunty verses such as: 'All my Delight is a Cunny in the Night' (1720). The pronunciation altered, the Dictionary speculates, through 'a desire to avoid certain vulgar associations with the word [unprinted] in the *cunny* form'. *Condom* was excluded (one of the voluntary readers felt that it was 'too utterly obscene' for inclusion),[17] though it was well documented in the eighteenth century, as can be seen from the witty entry from Francis Grose's *A Classical Dictionary of the Vulgar Tongue* (1785) reproduced as figure 4.2. (It was principally the AIDS panic of the mid 1980s which abruptly brought *condom* out of linguistic hiding and into general parlance.) *Twat* was, however, included, the reader being informed that it was 'low' and directed to Nathaniel Bailey's definition of 1727, in Latin.[18] Perhaps the funniest reading in the *OED* is the observation that the word was 'erroneously used by Browning under the impression that it denoted part of a nun's attire'.

One consequence of this communal and traditional censorship was that the thriving low-life sexual histories of *spend*, *debt*, *come*, *die* and *swink* (an archaic word for 'to labour') were largely obliterated. In Chaucer's *Canterbury Tales* the Wife of Bath's studied inversion of the marriage contract (as set out in her Prologue) uses these traditional financial and feudal terms with quite explicit sexual meanings.[19] *Come* is amusingly recorded in a saucy lyric of the mid-seventeenth century: 'Then off he came, & blusht for shame, soe soone that he had endit.'[S] *Die* certainly has a similar sexual innuendo in many Elizabethan contexts, for instance in Cleopatra's question of mock-astonishment concerning Antony's Roman wife: 'Can Fulvia die?' With many 'indecent' or 'obscene' words being driven out of use, hosts of risqué euphemisms or code-words took their place.[20] Most of these remained unexplained by the *OED*, and were decoded by Eric Partridge in his pioneering study of 1947, *Shakespeare's Bawdy*. The *Supplement*, in covering many of these omissions, has made the *Dictionary* a comprehensive record of what Wordsworth termed 'the language of ordinary men'.

EVOLUTION OR DEGENERATION?

As has been stressed already, printing made words mobile. They no longer moved in the slow flux of the speech-community, but travelled at speed across continents in books. They were pressed into service, made to plead the causes of the Reformation, of nationalism, of commercial and political interest. Prime meanings could be warped and registers mixed to achieve the desired effects of emotion, rationality or anaesthesia. The following chapters trace these developments in greater detail.

Today it is fashionable to see language change as virtually inevitable, a fact of life, and consequently to decry criticism of this fact and to pour scorn on those who disapprove of such changes. Such an attitude may seem rational and realistic, but it is important to distinguish between changes which are natural, evolutionary and symbiotic with social changes, and those which are artificially contrived or cynically imposed by an oligarchy. In this study I have sought to demonstrate the techniques and motives of vested interests which seek to bend language to their own purposes. I do not claim neutrality nor the 'massive impartiality' which Raymond Williams attributes (with some irony) to the *OED* (1976, p. 16). Language is a vital source, not only of communication, but of trust between people. If the tone of what follows is not always measured, it is because I believe that in vital areas of our social existence the contractual obligations of shared meanings have too often been abused.

The great Italian thinker Giambattista Vico distinguished, in his characteristically triadic style, three kinds of language, corresponding to his formulation of the Three Ages: that of gods, that of heroes and that of men (Vico, 1948, pp. 306–7). In analysing a particular segment of his cyclical theory of history, Vico is tracing a decline in civilization, a lost potency of language. In his brilliant insight, language changes, as society develops, from being initially hieratic, numinous or sacred, then poetic or rhetorical, then conventional or trivial. The theme of decay or decline was common in eighteenth-century historiography. Johnson gave out the general law that 'Tongues, like governments, have a natural tendency to degeneration'; Pope had articulated similar, but local, concern in 1728:

> Our sons their fathers' failing language see,
> And such as Chaucer is, shall Dryden be.
>
> *Essay on Criticism*, ll. 482–3

Alternatively, how valid is Otto Jespersen's optimistic, Victorian view of English showing, like Chinese, 'a progressive tendency towards a more perfect structure'?[21] Which theory adequately accommodates modern mass jargons? Reflecting the *anomie* or normlessness which Durkheim diagnosed as the distinctive malaise of modern society, these seem to represent the furthest remove from philosophical 'realism', in which words are regarded as the symbolic reflections of eternally stable, archetypal ideas. They show, instead, the chaotic nominalism shrewdly observed by Hobbes in what is often regarded as the first of the modern books, *The Leviathan* (1651): 'Words are wise men's counters; they do but reckon with them; but they are the money of fools' (part I, chapter 4). Nevertheless, the study of most verbal currency, no matter how debased or manipulated, is revealing.

NOTES

1 See, however, Robert Burchfield (1985), p. 18, where he argues that this 'enduring myth' is 'no more than a half-truth', on the grounds that *veal*, *beef*, *venison*, *pork* and *mutton* could mean in earlier times the animal as well as the flesh. This does not really affect the marked split in the nomenclature, which makes the field a frequent example in standard works.
2 Hobbes, *The Leviathan*, pt I, ch. 13.
3 Zipf argues that, theoretically, the ideal *speaker's economy* would consist of a few general-purpose words, while the ideal *auditor's economy* would consist of a vast, precise vocabulary.
4 The term, though rare, is recorded from 1569°.
5 See Robert Burchfield (1973), pp. 26ff.
6 The following categorization is an updated version of broadly similar treatments found in the standard histories of the language, such as Simeon Potter (1963), ch. 9 and C. L. Barber (1964), ch. 14.
7 Lewis is surely right when he says that 'the greatest cause of verbicide is the fact that most people are obviously far more anxious to express their approval and disapproval of things than to describe them' (1960, p. 7).
8 This apparent barnyard poem reaches an obviously phallic consummation:

And every night he percheth him
In mine ladye's chaumber.

9 Three useful discussions on register are to be found in G. L. Brook (1973), pp. 81–121, Philip Howard (1984), pp. 1–22 and Martin Joos (1961).
10 Their skilful exploitation of contrasting registers is dealt with more fully in chapters 2 and 4.
11 See John Nist (1966), pp. 8ff.
12 This view was put with vehement chauvinism a century ago by E. A. Freeman (1875–9), vol. V, p. 547: 'This abiding corruption of our language I believe to be the one result of the Norman Conquest which has been purely evil.' Orwell (1958) favours the Saxon element in the language over the

French and Latin (in a more temperate fashion) in his essay 'Politics and the English Language'.

13 The quotations are from Francis Grose's most entertaining *Classical Dictionary of the Vulgar Tongue* (1785), of which there is a sample reproduced as figure 4.2.

14 This brief survey of the earlier research in the field is not intended to be comprehensive, but simply to lead up to the use of the field approach. An interesting early formulation was that of Hans Sperber in 1922: 'If at a certain time a complex of ideas is so strongly charged with feeling that it causes *one* word to extend its sphere and change its meaning, we may confidently expect that other words belonging to the same emotional complex will also shift their meaning.' (Quoted in Ullmann (1957), p. 254.)

15 Preface to vol. IV, p. x. See also his discussion, 'Four-letter words and the *OED*', *TLS*, 13 October 1972, p. 1233.

16 Quoted in a letter from Arthur Hugh Clough to F. J. Child in 1854 concerning how thoroughly to gloss Chaucer's bawdy tales in a proposed edition.

17 From p. 195 of Murray's biography, *Caught in the Web of Words*, by his granddaughter, K. M. Elisabeth Murray (1977). In her discussion of the whole problem, she regards Murray as being 'forced to omit' the offending words by 'contemporary opinion'.

18 This accords with the advice of Dr J. S. Farmer (who became involved in a lawsuit for breach of contract when his publishers refused to publish obscene words).

19 See especially ll. 130–2, where she asks how

> That man shal yelde to his wyf her dette. . . .
> If he ne used his sely instrument?

In ll. 201–2 she recalls nostalgically:

> As help me God, I laughe whan I thynke
> How pitously a-nyght I made hem swynke!

20 Hugh Rawson's *A Dictionary of Euphemisms* (1981) treats this area of the lexicon fairly comprehensively.

21 Quoted by Randolph Quirk in the Foreword to the Tenth Edition (1982) of Jespersen's *Growth and Structure* (from a lecture to the British Academy in 1928).

2

Words of Conquest and Status: The Semantic Legacy of the Middle Ages

A Knight ther was, and that a worthy man,
That fro the time that he first began
To riden out, he loved chivalrye,
Trouthe and honoure, fredom and curteisye.

Chaucer

The age of chivalry is gone. That of sophisters, economists and calculators has succeeded.

Burke

ONE of the 'givens' of the Middle Ages is that it was an Age of Faith. The great physical constructs, such as the cathedrals, and the no less impressive architecture of the mind, such as the *Summa Theologica* of Aquinas and Dante's *Divina Commedia*, were all created within an explicit religious framework. Today man's great achievements are technical, secular and commercial: only one cathedral has been built in England in the last century (Liverpool), while in the past twenty years or so over a thousand churches have been demolished, reflecting the slow decline of several Christian denominations, notably the Anglican.[1] Ours is an age of doubt, scepticism, even cynicism. Religious authority figures do not excite their previous awe: kings, emperors and dictators are no longer meaningfully excommunicated or anathematized.

With the secularization of society, and the accompanying rise of individualism and materialism, there has been a reflective shift in key value-terms. The traditional canon of the Seven Deadly Sins has, for example, undergone a revealing alteration. (They are, or were: *Pride*, *Wrath*, *Envy*, *Lust*, *Gluttony*, *Avarice* and *Sloth*.) One is immediately struck by the interesting fact that expressions of popular culture such as pulp fiction, television soap-operas and the majority of advertisements one encounters nowadays amount to endorsements, blatant or latent, of precisely these qualities, with the sole exception of *Wrath*.

Under the modern ethos of conspicuous consumption, a form of competitive materialism, these traditional vices are becoming desirable and respectable. As this happens, so the terms in question will develop more favourable connotations, undergoing **amelioration**. *Pride* obviously does not carry the same negative connotations that it used to: it has also become strongly politicized as an expression of individual and racial assertion. Its cousin *Vanity* is now entirely acceptable in the form of feminine accoutrements such as the *vanity bag*, *vanity case*, *vanity basin* and so on.

Though *Wrath*, or its modern equivalent *Anger*, will always be too disruptive to become respectable, it is no longer regarded as something absolutely vicious or opprobrious. The notion of justifiable anger, the right to lose one's temper under extreme provocation, is now accepted. And public spectacles of anger, such as those increasingly witnessed in the arenas of politics and sport, no longer receive total condemnation: indeed, they are often publicized and relished as exhibitions of *aggro*. It seems significant that an orgy of mafia vengeance in a work of fiction should have given us the modern sense of *godfather*.

With the growth of the ethos of conspicuous consumption, *Covetousness* or *Avarice* and *Envy* have become almost respectable as the driving forces of competitive materialism. 'Keeping up with – or ahead of – the neighbours' has become a full-time occupation in which consumers willingly participate in 'pecuniary emulation' (Veblen, 1970, p. 71).

Gluttony and *Lust*, in former times regarded as deadly to the soul, are increasingly assumed under the mode of 'the good life'. The ascetic imperative of medieval times has given way to the hedonistic imperative of our own. This takes the various forms of the blow-out, the carvery, the calorific challenge to 'Eat as much as you like for £$', or the sensual self-indulgence of sporting in the sauna, frolicking in the jacuzzi, having an affair or a fling (to add spice to one's marriage) or comparing orgasms with the columnists and 'researchers' of the women's magazines. The sex manual has replaced the spiritual manual, which advocated mortification of the flesh rather than its excitation. (Catalogues of firearms, it might be noted, are now called Gun *Bibles*.) Sexual therapy has, of course, made *Lust* into one of the mainsprings of the 'good sex life', and though the term has not shaken off all its negative connotations, it is fast doing so.

Finally, *Sloth*, *Idleness* (or *Accidie* in medieval times) has acquired the curious high status accorded by the work-ethic to those who can afford to do nothing. This development is reflected in the enormous ramifications of the leisure industry, and by the ultimate ambition of those in the 'rat race' to retire early and become 'gentlemen (or ladies) of leisure'. The replacement of the old term *recreation* by *relaxation* is also revealing. *Fun* in Middle English related to stupidity.

The generally archaic tone of several of the Sins is, of course, a reflection of their increasing desuetude. The same is partly true of the Cardinal Virtues (*Faith*, *Hope*, *Charity*, *Prudence*, *Justice*, *Fortitude* and *Temperance*). Here one notes that *Justice* has become politicized, while *Temperance* has never recovered from the fanaticism of Prohibition to become a term of general morality. Other terms which have been largely displaced from their central spiritual significance are *soul* (now mainly associated with artistic temperament and music), *damanation*, *salvation*, *purgatory* and *hell. Sin* is most commonly encountered in the phrase *living in sin.* If the popular press is to be believed, one pursuit exclusive to the upwardly mobile is Satanism.

In undertaking an enterprise of the scope of this chapter, one needs at the outset a description, at once cogent, accurate and panoramic, of the major social developments of English society during the past millennium. Few accounts, I suggest, would be able to rival the almost nonchalant brilliance of de Tocqueville's summation of French social history in the opening pages of his classic of 1835–40, *Democracy in America*. Unlike many social theorists and historians (who tend to claim objectivity for their insights) de Tocqueville anticipated his own prejudices by making the illuminating distinction between historians writing in aristocratic ages, who are inclined to attribute all occurrences to individual influence, and those writing in democratic ages, who 'assign great general causes to all petty incidents' (1863, vol. II, p. 79). In terms of his own distinction, de Tocqueville's thesis is essentially that of a 'democratic' historian, his argument delineating a broad evolutionary social dynamic of liberation. Though it is primarily concerned with developments in France from feudal times onwards, de Tocqueville's description provides a suitable model for parallel changes in England. At the time of the Norman Conquest, de Tocqueville explains,

> the territory was divided among a small number of families, who were the owners of the soil and the rulers of the inhabitants . . . force was the only means that man could act on man; and landed property was the sole source of power.
>
> Soon, however, the political power of the clergy was founded, and

began to assert itself; the clergy opened its ranks to all classes, to the poor and the rich, the villein and the lord; equality penetrated into the government through the church, and the being who, as a serf, must have vegetated in perpetual bondage, took his place as priest in the midst of nobles, and not unfrequently above the heads of kings.

[In time] the want of civil laws was felt; and the order of legal functionaries soon arose from the obscurity of the tribunals and their dusty chambers, to appear at the court of the monarch, by the side of the feudal barons in their ermine and their mail.

While the kings were ruining themselves by their great enterprises, and the nobles exhausting their resources by private wars, the lower orders were enriching themselves by commerce. The influence of money began to be perceptible in state affairs. The transactions of business opened a new road to power, and the financier rose to a station of political influence in which he was at once flattered and despised.

Gradually the spread of mental acquirements, and the increasing taste for literature and art, opened chances of success to talent; science [knowledge] became the means of government, intelligence led to social power, and the man of letters took part in the affairs of state.

The value attached to the privileges of birth decreased in the exact proportion in which new paths were struck out to advancement. In the eleventh century [in France] nobility was beyond all price; in the thirteenth it might be purchased; it was conferred for the first time in 1270; and equality was thus introduced into the government by the aristocracy itself. . . .

As soon as the land was held on any other than feudal tenure, and personal property began in its turn to confer influence and power, every improvement which was introduced in commerce or manufacture was a fresh element of the equality of conditions. Henceforward every new discovery, every new want which it engendered, and every new desire which craved satisfaction, was a step toward the universal level. . . .

From the time when the exercise of the intellect became the source of strength and of wealth, it is impossible not to consider every addition to science, every fresh truth, and every new idea as a germe of power placed within the reach of the people. Poetry, eloquence, and memory, the grace of wit, the glow of imagination, the depth of thought, and all the gifts which are bestowed by Providence with an equal hand, turned to the advantage of democracy. . . .

In perusing the pages of our history, we shall scarcely meet with a single great event, in the lapse of seven hundred years, which has not turned to the advantage of equality.

The crusades and the wars of the English [*sic*] decimated the nobles, and divided their possessions; the erection of communes introduced an element of democratic liberty into the bosom of feudal monarchy; the invention of firearms equalised the villein and the noble on the field of

> battle; printing opened the same resources to the minds of all classes; the post was organised so as to bring the same information to the door of the poor man's cottage and to the gate of the palace; and protestantism proclaimed that all men are alike able to find the road to heaven. The discovery of America offered a thousand new paths to fortune, and placed riches and power within the reach of the adventurous and the obscure. . . .
>
> Nor is this phenomenon at all peculiar to France. Whithersoever we turn our eyes, we shall discover the same continual revolution throughout the whole of Christendom.
>
> (1863, vol. I, pp. 2–4)

The breadth, brilliance and acuteness of de Tocqueville's description are arresting. However, the 'providential' certainty of equality is now obviously questionable, in the light of the manifestations of despotic fascism in Germany and Italy during this century, and of post-colonial and post-revolutionary tyranny in Russia, China and Africa. In fairness to de Tocqueville, it must be conceded that the most potent modes of social control, such as broadcasting, were undeveloped when he was writing, and little was known about crowd psychology and propaganda.

The flaw in assuming, as de Tocqueville does, that 'the gradual development of the equality of conditions . . . possesses all the characteristics of a divine decree' (1863, vol. I, p. 6), is that it presupposes genuine freedom and equality of opportunity, if not ability. Obviously, printing and firearms become egalitarian instruments only insofar as access to both is equal. The totalitarian regime, which achieves power largely by the monopoly of both, is not envisaged in de Tocqueville's description. And even in a capitalist democracy considerable finance is needed to reach the majority of the population for any persuasive purpose. It is notably ironic that de Tocqueville should argue that 'printing opened the same resources to the minds of all classes', naively assuming this to be an educative, liberating process, for this description, if given a cynical twist, would suit very well for propaganda or advertising imposed on the mass by an oligarchy.

It can certainly be shown, by way of corroboration of de Tocqueville's essential thesis, that the main semantic trend with which we shall be concerned is that of **generalization**. This reflects, in various ways, the broadening use of words which used to have specific meanings in the hierarchy of power. As we shall see, the trend is evidenced, variously, in the **moralization of status words** (such as *gentle* and *noble*); the **secularization of religious words** (such as *office* or *sanction*); the **democratization of status words** (such as *freedom* and *largesse*), and the **moralization of learning words** (evidenced in *lewd* and *brilliant*).

Generalization is also common in the **monetarization of transactional terms** (such as *fee* and *purchase*), which are the focus of the next chapter.

It must, however, be conceded that de Tocqueville's kind of thesis – of dynamic social evolution – though highly favoured today, does not hold the field alone. A noted American medievalist, D. W. Robertson, Jr., has been prominent in asserting that the medieval social order existed in 'quiet hierarchies' (Robertson, 1963, p. 51), and that it was only towards the close of the period (i.e., near the Renaissance) that those hierarchies started to break up. This traditional view, which sees the Middle Ages as basically static, has been questioned by progressively detailed studies which tend to support dynamic or evolutionary interpretations of the period, showing change in virtually every field, or rather, every furrow: social, political, literary, economic, agricultural, technological, demographic and even dietetic. Historians of recent years consider the potentially revolutionary effects of the stirrup, the horseshoe, the heavy plough and amino-acids.

Change has become ingrained in our thinking, as the semantic history of a word like *condition* shows. Though the *Human Condition* (recorded from *c.* 1814[S]) continues as a cliché resonating a vague, permanent pessimism, behaviourism has suggested, if not demonstrated, that people can be conditioned no less than air. The dominant early sense of the noun *condition*, 'mode or state of being', dates from *c.* 1340[O], but has slowly given way to less permanent notions of mental and psychological states. Previously, one *changed one's condition* primarily by getting married; now it is assumed that virtually any condition can be altered by *conditioning* or therapy. The verbal sense, dating from *c.* 1494[O], is mainly concerned in its earlier stages with making conditions in a political sense; the more drastic modern sense, 'to teach or accustom (a person or animal) to adopt certain habits' is recorded from *c.* 1909[S].

The violent upheavals of 1381, collectively known as the Peasants' Revolt, suggest that the notion of 'quiet hierarchies' is a projection itself, one sustained not so much by absence as by suppression of evidence. In these insurrections the traditional 'silent majority'[2] become vociferously angry and subversive. The evidence takes the form of the chronicles, which range from the clearly biased, such as that of Walsingham, to the occasionally deficient, such as that of Knighton,[3] and of a more substantial body of suggestive legal evidence in charters and statutes showing the growth of an acquisitive, competitive, profit-oriented ethos occasioned by the labour shortages brought about by the ravages of the Black Death (1348–9).

The most important of these documents is the Statute of Labourers

(1351), which aimed to keep wages down by forcing all able-bodied men to work at the wage-rates of 1346. The preamble speaks with overt hostility of 'the malice of servants who were idle and unwilling to serve after the pestilence without taking outrageous wages'. A Sumptuary Ordinance of 1363 sought to diminish unseemly displays of affluence by commoners through minute regulations for the apparel for all ranks. The Poll Taxes of 1377, 1379 and especially of 1381, made necessary by the disastrous progress of the war with France, 'precipitated the riots (particularly in Essex) which led to a general revolt'.[4] 'Tax has tenet us alle' ('tax has destroyed us all'), wrote the unknown author of an English poem on the rising. A petition of 1354 against foreign merchants, and a notice of 1355 against armourers 'attempting to sell all kinds of armour . . . at too excessive a price . . .' (Hughes, 1918, p. 171) both indicate the profit motive starting to take hold.

Within the Church the spirit of reform is evidenced in the rise of Lollardy, certainly aided by a general animosity towards ecclesiastical sinecurism; the establishment accordingly united to institute acts against this splinter-group, 'seeing that the ship of the church was daily being endangered by the incessant force of these and innumerable other horrors and unspeakable opinions . . .' (Hughes, 1918, p. 201). Charles Muscatine summarizes the state of ecclesiastical confusion:

> The century begins with the captivity of the papacy at Avignon and ends with the Great Schism, in which Europe was treated to the spectacle of two popes excommunicating and making war on each other. The virtual destruction of the papacy as a spiritual force is only the symptom, however, of general decline in ecclesiastical prestige.
>
> (Muscatine, 1972, p. 20)

The payment of dues to Rome occasioned angry protests tinged with xenophobia. This complaint (of 1376) against the Pope and cardinals is typical in its sarcastic indignation: 'Be it considered that God has committed His sheep to our Holy Father to be fed, not to be shorn. . . .' John Ball, a Lollard preacher, questioned the whole economic and moral basis of tithes, and gave an old religious saw a strong political twist by asking one of his huge audiences:

Whanne Adam dalfe and Eve span
Who was thanne a gentil man?

In short, it becomes quite clear that in fourteenth-century England, at any rate, the 'quiet hierarchies' are experiencing some turmoil within themselves and are in obvious conflict with each other.

REGISTER AND CHARACTER IN CHAUCER

For the purposes of this study, the period is very much the 'Age of Chaucer and Langland', because without their verbal skill, social observation and moral sensitivity, it would be difficult to sustain even a limited thesis relating semantic change and social change in the Middle English period. One of the most remarkable achievements of this period is the linguistic subtlety of Chaucer's portraits in the General Prologue to *The Canterbury Tales.* Given the fact that there were no dictionaries at all, let alone those which concentrate on etymology or dialect, it is quite astonishing how Chaucer deploys the semantic strata of the language to create characters out of contrasting registers. The oafish Miller, for example, is created, not simply defined, in all his dense muscularity in a profusion of old, rude, unpolished, powerfully monosyllabic Saxon and Norse words 'as deep as England':[5]

> *The Millere was a* stout *carl for the nones,*
> *Ful big he was of* brawn *and eek of bones;*
> *That proved wel, for overal ther he cam,*
> *At wrastling he wolde have alwey the ram.*
> *He was short-sholdred, brood, a thicke knarre;*
> *Ther was no dore that he nolde heve of harre,*
> *Or breke it at a renning with his heed.*
> (ll. 545–51)

Even the French borrowings, *stout* and *brawn*, are lacking in refinement and harmonize perfectly in such knotted and gnarled native company. Against this portrait, which contains nearly 100 per cent 'native content', one could hardly imagine, but Chaucer did, a more extraordinary contrast than this, the absurdly affected pseudo-French Prioress:

> And sikerly she was of greet *desport*,
> And ful *plesaunt* and *amiable* of *port*,
> And *peyned* hir to *countrefete cheere*
> Of *court*, and to been *digne* of *reverence*.
> She was so *charitable* and so *pitous*
> She wolde wepe if that she saugh a mous
> Caught in a trappe, if it were deed or bledde.
> (ll. 137–45)

Madame Eglentine is as ridiculously over-refined as the Miller is comically coarse, and so Chaucer has created her entirely in the language of Frenchified cliché, an idiom which is starting to sound rather passé in the 1390s when French, no longer the language of power, is starting to go out of fashion. Bearing in mind the general statistic that Chaucer's language contains an average of 12 per cent French borrowing, the rise to near 40 per cent in parts of this portrait is very pointed. Chaucer is particularly adept at revealing the corruption or worldliness of the Church by studiedly placing religious terms in incongruous or absurd contexts. In this passage *reverence* is mistakenly thought to derive from a grand social manner (*estatliche of manere*), while *charitable* and *pitous* are applied, not to human suffering, but – absurdly – to the mouse caught in a trap. Without realizing it, the Prioress shows the worst failing known to those who aspire to be fashionable: she is out of date. The re-establishment of English in the fourteenth century is well documented, so that the cultivation of a parochial form of French (*after the scole of Stratford atte Bowe*) would be seen as a splendidly ridiculous affectation.[6]

In the context of these two portraits, that of Chaucer's ideal Knight gains added verbal and moral significance, for it is a balanced blend of Saxon solidity and French *courtoisie*, of what Anthony Burgess once memorably termed 'the North Sea and the Mediterranean':

> A Knight ther was, and that a worthy man,
> That from the time that he first began
> To riden out, he loved *chivalrie*,
> Trouthe and *honoure*, fredom and *curteisye*.
> . . . .
> He was a *verray, parfit, gentil* knight
> (ll. 43–6; 72)

The balance is preserved in almost every line, but is synthesized most clearly in the qualities of chivalry:

> Trouthe and *honoure*, fredom and *curteisye*.

These three portraits are composed of different strata or vintages of the language. The words of the Miller's portrait have an ancient solidity and force; those of the Prioress's contain the jaded archaism of affectation, while those of the Knight suggest the nostalgic charm of traditional nobility, a fading medieval ideal.

THE LINGUISTIC LEGACY OF THE NORMAN CONQUEST

The Normans, while accommodating many Saxon words of status, largely defined themselves in their own terms. The medieval terminology of rank may be conveniently divided in the following fashion:

Anglo-Saxon	*Norman-French*
King	
Queen	
	Prince
	Duke
	Marquess
Earl	Countess
Lord	
Lady	
	Viscount
	Baron
Knight	
	Squire
	Franklin
Sheriff	
	Bailiff
Reve	
	Sergeant
Yeoman	
	Page
	Groom
Churl	Villein
	Serf

This layout confers a false clarity on an essentially fluid situation. Several of the terms – notably *baron* – are applied to a confusing variety of people. Some of the titles gain formal recognition only in the fourteenth century, when feudalism was in decline. The title of *duke*, for instance, appears in the English peerage for the first time during the reign of Edward III, and is first conferred upon the Black Prince in 1337. One reason for the confusion was the problem of translation. The *OED* records, in the entry under *duke*: 'From the Conquest till Edward III, *ealdormann* or *eorl* was rendered by *comes*, and *dux*, *duc*, *duk* was known only as a foreign title. Even William and Robert are known to the Old English Chronicle only as "earls" of Normandy.'

In his wonderfully punctilious essay on the Doomsday Book, F. W. Maitland faces almost immediately the problem of the lack of a 'settled and stable scheme of technical terms':

> often enough it is very difficult for us to give just the right meaning to some simple Latin word. If we translate *miles* by *soldier* or *warrior*, this

> may be too indefinite; if we translate it by *knight*, this may be too definite, and yet leave open the question of whether we are comparing the *miles* of 1086 with the *cnicht* of unconquered England or with the *knight* of the thirteenth century.
>
> (1965, pp. 30–1)

There is also a political aspect to the instability of terms. The creation of several of the titles must be seen as implying forced recognition after a power-struggle; they are not gratuities granted for services rendered in a stable situation, which is the basic modern convention of the award of titles, whereby civil servants, jockeys and footballers are raised to the peerage by an exercise in regal largesse. One notices that, in general, the lower the term, the less precise its denotation. As Dr Johnson commented, 'What precedence, sir, between a louse and a flea?' Consequently, *baron*, the lowest rank of nobility, was applied indiscriminately, partly as a result of overproduction of the title by Richard II. Likewise, *villeins* and *serfs*, originally quite different, were by the thirteenth century regarded as the same. Indeed, the whole history of the Feudal System is largely one of semantic shifts, complicated and enriched by ancient, regional terms which also obstruct understanding: 'England was already mapped out into **counties**, **hundreds** or **wapentakes** and **vills. Trithings** or **ridings** appear in Yorkshire and Lincolnshire, **lathes** in Kent, **rapes** in Sussex, while **leets** appear, at least sporadically, in Norfolk' (Maitland, 1965, p. 32). However, as Maitland puts it, 'These provincial peculiarities we must pass by', since our aim is to relate the development of terms of power and status to social changes.

Even before the arrival of 'Earl' William, the main social developments have their semantic reflections. The decimation of the Celts is given sparse memorial in the dozen or so Celtic words which have managed to survive, excluding, that is, those which are place-names or describe geographical features, such as *avon* ('river'), *dee* ('holy'), *torr* ('hill'), *bryn* ('mountain') and *cumb* or *cwm* ('valley'). The subjection of the human survivors is simply traced in the word *wealh* (the root of *Wales* and the second element of *Cornwall*). In earlier Old English it meant a 'foreigner' or 'Celt', but later deteriorated to take on the sense of 'slave'.[7]

The Viking invasions resulted in some revealing penetrations into the core vocabulary, an enclave which would normally be thought of as unassailable. (King Alfred had attempted, by a futile species of *apartheid*, to confine the Vikings to the Danelaw, an area of England to the East and North of the Watling Street, the old Roman road from London to Chester.) A centrally important word, such as *die* (ON *deyja*) drives the main native counterpart, *starve* (OE *steorfan*) into the specialization of 'to die of hunger', and *take* (ON *taka*) drives *nim* (OE *niman*) first into dishonest practices, and then into final obscurity.[8] Even more remarkable is the borrowing of the central pronouns *they*, *their* and *them*, which filter into Standard English from the Danelaw, displacing the natives *hie*, *hiera* and *hem*. The Scandinavian borrowings merge easily with the cognate Saxon word-stock, having the same blunt strength: *anger*, *wrong*, *ill*, *ugly*, *meek*, *cast*, *call*, *husband*, *fellow*, *rotten*, *steak*, *knife*, *sky*, *low*, *scream* and *want.* Their unrefined directness and generality place them naturally in the neutral or lower register.

At Hastings the archetypal fear of the Anglo-Saxons, harped upon in their poetry, the fear of being reduced to a *wræcca* or 'wretch', a lordless, destitute exile, became universal reality. 'By 1086 only about eight per cent of the land remained in the hands of the erstwhile Anglo-Saxon aristocracy' (Douglas and Greenaway, 1953, p. 22). Although some strong-minded prelates continued to preach in English, for 300 years the lingua franca ceased to be the language of the law, of court, of parliament, the obvious sources of power and prestige.

Whereas the Scandinavian borrowings are common, 'grass-roots' words, 'many of the French loan words reflect . . . cultural and political dominance' (Barber, 1964, p. 161). They are concerned with administration, law, war, ecclesiastical affairs, the chase, the arts, architecture and fashion. Even the small sample in the columns below attests to their blend of authority and refinement:

crown	*peace*	*religion*	*chase*	*colour*	*costume*	*arch*
court	*battle*	*service*	*scent*	*image*	*garment*	*tower*
power	*arms*	*saint*	*falcon*	*design*	*apparel*	*vault*
authority	*siege*	*miracle*	*quarry*	*beauty*	*dress*	*column*
parliament	*enemy*	*clergy*	*forest*	*music*	*train*	*transept*
government	*armour*	*sacrifice*	*retrieve*	*romance*	*petticoat*	*cloister*

The supremacy in the field of architecture is impressive, not only in the technical terms mentioned above but in those denoting large or aristocratic structures: *palace*, *mansion*, *chapel*, *manor* and *castle.* The dominance in sophisticated food terms, already alluded to in the 'cow/beef' distinction in chapter 1, is charmingly illustrated in this medieval recipe for *Oystres in gravey*:

Take *almondes*, and *blanche* hem, and grinde hem, and drawe hem thorgh a *streynour* with wyne, and with goode fressh broth into gode mylke, and

> sette hit on the fire and lete *boyle*; and caste therto *Maces*, *clowes*, *Sugur*, *pouder* of *Ginger*, and faire *parboyled oynons mynced*; And then take faire *oystres*, and *parboyle* hem togidre in faire water; And then caste hem thereto; And lete hem *boyle* togidre til they ben ynowe; and *serve* hem forth for gode *potage.*[9]

The vocabulary of law is especially revealing. With the exceptions of the Norse borrowings *law*, *by-law*, and *thrall*, the Norman dominance is overwhelming: *justice*, *judge*, *jury*, *court*, *suit*, *sue*, *plaintiff*, *defendant*, *felony*, *crime*, *fee*, *assize*, *session*, *damage*, and the distinctively inverted phrases *real estate*, *fee simple*, *letter patent* and *attorney general.* The movement of these two classes of borrowings is traced in the following way by C. L. Barber (1964, p. 162): 'French words tended to penetrate *downwards* in society, whereas the Scandinavian words came in on the ground floor.'

As the scheme at the beginning of this section makes clear, the Normans 'borrowed' the titles of *king*, *queen*, *lord* and *lady*, but they imported almost the whole vocabulary of power, as has just been demonstrated. They thus defined themselves in their own terms, as is often the case in the semantics of colonialism. The strong cultural separation between conqueror and conquered is reflected in a fairly clear separation of registers. The Anglo-Saxon term *eorl* is virtually unique in that it received promotion with translation to *earl*, replacing French *count.* This might have been because the Normans recognized in the English term an echo of their Old Norse title *jarl*, a viceroy, or – more speculatively – because they wished to avoid the disparaging associations of *cunt*, first recorded in *c.* 1230^{S} in the startlingly direct London name *Gropecuntlane.*[10]

THE MORALIZATION OF STATUS-WORDS

C. S. Lewis formulated this, a most conspicuous semantic development of the Middle English period, in that work of the last years of his life, *Studies in Words* (1960, p. 7). The phrase sums up the process whereby words such as *noble* and *villain* change from being terms denoting rank to terms which are evaluative of moral conduct. Together with *noble* (recorded from *c.* 1225°) are its familiar associates, *gentle* (also from *c.* 1225°), *frank* (*c.* 1300°), *free* (*c.* 900°) and *liberal* (*c.* 1375°). One notes that *gentle* and *noble* emphasize initially the positives of 'good standing' and 'good breeding', whereas *free* (the only Saxon term), *frank* and *liberal* are, initially, more negative in definition, meaning, respectively, 'not in bondage', 'not in serfdom' and 'of the arts and sciences, worthy of a free man, as opposed to servile or mechanical'[O].

Contrariwise, words which originally denoted inferior social status become terms of moral disapproval. These are more numerous and include *villain*, *knave*, *blackguard*, *wretch*, *slave*, *churl*, and the adjectives *lewd* and *uncouth*. The majority of these are Saxon terms, a fact which in itself would accelerate their post-Conquest deterioration. They now smack of literary archaism, or have an aristocratic flavour, whereas *gentle*, *frank*, etc., are still in general use.

Of the older terms, perhaps only *wretch* (A-S *wræcca*) originally carried very obvious moral implications, since the state of being an exile or outcast was probably the consequence of some heinous action. *Knave* (A-S *cnapa*, *cnafa*, 'a male child', from *c.* 900[O]) and *churl* (A-S *ceorl*, a general term of 'man' from *c.* 900[O], but capable in Old English of a great variety of meanings including 'hero' and 'prince'), both declined with the status of the Saxons. In fact, the aristocratic associations of *ceorl* did not prevent the word from becoming the invariable translation in the Anglo-Saxon laws of Latin *villanus* (one attached to a villa or farmhouse). Furthermore, the fact that the word echoed the aristocratic *eorl* meant that its antithetical associations were intensified in the rhyming formulas *eorl and ceorl*, *eorlisc and ceorlisc*, which are common in Old English. *Villain* and its variant form *villein* derive from OF *vilein*, ultimately Latin *villanus*, mentioned above. *Villain*, 'a low-born, base-minded rustic', as it is revealingly defined in the *OED*, is recorded from *c.* 1303, marginally earlier than *villein*, 'one of the serfs of the feudal system', recorded from *c.* 1325[O].

The breakdown of feudalism did not – as might have been expected – arrest the impulse to attribute bad moral quality to an individual on the basis of status. The trend toward deterioration is continued by *blackguard*: 'the lowest menials of a household' from *c.* 1535[O], followed by 'the vagabond loafing criminal class' from *c.* 1683[O]. *Lackey*, or *lacquey* (an Old French term for a footsoldier), takes the sense of 'a footman, a running footman' from *c.* 1529[O] but acquires its modern opprobrious sense, 'a servilely obsequious follower, a toady', from *c.* 1588[O]. In the case of *scullion*, recorded from *c.* 1483[O], the abusive and the denotative senses are not easily separated, though the abusive are fairly well established by the late sixteenth century. *Slave*, from Latin *Sclavus*, a *Slav*, is a denotative term from *c.* 1290[O], but acquires its contemptuous sense from *c.* 1521[O]. *Vassal*, fourteenth-century in origin, follows suit *c.* 1589[O]. Here we may quote the observations of Stephen Ullmann, an authority in the field of semantics, on the pejorative associations of captivity:

> The semantic ramifications of Latin *captivus* may serve to illustrate this. Starting from the idea of captivity, this word has acquired unfavourable meanings in various languages though not in all: Spanish *cautivo* still means 'prisoner'. In French it has become *chétif* 'weak, sickly, poor, miserable'; the connecting link was the idea of a man dominated and weakened by his passions (Bloch-Wartburg). The same associations led to a different result in Italian where *cattivo* means 'bad'. Yet another line of development is found in English *caitiff*, of Anglo-Norman origin, which is now archaic and poetical. This has evolved through three stages: 1. 'a captive, a prisoner'; 2. 'one in a piteous case'; 3. 'a base, mean, despicable wretch, a villain'. (Ullmann, 1962, pp. 231–2)

The semantic evidence reinforces the association between captivity and alleged immorality. A much earlier example, *wealh*, also shows this tendency.[11]

It emerges that the breakdown of feudalism intensified the process of deterioration in words applied to those of lower station. Service, being no longer an obligation, became a disgrace. The more thoroughly it was pursued, the more assiduously it was offered, the more it was despised. The process is continued in the deterioration of *servile* from *c.* 1526[O], and of *obsequious* from *c.* 1602[O]. (Both words had previously had neutral senses of the kind Johnson recorded in his definition of *obsequious* as 'obedient; compliant; not resisting'.)

On the other side of the coin, the spirit of free-enterprise capitalism, which in large measure led to the breakdown of feudalism, contributed to the amelioration of *free*, *frank*, *liberal* and *generous* by stressing magnanimity in material terms as 'bounty' or 'munificence'. (*Free* has this sense of personal generosity recorded from *c.* 1300; *liberal* from *c.* 1387; *frank* from *c.* 1484 and *generous* from *c.* 1623[O].)

That moral worth and social status are inextricably intertwined in the idiom of English should not come as a surprise to anyone who has reflected, even casually, on the numerous phrases involving *high*, *great*, *low* and *base*. But how is this important semantic development to be interpreted? Is the moralization of status-words reflected in fact? Is it a cynical reinforcement of class-distinction in altered terms? Is it a reflection of the breakdown of feudalism as a result of economic pressures from below?

The answers, if answers there be, are extremely complex. In such involved sociolinguistic developments, the catalysts of change are sometimes not explicit in their presence, which makes their subsequent detection the more difficult. The simplest explanation, that moralization was reflected in fact, is basically that advanced by Owen Barfield: 'That the Feudal System had an educative value and played its part in creating modern ideals of conduct is suggested by such words as *honest*, *kind* and *gentle*, which at first meant simply "of good birth or position" and only later acquired during the Middle Ages their later and lovelier meanings' (1954, p. 51). To this argument one might reply, using the other side of the semantic evidence, that the Feudal System manifestly did *not* have an educative function (of a beneficent kind) since the *villeins*, the *ceorls*, the *lǣwed* and the *uncuþ* became, apparently, morally worse. Furthermore, the behaviour of magnates in the medieval period is reflected in the early semantic history of *danger.* Old French *dangier* is derived from Latin *dominium*, 'power', 'authority', which is the basic sense of ME *daunger.* The high-handed and lawless behaviour of those in power effected the shift to the modern sense of 'liability or exposure to harm or injury', first recorded in Caxton *c.* 1489°.[12] There is also the 'subversive' idiom *as drunk as a lord.*

C. S. Lewis takes the argument much further, in his characteristically acute and incisive fashion:

> It [moralization] will be diagnosed by many as a symptom of the inveterate snobbery of the human race; and certainly the implications of language are hardly ever egalitarian. But that is not the whole story. Two other factors come in. One is optimism; men's belief, or at least hope, that their social betters [*sic*] will be personally better as well. The other is far more important. A word like *nobility* begins to take on its social–ethical meaning when it refers not simply to a man's status but to the manners and character which are thought to be appropriate to that status. But the mind cannot long consider those manners and that character without being forced on the reflection that they are sometimes lacking in those who are noble by status and sometimes present in those who are not. Thus from the very first the social–ethical meaning, merely by existing, is bound to separate itself from the status-meaning. (1960, p. 22)

This analysis obviously avoids the oversimplification of Barfield's so-called 'educative' position and takes us to the nub of the matter by prompting the related questions 'Where does this social–ethical meaning derive from?' and 'How can it take root in a word which refers only to status?'

One answer, I suggest, lies in a body of evidence which is usually ignored in these matters: the law. The Anglo-Saxon laws are largely concerned with punishment and show, through the highly developed concept of *wergild*, an equation between a person's status and material value, and a strong correlation between status and implied moral quality:

A twelve hundred man's oath stands for six *ceorl*'s oaths. If a *ceorl* is often accused, and if at last he is taken [in the act], his hand or foot is to be struck off.

If a man of Kent buys property in London, he is to have then two or three honest *ceorls*, or the king's town-reeve, as witness.[13]

It is thus manifestly obvious that although the words *ceorl* and *eorl* had no moral connotation, *eorls* and *ceorls* were not equal in the sight of the law, and that very damaging moral assumptions were made about you if you had the misfortune to be born a *ceorl.* But the corollary of manifest injustice is also present. The more the notion of 'churlish' behaviour is subsumed or written into the law, the more people are going to realize the injustice done to those 'two or three honest churls', and so the divergence between 'status meaning' and 'social–ethical meaning' will grow.

The potential for upward mobility would seem to be a decisive factor in the semantic process under discussion. Once it is possible for people to move from their inherited 'natural' or 'native' station in life, it becomes more reasonable to regard those still in lower stations as objects of criticism. This becomes equally evident in the opprobrium attaching to poverty in capitalist societies, and to illiteracy in literate societies.

All upward mobility amongst the Anglo-Saxons was, of course, cut short at Battle Hill in 1066. As a consequence of the Conquest, the associations of nobility attaching to such native terms as *ðegn* (later *thane*) and *eðel* (nobleman) were extinguished with the words themselves. A separation of registers on the bases of class and race took place, with the Norman terms rising and the Saxon sinking in status. *Villain*, *knave*, *blackguard*, etc., generally deteriorate in terms of conventional morality and though *churl* shows the same basic line of development, it never becomes as morally critical as the other words. *The Children's Book* of 1480 admonishes youth in the most endearingly familiar bourgeois terms: 'Pyke not þyne Eris ne þy nostrellis; if þu do, men wolle sey þou come of cherlis. ["Do not pick your ears or nose; if you do, people will say that you're common."]' Furthermore, the pecuniary gloss added to *free*, *frank* and *liberal* serves to focus the Renaissance development of *churl* on matters of the purse. In Deloney's *Jack of Newberie* (1598) we hear that 'John Winchcombe . . . would spend his money with the best, and was not at any time found a churl of his purse.' The growing power of money and its semantic effects are the theme of the next chapter. However, as has become clear already, the semantic correlatives of this new source of power are very pervasive, and reflect the increasing secularization of society as well as greater social mobility.

THE SECULARIZATION OF RELIGIOUS TERMINOLOGY

This trend is now so advanced that it seems almost pedantic to point out the religious origins of *sanction*, *sanctuary*, *rubric*, *doctrine*, *propaganda*, *novice*, *incumbent*, *conscientious*, *office*, *lobby*, *asylum*, *cell*, *anathema*, *pittance*, *lesson*, *passion*, *mercy* and many others. The enduring power-struggle between Church and State is shown in the movement of these words, and the process has been, in the past few centuries, largely a one-way trend as the State has taken over from its erstwhile rival establishment numerous terms of ecclesiastical authority and significance. (Secular *holidays*, for instance, now rival or outnumber religious *holy days* in many societies.)[14]

The politicization of religious terms is not solely a matter of secular borrowing (or theft), and must have been influenced by the political character and actions of the medieval church, as well as by the highly secular lives led by many of the clergy. The Papal Schism was political rather than doctrinal in nature, and many of the worldly corruptions within the clergy shown so vividly by Chaucer and Langland were not truly reformed before the Reformation.

It is noteworthy that several terms normally thought of as being exclusively religious are originally borrowings from the secular sphere. *Priest*, for example, is derived from Greek *presbuteros*, 'an elder'; *bishop* originates in Greek *episkopos*, meaning 'an overseer' (the first meaning given in Cawdrey's *Table Alphabeticall* of 1604), and is applied to various civil offices; and the bishop's *diocese* derives from the term used in the Roman Empire for the area of a governor's jurisdiction. Similarly, *ecclesiastical* originates in *ekklesia*, a Greek word for any regularly convoked civil assembly, and *basilica* denotes in Greek a royal palace or hall of justice.

St Augustine and his fellow converters of the British were shrewd enough anthropologists to realize the efficacy of established pagan terms if they were given a new Christian gloss. The festival of *Easter* was accordingly adopted (or rather baptized) from the Spring festival of the pagan fertility goddess *Eastron* or *Eastre.*[15] (The fertility associations still hover round Easter bunnies and Easter eggs, in an admittedly commercialized form.) *Bless*, such a serene, beneficent word, derives – via Anglo-Saxon *bletsian* – from *blot*, 'a bloody sacrifice', for the word had the original sense of 'to mark or sprinkle with blood', a form of sympathetic magic whereby the power of the sacrificed beast was transferred to the faithful. In similar fashion, the archaic word for the Eucharist, *housel* (found centuries later in *Hamlet* I. v. 77) derives from the Anglo-

Saxon term *husl*, 'a sacrifice'. Even the word *god* is distantly rooted in the notion of sacrifice. The names of the days of the week remind us of the pagan roots of our culture: *Tuesday*, *Wednesday*, *Thursday* and *Friday* commemorate the Scandinavian deities Tiw, Woden, Thor and Freyja, respectively, while *Saturday*, *Sunday* and *Monday* recall the classical astronomical deities Saturn, the Sun and the Moon. The Lord's day has remained unconverted, in contradistinction to the style of the 'Catholic' European forms, *domenica*, *dimanche* and so on.

When one moves from the native terms which were converted along with the speakers to the borrowed words which were later secularized, it is often hard to separate the different shades of meaning. For instance, the *Cursor Mundi* (*c.* 1300), uses *ransom* in all three major senses, viz., payment for release of a prisoner (in a military context), the figurative sense referring to Christ and his blood, and the action or means of freeing oneself from a penalty. Similarly, with *sanction*, *mystery* and *doctrine*, it is difficult to ascertain whether the secular sense preceded the religious or vice versa. In general, the borrowing of religious terminology by the other estates is a slow process, achieved only after an average of some two centuries of coaxing and encroachment, according to the admittedly simplified record of the dictionary.

The relevant data are set out in figure 2.1, which shows that the process of borrowing was a fairly consistent and steady business, with significant increments around 1400 and 1600. The interesting hiatus between 1650 and 1800, filled mainly by *conscientious* and *enthusiasm*, relates potentially to the growth of Puritanism and the growth of fanatical cults. The tide of borrowing is halted, and only those terms which can be used to reinforce the ethic of conscientious industry are converted. *Dogma* and *propaganda*, both late arrivals dating from the early seventeenth century, are natural candidates for generalization in the nineteenth century, owing to the emergence of the passionate creeds of nationalism and their dissemination.

These two terms remind us of a general trend of deterioration in religious terminology, a tendency which started with the stirrings of the Reformation and has increased ever since. Thus *heresy* was used in a broad critical sense from the fourteenth century, and as the Spanish Inquisition (initiated in 1478) became notorious for its severities in the sixteenth century, so *inquisition* itself became a dreaded word. *Sermon* acquired the sense of a tiresome or boring harangue from *c.* 1596° (in *The Taming of the Shrew*), while *stigma* started to take on the sense of a mark of opprobrium from *c.* 1619°. Impatience with religious fanaticism and inflexibility also gave rise to the critical sense of *dogma* (as in 'the grosse

FIGURE 2.1 The secularization of religious terminology

1100	clerk worship
1150	
1200	cell
1250	obedience temptation
1300	mercy faith gospel ransom beg pray reverence
1350	lesson prayer penance
1400	baptism heresy office passion pittance retreat doctrine mystery solemn miracle
1450	schism talent redeem
1500	
1550	devotion creed sanctuary inquisition
1600	adore bless confession rubric stigma tenet sermon
1650	conscientious asylum sanction
1700	enthusiasm cult
1750	recluse
1800	communion dogma hermit crusade
1850	propaganda
1900	
1950	

fanatick Dogmates [dogmas] of the Alcoran', from *c.* 1638[O]), with *dogmatic* following suit around half a century later. (The King James Bible had previously warned readers against *dogmatizing.*) The eighteenth century saw *pittance* (originally a 'pious donation'), *crusade* and *cult* follow suit, while the following century added such quasi-religious words as *indoctrinate* (from *c.* 1832[O]) and its contemporary *doctrinaire.*

Perhaps the most spectacular decline occurred in the sacred phrase *hoc est corpus*, used in the Eucharist. It emerged *c.* 1624[O] in the corrupted form *hocus pocus*, a conjuring formula, explained acerbically by Archbishop Tillotson in 1694 as 'a ridiculous imitation of the priests of the Church of Rome, in their trick of Transubstantiation'[O]. The isolated form *hocus* had a considerable low currency meaning a conjuror or juggler, later becoming a verb for the same activity, and subsequently acquiring the sordid specialization of 'to stupefy with drugs, especially for some criminal purpose'. As the original form receded from recognition, so *hoax* came into being, recorded from *c.* 1796[O].

URBANITY AND RUDENESS

'Our courtiers say all's savage but at court.' So says a character in *Cymbeline* (IV. ii. 33), articulating with clear irony a prevailing polarization between town and country, one which makes itself felt from late medieval times onwards. The tide of popular preference for these contrasting locales has alternated through history. Dunbar wrote around 1500 of London, in almost stilted aureate terms, as ‘Gemme of all joy, jasper of jocunditie’. Blake’s poem *London* (1794) depicts a nightmarish den of alienation, exploitation and misery, the begetter of the *slum* (recorded from *c.* 1825[O]) and the *ghetto*, a more complex term in its racial shifts since its origins in Venice. The main demographic development of the medieval period is the rise of towns and this has produced – predictably – its semantic correlatives.

Originally ‘the country’ was unsafe, so that the *burg* or *burh* (later *borough*) related to A-S *beorgan*, ‘to defend’, was generally ‘a stronghold’, a place in which private safety was ensured by communal defence. (Today, the situation is largely reversed, with *vigilantes* and *neighbourhood watch* guarding against or avenging *muggings* and the multifarious forms of *inner city* crime in the *concrete jungle*.) A law of 1285, the Statute of Westminster, ordained that roads should be widened and cleared within a range of 200 feet on either side by the destruction of bushes and trees so that there should be no cover for robbers lying in ambush. It commanded that the gates of walled cities be closed all night, and gave a generally perilous picture of life at the time. The *curfew*, now invoked in special emergencies and states of martial law, was then *de rigueur*, meaning simply a precaution against fire, from the Norman etymology *couvre feu*. In time the *burgh* became a centre for commerce, and special privileges were often conferred by royal charter. This was the status of the *borough* by *c.* 1380. Xenophobia and economic competition led to restrictive legislation against ‘foreign’ traders and correspondingly protected *denizens*, i.e., those who lived ‘in the city’, derived from OF *deinz la cité*.

The polarization of civic urbanity and rustic rudeness is already established by the fourteenth century. Clear disparagement rings through Ranulf Higden’s comment on the ‘uppishness’ of ‘Vplondisshe men [Latin *rurales homines*] who wil likne himself to gentil men, and fonde wiþ gret besynesse for to speke Frensce, for to be [more] i-tolde of.’ (‘Country bumpkins, pretending to class, will make absurd efforts to speak French, in order to be more respected’), from John of Trevisa’s translation of Higden’s *Polychronicon* (1387, vol. II, p. 159). *Civil* gains in force and range through the sixteenth century, to be joined *c.* 1623[O] by *urbane* (‘having the manners, refinement, polish, regarded as characteristic of a town’[O]). *Civilization* is a comparatively late formation from the Latin root *civis*, emerging in the late eighteenth century and excluded by Johnson from even the fourth edition of his *Dictionary.* The word’s association with the city now seems ironic.

These semantic shifts are counterbalanced and reinforced by the deterioration of such original rural terms as *clown* (from *c.* 1565[O]), *lout* (from *c.* 1548[O]), *bumpkin* (from *c.* 1570[O]), *boor* (from *c.* 1598[O]) and *rustic* (from *c.* 1585[O]). The synchronous quality of these shifts is impressive. Johnson was to define *rustical*, for example, in a manner we should regard as hostile: 'rough; savage; boisterous; brutal; rude'. We know, however, that for a great many writers, previous and contemporary with him, such as Shakespeare, Milton, Marvell, Gray and Goldsmith, the countryside and its inhabitants had charms. These were with increasing commonness conveyed in the term *rural*, while *rustic* was increasingly reserved for 'the more primitive qualities or manners attaching to country life'[O]. Today a traveller through the countryside is less likely to be confronted by 'a company of buzzardly pezantes', as a writer of 1576[O] calls them, than he would in medieval times. And, largely owing to the influence of Wordsworth and the Romantic school who transformed the English sense of beauty, as well as attitudes towards the country, he would be less likely to see them in such terms.

THE MORALIZATION OF LEARNING

The status attaching to education has been a perennially obvious social fact, even in times when monarchs, magnates and other dignitaries have been illiterate. The semantic development of two traditionally antithetical social terms, *lered* and *lewed*, into *learned* and *lewd* is the most striking evidence of this status, as well as of accompanying moralization. The ancient distinction in Anglo-Saxon was between *gelæwede* and *gehadode*, the laity and the ordained. As the clergy were often not literate in those times, a distinction could not be made solely on the basis of education, but by early Middle English *lewed* has the chief sense of 'uneducated'. Wycliff writes (in *Deeds*, IV, 13) that 'Thei [Peter and John] weren men unlettrid, and *lewid* men.' As education has become a matter of will and choice, so the word has deteriorated to mean 'ignorant', 'stupid', 'foolish', 'useless', 'worthless', often with an implication of sloth. The sexual specialization of the term can be inferred from a passage in Chaucer's 'Merchant's Tale', where the old lecher January uses 'olde lewed wordes', inviting his child-bride May to 'taken som disport' ('have some fun'), but this meaning is generally found later. One of the best examples is in Shakespeare's *Richard III*, where Buckingham, acting as Richard's publicity agent, extols the sobriety and sexual continence of his candidate, qualities which contrast him sharply with the incumbent (Edward IV):

He is not lolling on a *lewd* love-bed
But on his knees at meditation.
(III. vii. 71–2)

Mass-education, supposedly a democratizing force, has in fact intensified the awareness of individual differences, not just in education but also in ability. The moralization of literacy (evident in the status now attaching to *articulate*, *learned* and *educated*[16]) has been extended to terms of ability, such as *brilliant*, *intelligent*, *capable*, *able* and *genius.*[17] Just as these are increasingly arrogated to a status approximating to moral worth, so their antonymic counterparts imply worthlessness and moral inadequacy. *Idiot*, *moron*, *imbecile*, *cretin*, as well as *illiterate*, *uneducated*, *ignorant*, *inarticulate* reveal the trend. Several of these words are fairly recent: *moron* was coined by H. H. Goddard, the researcher into the measurement of intelligence, in 1910. The stress on the so-called Intelligence Quotient, and the purveying of education as an acquisitive, competitive, self-advancing process have naturally made people very self-conscious of *grades*, *degrees*, *graduations*, as well as of the stigma attached to being *backward*, or in a state of *arrested development*, or, worst of all, of being a *failure.*

As literacy and education became more widespread, so various shifts of value took place. For example, *clerk*, dating from *c.* 1085[O], is now almost entirely debased to a low administrative function, but initially denoted a learned man, as clerics commonly were. The universality of literacy and basic education in the West has obviously played a part in the decline of the word by making the functionary more common. Cotgrave's definition (1611) is virtually a semantic history in itself: 'A scholler, or learned person; hence also a churchman (who should be learned); also a clarke in an office; a lawyers clark and generally any penman.' *Scrivener*, recorded from *c.* 1375[O], has also been rendered obsolete by general literacy, as has *scribe*, which survives mainly as an artificial archaism in journalism. In similar fashion, *trivial*, which is recorded in its literal association with the *trivium* (Grammar, Logic and Rhetoric) from *c.* 1432[O], has steadily lost its high medieval status to mean 'commonplace' or 'worthless', as in Thomas Nashe's remark, 'a few of our trivial translators' (1598)[O].

The prestige of the classics (which the *trivium* endorsed) is well established long before the Renaissance, but the history of *classic* is worthy of comment. It is interesting that the qualitative meaning 'a work of the first class', dating from *c.* 1613[O], almost immediately attracts the association of the standard Greek and Latin authors. This is clearly because of the dominance of classical culture at the time, particularly in the literary field. The term was extended to the other arts, particularly architecture, carrying the stylistic implication of purity, simplicity and harmonious elegance. From there developed the meaning of a 'standard of excellence' (which might be Romantic, Modern or even Medieval). Latterly, *classic* has generalized (some would say democratized) widely to include ballet, film and the performing arts, indeed even to horse racing. Nowadays it has lost its elitist connotations to mean 'a perfect instance', as in 'a classic instance of managerial blundering', 'a classic cover-drive', and so on. The term has gained currency in most egalitarian societies. In fact its broadened use seems to bear out the pregnant observation of de Tocqueville: 'Aristocratic nations are naturally too apt to narrow the scope of human perfectibility; democratic nations expand it beyond reason' (1863, part II, p. 34).

The related word *class* is in general a later term, being first recorded only in Blount's *Glossographia* (1656), where it is applied both to people and to school or university. (Political 'class-terms', as is pointed out in chapter 7, are a nineteenth-century introduction, since 'Higher and Lower Orders were formerly used'[O].) The sense of a 'division of candidates or competitors according to merit' dates from *c.* 1807[O], though a quotation 'A conjuror of the highest class' is found in 1694[O]. The American convention of dating university graduates by the label, for example, 'class of 76' is recorded from *c.* 1828. As opposed to emphasis on rank within that class (being *cum laude*, *summa cum laude*, *proxime accessit*, etc.), the concern with fraternities, and the 'rating' of the university in question as being 'Ivy League', 'redbrick' and so on, demonstrates the obvious truth that higher education has its own class system, much of which is not at all meritocratic.[18] It is also clear that *degree* and *class*, which were in earlier times terms implying high status (as was *price*), have now become far more generalized.

Hierarchies are traditionally conservative, and consequently the rise of parvenus through remarkable personal qualities tends to be viewed by the establishment with a mixture of admiration and suspicion. In this respect, *precocious* and *prodigy* have revealing semantic histories. *Prodigy* shows almost complete amelioration. Originally it had an ominous signification (the counterpart of OE *wundor*, 'wonder, strange, alarming happening') from *c.* 1494[O]. The bad personal sense of a monster is memorably instanced in Clarendon's vituperative description of Cromwell in 1656: 'That prodigie of nature, that opprobrium of mankind ... who now calls himself our Protector'[O]. John Evelyn is accorded the first instance of the now-familiar concept of 'infant prodigy' in a touching entry of 27 January 1658: 'Died my dear son Richard 5 years and 3 days old only, but at that tender age a prodigy for witt and understanding.'[O]

Precocious, on the other hand, has not achieved the same wholehearted amelioration. The early association with botany has served to strengthen the association of 'unnatural'. The earliest recorded instance of *precocity* (1640[O]) relates to the fall of Satan through his 'precocity of Spirit'. Today, unlike *prodigy*, the nuances are not always favourable. Here one may observe that in a relatively class-conscious society, as is still found in Britain, terms such as *uppish*, *uppity* or being *above oneself* are still in use. In such a social context, a hostile nuance still attaches to the more competitive words for intelligence, such as *clever*, *smart* and even *shrewd.* In American society, which is more egalitarian and competitive, these words carry better associations than they do in Britain. So does *sharp* in the US. One observes in this respect the peculiarly English quality of such phrases as 'too clever by half' and 'clever-clever', as well as the greater hostility attaching to being 'forward' or 'presumptuous'. The difference between these usages is clearly a reflection of the sense of hierarchy and deference in the respective societies.

The general attitude towards education, its practitioners and its values requires consideration. Today both *intellectual* and *academic* (as nouns and adjectives) have an uneasy ambivalence of nuance. Both can be used critically to suggest an undue concern with the theoretical at the expense of the practical, a pejorative development which is surprisingly recent, given the perennial vulnerability of the academic enterprise to charges of impracticality. The critical senses were not even recorded in the original *OED*, but the *Supplement* gives an excellent first instance for *academic*, in this extract from *The Times* of 1886: 'This discussion partook of an academic character, for it was well understood that, whatever the result of the discussions might be, no practical step would be taken in the present Parliament.'

Intellectual, 'a person possessing or supposed to possess superior powers of intellect'[O], has similarly in this past century and a half acquired a slightly critical tone quintessentially captured in this quotation from 1898: '. . . the so-called intellectuals of Constantinople, who were engaged in discussion while the Turks were taking possession of the city'. An instance from *The Times* (1974), 'Russian history has set a pattern of alienated intellectuals'[S], shows a recent shift in the politicization of the word, which is now often assumed to be the exclusive property of the Left.

The semantic history of the familiar antithesis between *academic* and *pragmatic* is one of switching polarization. Today *pragmatism*, *practical* and their related synonyms are favourable terms, but in the more conservative, hierarchical ethos of three centuries ago they were invariably critical. They often carried the sense of dishonesty still apparent in *sharp practice*, evident in the first recorded instance (1494[O]): 'The towne of Seynt Denys . . . was goten by treson and practyse.' Even as late as 1863 the primary meanings of *pragmatism* were given as 'officiousness, pedantry'[O]. *Pragmatist* has the sense of 'a busybody' from *c.* 1640[O]; Johnson defines *pragmatick*, *pragmatickal* as 'impertinently busy; meddling; assuming business without leave or invitation'.

The recent amelioration of the 'pragmatic' field in relation to education has clearly been influenced by the increasing quest for utilitarian 'relevance'. (*Relevance* itself has now become a term of undefined general value, together with *awareness*, *concerned*, *consciousness* and *committed*, all of which seek to stress some 'relatedness' between social needs and academic discipline.) The relative status of the liberal arts and their servile or mechanical counterparts has changed radically as a result of the increasing importance and status accorded to science. The main semantic effects of this development are discussed in chapter 9, the Conclusion to this study.

The stereotypic antithetical clichés, *the ivory tower* and *the rat race*,[19] today synthesize the perennial opposition between what medievals termed 'the theoric' and 'the practick', between unreflective action and impractical contemplation, qualities which are, by themselves, inadequate. These clichés serve to intensify and exaggerate the opposition between these two world-views into a false antithesis, and to rigidify thinking about them. Veblen, who observed sardonically in his chapter on 'The Higher Learning' that learning was 'a by-product of the priestly vicarious leisure class' (1970, p. 367), also pointed out the irony that as the competition between educational establishments increased, so their leadership became filled with erstwhile 'captains of industry' (a phrase coined by Carlyle in 1843) who supplanted the 'priest' (p. 374).

The more education is made into a competitive activity, the more moralization will become associated with the extremes of the *gifted* and of the *failure*, a word which is comparatively new in our vocabulary. (It seems significant that one of the dominant senses of *failure* should now be educational, rather than spiritual or moral.) There is a pleasing irony in the first recorded use of the word: it is attributed to that most gifted of all prodigies, John Stuart Mill, in a quotation from 1865: 'If you elect me and I should turn out a failure. . . .'[O]

So far as the practitioners and purveyors of education are concerned, one notes that several of the terms have deteriorated. These include *pedant*, *pedagogue* and *schoolmaster.* While Florio [1598] glosses 'pedante or schoolmaster', Johnson [1755] defines the dominant sense of *pedant* with brilliant conciseness as 'A man vain of low knowledge; a man awkwardly ostentatious of his literature.' Criticism of the practitioners is directed more at the lower orders of the hierarchy, as is the case in other fields. *Professor*, *lecturer* and *researcher* have all managed to keep prestige, or at least neutrality, even in the anti-authoritarian ambience which has made *lecture*, *sermon* and *preach* terms of impatient criticism. The accusations of pedantry and impracticality may arise from reductive philistinism, but can also derive from that essential intellectual censor, common sense. This commodity is naturally unsympathetic to extreme excursions in the pursuit of knowledge 'for its own sake'.

CHIVALRY AND STATUS: THE RISE OF THE HORSEMAN

In the earlier discussion of the contrasting registers selected for the character of Chaucer's Knight, it was observed that the portrait shows a harmonious balance between the doughty Anglo-Saxon and the courtly French elements. The ancient Saxon roots of such seminal words as *trouthe*, *fredom* and *worthynesse* lead us to question Denholm-Young's assertion, 'It is impossible to be chivalrous without a horse' (1948, p. 240), even allowing that the remark may have been made only for its etymological wit (*cheval* being the root of *chivalry*). The dragon-slaying hero of the Anglo-Saxon epic *Beowulf* (who is never seen on a horse) perhaps lacks the panache and charm of the subsequent hero of romance, Lancelot, but he certainly matches him in courage, service, courtesy, honour and simple piety. Furthermore, he is concerned chiefly with nations in distress, rather than with damsels in the same condition. And, unlike Lancelot, he does not make treacherous and adulterous love to his lord's wife. The Saxons in *The Battle of Maldon*, those of them that have horses, dismount to do battle, while the cowards unchivalrously remount only to flee. The horse, like the ship, is simply a means of transport, neither of which was very developed in Anglo-Saxon times as a means of battle. Hence the naval losses to the piratical Vikings and the disaster at Hastings, where *eorl* and *ceorl* were cut down 'at the place of the grey apple-tree'[20] by a new and devastating weapon: fully armed men on horseback. 'The Anglo-Saxons used the stirrup [AS *stig-rap*, 'rope for mounting'],' writes Lynn White, Jr., in his stimulating, though questioned, book *Medieval Technology and Social Change*, 'but they did not comprehend it: for this they paid a fearful price' (1962, p. 28).

The Norman practitioners of mounted shock combat, who were often landless younger sons, became a new class, the knights. Their rise to power from *c.* 1100 is interestingly paralleled by the social elevation of the people who originally looked after the horses. Semantically, 'the boy who tends the mares', Old Teutonic *marhosskalkos*, Old French *mareschal*, becomes the *marshal*, rising to *Earl Marshal*, later *Field Marshal*. Likewise, 'the man who looks after the stable', Late Latin *comes stabuli*, becomes the *Constable*, principal officer to the Household of the early French kings. His rise to power is as dramatic as that of the Marshal, but – interestingly – he declines from the seventeenth century, possibly with the diminished use of cavalry or the obsolescence of literal 'horse-power'. A parallel rise and fall can be seen in *henchman*, of which the first element is related to A-S *hengest*, a horse. However, the word first appears *c.* 1360, and there are problems of interpretation. The generalized sense of 'right-hand man', 'trusty follower' is strong in Scotland from *c.* 1730[O], and the deteriorated political sense is recorded from *c.* 1839: 'A stout political supporter or partisan; esp. in U.S. "A mercenary adherent; a venal follower"'[O]. The uglier application to the body-guards and thugs of the underworld is not, surprisingly, pursued in the *Supplement*. The armed man on the horse, the *knight*, represents a seemingly arbitrary promotion of Anglo-Saxon *cniht*, meaning 'boy' or 'servant', the specialization of which term has been achieved by *c.* 1100. (Contrariwise, the other Anglo-Saxon term for boy, *cnafa*, almost as arbitrarily goes down in the world from *c.* 1205[O], to become one of the knight's most common enemies, the *knave*.) Amidst all this social mobility the *groom* is left behind, still holding the horses. (*Bridegroom* is a misnomer, the second element deriving properly from A-S *guma*, a man.)

It would be naive to assume that the knights initially embodied the code of chivalry as it is now understood. As Douglas and Greenaway explain, 'the Norman knight was distinguished from his fellows not by wealth or birth or social position, but by proficiency in arms: he was a soldier trained to fight in a specialized manner, and possessed of the weapons for so doing' (1953, p. 25). Lynn White, Jr., has pointed out that horses and their upkeep were expensive, as was a suit of armour, which apparently took an armourer about one year to make. From these facts he infers that the knights must have been people of some substance initially. Be that as it may, this new fighting elite formed a weapon which could be turned against its master, particularly if it lacked the land-grant to sustain its life-style. Pointing out that 'landless knights are a constant feature of early Norman society', Douglas and Greenaway outline some of their unchivalrous behaviour: 'Such, for instance, were the armed and mounted men who rioted outside Westminster Abbey during the Conqueror's coronation. . . . They were a dangerous class, and William in fact dismissed many from his own service in 1067' (1953, pp. 25–6). By this action he sought to reduce the tenure of power to a manageably small group of about four thousand trained soldiers, satisfying their territorial ambitions by supplying them with the lands of the Old English nobility and quashing any centrifugal, rebellious tendencies by requiring personal loyalty and service as a condition of such tenure.

The main semantic shift reflecting the slow break up of feudalism is the **democratization of status-words**, including terms to do with chivalry. This trend, which is an aspect of the **moralization of status-words**, concerns such terms as *courtesy*, *freedom*, *largesse*, *chivalry*, *honest* and *kind*. Today, it goes without saying, it is assumed that any person can attain a life-style characterized by these qualities, which were originally the exclusive preserve of the aristocracy. *Freedom* has changed, of course, from being a quality limited to the nobility to a democratic right. *Franchise*, originally an exclusive privilege (as it still is in its commercial sense) has likewise become the political guarantee of that right, in the form of the vote. The *OED* has an interesting note on the ulterior meaning of *free*: 'The primary sense of the adjective is "dear"; the Germanic and Celtic sense comes of its having been applied as the distinctive epithet of those members of the household who were connected by ties of kindred with the head, as opposed to the slaves.'

One of the central terms of medieval civilization, *courtesy* has, in the process of 'levelling down', become almost entirely debased, concerned only with outward forms, tokens, gestures, a ghost of its essentially dynamic, courtly former self. In its medieval forms, such as *courteisie*, it encapsulated the richly layered meanings of high medieval culture. These have been steadily diluted and eroded into the formal gestures which we now refer to (significantly) as *common courtesy*, also preserved in the *courtesy call* and *courtesy card*. This general modern sense is recorded from *c.* 1513[O] and seems to derive from the pragmatic Renaissance ethos of self-improvement, evidenced in the publication of numerous *courtesy-books*. In its most limited and stylized form of behaviour, it survives as the *curtsy*, recorded from *c.* 1545[O].

Chivalry dates from *c.* 1300, some two centuries after the institution of knighthood. Its early meanings are strictly martial, including such senses as 'knights or horsemen equipped for battle' (a doublet of *cavalry*), 'bravery and prowess in war', or 'a feat of knightly valour', as exemplified in this quotation from Robert of Gloucester (1297): 'He smot of his heued as liȝliche as it were a stouple [cork]; þat was his laste chiualerye.' *Chivalrous*, which is also fourteenth-century in its recorded origins, has an interestingly complex history. The *OED* remarks:

> In its original use ('having the character of a knight') this word becomes obsolete before 1600, perhaps shortly after 1530 (Lord Berners), for in Shakespeare, Spenser and the dictionaries *c.* 1600 it was merely traditional. . . . The word was revived in the late eighteenth century in writers of the romance of chivalry.

Burke's eloquent and intuitive complaint 'But the age of chivalry is gone. That of sophisters, economists and calculators has succeeded' (used as an epigraph to this chapter), was made at the time (1790) when chivalry, while largely defunct in fact, was about to be most vigorously recreated as a literary construct. This interesting juxtaposition gives some plausibility to the notion that idealized forms of literature are more likely to be compensations for 'real life' than imitations of it. On this moot point one may note the observation of Nietzsche: 'The appearance of pessimistic philosophies is not at all the sign of great and dreadful miseries' (1924, I, p. 48).

In the democratization of status-words and terms associated with chivalry, the basic criterion which emerges is that of action, rather than the privilege of birth. *Largesse*, *chivalry* and *courtesy* were naturally more centred in action from the beginning, but required a life-style unattainable by all. However, a developing sense of bourgeois pragmatism and competitiveness reduced *courtesy* to the polite form of manners necessary for self-advancement, and monetarized the notion of *largesse*, while insisting – not unreasonably – that it lay within the capacity of all men to be *honest* or *kind* or *noble* or *gentle*. In short, the terms which had been rooted in action became more concerned with acting, while those which had been rooted in birth became more concerned with behaviour. The notion of a moral democracy, which can be evidenced in Chaucer's poem on 'Gentilesse', is even older, as C. S. Lewis observes: 'Accordingly, from Boethius down, it becomes a commonplace of European literature that the true nobility is within, that *villanie*, not status, makes the villain, that there are "ungentle gentles" and that "gentle is as gentle does"' (1960, p. 22).

An essential aspect of loyal behaviour and chivalry concerns the notion of *truth*: even this undergoes a considerable change in the medieval period.

> Trouthe is the hyest thing that man may kepe,

says Arveragus, the worthy knight of Chaucer's 'Franklin's Tale' (l. 1479). The central and fascinating point in the semantic history of *truth* is that it evolves from being a private commitment to a publicly assessed quality. The form of the word even changes, so that *troth*, the private form, can, by the proof of arms, be asserted above even the claims of evidence or testimony, if need arises. (This medievalized form of *truth* is, of course, virtually the opposite of the modern notion, which is factual, demonstrable and essentially impersonal.) This concept is paralleled by the development of the notions of *trial* and *proof*. The primitive ritual of *trial by ordeal* gives way to the vicissitudes of *trial of arms*, finally evolving into the more logical *trial of evidence.* Similarly, the medieval knight *proved* things *with his hands* or by his *prowess* (which now means little more than sexual potency). Today such matters are proved by public argument, evidence and data. *Troth*, which is now plighted mainly in the marriage service in peace, takes on a different significance in martial society. There the *boast* is a serious undertaking which in peace sounds foolish and hubristic. This is because the medieval hero is a magical person who can make his words 'come true' by physically changing the world, as can the wizard or witch. Of course, the man who does not keep his boast is despised in all societies, and Anglo-Saxon heroic poetry is full of gnomic warnings about not being *ȝielpes to ȝeorn*, 'too eager to boast'. The decline of A-S *ȝielpan*, 'to boast' to the pathetic sense 'to yelp' has been partly paralleled by the fourteenth-century words *boast* and *vaunt.* These words underscore the basic recognition that credibility is the *sine qua non* of authority, a fact which modern politicians have ignored to their cost.

It is noteworthy that at the opposite end of the scale from the specifically aristocratic behavioural terms, *courtesy*, *chivalry*, *gentillesse*, three central terms for what is unremarkable, namely *common*, *ordinary* and *banal*, should have converged from very diverse, specific, medieval meanings. *Common* originated as a class-term referring to the Third Estate; *ordinary* had originally almost the opposite of its present sense, namely a judge or priest validated in his own right, as opposed to one specially empowered; and *banal* meant liable to the *ban* or obligation to do compulsory feudal service. Though *common* and *vulgar* were for centuries terms of abuse and criticism, their currency in these senses has fallen off very rapidly in the last few decades.

CONCLUSION

The Peasants' Revolt (now often styled more democratically 'the English Rising') came – temporarily – close to being a genuine revolution. It marked a radical, though temporary, shift of power, ostensibly towards genuine democracy, and more genuinely towards indi- vidual free enterprise by those peasants who sought to buy their way out of the labour obligations of the Feudal System.

While Chaucer mentions the main demographic catalyst, the Black Death, only twice, *en passant*, his subtle deployment of shifting value-terms among morally different characters in the Prologue shows his sharp awareness of the growth of an acquisitive, competitive, profit-oriented ethos. The central notion which is changing is that of *profit.* The traditional formula of *commune profit* (found in many a statute, ordinance and proclamation) is that of 'the well-being of the community', a sense upheld by his idealized Knight, Parson and Plowman in their lives of dedicated service. But *commune profit* is giving way to private profit, just as *common weal* was to give way to private wealth. Chaucer demonstrates this new mode of profiteering being achieved by violent competition (between Miller and Reeve for the profits of harvest, between Summoner and Friar for the lucrative market of 'pay as you sin'), by casual pre-emption of established privilege and cynical exploitation of the underprivileged laity by the corrupt clergy. In this process, a word such as *bisynesse* (previously meaning simply 'activity') starts to acquire its modern financial sense, while *winne*, previously a military term, acquires the sense of 'make money'. Chaucer pointedly applies these profiteering senses to the corrupt or venal ecclesiastics.

Another of the essential differences between relationships in medieval and modern times lies in the changed notion of *person*. For medievals, *person* denoted office, function, role, variously derived from the word's origin in Latin *persona*, a mask. For us it means the essential individual, conceived of as having a unique personality, physique and psyche. Shakespeare seems to have been one of the first to show the modern sense:

> For her own person,
> It beggar'd all description;
> (*Antony and Cleopatra*, II. ii. 205–6)

But he also uses the older sense:

> He comes to disfigure, or to present, the person of Moon-shine.
> (*Midsummer Night's Dream*, III. i. 62)

The phrase *in the person of* still preserves the older sense by formulaic fossilization. *Parson* (a doublet of *person*, originally sharing the same pronunciation) is a similar survival, since the *parson* was conceived of as being a representative of the divine. The same complex of meanings is present in *vicar*, from Latin *vicarius*, a substitute, and its survival *vicarious.* It is clear that much of the ambivalence and moral irony of Chaucer and Langland is perceived and created out of the ambiguity of *person*. Masks, roles and hypocrisy are consistently revealed by ironic comment or by the conscious literary exploitation of semantic changes.

Three other central terms reveal radical shifts between their medieval origins and their modern application. *Train*, one harbinger of the mass transport of the Industrial Revolution, was originally a regal word, referring (as it still does) to the elongated part of a dignitary's robe. The sense of a number of followers attending upon a person of rank is a fifteenth-century development, while the modern railway *train* is recorded from 1824[O]. Similar in origin and parallel in development is *progress*, referring to a state journey by a royal or noble personage (now largely democratized into *walkabout*, recorded in relation to royalty from *c.* 1970[S]). The general sense of 'continuous improvement or advance' dates from the late sixteenth century; as the *OED* notes, its history since then has been complex: 'Common in England *c.* 1590–1670. In the eighteenth century obsolete in England but apparently retained (or formed anew) in America where it became very common *c.* 1790.' Since then it has become the ideological obsession of the West and for decades had the special status of a capital letter.

But of all the words which simultaneously join and separate us from the medieval world, few are as sharp and vivid in their semantic change as *passion*. The dominant medieval sense was, of course, religious, referring to the agony of Christ's Crucifixion, the central act of Man's redemption. From this developed two related senses, that of a narrative or musical setting describing the sufferings of Christ, as well as a similar act of human suffering accepted by a martyr. The sense of 'extreme or overpowering individual emotion' is found in Chaucer as the 'passion of ire' (for 'the frenzy of rage'). But it was only from the Elizabethan period that the sense which is now dominant – of amorous or sexual desire – arose. From the period of Romanticism onwards, *passion* has become private and physical, often unsocial and even anti-social, taking the extreme form of *egoisme à deux*, the defiant rejection of the world or society by a passionate pair. The most significant aspect of the change, however, lies in the fact that the word previously signified dedicated, altruistic suffering for a cause, but now centres on pleasurable fulfilment which is personal, intense and obsessive.

These and many other words reflect the breaking up of the medieval hierarchies. Chaucer's wonderfully outrageous creation, the Wife of Bath, who refers with blasphemous subversion to 'Seinte Venus', who has distinct signs of proto-feminism in her determined pre-emption of *maistrie* (mastery) in the marriage contract, and who is sexually liberated enough to speak openly (and repeatedly) of the orgasm as a 'merye fit', is a fictional sign of future liberation. She is also a prosperous and aggressive self-made woman, with marketable skills and a capacity (when it suits her) for what may be called upward nubility. The rise of capital and of the individual profit motive are already visible in the fourteenth century. Their immensely important social and semantic effects are the theme of the following chapter.

NOTES

1 Between 1969 and 1986, 1108 churches were demolished. See Gavin Stamp (1986, p. 9).
2 Burke anticipated this cliché, without actually formulating it, in *Reflections* (1925, p. 93).
3 R. B. Dobson points out: 'Nearly everything written by their contemporaries about the rebels of 1381 was written by their enemies' (1970, p. 3).
4 Dobson comments (1970, p. 4): 'There is no serious doubt that the English government's desperate attempts to break out of a position of extreme financial insolvency precipitated the riots which led to a general revolt.'
5 From Ted Hughes's poem 'Pike'.
6 Froissart registered surprise at the currency of French in the English court in 1395. See May McKisack (1959, p. 524) and Baugh (1965, ch. 6) particularly the reference (on p. 167) to Walter Map's observation that provincial 'English' French was stigmatized as the 'French of Marlborough'.
7 The sense of 'Celt' is common in the earlier stages of the *Anglo-Saxon Chronicle*, e.g. *anno* 473: 'Hengest and Æsc gefuhton wiþ Walas' ('Hengest and Ash fought against the Celts'). In Ælfric, a later writer, the sense of 'slave' is usual: *min weal sprecþ* is glossed as *meum manicipium loquitur* ('my slave speaks').
8 *Nim* starts to be eclipsed by *take* around 1100, but 'after 1600 it reappears . . . as a slang or colloquial word in the sense of "to steal", and it is very common in this sense throughout the seventeenth century.'O
9 From a fifteenth-century cookery book, cited in Serjeantson (1935, p. 149); italics added.
10 Medieval street names seem to have been far less prudish than their subsequent counterparts. The number of streets indecorously termed *Pissing Alley* in London is legion.
11 Unfavourable extensions of A-S *wealh*, 'a Celt', are found in the use of the base-word to mean 'a shameless person', together with *wealh-word*, 'a wanton word' and the verb *wealian*, 'to be bold, wanton, impudent'.
12 For instance, during the reign of terror inflicted on the land by the nobles who built 'adulterine' castles (in defiance of King Stephen). See *The Anglo-Saxon Chronicle*, particularly *anno* 1137.
13 From the laws of Ine, 18 and the laws of Hlothere and Eadric, 16.

14 Fasting has also become an increasingly fashionable form of political protest, a form of blackmail far removed from the original religious motive of self-mortification.

15 Bede derived the word from *Eostre* (Northumbrian spelling *Eastre*), the name of the goddess whose festival was celebrated at the spring equinox. Her name is cognate with Sanskrit *usra*, 'dawn', and is thus related to Latin *Aurora.*

16 In *Keywords* (1976) Raymond Williams makes this bitter observation (under *educated*): 'There is a strong class sense in this use, and the level indicated by *educated* has been continually adjusted to leave the majority of people who have received an education below it.' Though Williams implies a conspiracy against the less educated, it is quite normal for terms of achievement to be raised or lowered in view of the general standards prevailing. Consequently *rich* has also been 'continually adjusted' to allow for inflation.

17 The literal sense of *brilliant* is first recorded in an edition of Blount's *Glossographia* (1681); the figurative emerges about a century later. Though the *Supplement* does not trace the subsequent development, the word is now used vaguely of virtually any achievement, without necessarily implying special skill or cleverness.

18 The Ivy League is in origin a football league, comprising the more prestigious Eastern colleges. The phrase seems to be first recorded in 1933[S]. *Redbrick*, appearing slightly later, from *c.* 1943[S], has a stronger class demarcation, as these quotations indicate: 'It may be natural enough for him to go on to Redbrick, but to . . . enter Oxbridge is something infinitely more exciting.'[S] 'Marriner took his professorship at that frightful redbrick university.'[S]

19 *Ivory tower* was cointed by Sainte-Beuve in 1837. He used it as a criticism of Alfred de Vigny's concern with an inspiration unmixed with practical matters. First used in English *c.* 1911[S], the phrase has steadily moved from contexts of art to those of education. *Rat-race*, originally pre-war American slang for a low grade dance, was first used in the general behaviourist sense *c.* 1939 and is now well established in English parlance.

20 *The Anglo-Saxon Chronicle*, MS Cotton Tiberius B iv, AD 1066.

3
Moneyed Words: The Growth of Capitalism

The old population, consisting of clergy, knights, and serfs, lived by the soil, the lower class working for the upper classes, who, from the economic point of view, were consumers who produced nothing. . . .

In this tiny, changeless world the arrival of the merchants suddenly disarranged all the habits of life, and produced, in every domain, a veritable revolution. To tell the truth, they were intruders, and the traditional order could find no place for them. In the midst of these people who lived by the soil . . . they seemed in some way scandalous, being as they were, without roots in the soil, and because of the strange and restless nature of their way of life. With them came not only the spirit of gain and of enterprise, but also the free labourer, the man of independent trade, detached alike from the soil and from the authority of the seigneur: and above all, the circulation of money.

Henri Pirenne

Blest paper-credit! last and best supply!
That lends Corruption lighter wings to fly!
Gold, imp'd by thee, can compass hardest things,
Can pocket States, can fetch and carry Kings.

Pope

Bad money drives out good.

Gresham's Law

OF THE huge agglomeration of words related to the capitalist mode of economic life, certain illuminating examples reveal in their semantic changes the major social developments of the past. It might clarify matters to look at some of these at the outset.

For centuries *purchase* meant something far more rapacious and disorderly than the present transactional sense denotes. The old senses of *purchase*, dating in ME from *c.* 1297°, were derived from *chase* and revolved around the actions of hunting and taking by force, whether the object were prey, person, plunder or pelf. (In Old French an *enfant de porchas* was not, as one might suppose, a child adopted or 'purchased' in slavery, but an illegitimate.) These meanings reflect an ancient, primitive time when *de jure* and *de facto* possession were often difficult to distinguish, more so than today. The original strong physical sense of *purchase*, we observe, is still used in contexts of leverage in physics and engineering.

The semantic development of *purchase* from these primitive roots reflects the differing modes of legitimate acquisition employed in Western society from the Middle Ages to the Renaissance. Around the time of Chaucer were added the meanings of 'shifting for oneself', particularly through begging and a legal sense, meaning 'acquisition by one's own action, as distinct from inheritance'. The modern sense of 'acquisition by payment' dates from much later, *c.* 1560[O], since when the term has acquired central significance.

One of the nearest semantic associates, *pay* shows a similar development. The earliest sense, 'to appease or pacify' (with strong martial connotations) is recorded from *c.* 1200[O]; the meaning of 'remunerate' is added about half a century later. *Pelf*, though never a word of central importance, shows similar development, from 'property pilfered or stolen' through a general sense of 'property or possessions' to the specialization of 'money, wealth, riches', current from *c.* 1500 to *c.* 1874[O], the word now being obsolete.

Fee and *finance* are revealing terms in that their dominant early senses concern obligation to settle a debt, whereas from the early sixteenth century the modern senses, implying greater freedom deriving from the use of money, begin to make their appearance. More specifically, *fee* is initially related to *feudal* (with which it is actually cognate) and concerns property held 'in fee', i.e., under terms of feudal service. The dominant modern sense of 'remuneration paid to a professional man' is recorded only from *c.* 1583[O] when Stubbes, in his *Anatomy of Abuses*, utters a familiar wish about a notoriously rapacious profession: 'The lawiers I would wish to take lesse fees of their clients.'[O] (It might be said that the whole change from feudalism to capitalism is summed up in the basic notion of *service* changing from 'something owed to a superior as an obligation' to 'something offered as a matter of choice, with profit in mind'.)

Finance (n.) moves from its plain etymological sense of 'end or ending' to 'settlement with a creditor; payment of a debt' (akin to the modern sense of 'paying a *fine*'). The practice was especially prevalent in that medieval form of martial enterprise, the payment of ransom: 'Where as the seid Countesse . . . hath made a lone of MCC li [£700] to the seid Erle of Somerset, for the payment of his fenaunce' (from the Rolls of Parliament, 1439). The modern sense of 'borrowing money at interest' (with quite different associations of *initiating* a transaction as an entrepreneur) is recorded only about a century later, from *c.* 1552[O].

Perhaps the most dramatic semantic evidence of the liberating effect of money, and the recognition of this fact during the Renaissance, is found in the word *fortune*. The earliest sense of 'chance' (dating from *c.* 1300) underwent amelioration from about 1400[O]. (One notes, in passing, that the earliest recorded sense of *luck* is that of 'good fortune'.) *Fortune* as 'an amount of wealth' seems to be first found much later, in Spenser in 1596, and abounds in Shakespeare. This new sense represents an obvious, but vital, change in perspective: *fortune* was formerly seen as something which controlled one, and is so embodied in the great medieval symbol of the Wheel of Fortune; from Elizabethan times it becomes something which can be 'made', allowing one control over one's life. As the Clown says to his father (in *The Winter's Tale*, upon the discovery of a hoard of gold):

> You're a made old man!
> (III. iii. 124)

The idiom has proved understandably resilient, for today the equation of power and money is obvious. This is because, through the monetarization of transactions, money has become more legal, more mobile, more efficient and altogether more convenient than any other mode of acquisition or settlement. The growth of money as a source of power is impressively evident in the semantic development of *rich.* The Anglo-Saxon form *rice*, related via Celtic *rix* to Latin *rex*, and cognate with German *Reich*, means essentially 'powerful', 'mighty', 'great' or 'noble'. The modern sense of 'wealthy', 'opulent', though also traceable to Anglo-Saxon, has now supplanted its rival, which survives only in the fossil *bishopric* ('bishop's realm' = diocese).

These key terms, together with *profit* (discussed at the close of the previous chapter) reflect fundamental changes in the use and status of wealth in the course of the past millennium. The most significant of these changes affected the serfs who, being originally bound to the land ('*ascriptae glebae*'), were unable to sell their labour freely. These labour obligations were gradually commuted into money payments and then slowly dissolved as the serfs became independent wage-earners. Profit and economic expansion tended to be inhibited by the Church doctrine of the 'just price',[1] by the cartelization of wages and prices arranged by the guilds, and by the lack of capital arising from the Church's opposition to usury. However, the lifetime of Chaucer has been described by M. M. Postan as 'the great breeding season of English capitalism' (1972, p. 165), the essential characteristic of which is competitive 'free enterprise' or 'private enterprise' funded not on obligatory general debt, but on individual initiative and credit. The system became increasingly widespread and powerful from the fourteenth century to the nineteenth, which was the heyday of *laissez-faire* capitalism. Today Britain represents a compromise between capitalism and socialism, allowing for considerable private enterprise and social mobility, but at the same time ensuring that there is adequate social security, little real poverty and general accessibility to good housing, education, health and employment.

THE SEMANTIC FIELD

The word-field is, expectedly, large and complex. A great number of general terms yield at least one financial or monetary sense, so that the first problem is that of defining the extent of the field. I have tended to use only the more obviously specific terms, ignoring such words as *rate*, *worth* and *value* which, although carrying strong financial associations in some contexts (as in *interest rate*, *net worth* and *market value*), do not claim such an obvious general affiliation with the vocabulary of capitalist finance as, say, *interest*, *market*, *debt* and *company*.

The words chosen are set out in figure 3.1. The division into the two broad categories of 'Original Terms' and 'Specializations' depends on whether the words have always carried an economic sense, or whether this sense has been added to a general term. In a case like *chattel* or *cheap*, where the word has a long and complex semantic history, the date of entry is that of the emergence of the modern sense.

The arrangements of the terms in such restricted formats involves, necessarily, great crudification of many rich and involved changes of meaning, and the more interesting histories are briefly outlined in what follows. The advantage of the arrangement, of course, is that it brings into focus concentrations of semantic change, and these can then be related to changes in the economic structure as a whole. The growth of the field shows an interesting, and not entirely predictable, shift in the growth of the two categories. Up to about 1400 the field is dominated by original terms, but thereafter these steadily diminish, for there is a great burgeoning of specialized terms from about 1550 to 1700. After 1700 there is diminution of growth in both categories to *c.* 1900. One might

FIGURE 3.1 The semantic field of economic terms

Original Capitalist Sense	*Date of Earliest Specialized or Dominant Capitalist Sense*
900 fee buy	
950 yield rich	
1000 fellow guild	
1050	
1100	
1150	
1200 tally tithe	
1250	pay wealth
1300 account control thrift usury debt exchequer	sell price rent
1350 money bargain salary tax exchange	wage customs
1400 broker magnate redeem mercenary expense levy	company save bill
1450 staple commodity revenue	loan charge
1500 farm excise duty	bribe market cheap
1550 monopoly trade mark	bank chattel interest (usury) purchase (n.) trade traffic credit finance goodwill dues
1600 capitalist cash tariff commerce pre-emption	embezzle fortune profit dividend share income invest corporation industry
1650 jobber	concession workhouse factory
1700 cheque	consumption demand economy fund note stock interest bull bear luxury security concern
1750 capitalist scab	budget business currency draft stock exchange
1800 exploitation trade union	exploit speculate/or firm strike crash
1850 entrepreneur	inflation blackleg limited (liability) nationalization
1900 boom (n.) devaluation	cartel dole welfare slump (n.) recession
1950 reschedule	depression

reasonably expect the increasing terminology required by the complexities of capitalist finance to be supplied from a stock of new terms, as has generally happened in the technological and scientific fields, but one finds, in fact, that terms like *dividend*, *consumption*, *demand*, *inflation*, *cartel* and *finance* all have older and broader origins, semantically speaking. The most likely explanation would seem to be that, since the economic aspect of our lives has gradually acquired central importance, it has necessarily used general, accessible and comprehensible terms, and not the abstruse jargon which surrounds those technical areas which are the province of a minority.

The general trend of the specializations reflects a monetarization of transactional terms, like *business*, *budget*, *duty*, *embezzle*, *finance* and *income*, which previously had broad senses before being absorbed into the financial field. Groups of terms support the familiar generalization that capitalism liberated private enterprise, which had previously been restricted under feudalism. The more restrictive terms, denoting traditional obligations imposed by the Crown or the State are all in force up to about 1550. These include (in approximate order of appearance): *fee* (in its older senses), *yield*, *tithe*, *debt*, *tax*, *levy*, *revenue*, *customs*, *excise*, *duty*, *monopoly* and *trademark.* To these must be added the important word *control*, which had the dominant early sense (from *c.* 1300^{0}) of 'to check or regulate accounts', before acquiring its general sense of administrative dominance two centuries later. *Account* itself, dating from the same period, shows an early split into financial responsibility and general responsibility, as well as the implication of being 'esteemed'. (These senses are shown in such phrases as 'give an account of yourself' and 'a man of some account'.)

From 1550 onwards one finds a growth of terms or dominant senses suggestive of money as a source of freedom, and as a mobile resource of enterprise. These terms, in order of appearance, include: *capital*, *cash*, *purchase*, *credit*, *finance*, *fortune*, *invest*, *concession*, *exploitation*, *speculate* and *entrepreneur.* To these may be added the dubious financial cousins *embezzle*, *workhouse*, *bribe*, *limited* (liability) and the hated *jobber*, of whom more will be said later.

So far as the organizational and institutional terms are concerned, one finds that these generally follow their referents in predictable fashion. Thus *guild* dates from *c.* 1000^{0} and *exchequer* from *c.* 1300^{0}. The 'Dialogue of the Exchequer' (*Dialogus de Scaccario*), the monumental twelfth-century classic on the institution, explains at the outset that the derivation of the name 'Exchequer' lies in the fact that the quadrangular board on which transactions take place 'has a shape similar to that of a chess-board' (Douglas and Greenaway, 1953, p. 494). *Exchange* is first found (1335) in Act 9 of Edward III: '. . . le table deschange soit a Dovorri'. *Bank*, *trade* and *traffic* date from *c.* 1550, followed closely by *dividend* and *share* in an influx of terms which supports the location of major capitalist development in the sixteenth century. It is around 1700, though, the period when the Bank of England is founded, that much of the institutional vocabulary emerges, invariably in the form of specializations of broader terms. *Economy*, *fund*, *security*, *concern*, *note*, *stock*, *cheque*, *consumption* and *demand* all date from this period, to be followed shortly by *budget*, *currency* and *draft*.

Middlemen are invariably suspected of parasitical profiteering, and it is not surprising to find that *broker* is used with hostility or contempt right from its earliest appearances, most of which are traced to the pages of Langland. The word has its origins in the wine trade: 'celui qui vend du vin au *broc*', i.e., broached and retailed. Some of the contempt assuredly derives from the low status of being a retailer dealing in small lots. Here one may compare the similar tone surrounding *monger*, *hawker*, *cadger* and *huckster*, all of which had related functions. But much of the hostility seems to have genuine financial causes. In the case of *huckster* (which, as the suffix *-ster* originally indicated, was a feminine term as *spinster* still is), there is the implication of being an *engrosser*, that is, an attempted monopolist who seeks to buy a whole stock in order to fix the retail price. A Statute in the *Burgh Laws* of *c.* 1400 seeks to prevent this engrossing:

> Hukstaris þat byis and sellis agane to wynning sal nocht by ony thing before þat undern be rungyn in wynter and mydmorne in somer.[O]
> [Hucksters who buy and then sell to make a profit shall not buy anything before the third hour is rung in winter and mid-morning in summer.]

Many quotations through to the mid-seventeenth century harp on the 'fraud and base arts' used by those who 'play the hucksters to enhanse the price'[O]. All the earliest references to *hawkers* seek to outlaw them. Acts 34 and 35 of Henry VIII (1542–3) denounce 'Euill disposed persons [who] vse daily the craft and subtilty of hauking abroad in the Country, to Villages and to men's houses, putting the same naughty ware to sale secretly.' The opposition to hucksters and hawkers (who would now be regarded as embodying private enterprise), came largely from the guilds, who sought to have their own monopolies, which were shared amongst the members.

COMMON AND INDIVIDUAL PROFIT

As has already been pointed out, 'profit' and 'wealth' change from being plural and general notions to acquiring materialist and individualist emphases. *Common profit*, found in many a royal and civil document, is roughly equivalent to what would now be termed 'the public interest', something assumed rather than defined. An Act of Edward II (1311) expresses very clearly this 'communality' of profit, justifying legislation as being 'to our profit, and to the profit of our people'[O]. (The modern capitalist parallel would be 'What's good for General Motors is good for America.') However, in the course of the fourteenth century one finds 'commune profit' being appealed to in an increasingly sectional fashion. The request for ordinances controlling the alien weavers in London (1362) speaks of 'the common profit of the land and of the City'[O] though the control would, in fact, be most profitable to the vested interests of the guilds and the Staplers. In the fifteenth and sixteenth centuries, as *profit* becomes more individualized, so the old formula drops out of use, being replaced by such phrases as 'the strength and flourishing estate of this kingdom', 'the benefit and advantage of our realm', and the like.

Wealth derives from *weal* (as does *health* from *heal*). *Weal* originally signified 'wealth' or 'riches' in Anglo-Saxon (before it was displaced by Norman *monnaie*) but it subsequently broadened into a general sense of 'prosperity' or 'welfare'. It seems fitting that the final quotation in the *OED* illustrating a traditional alliterating formula should have come from Queen Victoria in 1897: 'In weal and woe I have ever had the true sympathy of all my people.' As *weal* became obsolescent, so *wealth*, which is a later word (dating from *c.* 1250[O]), tended to take its place. *Commonwealth* is recorded from *c.* 1470[O], but *common weal* continued in currency for centuries. The general senses attaching to *wealth* passed out of use around 1600, and the materialistic specialization (of an abundance of worldly goods) became dominant. Unlike *profit*, *wealth* soon became more 'nationalized' in use and concept, so that the phrase 'the wealth of nations', traditionally associated with Adam Smith's famous title (1776), is first recorded in Dryden in 1666[O].

MONEY AND PROPERTY

The relations of money to fixed and moveable property are complex and various. The rich old word for property, *chattel*, splits in the sixteenth century into two forms: the Norman French half of the doublet, *cattle*, becomes confined to livestock, while the Parisian form, *chattels*, comes to designate moveable property. (The Latin root *caput* can be thought of as dividing into 'capital' on the one hand and 'head' on the other.) *Fee*, from Anglo-Saxon *feoh*, 'cattle', 'property' or 'money' has moved in a similar semantic direction from livestock to moveable property, but has completed the process of mobility by becoming 'money', just as Latin *pecus* became *pecunia*. *Fellow*, like *partner*, is originally a business associate, found in late Old English *feolaga*, 'one who lays down *feoh* or money'.

Farm (a peculiarly English word unknown elsewhere) originally designated (from around 1400[O]) a sum of money payable as rent tax or the like. It then developed into the broad sense of a lease, before acquiring (*c.* 1523[O]) the meaning which we recognize, 'a tract of land held on lease for the purpose of cultivation'. The only vestige of the original sense is found in the verb *to farm* (out). This meaning is frequently encountered in medieval contexts concerning matters of finance or taxation. The Saxon kings had levied taxes on their own account: these might be *Danegeld* – to buy off the marauding Vikings – or Land Taxes. The Normans instituted the practice of allowing the sheriff (literally the 'shire reeve') to 'farm' his shire, i.e., 'of paying the King an agreed sum for the shire and later recouping himself what he could actually raise from its inhabitants' (Douglas and Greenaway, 1953, p. 546).

TAXATION

Echoing the sentiments quoted in the previous chapter that 'tax has ruined us all', Dr Johnson in his famous denunciation called excise 'a hateful tax'. The examples of *Danegeld* and Land Tax previously alluded to bring up the subject of taxation, which has been a perennial source of discontent. The practice of taxation is, of course, immensely old (there is a reference in the *OED* to *tax* in a grant in Latin dated 680) and its exaction has always been the privilege of those in power, either autocratically or democratically. The primary sense 'obligation' is brought out in the origin of the word, for it is a metathetical variant of *task* (as the form *axe* used to be of *ask*).[2] However, over the centuries, there has been a radical shift in the notion and function of tax.

Previously it was exacted by those in the upper echelons of the hierarchy from their underlings. Trevelyan outlines some of the punitive 'servile dues' of the Middle Ages: 'Such were the *merchet*, the fine paid for marriage; the *heriot*, the seizure of the family's best beast on the death of the tenant; the compulsory use of the lord's mill for grinding the family corn at a monopoly price – and many more such galling instances of servitude' (Trevelyan, 1945, p. 34). The effect of these taxes was obviously to maintain the status quo. However, since the medieval period, tax has increasingly taken on a quite contrary rationale, of seeking to equalize the distribution of wealth. Some impositions seem to have had less of a rationale than others, such as the taxes on matches, on dogs and on windows (this last being instituted in 1695, denounced by Harriet Martineau in 1850 as 'a duty upon fresh air, sunshine and health', and abolished the following year). Not surprisingly, *tax* as a verb took on the senses of 'to take to task' (from 1569[O]) and 'to burden or persecute', from *c.* 1672[O]. Furthermore, occasional tax also has a habit of becoming permanent. *Income tax*, the chief bane of most people's financial existence, was first introduced as a war tax in 1709. When it was reintroduced in 1842 it occasioned the following naive comment: 'The existing income-tax should not be retained a moment after it can be dispensed with.' That was in 1846. Death duties and other estate taxes have brought about an ironic reversal of the medieval status quo, in that those at the top of the class hierarchy are now often unable to meet the tax bill on their inheritance without living in reduced circumstances.

BRIBERY AND CORRUPTION

It can be seen that the potential for profit has always been essentially related to position in the hierarchy. This is cynically apparent in the semantic development of the complex noun *bribe*, fascinatingly pieced together in the *OED.* It emerges that the modern sense of 'a consideration voluntarily offered to corrupt a person' is *preceded* by the sense 'a consideration extorted, exacted or taken by an official, judge, etc.':

> The transition is best seen in the agent-noun *briber*, where we have the series, 'beggar', 'vagabond', 'thief', 'robber', 'extortioner', 'exactor of black mail', and 'receiver of baksheesh' (the Baconian sense). The sudden and startling change from the Baconian 'briber' who received douceurs, to the modern 'briber' who gives them, can be explained only by taking the latter as a separate derivative of the verb in its latest sense.

Likewise, the word *cheat* derives from the corruption of a medieval office, that of the *escheator.* His function was to assess the value of an *escheat*, 'property reverting to the Treasury on the death of the King's tenant-in-chief for want of an heir' (Douglas and Greenaway, 1953, pp. 546ff.). However, *escheators* became so notorious for their rapacity and dishonesty that the dominant modern sense of *cheat* and *cheater* developed, and can be detected as far back as the fourteenth century. Fuller was to write in 1642, 'Receiving black money from cheatours, he pays them in good silver'[O], and Jeremy Taylor (1651) gives us the contextual link with the modern sense in his ironic juxtaposition: 'Cheaters of Men's inheritances, unjust judges'[O].

Purveyors, now very respectable suppliers of provisions to royalty, were the source of many complaints in the fourteenth century for abusing their royal privilege by not paying for the goods and services commandeered in the King's name. A statute of 1360 cleaned up this area of corrupt exploitation by insisting on ready payment. Fascinatingly, it also sanctioned the somewhat cynical substitution of terminology which Orwell has exposed in the modern period with clarity and irony, whereby Ministries of War are restyled Ministries of Peace. In the statute we read that 'le heignous noun de purveyour soit chaungé & nomé achatour' ('the odious title of purveyor shall be changed and styled buyer').

Delving amongst these interesting (though sordid) medieval roots should not, however, obscure the major semantic development in the field, whereby *corruption* itself has narrowed down from its broad moral sense to become particularly associated with materialism, venality and money. Thus, a 'corrupt' politician or clergyman would today not mean simply one who was unprincipled or abused his office, but especially one who could be 'bought'.

CURRENCY DEBASEMENT

'Black' money raises the subject of coinage and foreign exchange, which, being royal prerogatives, have been a perennial source of revenue to the Treasury. As kings became, through diminished prestige, less able to levy money or soldiers without the consent of parliament, they resorted to the debasement of the currency. Hence the appearance of 'black' money (or debased silver coinage, as opposed to 'white' money, which was sound), first noted in an Act of Edward III of 1335. In the Rolls of Parliament of 1423 there is this melancholy observation: 'For as muche as gret scarcite of White money is wyth inne this land, because that silver is bought [hoarded].' The 'beggarly denier', as Richard III calls it in Shakespeare's play, was most commonly referred to as *monnaie noire* once its silver content had become minimal. In the reign of Charlemagne it had been about 22 troy grains silver, about a pennyweight; under Henry III (1574–89) it became a copper coin.

The subsequent history of debasements and devaluation is lamentably familiar to denizens of this century. Today this governmental form of coin-clipping produces in an inured public a response of resignation and cynicism. With the currency terms set so strongly against it, private enterprise has needed considerable sharpness to profit. Signs of this initiative are to be found even in the fourteenth century. In the portrait of Chaucer's shrewd mercantile entrepreneur (penned late in the century) one notices the wry accuracy of the reference to illicit dealings in foreign exchange: 'He was expert in trafficking in *sheeldes* [French gold coins].' This is the first reference to the French *écu*, which was the only genuine standard gold coin available at the time.

Against this background of debasement, the development of *sterling* is significant. The Norman silver penny, derived from either the small star ('starling') or bird of the same name, developed from the sixteenth century the sense of 'genuine English money' in contrast to *currency*, which then meant the depreciated money of certain colonies. In one of his *Drapier Letters*, denouncing the debasement of the Irish currency, Swift points out the iniquity that 'the [Irish] tenants are obliged by their leases to pay Sterling.' As a 'pound of Sterlings' became abbreviated to the 'pound sterling' and then plain 'sterling', so there developed in the course of the seventeenth century the figurative meanings of 'sterling qualities', i.e., 'excellent, capable of standing every test'. (It was around this time that Sir Isaac Newton became the Master of the Mint and established the guinea to be worth 129.4 grams of gold, thereby giving the currency a permanent value.) Not surprisingly, with the subsequent withdrawal of the gold and silver standards, and numerous devaluations, the 'confident' sense of *sterling* just mentioned has become something of an archaism in the course of the twentieth century.

MERCANTILE FINANCE AND THE CROWN

Chaucer's Merchant is presented as a timeless capitalist, obsessed with his corner of the market and with profit. Ironically, the two trading towns which are the source of his extreme concern have all but disappeared, the one (Orwell) literally under the Suffolk sea, the other (Middelburg) into the footnotes of history. This reference to Middelburg (a Staple market from 1383 to 1388) suggests that he is to be identified with either the Merchants of the Staple or the Merchant Adventurers. Their rise to power exemplifies entrepreneurial opportunism responding to the technical and organizational complexities of the wool trade. Their success transformed England's economic character from that of a subsistence economy based on agriculture to one enriched by substantial commerce, trade and manufacture. The Woolsack, the traditional seat of England's Chancellor, symbolizes this source of wealth, as well as the support of the Crown in fostering the trade. While *adventure* has retained its general sense, traces of the Merchant Adventurers can still be seen in *business venture* and in *venture capital.*

Staple, on the other hand, has moved from its specialized medieval economic sense of 'a town, appointed by royal authority, in which a body of merchants have exclusive right to trade in a particular commodity' to the general sense of a 'principal industrial product or article of consumption'. The ancient sense is recorded from *c.* 1423: 'They may buy

Wolle . . . atte the Stapull of Calais'[O], while Captain Smith in his *Description of New England* (1616) gives us the modern meaning with his observation, 'The maine staple . . . is fish.'

Trade is, according to the *OED*, 'apparently introduced into English in the fourteenth century from Hanseatic Middle Low German, perhaps originally in nautical language for the "course or track" of a ship'. Consequently, *trade-winds* (recorded from *c.* 1650[O]) were so called because of their reliability, not for their commercial value, which was exploited later. ('The wind blowing trade' is recorded in Hakluyt's *Voyages* of 1600 and is the origin of the compound.) *Traffic* has moved from the main sense of 'trade' to that of 'transport'.

Merchants of all kinds – whether 'denizen' or 'alien' – i.e., local or foreign, were always potentially valuable to the Crown as a source of loans, if not of revenue. It is interesting, therefore, to discover that, from the early Middle Ages, the preponderance of merchants were foreigners, native merchants being generally of low status. The aliens were regarded with the kind of hostility which will be examined in chapter 8, and resented by their competitors, but were granted privileges by the Crown in return for loans. Though the interest rates were high, it is hard not to see in the arrangement the vestiges of a 'protection racket', since the foreigners were the objects of frequent royal confiscations, perennial malice and occasional massacre (Coleman, McDonnell and Pollard, 1957, p. 71).

The Jews were the first group of foreign merchants to establish themselves in England in 'Jewries' in various towns during the twelfth century. Being exempt from the canon laws against usury, they had an advantage in terms of capitalist entrepreneurship, but their alien status made them vulnerable to local hostility and they were expelled with popular approval in 1290 during the reign of Edward I. This fact of deportation makes the semantic extension of the opprobrious figurative use of the word *Jew* harder to explain; from *c.* 1606 is recorded the sense of 'a grasping or extortionate money-lender or usurer'[O], for example: 'Better we canot express the most cut-throat dealing than thus, you use me like a Jew' (1700[O]). It would seem to be a stereotypic creation based on hostility, suspicion, xenophobia and envy. Though they had lent substantial sums to the Church for the building of monasteries and cathedrals, Jews were forbidden under the Ordinances of 1253 to 'enter any church or any chapel save in passing through, nor stay therein to the dishonour of Christ' (Bland, Brown and Tawney, 1933, pp. 45–6).

Their place was largely filled by the Italian bankers and traders in the thirteenth and fourteenth centuries, although by this time English merchants of substance (such as the de la Poles of Hull) were rising in power. These men formed part of what Postan has described as 'a new race of war financiers and commercial speculators, army purveyors and wool monopolists' (1972, p. 165). However, if trade declined, or if the war ended, or ran against England, they stood to lose. All these things happened. Furthermore, working from the adage 'Put not thy trust in princes', the Italian bankers seem to have been slow in applying the mercantile corollary of 'Put not thy credit in kings':

> The king was not a good customer, and one by one all the foreign bankers had their fingers burnt. The Riccardi served Henry III and Edward I; the Frescobaldi who succeeded them fell with Edward II; the Peruzzi and the Bardi went bankrupt in 1345 under Edward III (as a result of the king's inability to pay them 1,500,000 gold florins).
>
> (Coleman et al., 1957, p. 72)

This quotation makes it clear how *Lombard* became synonymous with 'banker' from *c.* 1377 to *c.* 1709[O]. The most noted survival of the meaning is Lombard Street, still a centre of banking business in London.

BANKING, INTEREST AND CREDIT

Bank is originally (from *c.* 1050[O]) a bench. (*Bank* and *Bench* are, in fact, doublets, and it might be said that the divergent branches of the word symbolize structurally two pillars of the establishment in the modern state, money and law.) The literal force of the word is more clearly retained in the Anglicized form, *bench*, where the association with law is strong (e.g. *Common Bench* and *Queen's Bench*, originally found in Act 3 of Edward I (1275) as *Baunk le Roi*)[O]. It is a tempting speculation that the 'Italianate' form *bank* (from Italian *banco*) was used because of the role of Italian bankers in the Middle Ages. Recently the term has been generalized, with the addition of *blood bank* (*c.* 1938), *nerve bank* (*c.* 1945), *bone bank* (*c.* 1947) and even *foetal tissue bank* (*c.* 1959).[S]

Usury slowly became respectable, under the name of *interest*. A Petition Against Usury of 1376 denounced 'the horrible vice of usury [being] so spread abroad and used throughout the land that the virtue of charity, without which none can be saved, is wellnigh wholly perished'. The medieval opposition to usury had been modified by the end of the fifteenth century, but various ecclesiastics and reformers, such as Luther and Latimer, sought to protect the poor from extortion. Over the centuries interest rates have come to reflect free enterprise by floating free, according to supply and demand. *Interest* now carries no pejorative associations, since it is viewed as a right, not an unreasonable imposition, by the lender. *Usury* is also virtually unheard of, except as continuing the old sense of 'excessive or illegal interest', exemplified in this quotation from 1663: 'I hate this rack-renting; tis worse than usury.' Ezra Pound, obsessed by the rapacity of banking methods, coined the form *usurocracy* and revived the Latin form *usura* in a vehement passage in *Canto* XLV.

Today *credit* and *interest* are very near neighbours, but neither term was originally a commercial specialization. *To give credit to* meant originally (in the mid-sixteenth century) 'to believe', while a *letter of credit* was like a character reference, a credential. The commercial sense of *credit* sprang up contemporaneously. An Act of Henry VIII (1542–3) speaks of 'caterpillars of the commonwealth', wastrels who 'consume the substance obteined by credite of other men'[O]. A *letter of credit* in this sense is first recorded in John Evelyn's *Memoirs* in 1645, while the *credit system* is first recorded *c.* 1880[O] and *credit card* from almost the same period, from 1888. These originated in America and still appeared in inverted commas in some UK publications as late as 1958.

The post-Restoration period saw the emergence of a recognizably modern banking system, not without its share of problems and instability. Since many foreign bankers had been ruined by their dealings with royalty, the Bank of England was founded in 1694 'under pressure of acute embarrassment of the Exchequer' (Coleman et al., 1957, p. 196). In the 1660s and 1670s, 'blest paper credit', as Pope ironically referred to it (*Epistle to Bathurst*, l. 39), was increasingly used. (*Cheques*, for example, date from *c.* 1670.) By 1672 Charles II had accumulated debts of two and a half million pounds, of which £1,328,000 was owed to the goldsmiths, who had increasingly taken on the role of bankers. In that year the King was obliged to call a Stop of the Exchequer, repaying interest only but not the principal. Five goldsmiths were bankrupted. The money was still owing at the Revolution (1688), but, as a recent historian puts it blandly, 'a rudimentary form of long-term debt had been created' (Coleman et al., 1957, p. 196). The foundation of the Bank of England embodied the final transfer of the control of money from royalty to the government, a transfer reflected on both the images and the formulas on currency. The permanent 'National Debt' generated in these times was more dramatically (and more honestly) termed the 'Sinking Fund'.

SPECULATION AND THE STOCK EXCHANGE

Speculation acquired its capitalist sense only in the late eighteenth century, having for centuries previously been concerned with more sober philosophical matters of hypothetical reasoning and observation. Horace Walpole comments in a splendid quotation of 1774 on the fashionable speculative craze of the times: 'Next to gaming ... the predominant folly is pictures.'[O] However, the practice of speculation is obviously much older, for risk-taking and business are old partners.

Once the economically debilitating strain of civil and foreign wars had passed, capital was directed through joint-stock companies to such enterprises as sugar-refining (1669), fishing (1671) fire assurance (1680) and water works (1681). These became vehicles for the raising of capital and objects of speculation. The most spectacular notoriety surrounded the debacle of the South Sea Company. In a mere eight months the South Sea 'Bubble', as it came to be known, expanded as the stock rose from £136 to £1,000 and then burst, collapsing to £121. Many companies disappeared in the wreckage. Since they purported to deal in such commodities as hair, 'wheels of perpetual motion' and even, in one case 'a design which will hereafter be promulgated' (Richards and Quick, 1961, pp. 22–3), their demise was not altogether a bad thing. *Bubble* has become, not surprisingly, part of the idiom of finance and the Stock Exchange. Swift seems to have had a hand in the formation of the original phrase in a contemporary satire:

> The nation then too late will find
> Directors' promises but wind
> *South-Sea* at best a mighty *bubble*.

A slang verb *to bubble*, meaning 'to cheat' also acquired an understandable popularity in the eighteenth century.

Stock Exchange as a term is recorded only from *c.* 1773[O], but the institution had by then been active for nearly a century, being called originally 'Jonathan's' later 'New Jonathan's', often viewed with the familiar mixture of envy and hostility. Hence the pejorative associations attaching to *broker*, already commented on, and *stock-jobber*, recorded from 1626[O] in an unfavourable reference. Dr Johnson's definition (of 1755) combines contempt with his characteristic trenchancy: 'A low wretch who gets money by buying and selling shares in the funds.' In the year of the South Sea Bubble a poet solemnly commented:

> We madly at our ain expenses,
> Stock-jobb'd away our cash and senses.[O]

The corruption seems clearly spread to *job*, a word of uncertain origin and neutral meaning, first recorded from around 1626[O]. It soon acquired the sense (still current) of 'theft or robbery' in thieves' slang: 'It was always reckoned a safe job,' says Moll Flanders (in 1772) 'when we heard of a new shop.'[O]

In 1721 Colley Cibber, a noted Grub Street writer, or what would now be called a journalistic hack, penned this exchange:

> And all this out of Change-Alley?
> Every Shilling Sir; all out of Stocks, Tuts, Bulls, Rams, Bears and Bubbles.

He was introducing, in a knowing way, several of the terms from the financial jargon of the times, most of which are still current. It seems that *bear* made the earliest appearance in the phrase *bearskin jobber*, which prompted the noted essayist Steele to comment in 1709: 'I fear the word Bear is hardly to be understood among the polite people.' The explanation of the metaphor lies in the proverbial phrase 'to sell the bearskin before one has caught the bear', since the Bear sells shares he does not own in the expectation of a fall in the price so that he can then purchase the shares he owes at a profit. *Bull*, now meaning one who is generally optimistic about the market, originally denoted (from *c.* 1714[O]) an equally speculative investor. Cibber's *ram* has since been replaced by the *stag*, the third creature in the financial bestiary (or jungle). *Stags* (recorded from *c.* 1845[O]), apply for shares solely to sell at a quick profit upon flotation.

'DARK SATANIC MILLS' AND HUMANITARIANISM

The nineteenth century saw the great fruition of capitalism in the enormous increase of productivity of the Industrial Revolution. It also produced the counter-forces which sought a greater distribution of wealth and welfare. The schizophrenia of the Victorian Age – one of the 'givens' of the history of the period – is thus very evident in the economic field. The one face of the age endorses the Marxist critique of 'naked, shameless, direct, brutal exploitation'[3] by a capitalist class, evidenced in highly successful entrepreneurship quite ruthless in its exploitation of, for example, child labour. The other shows many forms of humanitarian concern, of Bentham over social security, of Elizabeth Fry over prison conditions, of Wilberforce over slavery, of Owen and Peel over the plight of women and children in factories. (The life of Robert Owen epitomizes both entrepreneurial success and socialist idealism.)

The word *factory* itself becomes something of a witness word. Since the late sixteenth century it had meant little more than 'a foreign branch of a mercantile business’, the base of a *factor* or agent. It now started to take on a sinister exploitative sense. Some of the clearest evidence is in the various Factory Bills (1802 and 1833 particularly) ‘passed for the regulation of factories in the interest of the health and morals of the persons employed in them’[O]. In a sarcastic quotation of 1833 a Mr John Wood is savagely denounced in Parliament: ‘He is perhaps a better judge of fat cattle . . . than of lean Factory boys and girls.’[S] *Industry* likewise shifts a long way from its early sense of ‘intelligent or clever working’ (1494[O]) to the more utilitarian establishment of the House of Industry, recorded from *c.* 1696[O], which is the base of the modern sense of the word.

Other semantic correlatives are seen in such words as *capitalist*, *capitalism* (a later formation much associated with Marx) *exploit*, *exploitation*, *entrepreneur*, *speculate* and *cartel* on the one hand, set against *socialism* (a coinage of the 1820s), *nationalization*, *trade union*, *strike*, *blackleg*, *dole* and *welfare* on the other. (This last term was originally often combined with *work*, *committee*, *policy* and the like.) Today *welfare* stands on its own, and many of the poorer population of the centre of Western capitalism are described as being ‘on welfare’. *Dole* goes right back to Anglo-Saxon times in the sense of a ‘portion or share’. The broad medieval meaning of a ‘gift given in charity’ is recorded from *c.* 1205[O], while the sense of ‘unemployment benefit’ emerges just after the First World War. This euphemistic phrase has since come to replace the older word, no doubt as a result of the humiliating overtones attaching to the context.

The emotional tenor of industrial relations today has its source in a long and bitter history of conflict between management and labour. The solidarity of the workers, which used to be a feature of the guilds, was eventually mobilized in the form of the trade unions only after intense opposition, combinations of workmen being frequently prosecuted under the conspiracy laws. The earliest cited reference to *trade union* (from the pen of an aristocratic lady in 1831) is typical in its virulence: ‘The tremendous Trade Union Club . . . I wish it could be put down and that someone would shoot O’Connell and Cobbett.’ Unions gave to the workers increased bargaining-power, without the restraints which a Master would in earlier times have been able to exert over his Journeymen and Apprentices. But perhaps the most emotionally charged words concern *scabs* and *blacklegs*, those who break ranks with their fellow-workers. *Scab*, which had acquired (like *scurvy*) an abusive sense from Elizabethan times, took on its confrontational industrial meaning two centuries ago, in a strike involving the Cordwainers in Bristol: ‘The conflict would not have been so sharp had not there been so many dirty scabs,' observed a writer in 1770[O]. A trenchant definition followed 15 years later: 'What is a scab? He is to his *trade* what a *traitor* is to his *country*.' *Blackleg* (recorded from *c.* 1771[O]), was originally a slang term for a turf swindler; the sense of 'strike-breaker' emerges only *c.* 1865[O].

The ideological connotation of terms is often a matter of context. For instance, *exploit* and *capitalist* can be used in a neutral or even positive tone by a capitalist to describe some feat of entrepreneurial skill, and in a quite pejorative sense by a Marxist to stigmatize the same activity. The hostile sense of *capitalist* has been in evidence since the word's first recorded appearance in 1792 in Arthur Young's *Travels . . . in the Kingdom of France*, where he speaks of a 'gross evil of moneyed men, or capitalists, escaping all taxation'[O]. In his novel of the Two Nations, *Sybil*, published in 1845, Disraeli has a character exclaim bitterly: 'The capitalist flourishes, he amasses immense wealth; we sink, lower and lower; lower than the beasts of burthen.' *Exploit* as a verb shows a fascinating development from its early martial meaning 'to fight a battle' (*c.* 1400[O]). It then acquired the sense of 'to prosper' (*c.* 1488[O]) before finally acquiring its favourable and unfavourable capitalist senses in *c.* 1838[O] in the heyday of the Industrial Revolution: Mrs Carlyle comments bitterly in a letter of 1847 of someone: 'exploiting that poor girl for their idle curiosity'[O].

MODERN DEVELOPMENTS

The competing socialist and capitalist ideologies have produced new social institutions and new terms to describe them. In the course of this century 'pure' capitalism has been steadily diluted in Britain by increasing nationalization, referred to also in various ideologically emphasizing formulas, such as 'public ownership', 'state control' and 'social control'. The process, which is intended to widen the distribution of power and wealth, started with 'essential services', such as railways, airlines and hospitals, being subsequently extended to bring various 'staple industries', such as coal and steel, under the aegis of the state. (The term *nationalization* was coined long before, in 1874, ironically in the heyday of entrepreneurial capitalism.) In addition, the socialist institution of the Welfare State was brought into being, with the major benefits of the National Health Service and organized 'social security'. The expression *Welfare State* has been attributed by Roger Scruton to Archbishop William Temple's *Citizens and Churchmen* of 1941, although the German compound *Wohlfahrtsstaat* has probably been influential in the formation of the phrase.[4] Welfare legislation had been introduced into several

European states in the course of the nineteenth century, but it was only after the Labour Party came to power in the United Kingdom in 1945 that similar programmes were initiated.

In the last quarter of a century this process has been reversed by a series of Conservative governments which ideologically prefer a greater measure of free enterprise to operate. A programme of 'denationalization' or 'privatization' has been implemented. Both terms, having a ponderous institutional ugliness, are fairly recent: *denationalization* is first in the field, dated as far back as 1921[S], while *privatization* is recorded from around 1959[S], with one of the earliest uses contained in this interesting ideological statement: 'Complete privatization was opposed by the Socialists, because they feared the little man selling out his shares to the big capitalists.'[S]

In the course of this century, economic matters have moved from the business pages to the front pages of newspapers, and they occupy an increasing amount of congressional and parliamentary time. One consequence of this is that a variety of economic terms have become household words. These include *inflation*, *depression*, *recession*, *slump*, *boom*, *reflation*, *cartel*, *sanctions*, *entrepreneur*, *exploit*, *growth* and *earnings.* It can be said that, in broad terms, three kinds of language have emerged. These might be called 'the language of crisis', 'the language of euphemism' and 'the language of obfuscating jargon'.

'This is the end of Western Civilization.' That remark, which one would have thought appropriate to, say, the Holocaust or Hiroshima, was in fact made by one of the chief advisers to President Roosevelt when the United States went off the Gold Standard in 1933. It is typical of the language of crisis which has become more prevalent with the removal of fixed convertible standards which once underpinned currencies as sources of permanent value. In recent years the chimaera of the collapse of the international monetary system has produced such phrases as 'The Debt Bomb', the title of a cover story in *Time* magazine, while wide currency is given to emotive terms such as *slump* and *crash.*

Slump seems to have transatlantic origins in a reference to a slump in stock prices in the Boston *Journal* of 1888[O]. The first hint of the financial sense of *crash* comes from a most unusual source, namely Coleridge's *Lay Sermons* of 1817: 'A rapid series of explosions (in mercantile language, a crash) and a consequent precipitation of the general system.'[O] The positive emotive term *boom* ('originally U.S.') is found in a reference of 1911 to the 'Land Boom', though Mark Twain wrote in a letter of 1871: 'My popularity is booming now.'[O] One consequence of the Great Crash of 1929 is that *boom* has come to connote an unrealistically rapid advance in prices, which will probably be followed by a sharp fall.

However, as is mentioned in chapter 5, there is the counter-tendency to euphemize situations of genuine crisis. It is one of the conventions of financial reporting that the term *panic* is virtually never used, except in reassuring negations such as 'there was no panic selling'. On 29 October 1929, the day of greatest panic selling in the Great Wall Street Crash, a Mr Lamont of the JP Morgan Bank announced tersely: 'There has been a little distress selling on the Exchange' (Cockburn, 1967, p. 97). On 'Black Monday', 19 October 1987, when an even greater fall was recorded, the Chairman of the New York Stock Exchange, Mr John Phelan, also eschewed the word *panic*, ironically preferring the catastrophic nuclear term *meltdown.* He seemed not to realize that panic passes, but a meltdown can be terminal; much more than fingers get burnt.

The euphemistic terminology of economic upheaval and currency fluctuation is, by and large, fairly recent. Significantly, *devaluation*, *depression* and *inflation* received no mention in the pages of the original *OED*, and only the first of this now-familiar trio was added to the 1933 *Supplement*, with references going back to 1914. The catastrophic experience of the Great Depression has had the semantic consequence that *depression* as a term ceased to be an adequate euphemism for *slump*, and has itself been replaced by *recession.* The word was coined in the 1920s by Wesley Clair Mitchell, a noted business cycle analyst, to describe a relatively mild transition from 'prosperity' to 'depression'. According to the *New York Times*, 'the word it was designed to replace was *crisis*' (Rawson, *Dictionary of Euphemisms*, 1981, p. 232). Other terms for similar economic conditions are *down-turn* and *technical correction.* Not all euphemisms derive from the financial establishment. Of late *strike* has been replaced, in a rather obvious piece of semantic sleight-of-hand, by the vague and slightly absurd misnomer *industrial action*, recorded from 1972^{S}.

Here one starts to move onto the fringes of the obfuscating financial jargon previously alluded to. Among such terms are: *cash shell*, *asset-stripping*, *stale bulls*, *smart money*, *reverse take-over*, *stop-loss selling*, *blue chips* (ironically, from high stakes at poker), *insider trading*, *synergy*[5] and dramatic pieces of journalistic 'colour', such as *bear squeeze* and *dawn raid.* While these all have reasonably agreed meanings amongst 'the professionals', they can be used to obscure the situation by confusing outsiders. Six hundred years ago Chaucer had observed this tendency in his shrewd portrait of the Merchant, who, while sporting a pseudo-aristocratic appearance (the medieval equivalent of a 'good image'), is actually in debt, but disguises this fact by the use of financial jargon.[6] It also emerges, through covert reference to his illicit dealings in foreign exchange, that he operates in the *black market.* (This ancient institution is first recorded lexicographically very late in the day, under that name, in 1931[S].) This irregular and unregulated market is demarcated by criminal euphemism, evidenced in recent terms such as *kickbacks*, *slush funds*, *laundering* money (of dubious origin) and various *fiddles* and *dodges.*[7]

The wider consequence of this obscuring or evasive terminology is that the abstraction of 'the economy' and the fluctuating markets of monetary and commodity value become less easy to understand. A simple example of confusion lies in the differing definitions of *million* and *billion* according to United States and English usage. Even US definitions of what constitutes the Gross National Product differ widely (Pei, 1970, pp. 201–2). But nowhere is the lack of understanding and clarity more evident than in the use of *inflation* and *reflation*. The literal sense of *inflation* is recorded from the fourteenth century, and there is an interesting application to language: 'when it is swollen with big or pompous words', dating from *c.* 1603[O]. The over-issue of paper money is recorded in United States contexts by *Webster* from 1864, when the term also started to acquire political overtones. Through a programme of contrived inflation, governments could (and still do) create a brief period of artificial prosperity, and then use this euphoric state to their benefit at the polls. Hence an outspoken criticism in 1878 of 'the illegal inflation authorized by President Grant'[O].

Essential confusion arises through the treatment of inflation as both cause and effect of the current economic malaise. Even the metaphor of the *inflationary spiral* shows the essential circularity of thinking on these matters. (Equally significant is the fact that *spiral* and *escalation* are themselves always used in an inflationary way, to imply increase, never decrease.) The use of *inflation* and *reflation* by governments is often misleading. This is largely because they wish *inflation* (which has bad political consequences, usually in the form of rising prices and unemployment) to appear to be the result of uncontrollable or unseen manipulative forces, such as the Arab oil sheikhs, the gnomes of Zurich, or that overwhelming financial entity, *force majeur.* Contrariwise, *reflation* (which has favourable political consequences following upon an upturn in the economy) is to be attributed to the government alone.

Governments commonly seek a semantic monopoly over the description of the economy, even in the West. The extent of their success depends upon the degree of freedom in the society in question. In an unusual development in September 1977, the Editor of *The Times* issued a directive to all staff stressing that *reflation* was to be used only when inflation had, in fact, been reduced in the proper literal fashion; all other so-called 'reflation' was to be referred to as 'increased inflation'. This seems a significant and hopeful development in the direction of responsibility.

The past decade or so has witnessed the challenging of the previously dominant capitalist mode of 'conspicuous consumption' by that of 'austerity' and 'economy'. The amelioration of *luxury* from its immoral origins (discussed in chapter 6) remains undiminished. However, *economy*, in its sense of 'careful management of resources' (what used to be called *husbandry*), has developed a generally favourable overtone, particularly since 1973, when the conservation of energy became a national necessity in many countries in the West, as a consequence of rising oil prices. Chapter 6 sketches the effects on the vocabulary used to market motor vehicles, but the effects extend beyond the obvious. In the United States, it is now quite common to hear the consumption of red meat criticized in terms of the amount of grain needed to produce it. Indeed, the notion of *energy* is changing from 'a source of power to be used or exhibited' (as in the space-race) to 'a resource of power to be husbanded'. As 'saving' becomes a favourable quality so it acts as a 'contextual magnet' which draws words like *thrift*, *austerity* and even *cheap* away from their associations of 'niggardliness' and 'parsimony' in the direction of 'prudence', 'husbandry' and 'efficiency'. This trend seems likely to continue.

CONCLUSION

Ideologues, who tend to intensify or exaggerate the differences between systems of thought or national life-styles for the sake of political capital, have tended to see capitalism and communism as absolutely opposed. Yet in practice the two systems accommodate within them elements of the rival system. Thus, from the time of Roosevelt's New Deal, 'welfare programmes' have become an increasing ingredient in the US budget, and the Welfare State has become a completely established social programme in Britain. Furthermore, the capitalist system is not without criticism among those of a Conservative persuasion. In 1973 Edward Heath, a Tory prime minister, spoke memorably of profiteering as 'the ugly and unacceptable face of capitalism'. In similar vein, much publicity has in recent years been given to the need for a programme of 'caring capitalism', a cliché current from late 1985. Meanwhile, from behind the Iron Curtain comes increasing evidence of the industrious solidarity of the 'home' ideology being undermined by the conspicuous consumption of alcohol and institutionalized black-marketeering, referred to as 'operating on the left'.

The problem extends beyond blocs. Increasing scepticism about the validity of individual currencies as a permanent store of value, and of governments to control their economies, has evolved into a fear of a systemic imbalance and collapse in the international monetary system. The defiant refusal of Chile, Peru and Brazil to pay even the interest on their vast loans has destroyed the polite fiction that debtor countries will eventually repay their debts. Indeed, the whole notion of 'debt' as a morally binding obligation is slowly being eroded and turned into an ideological issue. (It is noteworthy that the term *Third World* has shifted from what originated as a non-aligned political grouping in the Bandung Conference in 1955 to an economic sense of *developing*, a euphemism for 'underdeveloped' or 'poor'.) The semantic correlatives can be seen in the emergence of the now-familiar euphemism *reschedule* around 1968[S], and more strikingly in the recent extension of *default* from companies to national reserve banks. The unhappy South African equivalent is *standstill*, organized by a bureaucratic entity stultifyingly termed the *Standstill Co-ordination Committee.*

The problem is essentially one of credibility. The mysteries of the higher economics, seemingly so profound, are discoursed at a level well beyond the understanding of the layman. Furthermore, the semantics of explication indulged in by some of the exponents has reached quite cynical proportions. In a famous pronouncement in late 1967 designed to reassure the British public that the devaluation of sterling was not what it seemed to be, the then Prime Minister, Harold Wilson, an economist of note, explained: 'From now on the pound abroad is worth 14 per cent or so less in terms of other currencies. It does not mean, of course, that the pound in Britain, in your pocket or purse, or in your bank, has been devalued.'[8]

The chaotic collapse of the International Tin Market in 1985 was tersely analysed by John Howarth in the following terms: 'Several operators' *dictum* is no longer their *pactum.*'[9] The problem of trust is shown with transparent simplicity in the recent history of the banknote. Put simply, it used to be a contractual promissory note. The US dollar bore the words: 'This Certifies That There Is on Deposit in the Treasury of the United States of America One Dollar in Silver Payable to the Bearer on Demand.'

These Silver Certificate dollars have by now all either been hoarded away by individuals or burnt by the Federal Reserve Bank. Today in Britain a banknote's credibility is undermined by a peculiar formula of semantic tautology: 'I promise to pay the Bearer on Demand the Sum of One Pound.' In what commodity? How? The note (now signed only by the Chief Cashier for the Governor and Company of the Bank of England) in effect promises itself. Not surprisingly, the phrase 'safe as the Bank of England' does not enjoy much currency nowadays. In sum, the economic instability of inflation, together with that deriving from currency fluctuations, has created a general sense of insecurity and demoralization, a malaise characterized by a loss of faith in our capacity to control our economic destiny.

NOTES

1 M. M. Postan (1972, p. 255) observes: 'The church doctrine was that of the "just price". In the sense in which it was propounded by canonist writers the doctrine was much more than a mere injunction against overcharging. It linked the price system with the divinely ordained structure of society, by defining a "just" price as that which would yield the makers of goods and their sellers sufficient income to maintain them in their respective social ranks.'

2 *Metathesis* involves the transposition (over time) of neighbouring letters. The letter 'r' is particularly prone to this process, as is shown in Middle English *bridde* becoming Modern English *bird*, as *thurh* has become *through* (though we still have *thoroughfare* as a fossil of the old form).

3 From *The Communist Manifesto* (1848).

4 Roger Scruton (1982), *A Dictionary of Political Thought.* See also Norman Stone, *Spectator*, 10 May 1986, p. 28.

5 *Synergy* refers to a mystical financial notion, very prevalent in the United States during the growth period of the 1960s, whereby it was believed that the consolidated earnings of a conglomerate corporation added up – in theory at any rate – to more than the sum of the parts. This belief added motivation to the prevalent mania for take-overs. The theory is now largely discredited.

6 So estatly was he of his **governaunce**,
With his **bargaynes** and his **chevyssaunce**.
(ll. 281–2)

Chevyssaunce, which has a pseudo-aristocratic ring about it, since it resembles *chivalrie* and *chivachie*, is based not on the root *cheval*, a horse, but *chevir*, to make money. In his portraits of the Doctor and the Lawyer, Chaucer also shows professional jargon being used to obfuscate and impress.

7 Hugh Rawson (*Dictionary of Euphemisms*, 1981) has some interesting quotations on *kickback*, as well as this observation: '*kickback* puts the blame on the recipient, while *bribe* places the onus on the giver.'

8 Harold Wilson, Speech, 18 November 1967.

9 *Spectator*, 10 May 1986, p. 24.

4
The Mobilization of Words: Printing, the Reformation and the Renaissance

Erasmus tells of how he bent down in a muddy lane ecstatically when his eye lit upon a scrap of print, so new was the miracle of the printed page.

George Steiner

Things are preached not in that they are taught, but in that they are published.

Richard Hooker

Print created national uniformity and government centralism, but also individualism and opposition to government as such.

Marshall McLuhan

Here will be an old abusing of God's patience and the King's English.

Shakespeare

WHEN we speak of the *King's English*, *the body politic*, the *Church of England*, the *Roman Catholic Church*, a *religious fanatic*, a *Puritan* or a *Protestant*, we are referring to institutions, using clichés, labels and set phrases which came into being and were given great currency within a few decades of the invention of printing. The widespread effects of this technological innovation on Western society have been given central importance, though differing emphases, by many cultural historians.[1] In recent years much stress has been put on 'the ways in which the *forms* of experience and of mental outlook have been modified, first by the phonetic alphabet and then by printing' (McLuhan, 1962, p. 1). The printed word, being the first vehicle of mass media, introduced the experience of the modern world in various essential ways. Lexically, the press liberated words from their traditional social roots: words no longer moved with the slow flux of migrating peoples, but travelled at speed across continents in the form of multiple first editions, rapidly acquiring currency and then permanency.

The press gave the writer enormous power. This was used, variously, to resurrect the master-works of Classical culture in that intellectual enterprise we term the Renaissance, to influence the population's religious allegiances in the Reformation and, through the mass use of the vernacular, to weld a sense of national cohesiveness. All of these developments were controversial. Even the nature and extent of the lexical borrowings which came flooding into the language caused the linguistic contretemps historically known as the Inkhorn Controversy. In it strong claims were made, alternatively, for native terms or for classical borrowings. No writer could feel free from involvement or immune from criticism. Few missed the creative opportunities afforded by the whole new 'World of Words', to borrow the title of John Florio's collection of 1598. Exuberance, exploration and experiment, the intellectual and creative keynotes of the Elizabethan Age, infuse attitudes towards language no less.

Printing encouraged diverse publishing ventures and accentuated different kinds of language. The first is the educational, ostensibly neutral, mode employed by Caxton and various Renaissance translators and educators; the second is the promotional language which, in Caxton's case, arose out of his opportunity to market his books; the third is the statement of authority, usually on religious or political matters; and the fourth is that of polemical controversy, commonly deriving from these same religious issues, as the divisions of the Reformation intensified into sectarian strife.

Although it may be argued that, strictly speaking, the invention of printing *per se* had little *direct* result upon the semantic development of individual words, I shall seek to show that the authorial awareness of the power of the printing press encouraged writers to strain the semantic parameters of words when pressing their argument or case. One is dealing here with the effects of a powerfully persuasive medium of communication on the whole language, not simply with changes in a particular word-field, such as that of capitalism or politics.

Whereas writing is personal and individual, printing was often anonymous or pseudonymous. Prior to printing, verbal authority was resident, linguistically speaking, in the monarchical or papal *fiats* and decrees issued in unique handwritten documents. Printing allowed these forms of authority to be challenged on a wide scale, subverted and (in places) overthrown. (It is perhaps worth recalling that the roots of 'authority' and 'author' are very close.) The power of the medium also encouraged an emotive, inflated and polemical use of language. The consequence was a semantic division of authority: words like *heresy*, *enormity*, *idolatry*, *abuse* and *superstition* ceased to be the exclusive prerogative of the papacy. In the schismatic strife which ensued, the language tended to an even greater violence, often of an abusive nature bordering on hysteria.

The sheer volume of publication and its simultaneity made literate people aware of new developments in politics, religion and the language itself on a scale which had not been possible previously.[2] Whereas Wycliffe and his followers in the fourteenth century had taken a strongly reformist stance in religion and are credited with the borrowing of over a thousand words of Latin origin, they had been unable to generate the same volume of controversy as their successors, essentially because they worked in a manuscript culture.

Three overlapping genre-words record the enlistment of the press into controversial matters. The first is *tract*, used generally from *c.* 1432°, before acquiring a strongly propagandist sense from the seventeenth century. Likewise, *pamphlet* (in etymology a Latin amatory poem by one Pamphilus, 'a highly popular opuscule of the thirteenth century'^{O}), was used generally from the fourteenth century before acquiring its controversial sense early in the sixteenth century. Sir Thomas Chaloner writes scathingly in 1549 of 'some rotten pamphlet' (Baugh, 1965, p. 262). Finally, there is *broadside*, a variant of *broadsheet*: the sense of a polemical statement printed on one side of a large page is recorded from 1575°, antedating by over 20 years the related meaning of 'simultaneous discharge of naval artillery'. In each case the term of the format came to imply controversy; the volume of reproduction added power to the polemic.

Subsequent semantic witnesses to the print revolution are *slogan*, *cliché* and *stereotype*. *Slogan* is in origin an Irish war-cry first recorded in English *c.* 1513°. *Cliché* surfaced *c.* 1832°, contemporaneously with the rise of mass-circulation newspapers. Deriving from the French root *clicher*, 'to set together, to consolidate', it referred to the practice of typesetters, who would keep recurring 'set phrases' in a special compartment of their print-trays in order to save the time and labour of repeatedly compositing them each time they appeared in the text. *Stereotype*, dating from *c.* 1798°, started to take on its broader human sense *c.* 1850, while the first reference to a stage character being 'something of a cliché' occurs *c.* 1895°. All of these have potent consequences in mass communications which extend beyond their linguistic origins.

PRINTING AND THE BALANCE OF THE ECONOMIES OF SPEECH

The illuminating linguistic model posited by Zipf and discussed in chapter 1 describes the linguistic situation as a conflict of verbal economies, that of the speaker set against that of the auditor. In this theory, the ideal verbal economy from the auditor's point of view would consist of a vast, specific vocabulary, thereby ensuring complete clarity, while the ideal speaker's economy would consist of a few, extremely flexible general terms, which would convey the maximum of information.

Like many theoretical models of discourse, Zipf's has an artificial quality about it, in that it separates the processes of communication to the point that little can, in theory, take place. Nevertheless, we can recognize extreme examples of contrasting verbal economies in, say, the formal linguistic mode of an elderly British academic, in which the thesaurus of the language will be thoroughly and liberally exposed, against the 'loose', vague mode of American youth, in which the absolute minimum of vocabulary is employed. (The extreme example is 'Valley Talk', or 'Valspeak', an almost monosyllabic argot originating from the San Fernando Valley near Los Angeles, in which fragmentary phrases such as *like, you know* feature prominently.) The one 'speaks like a book'; the other like Neanderthal Man.

The curious sense of alienation which Zipf describes, of two races (speakers and auditors) confused by language, becomes more recognizable once the printed, rather than the written, word, has become the medium of communication. The reasons for this alienation are simple. The printed word is often anonymous, and uttered without the censoring presence of an immediate audience. The fewer the presses and the stricter their control, the greater their power, as Orwell has so cogently shown in *Nineteen Eighty-Four*. In his totalitarian dystopia the media are monopolized by the state, newspapers may not be kept, and thus 'the news', 'history' and even political dramatis personae can be fabricated or eliminated at will by the controlling oligarchy. In print culture the 'audience' tends to become steadily more passive, usually acquiescing to the power of those behind the press. It seems significant, indeed, that in those areas where an audience is 'live' and literal, as in the theatre, it has become much more accepting and uncritical than in the past, when productions were not infrequently booed and hissed off the stage. Walter Lippmann uses the metaphor of the theatre to describe the alienation of the ordinary citizen from involvement in current affairs:

> The private citizen has come to feel rather like a deaf spectator in the back row, who ought to keep his mind on the mystery off there, but cannot quite manage to keep awake. . . . He lives in a word where he cannot see, does not understand, and is unable to direct.
>
> (*The Phantom Public*, cited in Hoch, 1974, p. 175)

In short, the invention of printing signals a decisive shift in the balance of power between the speech economies, a shift in favour of the speaker/writer. Hereafter the writer can choose not only the terms in which to argue, but can also choose to manipulate the senses of those terms. The writer can, in brief, usurp 'the freedom of the press' in matters of controversy, and dominate the market in the varieties of advertising and publicity.

The effect of the printed word upon the reader is complex. At the one extreme is the attitude of 'print credibility' widely evidenced amongst those who 'believe what they read in the papers'. At the other is the cynicism born of the 'credibility gap' which advocates the simple cautionary test that one should 'never believe a thing until it has been officially denied'. This scepticism derives from the awareness that the press has increasingly become the tool of propaganda, whether it be religious, political or commercial.

The awareness that language is manipulated for public effect is by no means recent. Shakespeare consistently dramatizes the ironies of political language in his Roman tragedies and English histories. It is in one of the earliest works, *Richard III*, that we find an illuminating vignette. The execution of the Lord Hastings by the controlling oligarchy is combined with character assassination in a manner which anticipates the now-familiar pattern of the purges seen in recent times in totalitarian states:

Enter a Scrivener with
a paper in his hand

Here is the indictment of the good Lord Hastings,
Which in a set hand fairly is engrossed
That it may be today read o'er in Paul's.

. . . .

And yet within these five hours Hastings lived,
Untainted, unexamined, free, at liberty.
Here's a good world the while! Who is so gross
That cannot see this palpable device?
Yet who so bold but says he sees it not?

(III. vi. 1–14)

The Scrivener is a press with a voice and a conscience. He is ashamed that his 'set hand fairly' puts a gloss on political dirty work, and he sees himself as part of a conspiratorial language-game played by the ruthless survivors against the dead man.

CAXTON

Though Caxton was not a highly significant or influential figure as a literary artist or a linguistic force, certain contemporary problems of correctness, use of register, bourgeois censorship, stylistic appropriateness and linguistic inflation do emerge with clarity in his writings. He is justly famous for the introduction of printing into England and is credited, mainly through his translations, with the absorption of numerous words into the English vocabulary. However, from the study of his 'own' language, that is to say, the language of his Prefaces, Prologues and Epilogues, Norman Blake has shown that his natural linguistic bent was fairly conservative.[3] Caxton's overt and immediate concern was with the 'dyversitie and chaunge' in English, an aspect referred to in his famous Prologue to the *Eneydos* (*c.* 1490):

> And certaynly our langage now used varyeth ferre from that whiche was used and spoken whan I was borne, for we Englysshemen ben borne under the domynacyon of the moone, which is never stedfaste, but ever waverynge: wexynge one season, and waneth and dyscreaseth another season.
>
> And that comyn Englysshe that is spoken in one shyre varyeth from another. In so moche that in my dayes happened that certayn marchauntes were in Tamyse for to have sayled over the see into Zelande. And for lacke of wynde thai taryed atte forlond [offshore] and wente to lande for to refreshe them. And one of theym named Sheffelde, a mercer, came into an hows and axed [asked] for mete [food] and specially he axyd after eggys. And the goode wyf answerede that she coude speke no Frenshe. And the marchaunte was angry for he also coude speke no Frenshe, but wolde have hadde egges; and she understoode hym not. And thenne at laste another sayd that he wolde have eyren; then the goode wyf sayd that she understod hym wel. Loo! what sholde a man in thyse dayes now write, 'egges' or 'eyren'? Certaynly it is harde to playse every man bycause of dyversitie and chaunge of langage.

Caxton's story is entertaining and pointed. I have quoted it at some length so as to give a sense of the spelling variants which emerged even on his printed page. The point of comic confusion is that *eggys* would have been more current in the North of England, *eyren* more common in the South, just as *bairn*, hay-*stack*, *beck* and *dizzy* are Northern terms for what are known in the South as *child*, hay-*rick*, *brook* and *giddy*. These variants are one consequence of King Alfred's ceding of the Danelaw to the Norse-speaking Vikings in the ninth century.

One suspects that Caxton's exasperation and his numerous declarations of 'sympleness' are a *captatio benevolentiae*, a rhetorical pose designed to gain sympathy with an audience. For elsewhere he reveals that his own linguistic history, both in England and on the Continent, would have experienced him in regional variants. The root cause of Caxton's naive querulousness is not, therefore, linguistic diversity *per se*. It is the necessary imposition of a linguistic standard which the print format naturally imposes, just as the varieties of handwriting, dialect and speech bring with them the expectation of a diversity of transcription. The example of Chaucer is worth recalling. He too had complained a century previously about 'the gret diversitie in Englissh and in writyng of oure tonge' and hoped that none would 'myswrite' his work.[4] Yet he could spell *sweet* as *swete*, *sote* or *swote*, and in 'The Reeve's Tale' used dialect in a pointed sociolinguistic fashion for the first time, when he has the two opportunistic Cambridge students assume a Northern dialect when they pretend to be simpletons.[5] Caxton's situation was different. Almost without realizing it, he was being forced by the use of his press at Westminster to produce a form of Standard English. Had he used a group of scriveners (of necessity drawn from different parts of the country) the problem of diversity would not have exercised him so much.

The problem of variant forms is not the only one which Caxton regards as being foisted on him: there is also the choice between registers, the linguistic modes appropriate to different stations and situations:

> For in these dayes every man that is in ony reputacyon in his countre [district] wyll utter his commynycacyon and maters in suche maners and termes that fewe men shall understonde theym. And som honest and grete clerkes [scholars] have ben wyth me and desired me to wryte the moste curyous [rarefied] termes that I coude fynde. And thus bytwene playn, rude and curyous I stande abasshed.
>
> (Prologue to the *Eneydos*, cited in Blake (1973), p. 80.)

Caxton's attitude towards 'rude' language is also important and formative. This designation could mean 'broad', 'coarse', 'vulgar' or 'lewd', and he was clearly embarrassed by it. So had Chaucer been a century before, but he had got round the problem by creating a dramatic framework, and claiming that – as the pilgrim-narrator – he was merely repeating, for example, the 'cherles tale' (vulgar or dirty story) of his Miller: those with delicate sensibilities could simply turn the page. Consequently, *The Canterbury Tales* is a rich linguistic mine in which every stratum of the language is liberally exposed, and often hilariously juxtaposed. The Wife of Bath demonstrates her renowned versatility in 'the olde daunce' of love in her remarkable confession, the Prologue, by working up and down the scale of register of terms for the *pudendum muliebre.* The range extends from the coarse, direct term *queynte*, through the common euphemism *thinge*, via mock-courtly French *bele chose*, pseudo-academic Latin *quoniam* to 'flowery mythological' *chambre of Venus.* The 'Miller's Tale' is, perhaps, the most exuberant mixture of courtliness and farce. The lascivious lodger, Nicholas, dispenses with the decencies of foreplay, seeking instant gratification in monosyllabic language which combines heavy breathing with bogus idealism:

> And prively he caughte her by the queynte [cunt],
> And seyde, 'Ywis, but if ich have my wille,
> For deerne [secret] love of thee, lemman [lover], I spille.'
> And helde her harde by the haunchebones,
> And seyde, 'Lemman, love me al at ones
> Or I wil dyen, also God me save!'

(*Spille* and *dye* might have premature ejaculatory senses.)[6] The response from the eager Alison is one of calculated coyness and mock gentility:

> 'Do wey your handes, for your curteisye!'
> ['Take your hands off me! Where are your manners!']
> (ll. 3276–87)

Subsequently in the tale, within the space of ten lines, Chaucer shifts the register from lyricism modelled blasphemously on the Song of Songs:

> 'What do ye, hony-comb, sweete Alisoun,
> My faire bryd, my sweete cynamome?'

to the crude rejection by the propositioned adulteress:

> 'Go fro the wyndow Jakke fool,' she sayde;
> 'As help me God, it wol not be "com pa [kiss] me."'
> (ll. 3699–709)

Caxton did not have the dramatic device of evasion. And perhaps he did not have the nerve to use 'broad' language in print. At any rate, the history of censorship of risqué language in print began. In the Winchester manuscript of Malory's *Morte d'Arthur* we read of the devastating effects of a truncheon being drawn out of Sir Lancelot's side: 'And [he] gave a great shriek and a grisly groan, so that the blood burst out, nigh a pint at once, that at last he sank down upon his arse and so swooned down, pale and deadly' (from 'The Fair Maid of Astolat', in *The Works of Sir Thomas Malory* (1947), vol. III, p. 1074). In Caxton's edition *arse* is edited out and replaced with the 'decent' variant *buttocks.* His successor at the press, Wynkyn de Worde, published in 1511 *The Demaundes Joyous*, a collection of riddles, some of which were coarse: *Question*: 'What beast is it that hath her tail between her eyes?' *Answer*: 'It is a cat when she licketh her arse.' However, a comparison with the main French source shows that de Worde or his compiler 'rejected a great number of obscene and scatalogical' riddles.[7]

It would thus be wrong to blame Caxton exclusively for the whole strange history of subsequent linguistic prissiness and preciosity. But his eagerness to 'strike the right note' (and avoid the wrong ones) in his choice of register cannot be attributed solely to artistic motives. Printing was a risky business, commercially speaking, and he needed to reach a market which combined the wealthier upper-class readership with a more popular, burgher element. Once one accepts the marketing motive, one sees the function of the Prologues and Prefaces in a rather different light, as advertisements framed to appeal to the aristocracy and the upwardly mobile. The Prologue to *King Arthur* (31 July 1485) shows the inflated linguistic qualities of a 'blurb' or 'film trailer': 'For herein may be seen noble chyvalrye, curtosye, humanyte, frendlynesse, hardynesse, love, frendshyp, cowardyse, murdre, hate, vertue and synne' (cited in Blake (1973), p. 109).

Caxton's 'own' language tends to reflect his attitudes and situation. He prefers to use an established vocabulary with an aristocratic timbre, and make emotive appeals to old-fashioned values. This consistently emotive quality in his language is what makes it original, since it has such marked affinities with what we now recognize as advertising copy. It is worth recalling, in point of fact, that Caxton's very first printed work in England (*c.* 1477) was an advertisement, the first of its kind:

> If it plese ony man spirituel or temporel to bye ony pyes [church calendars] of two or three comemoracions of Salisburi Use enpryntid after the forme of this present lettre, which ben wel and truly correct, late hym com to Westmonester into the Almonesrye at the Reed Pale and he shal have them good chepe [at a good price].

Caxton's language has more affinities with that of Madison Avenue than might be expected. 'Fayne wolde I satysfye every man,' he remarks in the Prologue to the *Eneydos*, thereby revealing the profit motive that lies behind much of his language.

THE INKHORN CONTROVERSY AND THE GROWTH OF SEMANTIC FIELDS

Caxton referred on several occasions to the 'symple and rude English' of his translations, contrasting it with 'the fayr langage of Frenshe'. As Barber has observed, 'in part this is purely conventional author's self-deprecation' (1976, p. 65). Caxton regarded the problem of word-choice as simply a matter of balancing dignified literacy with wide acceptability. But within a century these issues had become ideological and controversial, coloured by strong feelings of linguistic nationalism, patriotism and xenophobia. The same attitudes have governed the contemporary controversy in France over 'Franglais', as it was contemptuously termed by Professor Etiemble in the opening salvo, the publication of *Parlez-Vous Franglais?* in 1963.

The Inkhorn Controversy, as it is termed by historians of the language, derived indirectly from the invention of printing in that it arose from the issues generated in translating the classics, which the dissemination of the press had made more popular and economical. In the 'new' sciences, many borrowed words were acepted as the basic technical vocabulary. Some of these terms, like *algebra* (1541), *alcohol* (1543), and *chemistry* (1605), came from the Arabs, but most of the word-stock came from Latin and Greek. These included *anatomy* (1528), *optics* (1579), *mathematics* (1581) and *physics* (1589 – though the Aristotelian term *metaphysics* had appeared 20 years earlier). From the pages of Francis Bacon alone we find first instances of such scientific neologisms as *dissection*, *acid*, *hydraulic* and *suction*.

The rate of semantic additions (new words) and of semantic extensions (new meanings accreting to established words) accelerates sharply with the coming of printing. This is largely because printing gave greater force to Horace's dictum *littera scripta manet* ('the written word remains'), since printing preserved words and archaic meanings far more efficiently than manuscripts could. Simultaneously, printing increased the mobility of words and accelerated their currency.

How can we arrive at some accurate estimate of the volume of new words and meanings which came into the language at this time? Working from the source of the *Chronological English Dictionary* (1970), in which the data of *The Shorter Oxford English Dictionary* are transposed from alphabetical to chronological sequence, the growth of the vocabulary

FIGURE 4.1 The growth of the vocabulary and related publications 1500–1800

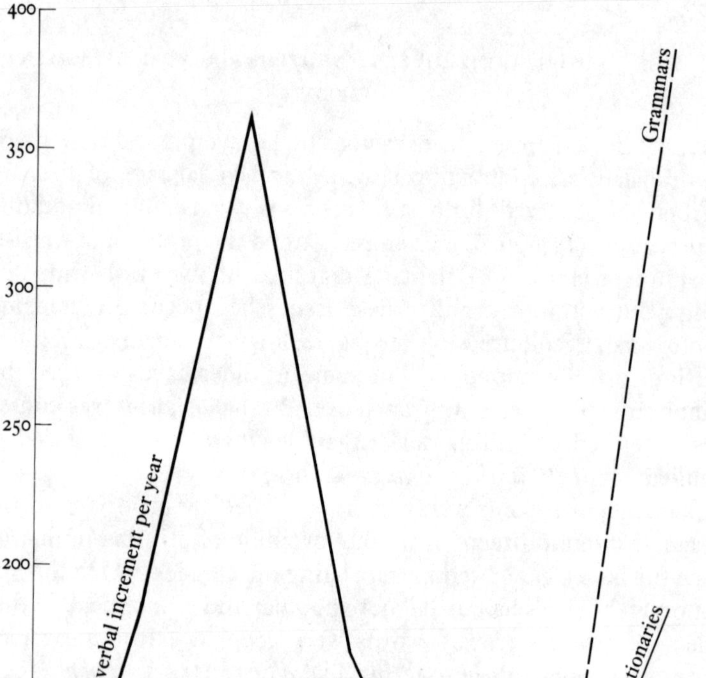

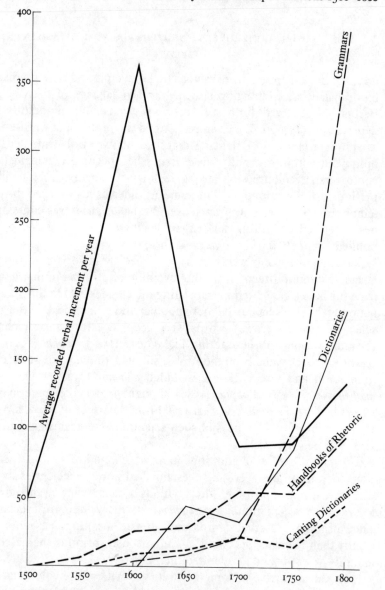

Sources: R. C. Alston, *A Bibliography of the English Language* (1965–)
A Chronological English Dictionary (1970)

can be plotted, as in figure 4.1. The graph shows an extraordinary sevenfold increase in the growth of the vocabulary from an average increment of 50 new words and meanings per year around 1500 to over 350 per year a mere century later. This massive influx caused a shift in the equilibrium of the language which aroused strong feelings and differences of opinion.

The participants in the Inkhorn Controversy have been categorized by Barber, more formally than is traditional, as the Neologizers, the Purists and the Archaizers (1976, pp. 79–100). The Purists and the Archaizers (who had basically the same linguistic sympathies) protested at what they regarded as the excessive borrowing of learned words of foreign origin, which they stigmatized as *dark* (= 'obscure') words. Contrariwise, the Neologizers insisted with equal vehemence that the new Greek and Latin borrowings were useful and necessary additions to the vocabulary of the new academic and cultural fields which the Renaissance scholars were rediscovering. Without these enrichments the language would, in their view, be *barbarous* (= 'crude, primitive').

The Purists had, however, a very strong argument in their assertion that learned loan-words were opaque and confusing to the unlettered. Malapropism, one of the semantic diseases of the language, derives precisely from this opacity. The symptoms are evident long before the gaffes of the famous Mrs Malaprop of Sheridan's *The Rivals* (1775): as far back as the fourteenth century one encounters in the pages of Langland a character who thinks that *restitution* means 'robbery', when it means the opposite, 'repayment, compensation' (B Text, 238). 'Your body is full of Englysch Laten,' complains a character in *Mankynd*, a morality play contemporary with Caxton. Furthermore, Purism acquired some ideological support from the Protestant insistence that the Bible be translated into the vernacular. Arguments raised over the suitability of English as a proper vehicle for Holy Writ produced polemical responses such as Tyndale's remarks in *The Obedience of a Christen Man* (1528): 'They wil say it cannot be translated into oure tonge it is so rude. It is not so rude as they are false lyers.'

The most noted Purist was Sir John Cheke, who despite being the first Professor of Greek at Cambridge, expressed his strong opposition to loan-words in a letter appended to Hoby's well-known translation of Castiglione's *The Courtier* (1561): 'I am this opinion that our own tung should be written cleane and pure, vnmixt and vnmangeled with borrowing of other tunges, wherein if we take not heed by tijm, euer borrowing and neuer payeng, she shall fain to keep her house as bankrupt.' Cheke studiedly insists upon the native term *tung* (instead of *language*), and seeks to restore *clean* to its older, general, use, but he nevertheless draws on the borrowings *pure* and *bankrupt*. In his translation of St Matthew's Gospel he was to coin such quaint and unfamiliar native formations as *freschman* for 'proselyte', *gainrising* for 'resurrection', *groundwrought* for 'founded' and *moond* for 'lunatic'. The translation was not published until the nineteenth century, but in 1573 another Purist, Ralph Lever, published a book on logic, or as he preferred it, *witcraft.* His coinages included *endsay* for 'conclusion', *foresay* for 'premiss', *naysay* for 'negation' and *yeasay* for 'affirmation'. Both Cheke and Lever have carried the principle of native preference (which is sound) to almost perverse lengths, so that the new native compounds themselves seem to be opaque and unnatural.

Whereas Cheke had used the strong and familiar argument that wholesale borrowing would debase the native word-hoard or currency, Thomas Wilson, in his *Arte of Rhetorique* (1553) brought other patriotic arguments into play:

> Among all other lessons this should first be learned, that wee never affect straunge [foreign] ynkehorne termes, but speake as is commonly received.... Some seeke so far for outlandish English, that they forget altogether their mother's language. And I dare sweare this, if some of their mothers were alive, thei were not able to tell what they say: and yet these fine English clerkes [scholars] will say, they speake in their mother tongue, if a man should charge them for counterfeiting the Kings English.

Wilson here uses the patriotic formula *the King's English* for the first time, and proceeds to stigmatize those who 'pouder their talke with oversea language', such as 'English Italienated', and those who 'so Latin their tongues, that the simple cannot but wonder at their talke'.

Spenser is commonly held up as the most celebrated of the Archaizers, for in the words of a contemporary estimation, he 'laboured to restore, as to theyr rightfull heritage such good and naturall English words, as haue ben long time out of vse and almost cleane disherited'. The same writer criticized borrowers who have 'made our English tongue a gallimaufray or hodgepodge of all other speeches'.[8]

Yet Spenser's archaisms are often so factitious and inaccurate that they are curious and comic 'antiques', not 'the language of ordinary men' (in Wordsworth's later formulation), but the language of no men at all, historically speaking. Ben Jonson's famous criticism that 'Spenser, in affecting the ancients, writ no language' is harsh, but not unjustified. He managed to coin archaisms and medievalisms such as *bellibone* – 'a fair maid', a *delve* – 'a pit', *eflin* – 'elvish', *gride* – 'to pierce' and *scruze* –

a portmanteau of 'screw' and 'squeeze'. From his evidently cursory reading of Chaucer he committed the juvenile howler of taking *yond* ('over there', 'far away') in the phrase 'a Tygre yond in Ynde' ('a tiger far away in India') to mean 'fierce'. He similarly took Chaucer's *dorrying don*, subsequently misprinted as *derrynge do* ('daring to do') as a compound noun meaning 'daring action, chivalry'. This pseudo-archaism ('deeds of derring do') was resuscitated as a cliché in the works of Sir Walter Scott and is still occasionally encountered. The final irony is that his most enduring coinage, *blatant*, seems to have been simply invented by Spenser in his description of a monster, 'the blatant beast'. The term for centuries meant 'loud, noisy, clamorous' and seems to have acquired its modern sense only about 1900. The point not to be lost is that print currency has legitimated what was originally **catachresis**, or illiterate usage. (See, however, the comments of Roy Harris on this term in *TLS* 3 September 1982, pp. 935–6.)

CANT AND CANTING DICTIONARIES

In addition to the 'literary' and 'acceptable' areas of the word-stock which have been discussed, cant, the secret language of the criminal underworld and vagabonds, occasioned considerable notoriety and excitement. Although Dr Johnson, in the later milieu of correctness in which he worked, regarded cant as 'unworthy of preservation', several of the earliest dictionaries deal exclusively and precisely with this clandestine, criminal code. In fact, as is shown on figure 4.1, they antedate what we would now call 'straight' or 'orthodox' dictionaries by half a century. Thomas Harman's pioneering work, *A Caveat or Warening for Comen Cursetors, vvlgarely called Vagabones*, appeared in 1567. Harman claims (perhaps with some self-interest) to be doing a public service in describing both the types and the nomenclature of 'these rowsey, ragged, rabblement of rakehells'. Two years previously there had appeared a similar glossary called '*The fraternitie of Vacabondes* . . . with theire proper names and qualityes. Also, the xxv Orders of Knaves . . .'. A typical entry concerns a denizen of what we still call *queer street*: 'A queer-bird is one that came lately out of prison and goeth to seek service. He is commonly a stealer of horses, which they term a prigger of palfreys.'

As can be seen in figure 4.1, the early growth-rate of these guides to the underworld was considerable. The titles were usually phrased so as to combine sensationalism with a calculated appeal of the illicit: *A Notable Discovery of Coosnage. Now daily practised by sundry lewd persons, called Connie-catchers and Cross-biters*, was Robert Greene's title of 1591. Most appealed openly to the need for self-protection, so that the purchaser would know the whereabouts of *coney-catchers* ('cheats and swindlers') and recognize their *coosnage* ('cosenage', 'trickery') through this indispensable guide to their argot.

Though much of this slang is ephemeral, there is a residue of common words, such as *cove* ('man, fellow, rogue'), *nipper* ('child'), *beak* ('judge') and *fence* ('receiver of stolen property'), which has survived the intervening four centuries without the support of respectability. (None of them was included in Johnson's *Dictionary*.) Nevertheless, these early canting dictionaries had the effect of reinforcing the separation of registers, so that low, criminal jargon was isolated from polite, acceptable usage. The tradition of recording the argot of the underworld and the coarser language of the street continued in the form of Captain Francis Grose's racy and readable *Classical Dictionary of the Vulgar Tongue* (1785), which can be sampled in figure 4.2, *The Swell's Night Guide* (1841) and a few others.

SHAKESPEARE

In this context of semantic controversy, the magisterial example of Shakespeare is revealing. Although committed to communication with a disparate audience (as Spenser, for example, was not), he contrived to exploit creatively all the varied resources of the language of his time. He was especially adept at playing off the Latin register against the Saxon element.[9] In the early plays there is an exhibitionist or mechanical quality in this word-game. *Richard III* abounds in such artificial embellishments, underscored by alliteration (latinized terms in bold):

> ... the **lascivious** pleasing of a lute.
> (I. i. 13)

> Unless to see my shadow in the sun
> And **descant** on mine own **deformity**.
> (I. i. 27–8)

However, in the mature tragedies, this juxtaposition is more daringly creative, profoundly revealing of character and psychology. Macbeth, unable to articulate directly the words *blood* and *death* because of his intense feelings of guilt, takes refuge in rarefied Latinized euphemisms or suggestive Saxon terms:

> If it were done when 'tis done, then 'twere well
> It were done quickly; if the **assassination***
> Could **trammel*** up the **consequence**, and catch

FIGURE 4.2 A glossary for the uninitiated: a page from Francis Grose's *Classical Dictionary of the Vulgar Tongue* (1785)

CUN

CRUSTY FELLOW. A surly fellow.

CUB. An unlicked cub; an unformed, ill-educated young man, a young nobleman or gentleman on his travels: an allusion to the story of the bear, said to bring its cub into form by licking. Also, a new gamester.

CUCKOLD. The husband of an incontinent wife: cuckolds, however, are Christians, as we learn by the following story: An old woman hearing a man call his dog Cuckold, reproved him sharply, saying, 'Sirrah, are not you ashamed to call a dog by a Christian's name?' To cuckold the parson; to bed with one's wife before she has been churched.

CUCUMBERS. Taylors, who are jocularly said to subsist, during the summer, chiefly on cucumbers.

CUFF. An old cuff; an old man. To cuff Jonas; said of one who is knock-kneed, or who beats his sides to keep himself warm in frosty weather; called also Beating the booby.

CUFFIN. A man.

CULL. A man, honest or otherwise. A bob cull; a good-natured, quiet fellow. *Cant.*

CULLABILITY. A disposition liable to be cheated, an unsuspecting nature, open to imposition.

CULLY. A fop or fool: also, a dupe to women: from the Italian word *coglione*, a blockhead.

CULP. A kick or blow: from the words *mea culpa*, being that part of the popish liturgy at which the people beat their breasts; or, as the vulgar term is, thump their craws.

CUNDUM. The dried gut of a sheep, worn by men in the act of coition, to prevent venereal infection; said to have been invented by one colonel Cundum. These machines were long prepared and sold by a matron of the name of Philips, at the Green Canister, in Half-moon-street, in the Strand. That good lady having acquired a fortune, retired from business; but learning that the town was not well served by her successors, she, out of a patriotic zeal for the public welfare, returned to her occupation; of which she gave notice by divers hand-bills, in circulation in the year 1776. Also a false scabbard over a sword, and the oil-skin case for holding the colours of a regiment.

CUNNINGHAM. A punning appellation for a simple fellow.

CUNNING MAN. A cheat, who pretends by his skill in astrology to assist persons in recovering stolen goods: and also to tell them their fortunes, and when, how often, and to whom they shall be married; likewise answers all lawful questions, both by sea and land. This profession is frequently occupied by ladies.

CUNNING

With his **surcease success**; that but this blow
Might be the be-all and the end-all . . . .
(I. vii. 1–5)

(The bold type indicates the latinisms; the asterisk denotes that this is the first recorded usage.)

Like Chaucer, Shakespeare relied largely on his intuition to contrive these contrasts, since the first, very rudimentary, 'respectable' dictionary, Robert Cawdrey's *Table Alphabeticall of Hard Vsuall English Words*, of which a sample appears in figure 4.3, appeared only in 1604. Shakespeare's peculiar felicity was in the creation of words which were sufficiently rare to reflect extreme, tragic experience, but not so opaque as to lose the audience. Perhaps the most dramatic and daring oscillation between registers is found in Macbeth's extraordinary lines:

. . . this my hand will rather
The **multitudinous*** seas **incarnadine***,
Making the green one red.
(II. ii. 62–4)

The use of the rare word is subtly varied. Regan's bogus declaration of love to Lear is signalled by a suitably artificial, stilted word:

. . . I am alone **felicitate***
In your dear highness' love.
(I. i. 77–8)

Lear, furious at Cordelia's apparent rejection of him, mixes fiery new coinages with the base idiom of the market place, dehumanizing and reifying his 'sometime' daughter. He insultingly solicits Burgundy:

Will you, with those **infirmities** she owes,
Unfriended*, new-**adopted*** to our hate,
Dower'd* with our curse and **stranger'd*** with our oath,
Take her, or leave her?
(I. i. 205–8)

The strangeness of the formations reflects the unnaturalness of what Lear is doing, but the meaning is always clear. *Antony and Cleopatra* shows Shakespeare's language at its most sumptuous and malleable: there are at least 33 new formations in it.[10]

In another vein entirely, Shakespeare makes comic capital out of the malapropisms of officialdom, exemplified by Dogberry, Chief of the Watch in *Much Ado About Nothing*, some of whose nonsense words and logical inversions have, perhaps, a subversive and satirical sting in them,

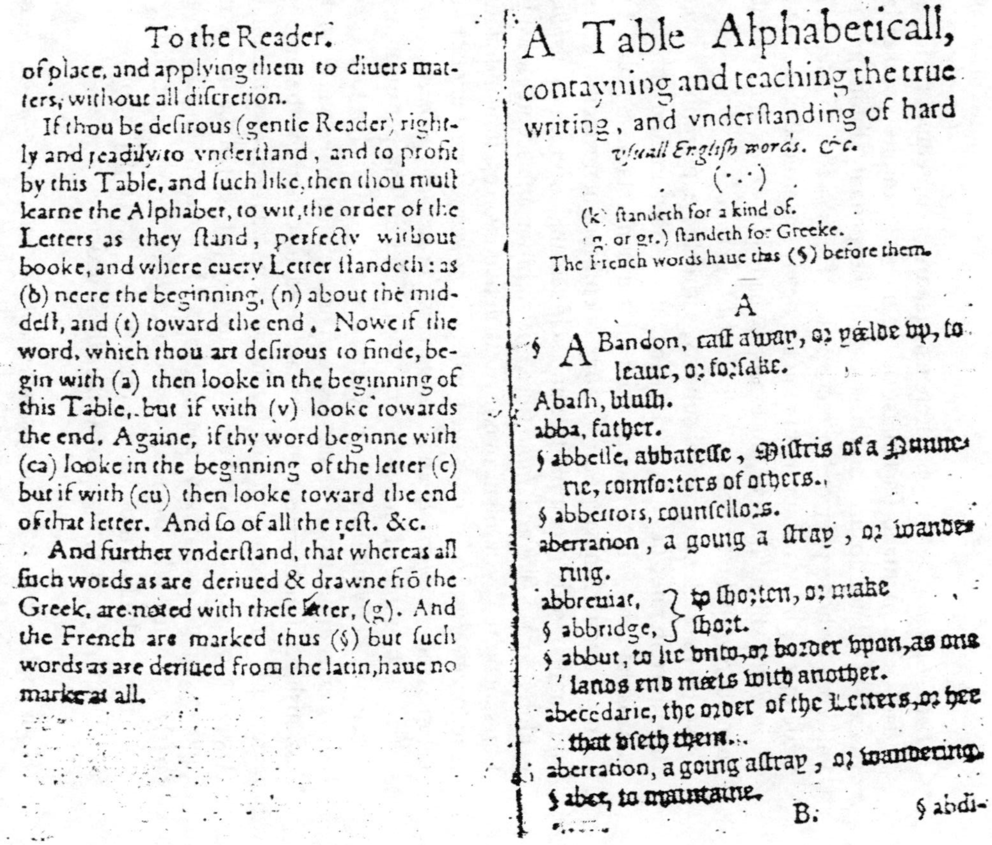

To the Reader.

of place, and applying them to diuers matters, without all discretion.

If thou be desirous (gentle Reader) rightly and readily to vnderstand, and to profit by this Table, and such like, then thou must learne the Alphabet, to wit, the order of the Letters as they stand, perfecty without booke, and where euery Letter standeth: as (b) neere the beginning, (n) about the middest, and (t) toward the end. Nowe if the word, which thou art desirous to finde, begin with (a) then looke in the beginning of this Table, but if with (v) looke towards the end. Againe, if thy word beginne with (ca) looke in the beginning of the letter (c) but if with (cu) then looke toward the end of that letter. And so of all the rest. &c.

And further vnderstand, that whereas all such words as are deriued & drawne frō the Greek, are noted with these letter, (g). And the French are marked thus (§) but such words as are deriued from the latin, haue no marke at all.

A Table Alphabeticall,

contayning and teaching the true writing, and vnderstanding of hard vsuall English words. &c.

(·.·)

(k) standeth for a kind of.

(g. or gr.) standeth for Greeke.

The French words haue this (§) before them.

A

§ ABandon, cast away, or yeelde vp, to leaue, or forsake.

Abash, blush.

abba, father.

§ abbesse, abbatesse, Mistris of a Nunnerie, comforters of others.

§ abbettors, counsellors.

aberration, a going a stray, or wandering.

abbreuiat, } to shorten, or make

§ abbridge, } short.

§ abbut, to lie vnto, or border vpon, as one lands end meets with another.

abecedarie, the order of the Letters, or hee that vseth them.

aberration, a going astray, or wandering.

§ abet, to maintaine.

B. § abdi-

FIGURE 4.3 A glossary for the unlearned: a page from the first, rudimentary dictionary, by Robert Cawdrey (1604)

making fun of pompous officialdom which boosts itself by confusing language:

> You are thought here to be the most senseless and fit man for the constable of the watch; therefore bear you the lanthorn. This is your charge: you shall comprehend all vagrom men.
>
> (III. iii. 20–5)

Love's Labour's Lost is a comprehensive satire of contemporary linguistic fads: Don Armado ('a fantastical Spaniard') exhibits 'oversea language' in all its absurd bombast, while the pedant Holofernes is a ludicrous orthographer or 'correct speller'. He is such a stickler in his trade that he insists on pronouncing the newly introduced etymological 'b' in *debt* (which Chaucer, for example, had spelt *dette*), and produces such alien verbal monsters as *honorificabilitudinitatibus.*

No play is lacking in verbal subtlety, satire and exploration. In many there are reiterated key words which in their crucial semantic ambiguities encapsulate the value-structure and ethical conflicts of the play. One example is *nature* in *King Lear*: is *natural* behaviour benevolent, altruistic and familial, or is it competitive and self-seeking? Another is *ambition*, explored in *Macbeth* and *Julius Caesar*: is ambition an acceptable aspiration sanctioned by heroism, or is it a destructive, overreaching individualistic force? *Henry IV* studies the concept of *honour*; *Hamlet* explores the complexities of *conscience* and *vengeance*, while *jealousy* in *Othello* hovers between the sense of 'suspicion' or 'doubt' and the sharper meaning of 'insecurity deriving from fear of a sexual rival or betrayal in love'.

The sheer quantity of Shakespeare's contribution to the word-stock is astonishing. On the basis of the data used to construct the graph in figure 4.1, it can be shown that for the years he was active as a dramatist (1590–1610), he contributed approximately 10 per cent of the new words and meanings accreting to the language. His total vocabulary is variously estimated at between 20,000 and over 30,000 words (as against 8,000 for Milton). Unlike those of any other writer, his contributions are not solely 'literary', but range across the whole lexicon:

High register: *assassination*, *festinate*, *compunctious*, *misanthrope*, *obscene*, *perusal*, *prodigious*, *protractive*, *sanctimonious*, *sanctuarize*

Foreign register: *ambuscado,*, *antre*, *barricado*, *bastinado*, *hurricano*, *mutiny*, *palisado*, *pell-mell*, *quietus*, *renegado*

Common register: *amazement*, *blanket* (vb), *critic*, *crop* (vb), *dwindle*, *fitful*, *humour* (vb), *humorous*, *hunch-backed*, *hurry*, *leap-frog*, *lonely*, *pedant*, *queasy*, *weird*

Low register: *boggler*, *beetle* (vb), *buzz* (rumour), *choppy* (chapped), *fee faw fum*, *foppish*, *gibber*, *barefaced*, *puke*

The permanent contribution of idioms is likewise remarkably copious:

High idiomatic: *hoist with his own petard*, *caviar to the general*, *more honoured in the breach than in the observance*, *to the manner born* (all from *Hamlet*)
Common idiomatic: *to out (Herod) Herod*, *full of sound and fury*, *one fell swoop*, *pound of flesh*, *it's Greek to me*, *be-all and end-all*, *foregone conclusion*, *what the dickens*, *household words*
Low idiomatic: *fob off*, *do famously*, *cheer up*, *small beer*, *seamy side*, *beast with two backs*, *hob nob*, *what ye call it*

As F. P. Wilson pointed out in 1941, 'His instinct for what was permanent in the colloquial language of his day is stronger than that of any contemporary dramatist.'[11] Shakespeare's avoidance of the easy laugh from the topical gag becomes very apparent when one compares his text with those of many a contemporary comedy, where copious footnotes now seek to explicate the irretrievably passé.

This brief survey can in no way do full justice to the mastery and the magical skill of Shakespeare's exploitation of the resources of the language of his time, nor of his remarkable linguistic creativity. His intuitive understanding of the strengths and follies, charms and banalities of the tongue is as profound as it is of other aspects of human behaviour.

Of the other contemporary Neologizers, one of the more famous and perceptive was Sir Thomas Elyot. In his treatise on education (a word he coined) called *The Governour* (1531) he introduced such borrowings as *dedicate*, *animate*, *encyclopaedia*, *frugality*, *metamorphosis*, *modesty*, *persist* and many others. He sensible followed the traditional practice of pairing his neologisms with established words and phrases in order to make their meaning comprehensible. Examples of these pairings are: '*animate* or gyue courage to others'; 'the beste fourme of *education* or bringing up of noble children'; '*persist* and continue'. But what makes Elyot virtually unique in his time is his acute understanding that to introduce a new term is to disturb an established semantic field by displacing the synonyms which already exist. This understanding is most clearly evidenced in his remarks justifying the introduction of *maturity* 'wherevnto we lacke a name in englisshe':

> Maturitie is a meane between two extremities / wherein nothing lacketh or excedeth. . . . Therefore that worde maturitie is translated to the actis

> of man / that whan they be done with such moderation / that nothing in the doinge may be sene superfluous or indigent / we may saye / that they be maturely done: reseruing the wordes ripe and ready to frute and other thinges seperate from affaires / as we haue now in vsage. And this do I nowe remembre for the necessary augmentation of our langage.

Fascinatingly, Elyot has described *in advance* the separation of registers which has in fact subsequently taken place between the native term *ripe* and the borrowed Latin word *maturity*. The borrowed term has acquired an abstract, intellectual register, while the native word has moved to a more physical, concrete register. We would not thus speak of a 'ripe man' or a 'ripe taste', any more than of a 'mature avocado' or a 'mature crop'. Caxton, however, had written half a century earlier of London children who, 'at their ful rypyng' are 'chaff for the moste parte'.

The example of *mature/ripe* can be multiplied many times. This separation of registers can be ascribed, in sociolinguistic terms, to the high status accorded the classical languages in Renaissance times, particularly by educated men who would themselves be instrumental in the borrowing of Greek and Latin words. The high status of the classical languages has persisted long after their actual currency as intellectual instruments. Furthermore, it is curious that Latin continued as the medium of major intellectual statement in the sciences rather than the humanities. More's *Utopia* (1516) and occasional Latin poems by Milton and others, mark the petering out of the 'direct' classical tradition, so to speak.[12] (One reads with amazement of Hobbes writing, at the age of 84, an autobiography in Latin verse.) But, following the tradition of Copernicus, Galileo and Gilbert, William Harvey published his two great medical works in Latin in 1628 and 1651, and Newton's *Principia* was similarly issued in 1686. Since then the public schools and the grammar schools have sought to maintain the traditional prestige of the classical languages, in the face of general inutility.

By referring to *maturity* as a 'strange and darke' word, Elyot immediately reveals to us the subsequent separation from 'foreign' and 'obscure'. Of many similar examples we may note *ghostly*, later ousted from respectability by *spiritual*, and *clean*, reduced to the physical domain as *pure* has assumed dominance of the moral.

Although the Inkhorn Controversy raged for several decades, the ultimate resolution was a compromise for, as the great American historian of English, Albert Croll Baugh, observes in his discussion of 'Synonyms at Three Levels': 'Language has need for the simple, the polished, and even the recondite word' (1965, p. 255).

LANGUAGE AND AUTHORITY IN THE REFORMATION

The Reformation was essentially a struggle between the rights of received authority and individual experience in spiritual matters. The outcome of controversy over what was the 'true' manifestation of the Christian spirit was largely determined through the effective mobilization of the letter. The press became a very influential weapon, and contributed to the division of religious authority whereby previously 'dogmatic' words like *heresy*, *enormity* and *abuse* became relative and plural in meaning, as their use became dispersed among the disputants. Even Gutenberg's famous Bible (1452–6) was in its time a venture inspired partly by reformist sympathies, since the Church was generally against the free reading (and consequent individual interpretation) of Holy Writ.

Luther and his followers were to mobilize the power of the press with much more effectiveness than their opponents, who generally relied on private letters to Electors and Dukes. Luther's 95 theses, which precipitated the indulgences controversy, were printed and published, probably on the door of the castle church at Wittenberg, in 1517. According to the somewhat chauvinist account of Friedrich Myconius in his *Historia Reformationis*, the dispersal of information was so miraculously swift that 'It almost appeared as if the angels themselves had been their messengers and brought them before the eyes of all the people' (Hillerbrand, 1964, p. 47).

The language of the theses is fairly neutral, though their import is obviously subversive. However, within a short while the Pope is referring to Luther as 'a certain son of iniquity', 'a son of perdition' and – after he was declared a heretic – as a 'roaring sow of the woods [which] has undertaken to destroy this vineyard, a wild beast [which] wants to devour it' (Hillerbrand, 1964, pp. 56, 60 and 80). Luther was to reply in kind, challenging authority in vituperative language. He remarked, in his debate with Johann Eck in 1519, 'To say that indulgences are a blessing for a Christian is insane. . . . Completely unlearned sophists and pestiferous flatterers dream that the Pope can remit every punishment owed for sins in this and the future life' (p. 66). Satirical, often scandalous, cartoons, the pictorial equivalent of the polemical insult, were frequent from the beginning of the struggle. These emotive distortions were fairly common currency in the subversive, 'populist' press. One of the most powerful depicted Pope Leo as the Beast of Antichrist (his name making a convenient association with this leonine creature), flanked by other of Luther's opponents represented by means of 'visual puns' with the visages of a cat, a goat, a pig and a dog.

The press was much more daring in its reformist use on the Continent than in England. Tyndale's magnificent translation of the New Testament was printed at Cologne and Worms (1525–6), and many Lutheran pamphlets issued from the Continent. By contrast, none of Caxton's output could be regarded as controversial, though the proportion rises in the work of his successors, Wynkyn de Worde (1492–1535) and Richard Pynson (d.1539), so that, in the words of H. S. Bennett, 'Good tempered or bad tempered, a considerable volume of controversial works poured from the presses in the forties and fifties of the century' (1952, pp. 71–2). In 1521 (prior to the break with Rome) Henry VIII entered the fray with his treatise, the *Assertio Septem Sacramentorum*, denouncing 'the pest of Martin Luther's heresy [which] had appeared in Germany and was raging everywhere' (Hillerbrand, 1964, p. 47).

The general tenor of language employed in statements of authority becomes virtually indistinguishable in virulence and intemperance from that used in polemical controversy. There are two significant documents of the period which illuminate this point. The first is the 'Act of Supremacy' (1534), in which Henry VIII makes final the break with Rome by a '*coup d'église*':

> Albeit the King's Majesty justly and rightfully is and ought to be the supreme head of the Church of England, and so is recognized by the clergy of this realm in their Convocations; yet nevertheless for corroboration and confirmation thereof, and for the increase of virtue in Christ's religion within this realm of England, and to repress and extirp all errors, heresies and other enormities and abuses heretofore used in the same; be it enacted by authority of this present Parliament, that the King our sovereign lord, his heirs and successors, kings of this realm, shall be taken, accepted and reputed the only supreme head in earth of the Church of England, called *Anglicana Ecclesia*.
>
> (Hillerbrand, 1964, p. 332)

The Act is a virtual fiat, in which the King's authority is being fabricated out of words, not out of a causal explanation of heredity, for Henry has the *de facto* power, but not the *de jure* authority. Hence the awkward conjunction of '*is* and *ought to be*' in the opening clause. Consequently, the syntax of the Act is revealing. It is a huge, convoluted, circular argument in which the premise is simply repeated in more imposing language. With simple 'legerdemot' the Church *in* England becomes the Church *of* England, and is given the final respectability of a Latin style: *Anglicana Ecclesia*. Henry, by using terms such as *heresy*, *abuse* and *enormity*, is usurping the role of the erstwhile central defining authority (the papacy) in these matters. Within a century, the words will be used by any sect of its rivals. Politically, the new title is effective, since the Church of England and the Church of Rome are given the appearance of equal status, but separate geographical jurisdiction. A modern advertising agency could hardly have achieved a more effective change of image.

The 'Act of Supremacy' was reinforced two years later (1536) by an Act invalidating the authority of the 'Bishop of Rome' in England. This refutation of papal authority employs much more emotive language, as well as a syntactical 'filibuster' – sentences of enormous length and weight:

> Forasmuch as notwithstanding the good and wholesome laws, ordinances and statutes heretofore enacted, made and established . . . for the extirpation, abolition and extinguishment, out of this realm and other his Grace's dominions, seignories and countries, of the pretended power and usurped authority of the Bishop of Rome, by some called the Pope . . . which did obfuscate and wrest God's holy word and testament a long season from the spiritual and true meaning thereof to his worldly and carnal affections, as pomp, glory, avarice, ambition and tyranny, covering and shadowing the same with his human and politic devices, traditions and inventions . . . so that the King's Majesty, the Lords spiritual and temporal, and the Commons of this realm, being overwearied and fatigated with the experience of the infinite abominations and mischiefs proceeding from his impostures and craftily colouring of his deceits, to the great damages of souls, bodies and goods, were forced of necessity for the public weal of this realm to exclude that foreign pretended power, jurisdiction and authority . . . and notwithstanding the said wholesome laws so made and heretofore established, yet it is come to the knowledge of the King's Highness and also to divers and many his loving, faithful and obedient subjects, how that divers seditious and contentious persons, being imps of the said Bishop of Rome and his see, and in heart members of his pretended monarchy, do in corners and elsewhere, as they dare, whisper, inculce, preach and persuade, and from time to time instill into the ears and heads of the poor, simple and unlettered people the advancement and continuance of the said bishop's feigned and pretended authority. . . .
>
> (Hillerbrand, 1964, pp. 333–4)

The cynicism of attributing discord to the Pope by Henry, who in fact split the Church, is impressive in its audacity. In addition to this considerable distortion, the Act employs many effective techniques of propaganda. One of the most successful is the demotion of the Pope to the title of mere 'Bishop of Rome',[13] thereby making his 'pretended monarchy' illegal and subversive. Considerable semantic play is made out of *pretended* and *pretence*, which in the mid-sixteenth century were ambiguous terms which could be used both to corroborate and to question authority, depending on the context. (Thus we have the *Pretender* to the Throne, i.e., legitimate claimant, as opposed to the *pretender* to modesty, i.e., user of simulation.) By an artful ambiguity the historical claims of papal authority are recognized, but their current validity is questioned and rejected as 'the said bishop's feigned and pretended authority'. Indeed, it may be argued that the semantic development of *pretended* and *pretence* from being ambiguous terms to their present dominant sense of criticism implying dishonesty, is intimately related to the religious and political upheavals of the sixteenth and seventeenth centuries. As the central authority is subsequently divided amongst more and more claimants, so each *pretender* will see fit to cast aspersions on the *pretences* of rivals.

The Pope is cast in the role of Antichrist or the Devil, 'obfuscat[ing] and wresting God's holy word and testament a long season from the spiritual and true meaning thereof', having 'carnal affections', using 'politic devices' to 'rob the King's Majesty' and 'spoil his realm'. The notion of diabolical influence is ingeniously insinuated in language which appears to be simple polemical exaggeration: 'divers seditious and contentious persons, being imps of the said Bishop of Rome and his see. . . .' *Imp*, though an ancient word meaning 'shoot' or 'scion' in the phrase 'the King's imp', had recently acquired the less wholesome sense of a 'child of the devil', clearly implied here. And, should this diabolical innuendo not be effective, there are strong appeals to national solidarity ('loving, faithful and obedient servants'), law and order ('good and wholesome laws'), and property rights (for the Pope seeks dominion 'both upon the souls and also the bodies and goods of all Christian people').

The Act implies, in the now-familiar propagandist stereotype, that 'the gullible masses are being wickedly misled'. Yet the skilful semantic manipulation of the language of the Act is clearly designed precisely to take advantage of those same 'poor, simple and unlettered people'. This point is corroborated by the copious use of rarefied latinisms. *Obfuscate* is a first usage, *fatigate* is recorded only from the previous year, while *contentious* (in application to people) dates from only three years previously. This instance of *imposture* antedates the first dictionary citation by one year. *Discontentation* is previously recorded in 1528, also in a usage attributed to Henry VIII, suggesting that the term enjoyed royal favour. *Inculce* is quite unrecorded in the *OED*, though there is a citation for *inculk*, dating from 1528[O], and regarded as a variant of *inculcate*. In all, this barrage of impressive rarities would make this Act a most effective propagandist statement for the year 1536.

RELIGIOUS CONTROVERSY: BROADSIDES AND TRACTS

In effective propaganda, the art is to conceal the art, to prevent, in the terms of Keats's dictum, the design from becoming too palpable. By and large, the Act of 1536 succeeds in avoiding the emotive extremes that were soon to become current. Its language appears extremely temperate, in fact, when set alongside that of a controversialist John Bale who, in his pamphlet of 1543, *Yet a course at the Romyshe foxe*, referred to his Catholic opponents as 'fylthye whoremongers, murtherers, thieves, raveners, idolatours, lyars, dogges, swyne . . . and very devyls incarnate' (Bennett, 1952, p. 73).

As this and many other broadsides and tracts indicate, the initial controversies were marked by a vehement anti-Catholic feeling, bred of xenophobia and nationalism, viewing the papacy in very much the light of the Act of 1536. A fair number of the terms used in contemporary polemic had been in currency since the fourteenth century, many of them deriving from the Wycliffite movement for reform. *Pope-holy*, with strong associations of hypocrisy, is first recorded in Langland. *Rome-runner* is a contemporary term, critical of direct papal taxation, traditionally called 'Peter's pence', which began in Anglo-Saxon times and continued to be a source of annoyance well beyond the Reformation.[14] Henry Brinklow added an ironic gloss in 1542: 'Papa means pay pay' (Brinklow, 1874, p. 39), but the denunciations of papal simony by the Puritan preacher Thomas Adams are of a quite different order of vehemence: 'the Pope is rich, and needs must, for his commings in be great: he hath Rent out of Heauen, Rent out of Hell, Rent out of Purgatory . . . he sells Christs crosse, Christs bloud, Christs selfe; all for money' (from 'The White Devil', preached 1612, cited in Chandos (1971), p. 180).

The continuing public use of anti-Catholic terms is noteworthy. In the Litany of the *Book of Common Prayer* (1549), the people prayed to be delivered 'from the tyranny of the Bishop of Rome and his detestable enormities'. The translators of the King James Bible (1611) acknowledge in the Preface (still often printed) that they may be: 'traduced by Popish persons at home or abroad, who therefore will malign us, because we are poor instruments to make God's holy truth to be yet more and more known unto the people, whom they desire still [always] to keep in ignorance and darkness. . . .' The Declaration of Right of William and Mary (1689) speaks of 'His highness the Prince of Orange (whom it hath pleased God to make the glorious Instrument of delivering this Kingdom from Popery and arbitrary power)'.

Subsequent additions to this verbal armoury include the use of *pope* to mean the effigy burnt on Guy Fawkes Night, a sense current from *c.* 1673[O] and recorded until the late nineteenth century. (November 5 was termed *Pope Day* at least until 1903[O].) David Hume in 1762 commented somewhat blandly in his *History of England*: 'One of the most innocent artifices . . . was the additional ceremony, pomp and expense with which a pope-burning was celebrated in London.' Dryden and Pope, with greater personal loyalty to Catholicism, have quotations in the *OED* which are not so tolerant. *The Pope's nose*, insultingly used for 'the rump of a fowl', is first recorded in Grose's *Dictionary of the Vulgar Tongue* (1796 edition) and was therefore presumably current for some time previously.

In such an atmosphere of fanaticism and suspicion it was virtually inevitable that general religious terms would deteriorate by becoming expressions of sectarian detestation and abuse. Amongst the older terms were *abomination*, *antichrist*, *carnal* and *superstition. Abomination* was generally spelt with an 'h' in Medieval Latin, Old French and earlier English, thereby suggesting the literal sense (from *ab homine*) of 'inhuman' or 'unnatural', as in 'the abhominable synne of Sodomye' (1366). The *OED* adds a note pointing out that the generalized emotive sense of *abominable* dates from at least the fifteenth century: '*Abominable* has occasionally been used, like *terrible*, *prodigious*, as a simple intensive. Juliana Berners (15th c.) writes of "a bominable syght of monks", i.e. a large company.'

Antichrist dates from *c.* 1300[O], is extended from Wycliffe (1370) onwards to the Pope or papal power, and by the sixteenth century the application was to become commonplace. *Carnal*, dating from *c.* 1400[O], moves from the literal sense of 'fleshly, sensual or corporeal' to that of 'temporal or worldly', with an implied antithesis to spiritual qualities. *Superstition* and *superstitious* are eagerly employed in this period to stigmatize belief in the sacraments, particularly that of transubstantiation: 'Shall we deny that it is a superstitious worshipping, when men do throw themselves down before bread, to worship Christe therein?' asks Thomas Norton in *Calvin's Institutes* of 1561.[O] A specifically anti-Catholic reference is found in 1566, alluding to 'The mass books and all other popishe and superstitious bookes.'[O]

Propaganda soon evolved into the policy of the physical destruction of Catholic establishments policed by Thomas Cromwell, culminating in the Dissolution of the Monasteries. In the upsurge of fanaticism in the following century the iconoclastic impulse was legalized by Parliament and various Puritan extremists set about defacing 'idolatrous' images and carvings in churches. William Dowsing, the most notorious of the iconoclasts, recorded his grim satisfaction at the reign of destruction he wreaked on local churches in his *Suffolk Journal* (1643–4): 'Clare, Jan. 6. [1643] We brake down 1000 Pictures superstitious; I brake down 200; 3 of God the Father, and 3 of Christ and the Holy Lamb, and 3 of the Holy Ghost like a Dove with Wings.'

Iconoclasm had the semantic consequence that terms referring to images acquired hostile overtones. *Idol*, *image* and *saint* were all affected, and in the case of a fanatic like Dowsing, it would appear that even *picture* has lost its neutrality. *Idol* becomes 'applied polemically to images or figures of divine beings and saints', with its first citation in 1545: '[He] set vp in the same place another idol of S. Iohan Baptyst.'[O] Other polemicists denounce 'this mischievous idol the mass'. *Image* too can be seen acquiring an emotive sense in Tyndale's (1526) rendering of Acts xv, 20: 'Abstayne themselves from the filthiness of ymages', a context in which Wycliffe (1387) had used *symulacres* and the King James Bible (1611) was to prefer *idols.* A *Homily Against Idolatry* (1563) warns: 'We should not have images in the temple for fear and occasion of worshipping them.'[O] A similar work, *Against Images*, also publishedin 1563, shows *saint* beginning to acquire emotive overtones: 'Such a creple came in and saluted this saint of Oke.'[O] Another significant extension of meaning is the application of the word by the Puritan sects to themselves: 'God, for thy grace . . . Ceis not to send thy Sanctis sume support' (1567). (The first reference to the Mormons, the Latter-Day Saints, is 1842.)

These essentially Puritan influences, while only temporary, extended to other religious terms such as *enormity*, *enthusiasm*, *zeal*, *profane* and *profanation.* Originally meaning 'a breach of the law or morality' from Caxton (1475) onwards, *enormity* acquires an intensified sense of 'extreme or monstrous wickedness' in the sixteenth century. But by 1614 Ben Jonson is using the term satirically: the hypocritical Puritan fanatic, Zeal-of-the-Land-Busy, rants his way through *Bartholomew Fair*, using *enormity* with an absurd, frenzied frequency, especially of such heinous activities as the eating of pork. *Profane* dates from Wycliffe in its strict religious sense, but also broadens in meaning to the point that tobacco is comically castigated in a quotation of 1606 as 'a pagan plant, a prophane weede and a most sinful smoke'. *Profanation*, first recorded in *The Book of Common Prayer* (1552), soon joins the vocabulary of polemic, in a pamphlet of 1588: 'You have ioyned the prophanation of the magistracie to the corruption of the ministreie' (1588).[O]

Enthusiasm, a particularly rich word which has attracted several major studies,[15] is a classic example of semantic change reflecting social pressures. The earliest instances (around 1579) denote 'prophetic and poetic inspiration' in a neutral fashion, the sense deriving from the Greek root *theos.* (A less inspired association links *giddy* to *god*.) However, within a few years there emerges the fanatical sense of *enthusiast*: 'one who erroneously believes himself to be the recipient of special divine communications'.[O] It is this notion which Thomas Adams denounces in his sermon 'The Devils Banquet' (1614): 'Sottish Enthusiastes condemn all learning, all premeditation.'[O] Increasingly critical definitions, such as that of John Wesley ('religious madness, fancied inspiration'), reflect the fanaticism of the times. The rationalism of the Enlightenment underscores the definition in the *Grub Street Journal* of 1735: '*Enthusiasm* is any exorbitant monstrous Appetite of the Human Mind . . . against the Light of Reason and Common Sense.' We can see generalization away from the religious contexts to which the word had previously been limited. With increasing religious stability and tolerance, and as religious issues became less central, *enthusiasm* took on a milder meaning and has subsequently undergone amelioration in all its forms.

Fanatic, however, still retains its sense of violent religious frenzy. Deriving from similar roots, 'pertaining to a temple (*fanum*), inspired by a deity', the term surfaced in the troubled times with which we are concerned, around 1533. Its early history is neatly summarized as 'a mad person; in later use, a religious maniac.'[O] Swift contributed this caustic observation in his fearless religious satire of 1704, *A Tale of a Tub*: 'The two principal qualifications of a fanatic preacher are, his inward light and his head filled with maggots; and the two different fates of his writings are, to be burnt or worm-eaten.' The jocular abbreviation *fan* originally reflected the old strong sense. The first reference is an ironic comment on religious zealots, termed 'loyal Phans' (as they are quaintly spelt) in a satirical work called *New News from Bedlam* (1682). Although *fan* is now used almost exclusively in secular contexts, the original hysterical overtones are not entirely lost in modern applications to blood-sports, such as those ferociously enjoyed by soccer hooligans and boxing crowds.

The volume of religious polemic is as astonishing as its vehemence. As sectarian strife intensified, so (predictably) did the violence of tone, to the point that almost the entire religious and spiritual vocabulary became part of a verbal armoury. Probably the most virulent philippics occurred in contemporary pamphlets and tracts, usually brief, inflammatory and anonymous or pseudonymous. In the earlier stages of the Reformation these were concerned with matters of doctrine and observance, as we have seen. Soon there were attacks on hierarchy in general and individual dignitaries. Probably the most famous of these were the pamphlets, secretly printed in 1588–9, and written under the pseudonym of Martin Marprelate. 'The pseudonymity was essential,' Charles Barber has explained, 'for it was perilous to attack the established order; one of the probable authors, John Penry, was executed for his seditious views, and another, John Udall, died in prison' (1976, p. 42). The following passage (p. 43) is typical in its contempt for episcopal authority and in its personal abuse:

> Therefore our Lord Bishops Iohn of Canterburie, Thomas of Winchester (I will spare Iohn of London for this time for it may be that he is at boules and it is pitie to trouble my good brother lest he should sweare too bad), my reuerend prelate of Litchfielde and the rest of that swinishe rable are pettie Antichrists, pettie popes, proud prelates, intollerable withstanders of reformation, enemies of the gospell and most couetous wretched priests.

In time the overtly propagandist mode of the pamphleteers spread to the writers of contemporary religious history, the most famous being John Knox's *History of the Reformation in Scotland* (1587–8) and John Foxe's *Actes & Monuments* of 1563, better known as *The Book of Martyrs*, 'containing an account of the sufferings and death of the Protestants in the reign of Queen Mary the First'. Though Foxe's basic accuracy has been corroborated (Mozley, 1940), his partisan tone can be gauged from his ironic remark that 'Tyndale's translation of the New Testament, with notes, drew a severe condemnation of the clergy, there being nothing in which they were more concerned than to keep the people unacquainted with that book' (Foxe, 1732, p. 198).

Some sense of the extreme counter-measures taken by those in authority to suppress the possession of Holy Writ in print and in the mother tongue[16] is indicated in this proclamation by Henry VIII in 1546: 'From henceforth no man, woman or person of what estate, condition or degree soever he or they be . . . shall have, take or keep in his possession the text of the New Testament of Tyndale's or Coverdale's translation in English' (Foxe, 1732, v, p. 565).

It now seems profoundly ironic that such fearsome prohibitions should have been directed at Tyndale's pioneering translation since 'one third of the King James Bible of 1611, it has been computed, is worded exactly as Tyndale left it' (Potter, 1963, p. 53). Space does not allow proper treatment of either the prototype or the later work, described by George Saintsbury as 'probably the greatest prose work in any language'. He continues:

> The plays of Shakespeare and the English Bible are, and ever will be the twin monuments, not merely of their own period, but of the perfection of English, the complete expressions of the literary capacities of the language, at the time when it had lost none of its pristine vigour, and had put on enough, but not too much of the adornments and the limitations of what may be called literary civilization.
>
> (*History of Elizabethan Literature*, cited in Potter, 1963, p. 54)

CONCLUSION

Looking back over the period, it is impossible not to be impressed by the ferment and excitement which language itself generated, nor by the way in which words were used as weapons of power. The scorn and the wit of the Inkhorn Controversy have seldom been matched. The berating of those who 'pouder theyr bokes with ynkehorne termes, although perchaunce as unaptly applied as a gold rynge in a sowes nose' was met with equally sharp ripostes: 'Some people, if they spy but a hard word are as much amazed as if they had met with a Hobgoblin.'[17]

Simeon Potter, taking up Saintsbury's 'pristine vigour', argues memorably that 'Words were still clean and bright: they had not lost their sharp cutting edge. Words had not yet gathered about themselves all those connotations, associations and subauditions which, for good and evil, cling to a language so widely diffused as ours' (1963, p. 54).

Persuasively written as that may be, it is surely an overstatement. Of the creativity shown in Elizabethan English there is no dispute. But the vehemence of social divisions took its toll. We have seen how political extremism and spiritual hysteria took much of the potency out of the language of outrage: *abominable*, *enormity*, *abuse*, *profane* and many others had already undergone marked weakening, by exaggeration and over-use in the war over God's Word. Verbicide was already causing the language of extreme expression to decay. Two witness-words refer revealingly to the catastrophes of the times, the Great Plague and the syphilis pandemic. Originally the Plague was called simply and starkly 'the Death'. But by the time of Henry VIII *pest* refers to anything noxious, destructive or troublesome. *Pestilential*, *pestiferous*, *plague* and *plaguey* become vogue-words of annoyance or abuse, even though the plague still visited sporadically. In distant America the word was to lose its etymological link and become *pesky*. Much the same pattern of weakening was to occur with *pox*.

Hobbes, whose pragmatic shrewdness is now a byword, seems in *The*

Leviathan to have underplayed the significance of printing: 'The invention of *Printing*, though ingenious, compared with the invention of letters, is no great matter' (part I, chapter 4). In fact, the press became associated almost immediately with institutionalizing the three roles to be discussed in chapters 6, 7 and 8, namely the language of advertising, the language of politics and the language of propaganda. In leaving the early functions of the press, one may observe that, as a matter of controversy, religion has been displaced almost entirely by secular issues involving politics, economics, sexual mores, sport, fashion and the entertainment industry in general.

NOTES

1 H. J. Chaytor (1945) stresses the important differences in cognition and memory between medieval and modern approaches to a text. In addition to McLuhan's numerous works on this theme, there are several by Walter Ong. Ong argues that the technology of printing, 'bringing new ideas about how to arrange the spoken word in space', introduced a new 'typographical culture' with altered notions of logic and dialectic (1958, pp. 75 and 97).
2 By 1500, 35,000 books had been published in Europe and 20,000 English titles had appeared by 1640. (The latter statistic would yield an average annual production of 125 books per year from the inception of printing.)
3 Blake notes: 'His own vocabulary was not very extensive and it appears that he did not go out of his way to enrich it. His own prose contains few examples of first occurrences in English' (1973, p. 32).
4 *Troilus & Criseyde*, V. 1793–5.
5 In the Wakefield *Second Shepherd's Play*, Mak the sheep-stealer assumes Southern forms of speech when he wishes to evade recognition.
6 Generally, these sexual senses are recorded only around Elizabethan times.
7 *The Demaundes Joyous*, ed. John Wardroper (London, Gordon Fraser, 1976), p. 4.
8 From the Preface to *The Shepheardes Calendar*, by Spenser's friend 'E. K.' (possibly Edward Kirke).
9 One of the best treatments of this feature is by another poet, John Crowe Ransom, in his essay 'On Shakespeare's language', *Sewanee Review* (1947), pp. 181–98.
10 Among these are *boggler*, *congealment*, *carbuncled*, *enthroned*, *gipsy*, *queasy*, *transmigrates*, *unpolicied* and *word* (used as a verb).
11 F. P. Wilson, 'Shakespeare and the Diction of Common Life' (British Academy Lecture, 1941).
12 More's classical bent is very apparent in his borrowings, which include *absurdity*, *acceptance*, *anticipate*, *contradictory*, *exaggerate*, *exasperate*, *paradox*, *pretext* and many others.
13 This demotion of the Pope can be traced as far back as Wycliffe, but was given renewed vehemence in Reformation times.
14 Chapter 2 mentions other hostile references.

15 The two most important recent studies are those of Ronald Knox, *Enthusiasm* (Oxford, OUP, 1950) and Susie I. Tucker, *Enthusiasm* (Cambridge, CUP, 1972). There are several earlier works, dating back to Meric Casaubon, *A Treatise Concerning Enthusiasme* (1655).

16 The first recorded use of *mother tongue* is in this typically polemical passage from Wycliffe: 'Secler lordys schuld, in defawte of prelatys, lerne and preche þe lawe of God in here modyr tunge.' ('Secular lords ought to make up for the deficiencies of the clergy by teaching and preaching the law of God in their mother tongue.')

17 The first combatant is Sir Thomas Chaloner; the reply is by Edward Phillips in his *New World of Words.*

5
The Fourth Estate: Journalism

Burke said that there were Three Estates in Parliament; but in the Reporters' Gallery yonder, there sat a *Fourth Estate* more important far than they all.

Thomas Carlyle

Well . . . of course, people don't actually read newspapers. They get into them every morning like a hot bath.

Marshall McLuhan

The speaking in a perpetual hyperbole is comely in nothing but love.

Bacon

. . . a very considerable Branch of the English Commerce.

Daniel Defoe

The first freedom of the press consists in its not being a trade.

Marx

INTRODUCTION

THE VIRTUAL saturation of the literacy market achieved by the various forms of Western journalism has had very diverse semantic effects: many individual words have undergone generalization and weakening, often to the point of verbicide, but clichés and set phrases have gained enormous currency and force. The first section of this chapter gives a brief history of English journalism, showing how 'popular journalism' has in the past century taken over a market formerly monopolized by 'quality journalism'. Newspapers have also tended to reflect the class structure, being categorized in broadly hierarchical fashion as 'quality', 'popular' and 'tabloid', employing different news-styles and language, which are analysed. The second section analyses the varieties of headline language (now virtually a language in its own right in terms of vocabulary and syntax) and the differing exploitation of register found in English and American journalism. The final section considers common journalistic characteristics, such as the use of cliché, categorization, the fabrication and suppression of news. It analyses the causes and effects of semantic disintegration, arising partly through sensationalism, and partly through English expanding to become a world language, thus being made responsive simultaneously to local and international perspectives.

A Brief History of the Varieties of English Journalism

Within forty years of Caxton setting up his press at Westminster, the first vestiges of journalism appeared when one Richard Faques printed an illustrated news pamphlet on the Battle of Flodden (1513). It claimed to be, in modern categories, both a 'scoop' and a 'confirmed report', announcing 'the trewe encountre of the batayle lately don betwene Englande and Scotlande'. The 'headline', though not in capitals, is set out above a block illustration, and – as is proper – contains the 'highlight': '. . . in which batayle the Scottishe Kynge was slayne' (Steinberg, 1966, p. 241). One is struck by the sobriety of the language, in comparison with that of a modern popular newspaper. This instance makes the point that originally journalism was 'occasional', responding to 'the event', which was of sufficient moment to require report and comment. Being inherently *newsworthy* (to use a term first recorded in *Time* magazine in 1932[S]), the event did not require special linguistic emphasis. In modern times, in strict etymological agreement with the root of the word *journalism* in French *jour*, 'day', newspapers and periodicals appear on a regular or daily basis, regardless of whether anything of importance has happened.

Nathaniel Butter, who from 1602 'published Corantos, Avisos, Passages, Newes, Relations, etc.', is commonly thought of as 'the father of English journalism' (Steinberg, 1966, p. 244), though the *Daily Courant*, begun in 1702, is generally regarded as the world's first daily *newspaper*, a word which had been coined only in 1670[O]. Financially, newspapers have become increasingly dependent on advertising revenue, which is geared to circulation within certain significant sectors of the population. The consequence is that 'news' is programmed by deadline, and has often to be fabricated out of trivia or 'pseudo-events', commonly proffered in inflated language.

To a considerable extent, the themes of the chapter are summed up in the semantic histories of the words *journalism*, *journalistic* and *journalese*, all of which emerged in the nineteenth century. *Journalism* dates from *c.* 1833[O], and in the course of the century the tone of the word shifts from respect for its power to contempt for its glibness. The pronouncements of two Victorian sages sum up these attitudes. Carlyle castigated the occupation and the product, writing in 1883: 'Journalism is just ditch-water.'[O] Matthew Arnold, on the other hand, responded more positively (in 1887) to the developments of popular journalism: 'We have had opportunities of observing a new journalism which a clever and energetic man [Northcliffe] has invented.'[O] *Journalistic* is first recorded a few years earlier than *journalism*, in 1829[O] in the writings of Carlyle. It soon acquired the modern pejorative tone, obvious in George Eliot's comment (in 1879) about 'Journalistic guides to the popular mind'.[O] The awareness that much journalistic writing is in a code of its own emerges in the ironic contemporary formation *journalese*. An essay in the *Pall Mall Gazette* of 1882 comments on a piece being 'translated from "Journalese" into plain English'[O], while a contemporary barb in *Harpers* observes: 'The phrase "newspaper English" has come to have a significance which is not flattering to newspapers.'

Journalism is, of course, not solely concerned with news. In the eighteenth century, with the liberation of the independent 'man of letters' from the previous system of patronage, there emerged a new, authoritative stylist, the serious essayist. Unlike the pamphleteers treated in the previous chapter, who used language in a highly emotive, polemical, even vitriolic fashion, the new essayists and exponents of high journalism used a style which is uniformly authoritative and serious: consequently the register is steadfastly high, full of latinization, aspiring to classic dignity. A characteristic passage from Dr Johnson's *Rambler* illustrates these features splendidly:

> Pedantry is the unseasonable ostentation of learning. He is undoubtedly guilty of pedantry, who, when he has made himself master of some abstruse and uncultivated part of knowledge, obtrudes his remarks and discoveries upon those he believes unable to judge his proficiency, and from whom, as he cannot fear contradiction, he cannot properly expect applause.
>
> (*Rambler*, no. 173, on 'Pedantry')

The vehicles for these independent commentators on public affairs were the new, usually one-man journals such as Steele's *Tatler* (1709–11), Addison and Steele's *Spectator* (1711–12), Johnson's *Rambler* (1750–2) and *Idler* (1758) and Goldsmith's *Bee* (1759). Many of the essays had a tone and function similar to the weighty newspaper editorials of later times. This style of journalism has not died out entirely: indeed, the

Spectator (revived in 1828) still flourishes, as do many literary periodicals, but they now form only a corner of the market.

The main genre of journalism was of a decidedly lower order:

> In the early years of the eighteenth century, journalistic partisanship was vehement and vituperative; newspaper content was also bawdy and licentious. . . . In 1712, Parliament retaliated by enacting a stamp duty on publications . . . the stringency of which measure may be inferred by Swift's complaint 'that all Grub Street is ruined by the Stamp Act'.
>
> (Koss, 1981, p. 31)

The stamp duty was raised successively from the original penny a sheet, through the nervous years of the French Revolution, to $3\frac{1}{2}d.$ in 1797, since newspapers were 'regarded as vehicles of turbulence' (Koss, 1981, p. 33). The duty was finally repealed in 1855.

The most significant trend undergone by the genre from the mid-eighteenth century to the present has been the rise of popular journalism. To a great extent this development seems to validate T. S. Eliot's mordant observation on modern culture exhibiting 'the indomitable spirit of mediocrity'. For *The Times* (started in 1785) reigned supreme without a real competitor through the first half of the nineteenth century, after which it was surpassed in circulation, but not in status, by the first popular daily, *The Daily Telegraph*, started on the day when the repeal of the stamp duty came into effect. The *Telegraph* succeeded, as have most popular dailies, by using a news-style and contents which approximated to that of the most successful Sunday papers, *Lloyd's Weekly News* and the *News of the World.* This was a formula of 'crime (especially when violent), sex (suitably shrouded) and sport' (Francis Williams, 1957, p. 103).

Northcliffe's *Daily Mail* (started 1896) exploited the typographical expansion of dramatic headlines across columns (first used by Pulitzer in the United States) and large poster advertisements. Together with sensationalized copy, these technical innovations combined in a formula for certain success: the first number sold 400,000 copies. Realizing that there was a new mass audience to be tapped, one which – in his view – 'has no interest in society, but will read anything which is simple and sufficiently interesting' (Raymond Williams, 1975, p. 196), Northcliffe set about changing the whole face of British journalism. In fact, only the original *Daily Mirror*, the first tabloid (started 1903), could – temporarily – be termed a failure. When it seemed to be foundering after being launched as 'the First Daily Newspaper for Gentlewomen', Northcliffe's solution was simple: cut the price and replace words with images.

Reduced to a halfpenny and 'turned into the first picture-newspaper', the *Mirror* became in 1911–12 the first newspaper to reach a circulation of a million (Williams, 1975, p. 228). Not without cause did A. G. Gardiner condemn Northcliffe in terms of 'his eager interest in the moment, his passion for sensation, his indifference to ideas, and his dislike for abstract thought' (Koss, 1981, p. 7).

The term *tabloid* has an interesting entrepreneurial twist in its history. It was originally registered as a trade mark by Burroughs, Wellcome in 1884. When, some 15 years later, Northcliffe used the term of half-size, compact newspapers, the owners of the trade mark got an injunction preventing the term from being applied in this way. However, a Mr Justice Byrne pronounced in 1903 that through the popularity of the primary pharmaceutical meaning, the word had 'acquired a secondary sense in which it may legitimately be used'. The phrase *tabloid journalism* (which is recorded as far back as 1901[O]) was originally a complimentary expression for concentrated and compressed journalism, similar in quality to the original drugs. It has since become derogatory, implying that the journalism is superficial, sensationalist, limited, bigoted and cheap in all senses.

Newspapers survive or fail as advertising media. This point is well made by Raymond Williams in his analysis of the steady demise of seemingly well-established newspapers:

> The last available figures for the five national newspapers which have been closed show sales of over two million (*Empire News*), one and a half million (*Dispatch*), and over one million each (*News Chronicle*, *Graphic*, *Sunday Chronicle*). Such figures show that it cannot be said that these papers had to close because people would not buy them. . . . Papers with much lower circulations, such as *The Times* and the *Guardian* (about a quarter of a million each), survive because the nature of their readership (people with higher incomes and more social influence) enables them to get advertising revenue at higher rates.
>
> (Raymond Williams, 1970, p. 28)

It emerges that the fate of a newspaper depends on its efficiency as an advertising vehicle to penetrate the 'social grades' posited by advertisers in their classification of the population. These grades range from 'AB', the managerial, professional class, to 'DE', the semi- and unskilled manual worker (Carter, 1971, p. 89). Paul Hoch quotes an ironic observation and comments on the consequences, both ideological and practical, of having to appeal to certain 'social grades':

> in order to maintain its attractiveness to élite advertising, the American *Saturday Evening Post* had to *fire* four million of its readers!'

> Similarly, the necessity of not alienating too many of their AB readers imposes a neat upper limit on the 'radical' tendencies of the *Manchester Guardian*, the *Washington Post*, or even the *New Republic.*
>
> (Hoch, 1974, p. 197)

The categorization of the press, which the advertising target market now underwrites, evolved in the last century. Lord Ellenborough, explaining the Government's aims in the Newspapers Stamp Act of 1819, used a familiar distinction, that of the 'respectable Press' as opposed to the 'pauper Press'. The polarization is no longer as simple, though much currency is given to such labelling clichés as 'the gutter press', 'the alternative press', 'the yellow press', 'the popular press', 'the responsible press' and so on. The social status of the papers is now rather less stressed, while political affiliation is more emphasized. *The Times* is considered, in hierarchical terms, to be a 'better' newspaper than the *Sun*. So it is, in terms of range of information and responsibility of comment, but it is important to see, in terms of the point made by Williams and Hoch, that each paper maintains its role and news-style for strong economic reasons. If either paper started to read and look like the other, it would start to lose readers and thus advertising revenue.

A comparison of the composition of the market over the past half-century is revealing. Between 1937 and 1957 the tabloid dailies gained substantially (from 20 to 35 per cent of the market), but this gain was achieved wholly at the expense of the popular papers; the quality dailies rose marginally from 8 to 9.5 per cent (Raymond Williams, 1975, p. 234). This trend has continued. The breakdown 30 years later shows that the tabloids are now dominant, with over 60 per cent of the market, though the quality papers have edged up to around 11 per cent. Indeed, the launching of the up-market *Independent* in 1986 shows that – at least in the analyses of market researchers – there is a place for another quality paper.

The 'popular' and tabloid press therefore hold 90 per cent of the market. But newspaper sales are generally in decline. In 1957 Francis Williams calculated that 'nearly ninety per cent of the adult population of this island reads regularly at least one national morning paper every day' (p. 1). However, even by the end of 1964, television was in 'about ninety per cent of the homes of Britain' (Belson, 1967, p. 1), and by 1983, largely as a result of the competition of television, the total number of dailies was reduced to just over 100, down from 150 in 1968.

The consequences of the division of the newspaper market are illuminating in both style and content. The more serious category has become associated with the authoritative and 'opinion-forming' pronouncements of editors, referred to as *leading articles* from *c.* 1807[O]. The abbreviation to *leader* is found, most appropriately, in the writings of Disraeli: 'Give me a man who can write a leader', he wrote in his novel *Coningsby* (1844), where is also to be found the aphorism 'Opinion is now supreme, and opinion speaks in print.' It was in this epoch that *The Times*, unchallenged in authority, earned the nickname of 'the Thunderer'.

The popular and tabloid sectors of the market, contrariwise, have generated numerous by-products, most of them non-verbal, to entertain and divert the attention of their readers. These include *gossip columns*, first recorded in George Eliot's ironic reference (in 1859[S]) to 'literary gossip columns'; *comics*, first referred to *c.* 1889[O] in a hostile quotation, 'the comics, to which you object' and later by H. G. Wells as 'the cheap boys' "comics" of today' in 1910[S]; *crossword-puzzles*, largely an American invention, dating only from *c.* 1914[S], and *pin-ups*, of similar origin and first recorded in 1941, when *Life* noted that 'Dorothy Lamour is No. 1 pin-up girl of the U.S. Army.'[S] *Kiss and tell*, the euphemistic formula for 'exclusive' sexual scandal, derives, with amusing irony, from William Congreve's Restoration comedy *Love for Love* (1695), though the modern mercenary motive was not then a feature of this form of amorous betrayal.

The *cartoon*, which is common to all categories, has undergone an interesting semantic development. Its first recorded sense (in the pages of John Evelyn in 1671) concerns the world of serious art, namely 'a drawing as a design for a painting, mosaic, sculpture etc.'[O] The *OED*'s earliest instance of the modern comic sense is only in 1863, which the *Supplement* pre-dates with a reference to 'several exquisite designs, to be called Punch's Cartoons' in 1843. However, the signal examples of Hogarth's much earlier satirical work (*c.* 1726–64), followed by Rowlandson (*c.* 1784–1820) and George Cruikshank (*c.* 1811–48) must obviously have influenced the emergence of the present meaning. (The animated cartoon, parent of the strip cartoon, dates from *c.* 1916[S].)

DIFFERENCES IN NEWS-STYLE

The Press in Britain

Certain broad generalizations can be made about the news-style of the 'quality' press, as opposed to the 'popular' press. The 'popular' press relies on a sensational treatment of a small segment of the news, one which may be banal or momentous. This it achieves by emphasis on a few 'stories' arranged hierarchically on the front page, with top priority given to 'human interest' or rarity items. These are dramatized by large headlines, powerful emotive language and the impact of sizeable, close-up photographs invariably 'cropped' out of their original shape. Contrariwise, the 'quality' paper attempts to give a more balanced and sober 'spread' of news with emphasis on world events presented in neutral language, with smaller, rectangular photographs being used to create interest, but not drama.

The difference in language used by newspapers is obviously one of the main ways they can be categorized. Raymond Williams made a revealing comparison of the headlines used over a week in 1961, and Colin Seymour-Ure has similarly compared the treatment of a speech made by Enoch Powell on immigration to a small audience of Birmingham Conservatives on 20 April 1968. These appear as figures 5.1 and 5.2, respectively. Figure 5.3 contrasts layout and news-style in various Sunday papers appearing on 1 March 1987. A comparison reveals (most clearly in the dailies) a hierarchical separation of registers, the quality papers preferring conservative, neutral diction, as against the popular and tabloid news-style, which seeks more idiomatic, emotive and powerful registers, often exploiting metaphors of violence and sex.

Figure 5.1 is especially revealing of the different emphases put on 'the news' by the different kinds of papers: only on the Wednesday were all the papers focusing on the same event, the arrival of the Soviet cosmonaut, Major Gagarin. On the other days *The Times* and the *Guardian* generally gave prominence to the same event, while the *Mirror* and the *Sketch* usually sensationalized some triviality, as in '1-TON WHALE AMOK AT KEW'.

The difference in register employed by different papers is shown most clearly in the headlines for Monday, Wednesday and Friday. The treatment of the BOAC strike is particularly revealing: 'STRIKE HALTS BOAC' runs the *Mail*, while the *Express* is slightly more dramatic with 'STRIKE STOPS PLANES', but both are sober alongside the *Sketch*'s sensationalism 'BOAC STRUCK DEAD', even allowing for the pun.

Figure 5.2, focusing on the coverage of a single event, makes linguistic comparison easier, and also reveals political affiliations more clearly. The difference in register on Sunday, Monday and Tuesday is plain to see. By the Wednesday different constructions are being put on the situation within the Conservative Party, with the pro-Tory *Daily Mail* implying calm after the storm: 'Hogg Takes It Off The Boil', while the pro-Labour *Sketch* suggests continued dissension: 'Hogg Lashes Out At "Disloyal" Powell'. By the following Saturday the difference between the 'responsible' and the 'sensationalist' press is clear in both stance and language. The *Sketch* is inflammatory: 'Now Ennals Stirs It Up – "Dockers Are Like Nazis"', while *The Times* is placatory: 'Ministers Act to Cool Race Feeling', supported by a leader: 'Appeal for Tolerance'.

The sober language of *The Times* is part of its institutional character, for it 'has traditionally claimed a role above party.... The Editor, William Rees-Mogg, described this stance in 1969 as "*The Times* idea... that's to say the idea of an impartial, independent, comprehensive newspaper ..."' (Seymour-Ure, 1974, p. 164). The Library of Congress Survey, *The European Press Today* (Washington, D.C., 1949) concluded that *The Times* had more of an establishment character: '[It] usually reflects government views, particularly on foreign affairs, and thus assumes a semi-official character which it maintains despite change of government.'[1] *The Times* has, however, been subjected at regular intervals to proprietary pressure to become more popular and thus more profitable. Northcliffe, who took an indecently strong hand in editorial matters, instituted the daily page of pictures in 1922. Partly to avert the imminent Thompson take-over, the paper later changed its format most radically (on 3 May 1966), placing the news on the front page, where previously there had been only classified advertisements. Other changes, designed to make the paper more popular and effective as an advertising medium, included the introduction of a gossip column, cartoons, a woman's page and the placing of advertisements on the main news pages. On more than one occasion there has been resistance near to a palace mutiny to these popularizing tendencies. By and large, '*The Times* idea' has prevailed, but, equally, other newspapers have seen it as their right to adopt a more partisan role in the reporting of events.

Headline Language

Headline language as used in the popular press now tends to be similar the world over. Great currency is given to words which are short, emotive, low register to the point of being vulgar, and commonly incorporating metaphors of violence. The currency given them by newspapers means that, in terms of semantic development, such words have become generalized in meaning and flexible in grammatical function. (For instance, *axe* was rarely used as a verb before it became 'journalese', the first recorded use being a quotation from the *Glasgow Herald* in 1922[S]). The same can be said of *slash*, *blast*, *slate* and many others.

'Headlinese' (first recorded in an American reference in 1927[S]) tends to be most developed, predictably in those areas familiar in politics such as confrontation, alliance, agreement and disagreement. These developments are described, variously, as being *clashes*, *rows*, *battles* and *fights*

FIGURE 5.1 Headlines during a week in 1961

MONDAY

Times	RUSSIA DISPLAYS HER AIR POWER
Guardian	RUSSIA SHOWS OFF HER AIR POWER
Telegraph	RUSSIA DISPLAYS HER MISSILES
Mail	MR K'S SKY-OPENER
Express	KRUSCHEV SHOWS OFF
Herald	THE MIGHTIEST OF ALL AIR SHOWS – BY MR K
Worker	PRICE-RISE, PAY-PEG PLAN
Mirror	CRUTCHES FOR THE DUKE
Sketch	ROPED CHILD FOUND IN LAKE

TUESDAY

Times	MR KENNEDY ORDERS DEFENCE REVIEW
Guardian	MR KENNEDY ORDERS DEFENCE REVIEW
Telegraph	MENZIES CLASH ON COMMON MARKET
Mail	SIX SAY: LET'S TALK
Express	SANDYS C AND B MENZIES O
Herald	THE SIX CALL BRITAIN TO TALKS ON AUGUST 1
Worker	WELCOME SPACEMAN!
Mirror	STUFFED SHIRTS IN THE SPACE AGE
Sketch	RAF BOFFIN WILL QUIZ GAGA

WEDNESDAY

Times	CHEERING CROWDS HAIL MAJOR GAGARIN
Guardian	HERO'S WELCOME FOR MAJOR GAGARIN
Telegraph	GAGARIN LUNCH WITH QUEEN
Mail	SHAKE! 2,000 TIMES
Express	FANTASTICHESKY
Herald	LONDON GIVES LITTLE YURI THE BIG HAND
Worker	A REAL HERO'S WELCOME
Mirror	RADY VAS VIDJETJI
Sketch	GA-GA OVER GAGA

THURSDAY

Times	US MISSILE DETECTOR LAUNCHED
Guardian	MISSILE TRACKER IN ORBIT
Telegraph	COMMANDOS WILL QUIT KUWAIT
Mail	PREMIER TO WARN
Express	RED EXPERTS PERISH
Herald	US PUTS 'SPY IN THE SKY' OVER RUSSIA
Worker	PANZERS HERE IN AUTUMN
Mirror	THE GIRL WHO GAVE YURI A KISS
Sketch	1-TON WHALE AMOK AT KEW

FRIDAY

Times	EMERGENCY ACTION TO RESTORE ECONOMY
Guardian	SHIPYARDS INQUIRY BY GOVERNMENT
Telegraph	PREMIER ANXIOUS BUT 'NO FEARS'
Mail	MAC PLAYS IT CALM
Express	WORRIED – NOT AFRAID
Herald	I'M WORRIED BUT NOT AFRAID, SAYS PREMIER
Worker	BAN-BOMB: SMASHING VICTORY
Mirror	BURIED ALIVE!
Sketch	THIS IS MY AXE

SATURDAY

Times	GEN. KASSEM RENEWS CLAIM TO KUWAIT
Guardian	FBI MISGIVINGS ON COMMON MARKET
Telegraph	TUC TO MEET ON ETU CRISIS
Mail	STRIKE HALTS BOAC
Express	STRIKE STOPS PLANES
Herald	THE CRISIS: TORIES NOW TURN TO PLANNING
Worker	MAC PLANS A WAGE CUT IN DISGUISE
Mirror	TUC PROBE SHOCK FOR RED UNION
Sketch	BOAC STRUCK DEAD

Source: Raymond Williams, *Communications* (1970), pp. 71-2

Figure 5.2 Daily paper coverage of Enoch Powell's Birmingham speech and aftermath

	Daily Mirror (Lab.)	*Daily Express* (Con.)	*Daily Mail* (Con.)	*Sun* (Lab.)
Mon. 22nd	'Sack for Powell In Tory Race Row' (Hostile leader)	'Heath Sacks Powell Over Race Speech' (Pro-Powell leader)	'Powell Sacked For Race Speech' (Hostile leader)	'Heath Sacks Powell' (Hostile leader)
Tues. 23rd	'Heath Slaps Down Powell Innuendo'	'Tory "Cabinet" Backs Heath'	'Powell Swipe – Then Heath Wins Vote'	'Powell Accuses Heath of Cowardice'
Wed. 24th	'Thousands Back Powell With Strikes' (Hostile leader)	'Race Bill Stirs Up Tory Storm' (Pro-Powell leader)	'Hogg Takes It Off The Boil' (Leader on Race Bill)	'24 Tory MPs In Vote Revolt' (Hostile leader)
Thurs. 25th	'"Back Enoch" Immigration Man is Suspended' (Pro-Powell leader)	'Airport "Back Powell" Man Suspended' (Pro-Powell leader)	'Callaghan Orders Airport Race Inquiry'	'Callaghan Acts In Airport Race Row' (Hostile 2nd leader)
Fri. 26th		'Back-Enoch March May Shut The Docks'		'Powell Pulls Out of Varsity Speech'
Sat. 27th	'Racial Agitators Lead "Back Enoch" Strikes, Says Heath (page 2)			
Mon. 29th				'Arrest Powell, Say 1500 Quiet Marchers' (Hostile leader, page 5)
Tues. 30th	'We'll Pay Immigrants Fares Home – Callaghan'	'Immigration: New Storm' (Callaghan)		'Callaghan Offers Fare Home to Immigrants'

	Sketch (Con.)	*Guardian* (Lab.)	*Daily Telegraph* (Con.)	*The Times* (Con.)
Mon. 22nd	'Why I Spoke Out – Enoch Powell' (Leader hostile to language)	'Mr Heath Dismisses Mr Powell For "Racialist" Speech' (Hostile leader)	'Heath Sacks Powell For Race Speech' (Pro-Powell leader)	'Powell Out of Shadow Cabinet. Heath Attacks "Racialist" Speech' (Leader: 'An Evil Speech')
Tues. 23rd	'Powell Accuses "Too Cool" Heath' (Leader on Race Bill)	'Mr Powell Accuses Mr Heath of Bowing to "Clamour": Tory Leaders Still Torn Over Policy on Race Bill' (Leader on Race Relations)	'Powell Rebukes Heath On Race' (Leader hostile to language)	'Mr Heath Gets Full Backing From His Shadow Cabinet'
Wed. 24th	'Hogg Lashes Out At "Disloyal" Powell' (Leader on race)	'22 Tory M.P.s Abstain In Race Bill Vote' (Leader on Race Bill)	'24 Tories Abstain on Race Bill: 3-fold Demand for Effective Policy: Powell Votes With Party Line' (Leader on Race Bill)	'24 Tories Abstain Over Race Bill: A Majority of 104 for the Government' (Leader on Race Bill)
Thurs. 25th	'Immigrants: The Voice of Britain' (Poll) (Leader on immigration)	'Mr Callaghan Suspends Immigration Officer'	'Airport "Revolt" on Immigrants: 39 Officers Write to Powell: Discipline Inquiry by Callaghan' (Leader: 'Race and Conscience')	'Widespread Split Over Powell's Race Speech' (Leader on Race Bill Vote)
Fri. 26th			'Brown Accuses Powell: "Opting In" to Race for Leadership: Commons Storm on Airport Inquiry'	'Midland Tories Cheer Heath Over Powell Dismissal'
Sat. 27th	'Now Ennals Stirs It Up – "Dockers Are Like Nazis"'	'Mr Heath Lays Blame On Racialist Agitators'	'Powell Dockers Jeer Mikardo: Heath Attacks "Nasty Vicious Reaction"'	'Ministers Act to Cool Race Feeling' (Leader: 'Appeal for Tolerance')
Mon. 29th	'Anti-Powell Protest Is a Wash-Out' (page 2)			
Tues. 30th			'Fare Home Aid for Immigrants'	

Note: Page 1 headline except where indicated
Source: Colin Seymour-Ure, *The Political Impact of the Mass Media* (1974), 106-9

FIGURE 5.3 Varieties in news-style and register in British Sunday newspapers for 1 March 1987

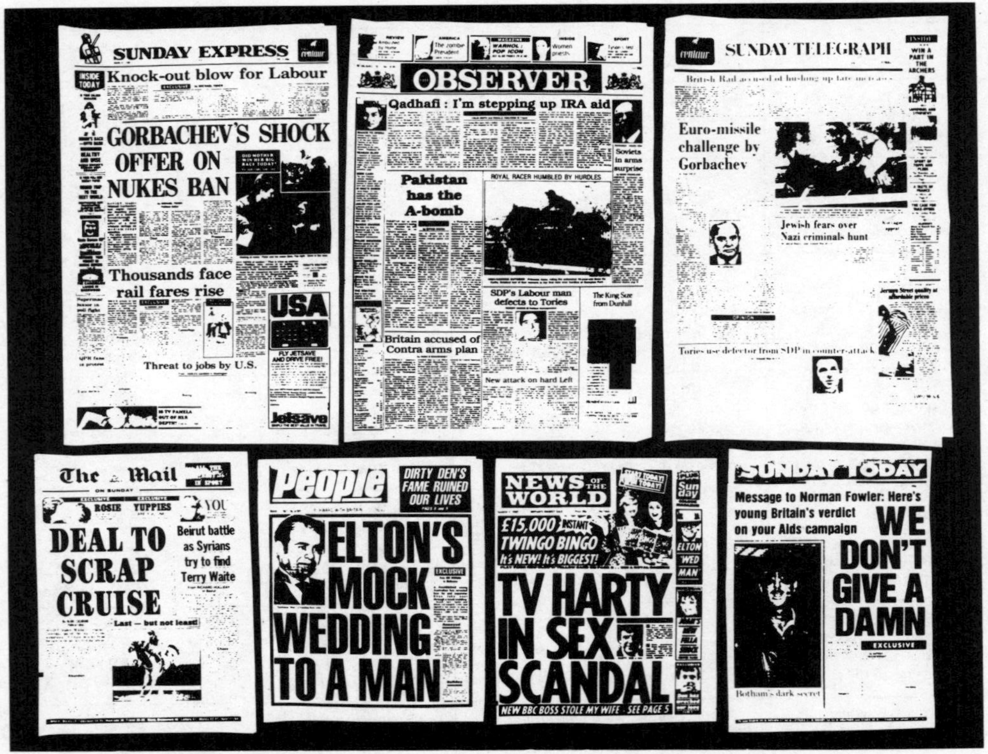

on the one hand, and *pacts*, *pledges* and *deals* on the other. In place of *criticize* the most favoured terms are *blast*, *slam*, *slate*, *hit* and *attack.* Surprise developments (which are invariably unpleasant, giving rise to the adage that 'no news is good news') are referred to as *blows*, *shocks* and *bombshells.* In place of the neutral words *increase* and *decrease* are *soar*, *rocket* and *boom* on the one hand, and *slash*, *cut* and *axe* on the other. Similarly, gold *tumbles*, sales *slump* and firms *go bust*, an investigation becomes a *blitz*, a *probe* or a *swoop*, and *power* is physically characterized as *punch*, *clout*, *muscle*, *bite* and even *teeth.*

Idiomatic exclamations and expressions which would not have been granted the dignity of print before the Second World War are now common in the popular press of the United Kingdom. The *Daily Mirror* reprimanded Mr Krushchev's boorish behaviour in the United Nations with the exhortation 'DON'T BE SO BLOODY RUDE!' and in the midst of one of Britain's financial crises in 1974 the same paper asked despairingly on its front page the question 'IS EVERYBODY GOING BLOODY MAD?' The assassination of Lord Mountbatten was denounced with the headline 'MURDERING BASTARDS!' The London *Evening Standard* (2 October 1978) reported a confrontation at the Labour Party conference at Blackpool in the words 'JIM [CALLAGHAN] TOLD: GET STUFFED'. Obviously, such expressions would not find a place in *The Times* or the *Guardian.* Although the distinction drawn between the register employed in 'quality' and 'popular' journalism is still valid in the main, there are exceptions, as the following sample shows:

page 7 : FIRST DEGREE AS PASSPORT TO THE DOLE QUEUE.
page 9 : PUSSY CAT, PUSSY CAT, WHAT HAVE YOU SEEN?
page 10: PROBLEM OF SELLING PHYSICS AS A WAY OF LIFE.
page 12: OIL BOOM ALASKA TOPS CHARTS IN EDUCATION SPENDING.
page 28: HOW THE PM'S RUSKIN SONG HAS UPPED THE STAKES.

These headlines all featured in the *Times Higher Educational Supplement* (5 November 1976). Only the content of some of the headlines indicates the publication, for the style is frankly popular. Descents to uncharacteristic register are all too apparent in such headlines from *The Times* as 'The Bloke George Eliot Lived With', a Saturday Review article on G. H. Lewes (30 March 1968), and 'Cool, Real Cool, this Young Man in a Hell of a Hurry to Win Gold', from an article on an athlete (16 July 1971). More recent lapses in taste include an article by George Hutchinson under the headline 'The hotheads were raring to go on the issue of "Who rules?" or the Red conspiracy' (by-lined in the *Star* of 11 March 1974), and one by Bernard Levin entitled 'Mr Thorpe Blew It' (by-lined in the *Star* of 12 March 1974). Coarse or contemptuous language, the register of common insult, is increasingly encountered in 'quality' papers: President Reagan is written off in *The Observer* (1 March 1987) as 'The Zombie President', while the newspaper magnate Rupert Murdoch was summarily dismissed by Auberon Waugh in the *Spectator* (3 January 1987) as 'a hairy-heeled, tit-and-bum merchant from Oz'.

A study of the Sunday newspapers for 1 March 1987 (figure 5.3) suggests that there has been a general 'levelling-down' in comparison with the earlier samples by Raymond Williams for 1961 and by Colin Seymour-Ure for 1968:

Sunday Telegraph: British Rail accused of hushing up fare increases
Observer: Qadhafi: I'm stepping up IRA Aid
Sunday Express: GORBACHEV'S SHOCK OFFER ON NUKES BAN
Mail on Sunday: DEAL TO SCRAP CRUISE
Sunday Today: WE DON'T GIVE A DAMN

In keeping with tradition, what especially distinguishes the tabloids is the concentration on one sensational story, with headlines covering up to half of the available area:

People: ELTON'S MOCK WEDDING TO A MAN
News of the World: TV HARTY IN SEX SCANDAL
Sunday Mirror: WHY THE QUEEN **NEVER** WISHES TO SEE THOSE EARRINGS AGAIN

When one turns to the 'alternative' or 'underground' press, there are absolutely no taboos. *Cunt Power Trials* was an exhibitionist headline in *Oz* (no. 33, February 1971), which also referred to pornographic films unsqueamishly as *fuck films*. In similar tone the *International Times* (27 October 1967) asked the provocative question: *Isn't Quintin Hogg an unremitting shit?* – using a contrast of registers which is effective because of its extremity.

The constrictions of the headline contribute to flexibility of usage. Nouns take on an adjectival function simply by being placed in a sequence, as in *New Peace Move*, *Omnibus Firework Tragedy*, *New General*

Election Sensation, *London Street Explosion Panic* and *Wood Murder Charge Court Scene* (all cited in Straumann, 1935). Michael Frayn (1966) has a satirical divertissement on headline language in *The Tin Men*:

> UHL was Unit Headline Language, and it consisted of a comprehensive lexicon of all the multi-purpose monosyllables used by headline writers ... if they could be used in almost any order to make a sentence they could easily be randomised.... Or the units could be added cumulatively:
>
> STRIKE THREAT PLEA
> STRIKE THREAT PLEA PROBE
> STRIKE THREAT PLEA PROBE MOVE
> STRIKE THREAT PLEA PROBE MOVE SHOCK
> STRIKE THREAT PLEA PROBE MOVE SHOCK HOPE
> STRIKE THREAT PLEA PROBE MOVE SHOCK HOPE STORM
>
> Or the units could be used entirely at random:
>
> LEAK ROW LOOMS
> TEST ROW LEAK
> LEAK HOPE DASH BID
>
> With UHL, in other words, a computer could turn out a page whose language was both soothingly familiar and yet calmingly incomprehensible.
>
> (chapter 12, pp. 57–9)

The growth of the 'all noun' headline was originally accentuated by a curious taboo in headline language, namely the avoidance of the -s form of the present tense of the verb. The enforced absence of this, one of the most natural grammatical forms for use in a headline, meant that the commonest form of the simple sentence could not be used, and an unnatural syntax resulted. In his study of newspaper headlines, Heinrich Straumann heralds the arrival of the -s form in an American paper reporting the Battle of Gettysburg. It is an interesting example of content affecting style: 'in 1863, after the battle of Gettysburg, the [New York] *Sun* even applied the verbal -s form 'comes', forty years before the English papers started using it regularly: VICTORY – INVASION COMES TO GRIEF – LEE UTTERLY ROUTED (Straumann, 1935, p. 99). Claud Cockburn amusingly recalls how his proposed headline for *The Times*: QUEEN VISITS CHINA was promptly emended to the more cumbersome, traditional style: QUEEN'S VISIT TO CHINA (1967, p. 71).

Today the taboo no longer holds, but few people would claim that there is much similarity between the syntax of headline language and that of common speech. One can hardly imagine two people in a bus queue using verbatim in a conversation such phrases as 'new Kissinger peace dash' or 'glory day for Tottenham'. Headlinese, in terms of both vocabulary and syntax, has become a sub-language in its own right: though many of the terms in common journalistic use have become generalized, its distinctive syntax is usually too ambiguous and opaque to be adopted generally by the speech-community. It represents, together with 'telegraphese', the furthest limit of communication which can be achieved through the flexible medium of an uninflected language. In many respects, it is a kind of pidgin English, with one basic tense (the present), the most opaque of the verbal forms (the past and present participles) and a few, simple, general-purpose nouns which are frequently converted into adjectives and verbs.

Register in US Journalism

When one turns to journalism in the United States, one is struck by two features. The first is the 'democratization' of the language, for the ideology of the 'melting pot' has its linguistic equivalent and there is a rich seam of slang running through all categories. The second, the result of competition, it would seem, is that the whole verbal texture resembles a conglomerate of registers made up of the recherché, the literary and the common slang terms. This verbal pot-pourri is quite different in all respects from the higher journalism of eighteenth-century England and the hierarchical division between 'quality' and 'popular' journalism of the twentieth. In contrast to the dignified classicism of Addison, Steele and Johnson, described by McLuhan as 'equitone',[2] American journalism is characterized by 'thesaurustone' or 'gamutone', an extension of the semantic field in all directions, regardless of clashes in tone and colour. For instance, *Time* magazine (8 November 1976) contained the following headlines: *Kim's Ill Economy*, *Cabinet Fratricide*, *The Seoul Brother* (puns of this sort are generally unacceptable in serious British journalism), *A Spicy Set of State Races* [Elections], *A Game of Chicken Over Sterling*, *The Spreading Boycott Brouhaha* and *Desexing the Bible.* The edition of 24 May 1976 contained the following examples of 'thesaurustone' and contrived alliteration in its headlines: *Disciple of Despair*, *Feuding Fiefs*, *Brash Gamble on an Economic Miracle*, *Cooking Cancers*, *Flotilla of Fun*, *Dandied Breed*, *The Great Iranian Swap* and *Global Glut.* More recent examples (from *Time* of 16 March 1987) are: *Trying a Comeback: Reagan concedes error in Iranscam*; *G-Man among the Spooks* (on the new head of the CIA); *Everybody's Doing it* (selling arms to Iran); *Pizza Penance* and *From Mozart to Megabytes.*

Compound epithets abound in US journalism. On every page one encounters examples, often with a colloquial flavour and with a touch of descriptive colour: 'paunchy, silver-haired Antonio Perelli', '40 revolving-door governments', 'hard-working, button-down Communists', 'an accomplished, if reluctant flesh-presser' (all from *Time*, 14 June 1976). Yet the same article uses much more literary vocabulary in referring to 'the scion of petty aristocrats', 'a voracious reader', of 'café habitués', and of Henry Kissinger warning 'Cassandra-fashion'. Examples of the ostentatious use of the rare synonym (an aspect of thesaurustone) in the *New York Times* (25 November 1974) include *U.S.* **Lauds** *Move*, *Women's* **apparel** *is up 4 per cent in sales.* The front page of the edition of 7 November 1974 carried the headline *Reduced Diets in* **Affluent** *Lands Proposed at World Food* **Parley**.

Thesaurustone leads to the word-stock becoming a hoard to be ransacked in a competitive fashion, like any other resource. (As we shall see in the following chapter, this process is far more developed in advertising language.) But the informal, common touch is never neglected. Daniel J. Boorstin devoted nearly 40 pages of his great social history, *The Americans* (1973), to 'American Ways of Talking'. Discussing 'the conditions most favourable to the creation of slang', he cites (p. 351) among other factors:

> 'the democratic mingling between sub-groups and the dominant culture'.... Since in America the boundaries of standard speech were even vaguer than elsewhere, the distinction between slang and 'correct' usage was also vaguer. And the distinction became vaguer and vaguer as the American word-stock grew, as American civilization became more confident of itself.[3]

Reading those lines, one is struck by how little things have changed, and how contemporary is the description implied in his chapter-heading, 'An Ungoverned Vocabulary'. Boorstin goes on to say that the 'American language became the apotheosis of slang' (p. 351).

The innovatory influence of US journalism upon the British variety is a feature to be stressed as much as its special breadth of vocabulary. '*Interviewing* is confined to American journalism', wrote the New York *Nation* in 1869[0], in what is apparently the first recorded usage of the word in a journalistic context. (The word *interview* dates, as noun and verb, from the sixteenth century.) Today the borrowing of words of US origin (*caucus*, *mass-meeting*, *squatter*, *commuter*, *executive*, *teenager*, *radio*, *can* (for *tin*), *date* (verb), *mail* and *know-how*) does not excite as much interest and linguistic xenophobia as it did previously. Many of these borrowings have come about largely through the medium of journalism.

American usage has greatly accelerated the flexibility of grammatical function, particularly the 'conversion' of nouns into verbs. For instance, the *OED* remarks of *notice* (used as a verb): 'not much used before the middle of the 18th century, after which it becomes common in American use'. More journalistic in timbre are the following original American instances of uses as verbs (with first recorded *OED* date): *jeopardize* (1828, only grudgingly accepted by Webster), *boost* (1848), *splurge* (1848), *corner* (a market) (1857), *coast* (on a sled) (1859), *itemize* (1864), *enthuse* (1869), *engineer* (1873), *bulldoze* (1876) and *boom* (1879). Other journalistic formations which are still largely confined to the world of printers' ink or the green screen are: *know-how* (1838), *scoop* (1874), *hype* (1926 – originally 'a confidence trick'), *mothballed* (1943) *showbiz* (1945) *lookalike* (1947) and *jet-set* (1951).

The process of conversion is not, of course, confined to US journalism; the use of the following words as verbs has, however, been encouraged by general journalistic practice: *fuel* (though recorded from 1592[O], noted as 'Obs. rare'[O]); *cost* (recorded from 1884[O] in its now common commercial sense); *police* (1851[O]); *impact* (1916[S]); *schedule* (1862[O]); *host* (although Middle English, revived *c.* 1939[S]) and *star* (recorded from *c.* 1824[O], in contexts of repertory theatre, before it became part of the Hollywood language of promotion).

COMMON LINGUISTIC ASPECTS OF JOURNALISM

Cliché and Journalistic Categorization

Most journalism is interpretative rather than descriptive, no matter how much its defenders may boast, in the slogan of the trade, of 'telling it like it is'. Popular journalism invariably trivializes thought, or oversimplifies situations. It does this in order to 'make sense' of the world, and because it assumes (perhaps rightly) that simplification is necessary to reach a mass readership. After all, language itself puts a simplified pattern over the complexity of life; different languages modify experience in distinctive ways, as Whorf and others have argued.[4] 'If Aristotle had spoken Dakotan,' Fritz Maunther observed, 'he would have had to adopt an entirely different logic or at any rate an entirely different theory of categories' (cited in Ullmann, 1964, p. 217). A character in Tom Stoppard's play *Jumpers* succinctly observes: 'Language is a finite instrument crudely applied to an infinity of ideas' (1972, p. 63). Furthermore, the sheer volume of repetition generated by the modern press means that even serious and intelligent journalism becomes transformed into near-cliché. A brilliant insight (for example, the Oedipus complex) becomes crudified into a mass-produced stereotyped idea used to explain any familial tension. An incisive analytical phrase (such as 'the survival of the fittest') becomes, similarly, a facile rationalization for any form of competition.

A revealing recent example has been the 'Territorial Imperative', which has undergone, through a process of constant repetition, a qualitative transformation from hypothesis to supposed 'fact'. Robert Ardrey's interesting book was published under that title in 1966. In a few years it has been transformed by the powerful pulse of the printing press, first into a catch-phrase, then into a received idea, then into a cliché, then into an established behavioural fact, and finally into a species of natural law. It is incorporated into the zoological sense of *territorial* (recorded from 1920) in the *Supplement*, though there continues to be dispute as to whether man is a territorial creature. (One notices that most of these categories, such as 'catch-phrase', 'received idea' and so on, are near-clichés: a *hackneyed cliché* is a hackneyed cliché. The world of mass media is one of self-reflecting mirrors.)

Similar journalistic categorization has produced, within a few years, a whole range of pseudo-sociological 'societies', such as 'The Affluent Society', 'The Permissive Society', 'The Stagnant Society', while at the same time perpetuating the growth of such hardy perennials as 'The American Dream', 'The Beautiful People' and 'The Silent Majority'. Any such list is incomplete without 'The Human Condition', seemingly so profound, and yet actually so vague. The use of the definite article as a foundation for the formula imparts a spurious authenticity to the concept, apparently reifying it, a process which is aided by the capitalization. The practice of Humpty Dumpty is apposite here: he endowed words with capitals when he wanted them to mean more.

Certain fields of journalism, such as finance and sport, are more prone to cliché than others. This is because the pattern of events is in each case fairly limited, repetitive and predictable: teams win, draw or lose; company profits and stock markets rise, fall or stay the same. In both fields metaphors of violence have proliferated in recent times. *Battles*, *fights*, *massacres*, *slaughters*, *carnage* and *blitzes* abound. It seems notable that as soccer has become more violent (amongst both players and spectators) the basic positional terminology has taken on a more aggressive, military register: the older terms *backs*, *forwards* and *inside-forwards* have been 'militarized' into *defenders*, *attackers* and *strikers*. However, the general totemization of sport, and the idolization of the star performers, has brought in a higher register: writers and commentators now tend to use portentous terms such as *philosophy*, *commitment*, *strategy*, *artistry* and *classic* to elevate the proceedings. Typical of this 'boosting' style would be: 'Botham responded eloquently to his critics with a flawless 87.'

Financial reporting employs two kinds of register, one of emotive sensationalism, and one of abstract euphemism. The ideology of capitalism, being that of growth, requires that increase in profits should be publicized emotively and positively, but that serious falls should be described in more euphemistic terms, lest panic should ensue. The emotive register of stock-market reporting centres on 'muscular' metaphors in which some sexual innuendo is apparent. Since the Stock Market is, traditionally, a male domain, it thus *firms* or *hardens*, occasionally *spurts ahead*, and when the gold price *leaps*, the movement *spills over* into mining financials; the professionals or 'shrewd operators' *make a killing*, selling at the top, having bought when the 'small men' were disburdening themselves in a *selling climax* (Pei, 1970, p. 207). The euphemistic register of abstract latinisms like *recession*, and *technical correction* replaces the old traumatic terms like *slump* and *crash*, discussed in chapter 3. Even on the worst days, there is no 'panic selling': 'the bears' are 'having a picnic' or 'the bulls' have 'burnt their fingers'.

Cliché, discussed at the opening of chapter 4, is apparently first recorded *c.* 1832°. Today the term is greatly generalized, so that Eric Partridge includes, for example, in his *Dictionary of Clichés*, idioms, proverbs, stock phrases, foreign phrases and literary quotations. I am chiefly concerned, as should be already apparent, with the 'artificial cliché', the product of printing volume and perhaps only a single writer or journalist, in contradistinction with the proverb, which is a time-honoured residue of traditional wisdom and collective attitudes.

Journalistic categorization is most pronounced in the areas of politics and economics, dealt with in chapters 3 and 7, respectively. Simplistic antithetical categories, the linguistics of confrontation, are invariably employed. Generally speaking, the more colourful the metaphor of antithesis, the more it is favoured by the press: the metaphor prevents the analysis from becoming too exact, while allowing it to remain suggestive. Thus, *doves* and *hawks*, *Young Turks* and *Old Guard*, *hardliners* and *Wets* (from factions within the Conservative Cabinet *c.* 1980) continue to enjoy currency.

To some extent journalistic categorization arises out of the imposition of the rigours of syntax upon the confused flux of events. This can be seen in quite simple formations. Whether or not a sentence has a verb – and increasingly it has not – it must have a subject, a source of action, speech or information. In much political journalism the conflict between syntax (with its requirements of clarity, causation and sequence) and fact (elusive, complex and often incoherent) is very evident. In the stress resulting from this conflict the main protagonists become subtly changed. In the first place, the source of much news is obscured. 'Reports', confirmed, unconfirmed or authoritative, vie with 'observers', 'sources' and 'commentators', who are further labelled as 'informed', 'reliable', 'experienced' and so on, in a hierarchy which the layman cannot usually decode. They fulfil, however, the vital function of supplying the subject, in both senses, of providing the impetus and the direction of the sentence. False personifications and national entities provide a useful alternative: 'Canberra takes the view . . .', 'Washington is suspicious . . .', 'Bonn is optimistic . . .'. These formulations have become quite common in fairly respectable journalism. The popular caricatures, John Bull (the invention of Dr John Arbuthnot in 1712), Uncle Sam (originated during the War of 1812) and the Russian Bear, are cruder only in that they are more picturesque and smack of the cartoon.

Too often a false consensus is implied in such formulations as *the West*, *the superpowers* (is China a superpower?) and *the Third World*. Often the formulas are compounded, which makes them more suggestive but less specific, as in *low-key*, *feedback*, *grass-roots*, *low-profile*, *hard sell*, *soft sell* and *in-depth*. Individuals are categorized according to background, schooling or social group. Hence the tripartite divisions of British society, and the use of formulations like a *working-class background*, or the *upper crust*, as if they were decisive explanations and predictions of character. *The Prestige Press*, a study dealing with the most influential newspapers in the world, contains a formidable array of these quasi-sociological categorizations:

> The editors of the London *Times* for seventy-one of the past seventy-three years have been public school men and for sixty years have been Oxford men. Three of them have been related to the nobility, and five out of six come from prominent English families. In America, on the other hand, the editors have generally been Main Street boys who made good. They all came from towns with a population of under 25,000.
>
> (Pool, I. et al., 1970, p. 67)

'Main Street boys who make good' is echoed in an article in *Time* magazine (24 May 1976), *Why Small-Town Boys Make Good.* Both are formulations made up of two seminal American clichés, with the American Dream hovering in the background; they are variations of the myth immortalized by Abraham Lincoln, that of progress from Log Cabin to White House. The widespread use of cliché and categorization in the popular press thus becomes mass-connivance in naivety.

Two Styles of Crisis: Sensationalism and Euphemism

Crisis was originally a pathological term, denoting 'a sodayne chaunge in a disease' (1543[O]). The figurative sense, first recorded in a parliamentary crisis, dates from *c.* 1627[O]: 'This is the Chrysis of Parliaments; we shall know by this if Parliaments live or die.' Since then crises have become more a matter of opinion, mostly mediated. When the situation is not considered so serious that a news embargo has to be placed on it, the linguistic effects are interesting. The most common result is the use of abstract or euphemistic terminology, chiefly latinized, which serves to cool emotions of fear or anger. Two observations on the definition and response to a crisis are pertinent here:

> When is something a crisis? One answer is: when the media say it is. Lord Boyle has been quoted as saying that the cabinet uses as one guideline for the priorities of its business (apart, obviously, from routine and administrative matters) the agenda set out by the media.
>
> (Seymour-Ure, 1974, p. 39)

> I scarcely began to guess how bad the situation [the Great Crash] really was until Hinrichs, in a low voice, said to me: 'Remembering when we're writing this story the word "panic" is not to be used.'
>
> (Cockburn, 1967, p. 96)

These quotations show how 'the media' can radically affect 'the climate of opinion', if not actually control it. In economic matters, particularly when currency devaluations are concerned and opinion or rumour is transformed into fact very quickly, journalism is very influential. Consequently, an embargo is often put on any such unsettling news, removing from newspapers their usual and proper informational function. A political instance cited by Paul Hoch involved the suppression of a story for *Time* magazine filed under the ideologically devastating title, THE WAR IN VIETNAM IS BEING LOST (1974, p. 102).

The coverage of the 1976 riots in the black townships in South Africa showed an interesting shift from sensational to anaesthetic language. When the riots started the facts of suffering and death were clearly emphasized: SIX DIE IN RIOTS was the banner headline in the *Star* (16 June 1976); FLAMING NIGHT: POLICE STATIONS ARE BESEIGED AS MOBS GO ON THE RAMPAGE (*Rand Daily Mail*, 17 June); VIOLENCE SPREADS: 54 NOW DEAD IN TOWNSHIP RIOTS (*Rand Daily Mail*, 18 June). The following *Sunday Times* tried to defuse the situation with enormous banner headlines NOW THE CALM. However, as the days went by, and the killing continued, so the white press started to shift its perspective and its language. The focus changed from black suffering to white safety; euphemism became extensively employed. Terms like *unrest* and *incident* increasingly took the place of the more specific words previously used. In the Government-controlled news media, the use of euphemistic formulas was highly pronounced: *Isolated incidents of stone-throwing have occurred, but the situation has returned to normal after the use of tear-smoke.* Variations of this formula have become common. In this 'anaesthetic' vocabulary, *casualty* is preferred to dead, *explosive device* to bomb, *stay-away* to strike, *demonstrators* to rioters, *tear-smoke* for tear-gas and *quirt* (a South American word for a rancher's whip) for the traditional *sjambok.* Favoured abstract latinisms include *emergency*, *operation*, *element* and others, discussed in chapter 8, under 'The Semantic Disguise of War'.

One inference to be drawn from the treatments of crisis is that when the status quo or system which the newspaper tacitly or openly supports is seriously threatened, it resorts to a euphemistic news-style to prevent panic spreading. On the other hand, when there is a power-struggle of a peripheral nature, unlikely to change the basic *realpolitik*, the treatment is likely to be sensational, particularly if there is a paucity of 'real' news.

The difference in news coverage dealing with real crises, as opposed to 'pseudo-crises' is paralleled in the difference between the status accorded 'personalities' and that accorded ordinary people. 'Personalities' or 'celebrities' are people familiar to the public simply because of their publicity: they are products of the media who become magnified in the public consciousness as being larger than life. George Bernard Shaw seems to have been one of the first people to use *personality* in this modern, public sense, in 1889[S]. Daniel J. Boorstin, in his study *The Image* (1962), has a very shrewd analysis of the 'celebrity'. Pointing out that this 'new kind of eminence' is steadily overshadowing previous notions of heroism, sainthood and martyrdom, Boorstin defines a celebrity as 'a person who is known for his well-knownness' (pp. 66–7). The growth of the celebrity market is most commonly achieved through an alliance between the media and the entertainment industry. The 'news-value' of celebrities and their 'entertainment-value' is fabricated by advance publicity. Their movements, which aptly qualify for Boorstin's definition of 'pseudo-events', almost invariably oust the real tragedies of ordinary people from the front pages. A pseudo-event, Boorstin observes, 'is not spontaneous, but comes about because someone has planned, planted, or incited it. Typically, it is not a train wreck or an earthquake, but an interview' (1962, p. 22).

Competition between newspapers for the dramatic and sensational can, alternatively, lead to more corrupt and dangerous forms of fabrication, as occurred in the last century when two newspaper barons, Pulitzer and Hearst, competed ferociously for readers, inventing *yellow journalism* in the process. The name derives from the appearance in 1895 of a child in a yellow dress ('The Yellow Kid') as experiment in colour-printing designed to attract purchasers. Stylistically the term refers to journalism of 'a recklessly or unscrupulously sensational character'[O]. A quotation from 1898, 'The Yellow Press is for a war with Spain at all costs',[O] seems to corroborate 'the frequently reiterated statement that if Hearst had not challenged Pulitzer to a circulation contest at the time of the Cuban insurrection, there would have been no Spanish-American War' (Mott, 1967, p. 527).

Since 'Cuban atrocity stories proved to be good circulation pullers', Hearst sent Frederick Remington, a famous illustrator, to Cuba. Remington did not like the assignment, and the following exchange of cablegrams is said to have taken place:

> [To] HEARST, JOURNAL, NEW YORK:
> EVERYTHING IS QUIET. THERE IS NO TROUBLE HERE.
> THERE WILL BE NO WAR. WISH TO RETURN.
> REMINGTON.
>
> [To] REMINGTON, HAVANA:
> PLEASE REMAIN. YOU FURNISH THE PICTURES
> AND I'LL FURNISH THE WAR.
> HEARST.[5]

The excesses of yellow journalism remind us of the liberties which can be taken with the freedom of the press. On this point Walter Lippmann wrote caustically in 1919 of a curious double-standard:

> If I lie in a lawsuit involving the fate of my neighbour's cow, I can go to jail. But if I lie to a million readers in a matter involving war and peace, I can lie my head off, and, if I choose the right series of lies, be entirely irresponsible. Nobody will punish me if I lie about Japan, for example.
> (cited in Hoch, 1974, p. 108)

Attitudes towards the establishment have altered radically in the past half century. The scandalous romance between Prince Edward and Mrs Simpson in the thirties produced an astonishing range of reactions. From 1931 the movements of the couple were fairly open, with Mrs Simpson's name appearing more than once in the Court Circular. However, the British press maintained a resolute silence, largely through a gentleman's agreement between the major proprietors, Beaverbrook and Rothermere (as he was to become), Dawson (Editor of *The Times*) and Stanley Baldwin. The American press, on the other hand, sensationalized every development. As the abdication crisis intensified in 1936, the distributors of *Time* magazine in London even scissored out all potentially libellous stories to do with the affair. Today, with the 'bourgeoisification' of the 'royals' (in journalese), the popular press assumes itself to be on first-name terms with 'Randy Andy' or 'Dazzling Di', the 'Queen Mum' and so on, and to have the right to sensationalize the most intimate and trivial details of their private lives.

Private and National Perspective; Semantic Disintegration

Today, the persistent sensationalization of trivia by the popular press is the most familiar form of prefabricated news. This sensationalism has meant that certain words, particularly those referring to suffering, have undergone weakening. *Tragedy* may now be used of a blunder by a football goal-keeper, the death of a favourite pet, or the loss of thousands of lives in an earthquake. Similar semantic elasticity is forced upon *crisis*, *disaster*, *outrage* and *massacre.* The use of these highly emotive words is likely to increase sales, and is often quite cynical. The origin of such semantic elasticity is, however, complex, reflecting the concentration of different perspectives in the same word. It relates to the fact that, as English has become a world language, so it has been pulled in many national directions at once. It has been made to serve simultaneously many private, sectional, national and international interests in what is called 'the world press'. It is increasingly used to justify conflicting national ideologies against each other.

The history of the American Revolution is particularly pertinent here. This revolution, the first colonial revolt to be carried on in 'the mother tongue', had the effect of semantic fragmentation in that both sides used the same language to justify their cause. The American colonies thus became 'rebels' to the English, while the King of England became a 'tyrant' to the colonies, 'the royal Brute of Britain', as Thomas Paine caustically referred to him. Minor incidents became turned into major outrages. Here, for example, is an account of the Boston Massacre, as reported in the *Boston Gazette* of 12 March 1770: 'The people were immediately alarmed with the Report of this horrid Massacre, the Bells were set a Ringing, and great Numbers soon assembled at the Place where this tragical Scene had been acted.' In fact, five men were killed, though many more were wounded. The description is a potent mixture, however, of journalistic exaggeration and sectional pleading of a kind which has now become very common.

CONCLUSIONS

Journalism as a Sub-Language

In assessing the influence of journalism on the language in general, one's findings are limited by subjective response. Yet the effects have not been uniform. The semantic trends of generalization and weakening are very pronounced, while grammatical flexibility has been encouraged. In this respect the use of nouns as adjectives is more common than the use of nouns as verbs, which involves greater grammatical daring. There are, however, several instances of adjectives and verbs being used as nouns: *great*, *first*, *must*, *hopefuls*, *young-marrieds* and *dash.* It is, nevertheless, fairly common nowadays to hear moderately conservative, educated speakers talking of 'top people', 'a rush job', 'the in thing', 'a fun party' and – if they have been to the United States – 'a hit man', 'a fall guy' and 'the now craze'. Yet probably only the first three examples would be acceptable in written English. And those same hypothetical speakers might use *shelve* as a verb, but not *blueprint*, *power*, *fuel*, *sideline*, *mushroom* and *spark*, which are common in journalism.

Broadly speaking, it would appear from these examples that spoken, and therefore informal, usage is more likely to become a source of acceptable written usage than an artificially selected, though flexible, vocabulary invented by journalists for their own convenience, but not used outside editorial offices. A similar point can be made from a different area of the word-stock, that of archaisms. Journalistic usage such as *slain*, *yule* (the original pagan Germanic winter feast) and flat-*dweller* would not be found in ordinary parlance. Nevertheless, these are at least genuinely ancient terms, unlike *aglitter*, from Dickens, first recorded 1865°; *aglow*, from Coleridge, 1817°; *aplenty*, originally American, *c.* 1830^{S}, *awash*, dating from *c.* 1833° and *agog*, the oldest of these pseudo-archaisms, recorded from *c.* 1542°.

The distinction between natural discourse and artificial journalese becomes clear when one puts newspaper argot into a natural situation:

Wife What sort of day did you have at the office, dear?

Husband A real bombshell. The Accounts Department is having a shock swoop as part of the office-wide probe to foil the splurgers. But Alan has hit out at this clamp and John has pledged his support in the clash with the get-tough gang. It's sure to spark an eyeball-to-eyeball between the Old Guard and the Young Turks. Oh, and Smithers has got a new secretary. She's a friend of Brenda's, that jet-setting, vivacious, good-time girl, Gloria Schmuck.

The contrast in usage is also apparent in the way that compounds made up of slang terms and metaphors, such as *roadhog*, *litterbug*, *dropout*, *rip-off* and *up-tight* have gained a genuine currency, whereas artificial and colourless compounds like *holidaymaker*, *rescue-worker*, *pace-setter* and *flat-dweller* are unlikely to move beyond their birthplace in columns of print.

Changed Notions of the Media

The final point which emerges is that a major redefinition of the notion of 'the media' has come into being. Until fairly recently *medium* was used to mean, literally, the means, instrument or intermediate agency by which meaning was conveyed. Thus Bacon observed nearly four centuries ago that 'cogitations' are conveyed by 'the medium of words'. Consequently, when people spoke of 'the medium of theatre' or of 'advertising media', they were aware of the particular interpretational quality of the means used to convey information.

In the 1960s, largely as a result of the highly publicized and controversial observations of Marshall McLuhan to the effect that societies are shaped more by the style of their media than by the content, 'the media' started to be thought of as an agglomerated informational entity in itself. (And, as Kingsley Amis observed in 1966: 'The treatment of *media* as a singular noun is now spreading to the upper cultural strata.') With the development of radio and television news 'bulletins' (which are compact and suggest completeness by the formula 'That is the end of the News' in ways that newspaper reporting cannot) there has developed increasing awareness of the capacity of the media to generate and suppress news, rather than simply to reflect it. In the case of the visual media, it can fairly be said that they have tended to move away from 'straight' reporting or analysis in the direction of dramatization. (This is apparent, to take a simple example, in the way that chess or bridge are rarely covered live on television since they are too 'slow'.) In political areas, selectivity is very influential, and highlights the inadequate and paradoxical relationship which an image must always have with 'reality' (whatever that may be). A picture may, in the journalistic cliché, 'tell a thousand words' and will, in a limited sense, always be 'true'. But when it relates to a general or widespread situation, it necessarily cannot tell 'the whole truth': it may even be totally misleading in ways which a verbal report could never be. 'The media' are not, then, simply 'mirrors' reflecting the world, but lenses with a particular focus, or prisms, giving the reader or viewer 'the news' refracted and coloured ideologically from pink to blue. The power of images to supplant words is not, of course, confined to journalism, as we shall see in the following chapters.

NOTES

Some of the newspapers cited as evidence in this chapter are more internationally familiar than others. The *Rand Daily Mail* (now defunct), the *Star* and the *Citizen* are all Johannesburg newspapers.

1 *'The Prestige Press'*, Pool et al. (1970), p. 66.
2 McLuhan invented this term to describe the 'new prose technique' of the early eighteenth century, which 'consisted in maintaining a single level of attitude to the reader throughout the entire composition' (*Understanding Media*, p. 219).
3 The quotation is from Harold Wentworth and Stuart Berg Flexner (1960), *A Dictionary of American Slang*, p. x.
4 Whorf (1974) noted that the American Indian Hopi language had totally different concepts of time and tense from European languages, and argued that linguistic structures determined mental categories.
5 It is not certain that Hearst expressed himself with such memorably arrogant wit. According to Winkler, a biographer of Hearst, he denied making the statement.

6

Advertising: Linguistic Capitalism and Wordsmithing

What's in a name? That which we call a rose
By any other name would smell as sweet. . . .
Shakespeare

Erik the Red named the country he had discovered *Greenland*, for he said that people would be much more tempted to go there if it had an attractive name.

The Greenland Saga

Invention is the mother of necessity.

Thorstein Veblen

Commerce, however necessary, however lucrative, as it depraves the manners, corrupts the language.

Samuel Johnson

Images now displace ideals.

Daniel J. Boorstin

ADVERTISING AND CONSUMPTION

LINGUISTICALLY, all modes of advertising now assume that the language is simply a resource, to be appropriated, abused, plundered or modified for any marketing purpose. This attitude to language derives from the profit motive, from anonymity and from the mass scale of advertising campaigns. One cannot imagine a Derbyshire baker marketing his product with the slogan 'Bakewell tarts add life!', since in a small community such a fatuous overstatement would be embarrassingly detrimental to his goodwill. But as a strident formula for a global saturation campaign for Coca Cola, the slogan gains hypnotic acceptance by repetition.

As was mentioned in chapter 4, William Caxton exploited the new medium of the press by producing the first printed advertisement in the language, offering spiritual handbooks for sale. He used the traditional formula of the 'Si quis' ('If anybody'), later institutionalized into the word *siquis*, recorded from *c.* 1597[O]. His Prefaces and Prologues are the obvious prototypes of advertising copy or 'blurbs', and he was, in fact, one of the first people to use the word *advertise* in something approaching its modern sense. Caxton sought to market a luxury product, and employed an approach very similar to that used by agencies today: the product is promoted as a status-symbol, with prospective purchasers encouraged to feel that they are acquiring not just a book, but 'class' and 'culture'. However, were Caxton to return to earth today and discover the enormous and ubiquitous growth-industry which has developed from such meagre beginnings, he would be astonished, and probably appalled. His response would most likely be along the lines wittily described by G. K. Chesterton: 'When I looked at the lights of Broadway by night I said to my American friends: "What a glorious garden of wonders this would be, to one who was lucky enough to be unable to read"' (quoted in Flesch, 1962).

The more technically advanced a society, the greater the saturation of advertising; in much of the West, it is now inescapable. Leaving aside plain announcements and 'for sale' notices, advertising varies enormously, from the most blatant verbal manipulation motivating consumers to purchase some product, to more subtle, virtually subliminal endorsements of certain life-styles and values which make it indistinguishable from propaganda. In recent years it has become quite difficult, indeed, to recognize advertisements of this second type. This is because of the emergence of the insidious practice known as *advertorial*, a recent portmanteau word (made up of *advertising* and *editorial*) as yet unrecorded in the dictionaries. It refers to the practice of a quid pro quo whereby a magazine or journal agrees to publicize particular goods or services in the form of a feature article, in return for a stipulated amount of advertising sold. The consequence is that the (admittedly tenuous) difference between 'advertising' and 'news' becomes obliterated to the point of indistinction.

Much of the argot of advertising is now generally current, since some of the terms were established decades ago. For instance, *blurb*, mentioned previously, is the coinage of the American humourist Gelett Burgess in 1907. The term referred, in Mencken's words, to 'a comic book jacket with a drawing of a pulchritudinous young lady whom he facetiously dubbed Miss Linda Blurb'.[1] In 1914 Burgess defined the word as 'a flamboyant advertisement . . . abounding in agile adjectives'. *Slogan*, in origin a Scots or Irish war-cry, has a long political history from which it is difficult to extricate a specific commercial sense. (The *Supplement* does not make this distinction.) Andrew Lang seems to have been one of the first to use the advertising sense when he wrote in 1887: 'Printers and authors had their emblems and private literary slogans.' *Plug* is found as far back as 1896[S] in the sense 'persuasive speech' or 'line'. The use of music and voice contributed *spot*, from 1926[S] and *jingle* from 1930[S], while *slot*, more associated with the electronic media, dates from around 1964[S]. The colloquial abbreviation *ad* seems first to have been used by Thackeray in 1841, when he threatened: 'I'll have my books properly reviewed: or else, I'll withdraw my ads.'

The volume of money now channelled into advertising is incredible. The growth in America has been especially dramatic. According to Paul Hoch, 'Advertising in the United States, which had been of negligible importance before the Civil War, climbed to $360 million by 1890, when the popular press was being created. By 1920 it was nearly $3 billion. By 1950, over $5 billion. By 1970, over $20 billion' (1974, p. 14). The television market is particularly lucrative. In late 1983, CBS was selling 30-second advertising 'slots' on prime-time for $175,000;[2] in 1985, the average prime-time network commercial cost $180,000, about three times more than in 1975.[3]

With enormous sums of this order involved, the pressure on advertising agencies to succeed in boosting their clients' products is great indeed. Yet advertisers often claim, somewhat defensively, that they cannot create markets, but merely locate them. It would certainly appear that the ethos of 'conspicuous consumption' was well developed long before the rise of high-pressure publicity. Thorstein Veblen coined this brilliant phrase and analysed the condition in his classic *The Theory of the Leisure Class* in 1899. In an industrial society, he noted, with his characteristic irony: 'The only practicable means of impressing one's pecuniary ability on . . . unsympathetic observers of one's everyday life is an unremitting demonstration of the ability to pay' (1970, p. 110).

Of course, it would be quite anachronistic to suppose that Veblen had diagnosed some new form of human behaviour. He himself consistently stressed the historical development through various cultures of 'conspicuous consumption' and 'pecuniary emulation'. Chaucer, for example, in his observations on the culinary largesse of his Franklin and the ostentation of the *nouveau riche* Guildsmen (and their no less socially ambitious wives), understood and illustrated conspicuous consumption very clearly: it is a manifestation of status insecurity shown in times of social mobility by those who are anxious, through lack of traditional credentials of class, to show their standing in society. In a strongly demarcated class-society like that of Britain, conspicuous consumption is seldom successful in its aim, since the spendthrift is stigmatized as *nouveau riche* by the upper class and as a *wastrel*, or *prodigal* by the others. In a comparatively classless society such as that of the United States, however, Veblen's general axiom is a *modus vivendi*. The Lynds, in their social study *Middletown in Transition* (1937), wrote of

> a culture hypnotized by the gorged stream of new things to buy . . . ; a culture in which private business tempts the population in its every waking minute with adroitly phrased invitations to apply the solvent remedy of more and new possessions and socially distinguishing goods and comforts to all the ills that flesh is heir to – to loneliness, insecurity, deferred hope, and frustration.
>
> (p. 46)

However, once the real consumption needs have been met, it becomes necessary, as Veblen, Marcuse and others have shown, to create new needs:

> We may distinguish both true and false needs. 'False' are those which are superimposed upon the individual by particular social interests in his repression: the needs which perpetuate toil, aggressiveness, misery, and injustice. . . . The result then is euphoria in unhappiness. Most of the prevailing needs to relax, to have fun, to behave and consume in accordance with the advertisements, to love and hate what others love and hate, belong to this category of false needs.
>
> (Marcuse, 1968, pp. 21–2)

The more advertising has become an essential service of capitalism in its promotion of consumerism, the more it has acquired the 'morality of success', which means that 'success' and 'morality' have, ironically, become divorced. (David Ogilvy (1966, pp. 113, 141) repeatedly insists – without seemingly being aware of the moral irony – that the successful advertisement should never draw attention to its methods of persuasion.) This does not mean, however, that advertising has simply become more blatantly dishonest with the passing of time. Increasing subtlety of technique has extended to manipulations of the truth; in fact, Daniel Boorstin has argued that advertising has profoundly altered the whole concept of 'truth'.

The advertising industry has grown to such proportions and in such varied directions that it is hard to categorize. Its boundaries are now indivisible from those of public relations, propaganda, journalism and art. Quality also defies general description. It ranges from the most original, acute and articulate achievements in persuasion (very often found in the promotion of luxuries) to the most banal, unchallenging, virtually moronic efforts whereby necessities are promoted in 'saturation campaigns' (a term recorded from *c.* 1957[S]).

The range in quality can in part be attributed to the classification of the populace into 'social grades' (AB to DE) by the market researchers themselves.[4] There are four classes in this grading, the substantial differences between this classification and the traditional, tripartite division of British society being the separation of the middle class into 'upper' and 'lower', and the working class into 'skilled' and 'unskilled'. Advertisements are then devised according to which sector of the market will be their target.

LINGUISTIC CAPITALISM

Advertising is, from a linguistic point of view, a dubious manifestation of free enterprise in which the language, the common property of the speech-community, becomes a natural resource which is exploited by agencies in the sectional interests of their clients' marketing programmes. Words have the added advantage of being free for the taking, unlike images and sounds, which cost money to make. This exploitation takes two obvious forms. The first is the familiar process whereby emotively favourable words (*luxurious*, *craftsmanship*, *fresh*, *pure*, *gentle* and *brilliant* will suffice) are abstracted from their familiar or contextual settings and forced into incongruous alliances: 'Such a *blissful* sink!' will serve as a typically outrageous example. More insidious, and therefore probably more effective, is the way in which similar terms, like *comfort*, *purity*, *emotion*, *pioneer*, *glad*, *agree*, *good luck*, *shield*, *sharp*, *sunlight* and *spring* have been simply appropriated as brand names for products. This amounts to buying their favourable overtones cheap (in fact, free) and using them for the purpose of 'image-building'. This appropriation of established terms for commercial purposes is a fairly recent development, and can be seen as reflecting an advanced stage of 'linguistic capitalism' by advertisers.

A natural consequence of capitalist competition is that terms which ought to be unique become widely appropriated and greatly generalized by being used very loosely. For instance, *Virginia*, a term which is presumably attractive for its associations of pure Elizabethan origins, can now be used of any flue-cured tobacco derived from Virginia-type seed. Only where there is a territorial watchdog to protect the legality of some distinctive name can the *appellation* remain *controllée*. Recent cases brought by vested interests eventually succeeded in restricting *champagne* and *sherry* to wines produced within the limits of Champagne and Jerez. Cheap imitations of luxury products commonly exploit the name of the original in various ways: hence *Babycham* (in fact made from pears and lacking any alcoholic content) or 'suede-type' leather, or the final cynicism, 'made of "genuine" suede'.

Some terms, like *excellence*, *pure*, *fresh* and *brilliant*, have always had favourable meanings or connotations. Others become 'plus words' (as they have been known in America since the 1950s) for special reasons, altering the 'image' or 'angle' of a product. Up to the early 1970s, speed and 'performance' were the most commonly stressed selling points of automobiles; then came a reaction and safety was more emphasized; with the dramatic increase in the price of oil from 1972 to 1984, economy became the major feature. Energy, which had previously been a commodity to be expended, now became a resource to be husbanded and conserved. Semantically, the result was an increasing preference for words which put a good gloss on the notion of economy, such as *save* and the various relations of *economy*. *Thrifty* was brought into play, *lean* no longer suggested 'emaciated', but 'athletic' and 'efficient'; even *mean* and *miser* started to undergo amelioration. The new Ford Cortina (launched in May 1977) was marketed as 'a lean and efficiently engineered athlete ... It's clean and uncluttered ... Moneywise it's mean. ...' The BMC *mini* (launched in August 1959, introducing the *mini-skirt* and a host of related terms) had previously been a 'compact' car; it now became the 'mini-miser'. Other models claimed to be 'big on range', to have a consumption which was 'bird-like' or to be 'the sipper'. Large American cars, previously marketed as symbols of potency,[5] have ever since been stigmatized as 'gas-guzzlers'.

Other ameliorated terms include *action*, *performance*, *tough*, *rugged*, *muscle*, *revolutionary*, *quality*, *design*, *styling*, *philosophy*, *sensational*, *blend*, *flavour*, *luxury*, *prestige*, *charisma* and *security*. The attraction of some of these words is more easily explained than others. *Action* and *performance* would seem to reflect the aimless or undefined notion of 'progress' which now dominates Western society, so that material development is regarded as a good in itself. *Tough*, *rugged* and *muscle*, most of them actually repulsive to earlier generations, now serve to promote durability and strength in a hostile environment. *Revolutionary* is the ultimate aggressive endorser of novelty. David Ogilvy's incisively titled chapter 'How to Write Potent Copy' stresses the point that the copywriter should 'always try to inject *news* into the headlines' (1966, p. 131). Of his listed 25 'words which work wonders', about a third stress novelty, also a recent and dubious 'good'.[6] G. N. Leech confirms the conformity, if not the efficacy, of Ogilvy's advice in his finding that *new* is the most commonly used word in direct address advertising; he comments drily that '*new* is a word which apparently cannot be used too often' (1966, p. 152). Nearly all the other previously listed terms are nouns, and most of them have acquired favourable overtones only in recent times. Some, like *blend* and *flavour* (much favoured in cigarette advertisements) are simply the preferred synonyms for *mixture* and *taste*. Others, like *quality*, *design action*, and *performance*, have moved from their neutral ground (of good or bad quality/design and so on) and are used to suggest exclusive or excellent achievements. This shift can be paralleled by the vocabulary of character used by an earlier age, in which *parts*, *character*, *taste* and *ability* were used as positives only.

One signal category of promotional success is to be found in those products in which proprietary names have become bywords. These include *Thermos*, *Primus*, *Hoover*, *Tampax*, *Formica*, *Anglepoise*, *Kleenex* and – less well known outside the United States – *Frisbee* and *Gunk.* (This last – together with *Brand X* – is an interesting example of the imperviousness of bad publicity, for the general sense of *gunk* is 'rubbish' or 'dirty waste', which may have grown up by association with Gunk, a degreasing detergent.) In general, however, copywriters simply plunder the rich veins of emotive or suggestive language to glamorize their product, nowhere more so than in the home of capitalism. One finds, for example, *Merit*, *Fact*, *Now*, *Vantage*, *Real*, *Life* and *Kool* used as brand names for cigarettes; the British equivalents stick, traditionally, to the name of the founding family: Players, Benson & Hedges, Rothmans, Wills, The House of Dunhill. This pattern of contrast turns out to be fairly general, no doubt reflecting the traditional bias of British culture and the more modern, innovative thrust of US culture. For example, traditional English names are more commonly current in the names of say, cars, biscuits, soap, sweets and many other products. The greater conglomeration of business corporations in the United States is probably a factor.

As befits luxury products, women's cosmetics are marketed under such typical transatlantic names as *Natural Wonder*, *Celebrity*, *Cover Girl*, names which promise success. A recent strategy is to call the product by the name of the wished response, ranging from the simple *Agree*, *Tickled Pink* or *Earth Born*, to the enthusiastically juvenile *Gee, Your Hair Smells Terrific!* The pairing of terms is to some extent replacing the compound: *Dark and Lovely*, *Short and Sassy*, *Soft and Dri*, *Long and Silky*, *Silk and*

Silver (for those who are 'Free, Gray and 51'). Lipsticks are invariably named with romantic, almost hallucinogenic, couplings such as *Pink Clover*, *Golden Vino*, *Mimosa Peach*, *Rosepearl*, *Marmalade Tea* and *Ginger Frost.*

A recent stage of exploitation is to be seen in the appropriation of the idiomatic resources in the language to reinforce a slogan. These idiomatic reinforcements can be used in any sector of the market. British examples include 'Every girl needs her Mum' (deodorant), 'Truth will in' (*The Times*), Digger, 'the down to earth garden tool', 'We have your interest at heart' (a responsible bank) and this coy pun endorsing breakfast sausages: 'Get off to a frying start!' From the United States comes *Hard as Nails* ('America's number one nail protection'), *No Nonsense* ('cotton-lined ventilated crotch panel'), 'Escape to Florida. Let National plot your jetaway', and 'I'm head over heels in DOVE' (soap), mentioned with pride by David Ogilvy in his *Confessions* (1966, p. 132). Increasingly, brand names are chosen precisely so that they can be used idiomatically, for example: 'Strong men come in a Jiffy' (condom).

Copywriters have come to assume that they can take two basic liberties with the language: to appropriate and to change. Increased grammatical flexibility will be discussed under the general heading of Techniques, but varieties of spelling require some discussion. Three main strategies can be distinguished. Firstly, there is the quaint, contrived archaism, such as *shoppe*, *olde*, *ye* and the like, often extended to become the verbal paraphernalia of the pseudo-baronial. More common is the jocular use of 'imitation-accents', to use national stereotypes, for instance, 'exotic' or 'sophisticated' imitation-French: 'Renault 5: fantastique, economique, chic sport-luxury from France; stunningly economique'. A US fashion advertisement runs: 'Go ahead. We derrière you to try the chic French look of our famous N'est ce pas (ness-pah) French fit jeans. . . .'

More disturbing, and more prolific, is the aggressively illiterate trend of the last few years. Product names like *Eet-sum-mor*, *sta-fresh*, *kar-kare*, *flint-kote*, *sno-freez*, *kwik-hot* and *litemaster* are now encountered with arresting frequency. There is a fairly determined excision of the silent consonant coupling *gh* and a phonetic rendering of the quirkish combination *qu* (a product of the Norman scribes, who summarily transliterated Anglo-Saxon *cwen* and *cwic* into *queen* and *quick*). Noah Webster, the American lexicographer, initiated the process of cutting into the undergrowth of silent consonants, so that *hiway* and *thruway* are now institutionalized US forms.[7] There seems, however, to be a limit of tolerance which makes forms like *thruout*, *hier* and *hiest* unacceptable.

Though it is often said that Webster's goal of phonetic spelling has not been attained, this is true only insofar as dictionary recognition is concerned. Commerce has readily continued where Webster left off, with *nu*, *nite*, *lite*, *donut*, *tuf*, *pak*, *ezkleen* (eezeekleen) and *kreem* littering the copy and the packaging. The abbreviated 'grunt form' for 'and' (''*n*') has spread far and wide from its US origins *c.* 1858[S]. (The first use is a facetious phonetic rendition by Oliver Wendell Holmes.) From copious usage in *rock 'n roll* it is now found in many brand-names suggesting ease and speed, such as *Nice 'n Easy*, *Turn 'n Tender* and the like. Most of these are offensive to the educated without being heinously deceitful. However, *kreem* is not an innocent illiteratism, since the spelling implies the existence of cream, but technically evades the guarantee of its being an ingredient. *Lite*, the streamlined illiterate parvenu, is being developed as a form applied to products which are allegedly non-fattening (Lite margarine) or non-filling (Miller's Lite Beer). *Light* is starting to appear stodgy by comparison. *Nite* is also being developed as a truly 'alternative' form of *night*; it is invariably used in contexts of 'nite clubs', 'nite spots' and so on, suggestive of exciting entertainment after dark, as opposed to boring, plain old *night.* The end result of this commercial interference is a regression to orthographical confusion which Johnson described as 'unsettled and fortuitous'.

KEY WORDS

The field of advertising is dominated by two significant notional terms, *luxury* and *prestige.* Both words were originally 'bad' words, both are now 'good' words, and may be regarded in Matoré's designation as *mots-clés*,[8] 'key words' expressive of a particular ethos. *Luxury* had as its earliest, dominant sense (from the fourteenth century) that of lasciviousness or lust, and meant generally sinful self-indulgence, usually sexual in nature, up to the time of Shakespeare and Milton. This sense is found much later in poetic contexts, such as that of Crabbe in 1812: 'Grovelling in the sty of shameless luxury'. The sexual connotation survives in the phrase 'the lap of luxury', an example of impacted archaism. Oliver Goldsmith's famous tirade in *The Deserted Village*, 'O luxury, thou curst by heaven's decree', might have been uttered at any time from the Middle Ages to the late nineteenth century. It would be unthinkable now, when 'the good life' is equated with the hedonistic imperatives of Western capitalist society. Today, luxuries have become converted into necessities; as an advertisement in the *New Yorker* revealing claimed: 'Yesterday you couldn't buy it, tomorrow you won't be able to do without it.'

The word began to lose its original, sinful sense by generalizing in the course of the seventeenth century, in the direction of *luxuriance.* It thus reflected the triumph of an assertive capitalist class which came into prominence as the two previously dominant groups, the Church and the nobility, lost power and influence.[9] Since this 'new class', usually termed 'the gentry', did not have traditional evidence of status (such as pedigree), it asserted itself by expenditure. Its model became the *cavalier* or *gallant.* Both words contain in their earliest senses an emphasis on panache or brio. *Cavalier*, in the sense quintessentially defined by Johnson as 'a gay sprightly military man', emerges before the general sense of 'knight'. *Gallant* (from various French roots meaning 'to make merry') has its dominant emphasis on 'showy in appearance, finely dressed, smart', 'fine-looking [of women]' from Middle English times, long before the present sense of 'chivalrously brave' emerged from around 1596.[O] (There is an interesting parallel in the course taken by the word *bravery*, which from *c.* 1580[O] took on the sense of 'display, show, splendour'. Miranda's famous exclamation in *The Tempest* 'O brave new world!' conveys the sense of 'magnificent'.) One can certainly see conspicuous waste at the heart of various social types which subsequently became fashionable. These include the *rake*, recorded from *c.* 1653[O] onwards, the *fop*, from *c.* 1672[O], the *beau*, from *c.* 1687[O], the *buck*, from *c.* 1725[O] and the *dandy*, from *c.* 1780[O].[10]

Luxury, in its ameliorated sense, has become a dominant word endorsing the ethos of conspicuous consumption. It is no longer even applied (in copy) to expensive items. The Kraft Corporation, seeking to remove the associations of niggardliness surrounding margarine, recently launched a brand called Luxury Blend, employing in the copy this comic excess of idiomatic reinforcement: 'Pure Unadulterated Luxury'.

Prestige carries in its semantic history a revealing witness of the methods of the public relations industry. In origin it is related to *prestidigitator*, the Latin *praestigium* meaning an illusion or delusion, usually performed by a juggler or conjuror. In its earliest English sense, recorded in a dictionary of 1656, it carries the basic sense of illusion, imposture or deception, meanings which are still found as late as 1881[O]. It is splendidly encapsulated in the comment of John Stuart Mill in 1838: 'The prestige with which Napoleon overawed the world is . . . the effect of a stage-trick'. From around 1815[O] the less morally damning sense of 'magic, glamour, blinding or dazzling influence' takes over, contemporaneously with the rise of popular newspapers. A writer of 1856 comments: 'The prestige of the gun with the savage is in his notion of its infallibility.' The 'proper' modern sense of 'reputation derived from previous character, achievements or success' follows fairly predictably, in the late nineteenth century, though the subtlety of the word makes the exact nuance difficult to isolate. In which sense, precisely, was Mark Pattison using the word when he wryly commented (in 1868) that 'Balliol can set off a prestige of long standing against a deficiency in the stipend'?

Today prestige is fabricated, by wordsmiths and image-builders, with much the same legerdemain as was used by the conjurors who brought the word into being. This 'improper' sense is used of luxury products or great corporations or even nations; the promotion, in every sense of the word, of *prestige* has been a great success. By contrast, its new companion, *charisma*, is used only of individuals. In origin it meant 'a favour specially vouchsafed by God; a grace, a talent'[O]. Today it is entirely a secular quality attributed wholesale to entertainers, from the conspicuously to the dubiously gifted. As we shall see in the following chapter, *charisma* is closely associated with 'the cult of personality'. In the present close association of *prestige* and *charisma*, the one originally expressive of divine grace, the other of human deceit, we can see the fundamental cynicism of the promotions industry.

EARLY HISTORY, ESPECIALLY OF PATENT MEDICINES

It is significant that in the period of *laissez-faire* capitalism in the eighteenth century, advertising claims were far more strident, exaggerated and blatantly fraudulent than anything encountered today. This was, perhaps, because the language was the sole mode of persuasion, as is not the case in modern advertising. Nevertheless, it is strange to find, in a work of high journalism (the *Spectator*), in a sceptically enlightened period, claims being made for an 'incomparable pleasant Tincture' which would not only 'certainly cure' loss of memory but also 'corroborate and revive all the noble faculties of the Soul, such as Thought, Judgement, Apprehension, Reason and Memory. . . .' Tobacco, now regarded in the words of the mandatory warning as being 'Dangerous to your Health', had the wildest claims made for it in the mid-eighteenth century. Readers of *The Times* were assured that a pipe of the famous Cephalick and Ophthalmick Tobacco 'is good for the Head, Eyes, Stomach, Lungs, Rheumatism, and GOUT, Thickness of Hearing, Head-Ach, Tooth-Ach or Vapours'. No doubt the promoters were assuming that readers had not encountered *A Counterblaste to Tobacco* by James I in 1604. Here he had denounced 'this filthie noveltie' in terms not without medical soundness, in spite of the extremity of the rhetoric:

'a custome lothsome to the eye, hatefulle to the Nose, harmfull to the braine, dangerous to the Lungs, and in the blacke stinking fume thereof, neerest resembling the horrible Stigian smoke of the pit that is bottomlesse'.

A range of similar, ridiculously boasting advertisements is cited by E. S. Turner, who also mentions the following claims for an exotic aphrodisiac in a London journal of 1772:

> The True Cordial Quintessence of Vipers.
> The most noble and grand Preparation in the whole Materia Medica, for the real substantial Cure of Impotency in Men and Barrenness in Women. . .
> A few Days of it only gives such a general Warmth, and so exceedingly delight the Vital and Animal Spirits, Senses and Nerves, as soon to show what it will do upon a little Continuance of it; for it not only promotes and prompts Desire, but also furnishes proper Matter for the Support and Establishment of a true and lasting Power and Inclination. Price 10s. 6d. a bottle.

Even these excesses were surpassed by the promotion of that nineteenth-century meliorist panacea, the Universal Pill. Morison's Universal Pills, Parr's Life Pills and Holloway's Pills and Ointment were attributed with an omnipotence which today produces mere amusement. As *Punch* ironically remarked in 1843: 'Mr Holloway, with the modesty which is the invariable attendant on real merit, declares that his "Universal Ointment" will mend the legs of men and tables equally well and will be found an excellent article for frying fish in.'

In 1892 the fraudulent recklessness of many cynical advertisers was curbed by the case brought against the Carbolic Smoke Ball Co. The company had been sufficiently rash to claim that '£100 will be paid by the Carbolic Smoke Ball Co. to any person who contracts the increasing Epidemic, INFLUENZA, Colds, or any diseases caused by taking cold after having used the Ball 3 times daily for two weeks according to the printed instructions supplied with each Ball.' A customer used the Ball, contracted influenza, claimed her £100, took the company to court when they refused to pay, and – hardly surprisingly – won the case.[11]

The history of patent medicines and their advertisement in the eighteenth and nineteenth centuries resembles the motif of the Overreacher. Puffery becomes so outrageous and rapacious that it comes into conflict with the law and is curbed. A revealing semantic trail is left in such words as *mountebank* (from *c.* 1577°), defined by Johnson as 'a doctor that mounts a bench in a market, and boasts his infallible remedies and cures'. This confidence trickster is soon followed by the *quacksalver* or 'bogus healer' (from *c.* 1579°), soon to be abbreviated to its familiar form *quack*, *c.* 1638°, damningly defined by Johnson as 'a boastful pretender to arts he does not understand', and then institutionalized as *quackery* *c.* 1709°. *Charlatan*, recorded from *c.* 1618°, describes a similar practice and derives from a notion similar to that of *quack*, since it is rooted in *cialare*, 'to babble'.

Probably as a consequence of the inflated puffery of the advertisements we have been sampling, the eighteenth century sees the growth of several terms for fraudulent medicine-mongers. Grose (in his dictionary of 1785) defines *apothecary*, when used as a verb, as 'to use hard [obscure] words; from the assumed gravity and affectation of knowledge generally put on by the gentlemen of that profession, who are commonly as superficial in their learnings as they are pedantical in their language'. The pejorative associations of *doctor*, when used as a verb, are recorded contemporaneously, from *c.* 1774°. They no doubt reflect on the morality and the methods of the profession at the time.

The more general word *puff*, used as a noun from *c.* 1732° and as a verb from *c.* 1735°, is a splendidly simple and descriptive word for 'inflated laudation', as the *OED* refers to it. *Puff* became a vogue-word, if not a rage-word. Fielding indulged in many ironic sallies on the Art of Puffing. One, a letter to *The Champion* of 19 December 1741, by one Gustavus Puffendorf, makes some disturbing comparisons: 'But what sets the antiquity of *Puffing* beyond all controversy, is the institution of Rhetoric, or the Art of Persuasion, which is but another word for *Puffing*.'[12] *Puffery*, recorded only from *c.* 1782°, was added to a word-field which was further institutionalized by the personification of Sheridan's Mr Puff in 1779. This satirical 'hero' of *The Critic* specialized in glowing reviews of plays he had never seen.

One of the strongest contemporary reactions to advertising came from Dr Johnson, in his periodical the *Idler* of 20 January 1761: 'Whatever is common is despised. Advertisements are now so numerous that they are very negligently perused, and it is therefore become necessary to gain attention by magnificence of promises, and by eloquence sometimes sublime and sometimes pathetic [moving, emotional]. Promise, large Promise is the soul of an Advertisement.'

MODERN DEVELOPMENTS AND TECHNIQUES

Modern 'puffers', 'hidden persuaders' or 'image-builders' are more limited in the general area of claim than were their counterparts two centuries ago. Yet in Britain it was only in 1939 that government legislation banned the advertising of cures for cancer, a move which was extended in 1941 to cures for Bright's disease, cataracts, diabetes, epilepsy, glaucoma, paralysis and tuberculosis. The title 'Doctor' or 'Dr' could not appear on products marketed after 1 January 1944. Similar limitations, promulgated in 1950, insisted that words like *laboratory*, *college* and *clinic* had to be used truthfully, though the last has since been appropriated as the brand name of a shampoo.

The field of medicine has remained almost the sole area of semantic restraint, and even within it Beecham's Pills persisted in the claim that they were 'worth a guinea a box'. Elsewhere dubious claims abound. We are informed that 'Guinness is good for you', that 'Butter is better' and that 'Beer is best'. Even the restrictions on cigarette advertising have been very slow and tentative.

Executives from Madison Avenue (referred to ironically as 'Ad Alley' and 'Ulcer Gulch') speak of 'legitimate puffery' when explaining a competitor's right to claim that his product is 'best'. The definition of 'puffery' became a legally crucial factor when Regimen Tablets (an appetite depressant) were brought to trial in the United States. During the trial 'puffery' was defined by an agency executive witness as 'the dramatic extension of a claim area' (Baker, 1969, p. 23). (The metaphor from the land-grab or the gold-rush is revealing.) The defence attorney claimed 'puffery' to be a 'normal, accepted, routine practice in the advertising industry' (1969, p. 23). As an example he gave the retouching of a photograph of a woman's hips to make them appear slimmer than the original photograph did. The presiding judge took a more straightforward view: 'There is no principle in law that I know of condoning puffery as a justification for deception. *Caveat emptor* [let the buyer beware] is no longer acceptable' (1969, p. 23).

Judgement went against Regimen Tablets. But there are still many advertisements which would, one feels, receive a similar verdict if their proponents were taken to court. The problem is who is going to have the financial backing for such a crusading enterprise, let alone the energy and the concern. In consequence, dubious advertising continues in the grey hinterland between linguistic peccadillo and fraud. Dorothy Sayers, who worked in an advertising agency, defined this limbo with academic stringency in the *Spectator* of 19 November 1937: 'Plain lies are dangerous. The only weapons left to [the copywriter] are *suggestio falsi* and *suppressio veri*, and his use even of these would be very much more circumscribed if one person in ten had ever been taught to read.'

The Weasel

Miss Sayers was describing a creature well known in advertising circles and referred to in the trade as 'the weasel'. The linguistic history of this verbicidal creature originates in America in the verb 'to weasel' and in 'weasel-word', recorded from *c.* 1900[S]. A 'weasel-word' is one which, by its calculated ambiguity, erodes the meaning of the phrase or sentence in which it is used. The verb means 'to equivocate or avoid commitment'.[13] Both terms were the *bêtes noires* of Theodore Roosevelt, who reminded his countrymen in a speech given in 1916 of the weasel's ability to suck out the contents of an egg without doing obvious damage to the shell. Weasels multiply in the unclaimed area between 'true' and 'false'. Often they take the form of 'open comparatives' or 'bogus superlatives':

> 'America's Best'
> 'The better quality cigarette'
> 'Longer than Kingsize and noticeably smoother'
> 'There's nothing just like Sego'
> 'The smoothest, happiest vodka of all'

In areas where there are semantic restraints – such as in patent medicines against the use of the word *cure* – ingeniously ambiguous suggestions of 'symptomatic relief' are offered instead:

> 'Brand X works fifteen ways to help relieve your cold'
> 'Scott [tissue] makes it better for you'

In journalism and politics one of the most effective weasel-words is *alleged.* In advertising some of the hardy annuals are *proven*, *tested*, *guaranteed*, *scientific*, *traditional* and *home-made.*

Daniel J. Boorstin has analysed many of these weasels in terms, not so much of legal evasion, but of what he calls 'the appeal of the neither-true-nor-false':

> The larger proportion of advertising statements subsist in this new limbo. They cannot be parsed in the old grammar of epistemology, because modern experience is newly ambiguous. . . . The advertiser's art, then, consists largely of making persuasive statements which are neither true nor false. He does not violate the old truth-morality. Rather, like the news-maker, he evades it.
>
> (Boorstin, 1963, pp. 217–18)

The Unique Selling Proposition

This describes a campaign built around a particular 'angle' which market research has shown to have a special appeal for the target public. Ironically, the 'USP' – as it is known in the trade – is usually not unique to the product, but has by chance been mentioned in the advertising copy. Two of the noted examples include that of Schlitz beer stressing that its bottles were 'steam sterilized' and Lucky Strike cigarettes fortuitously pre-empting the slogan 'It's toasted'. *All* other beer bottles were also steam sterilized, but publicizing the notion that Schlitz bottles were 'sanitized for your protection' evidently worked wonders. Likewise, 'Lucky Strike *were* toasted. So was every other American cigarette' (Boorstin, 1963, p. 218).

These examples of the hit-and-miss methods of advertisers cannot really be criticized in terms of semantics, since the slogans are telling some truth which has a mysterious appeal for the public. The strategy can, however, lead to the fabrication of the 'miracle ingredient', which is then stressed as the USP. Commonly, the ingredient is given a mystifying, pseudo-scientific name, such as *chlorophyll*, *lanolin*, *hexachlorophene*, *fluoride*, '*ammoniated*', *GL 70*, and so on. This technique is, of course, the modern version of that which the redoubtable Francis Grose referred to earlier under the heading of *apothecary.* In Victorian times droves of pseudo-Latin and Greek terms were invented to impress a public which generally held the classics in high regard: 'Teeth were stopped with "mineral marmoratum" or "mineral succedaneum"; raincoats were "siphonias"; hair cream was an "aromatic regenerator"; hair dye was an "atrapilatory". There were "pulmonic wafers" for the chest; there were Aethereal Oleine, Elme's Arcanum, Winn's Anticardium, Olden's Eukeirogenion, and Rypophagon Soap' (Turner, 1965, p. 57).

The modern names are more subtle in that they use genuine scientific terms (unlike the spoofs quoted above), though the motive of mystification remains the same. Today we cannot be unaware of the variety of fabricated (and less meaningful) names which are now in use: *nylon* (coined, but not trademarked, by Du Pont in 1938),[14] *bri-nylon*, *terylene*, *viyella*, *dacron*, *tricopress*, *vinyl*, *perspex*, *plexiglass*, *polythene*, *polystyrene* and so on. Perhaps *plastic*, recorded from *c.* 1905°, is a prime example of a synthetic substance which, though mass-produced, is not made to any specification of strength or durability, so that consumers do not really know what they are buying. The present ubiquity of plastic was predicted 60 years ago in this quotation from *Discovery*: 'These resins are but one more milestone on the road leading towards the transition from the metal age to the plastic age.'[S]

There is, of course, a case for using a new word for a new thing or substance, and it is probably better to have a totally new word (like *nylon*) rather than a factitious compound (like *fibreglass*). Hence the genuine need for *deodorant* (1869[O]), *aerosol* (1923[S]), *overdrive* (1929[S]), *moisturizer* (1957[S]) and *pantihose* (1967[S]). However, one passes over a shadowy border between definition and mystification when one reaches terms like *ergonomic*, *hydrolastic*, *instamatic*, *posturepedic*, *solid-state* and *leathercloth.* Here we have language which is designed to reflect and reinforce what Boorstin calls 'the complexity of the new manufacturing processes' (1963, p. 217).

Compounding and Flexibility

It will have been noticed that many of the terms immediately under discussion are compounds. Compounding is a fundamental method of word-formation in English, and is a general feature of the Germanic languages. Formations which have evolved over time, like *handbook*, *homesick* and *sea-horse* have a natural, assimilated quality, which is different from the typically artificial creations of copywriters, such as *fresh-tasting*, *hand-crafted*, *oven-fresh*, *king-size*, *see-through*, *all-round*, *space-saving*, *take-away*, *up-to-the-minute* and *do-it-yourself.* These are now the stock-in-trade of the 'wordsmiths' of advertising firms. They are not particularly original or arresting, but presumably seek increased impact which derives from using a 'double-barrelled' term such as *space-saving* in preference to *compact*. But in technical areas compounds proliferate greatly, since they produce an opaque jargon which impresses but mystifies the layman. He is informed that the latest car model has *hydromatic* drive (if it does not have *handy four-on-the-floor gearshift*), *servo-assisted brakes* in a *booster-assisted system*, a *uniweld* chassis, a *close-ratio* gear-box, a *v-type* engine with *fuel-injected* carburation, *wide-tracking* wheels, *radial-ply* tyres, *ergonomic* seats, *glance-of-the-eye* instrumentation and probably *you-dial-it*, *through-flow* ventilation. (A similar pastiche could be made up from the advertisements found in virtually any magazine.)

Often compounding is expanded into mere 'adjective-shunting'. Buyers of the 1968 Pontiac Bonneville were promised 'generous swathes of simulated burl grained Carpathian elm that abound on doors and dash';[15] a holiday in the Seychelles invited 'an exotic mix of lazy, sun-filled days and sizzlingly exciting tropic nights. Of French "laisser-faire" [*sic*] and Creole cuisine. Of surf, sport and sail-away-from-it-all tranquillity in an oo-la-la lifestyle'. The multiple compound forms create an increasing flexibility in the language, or, as G. N. Leech puts it: 'There seems, in fact, to be very little restriction on the kind of embedded structure that can occur in this pre-modifying position. Compounding is exceptionally free in the noun group not only in lexical productiveness, but also in variety of grammatical structure' (1966, p. 139).

In his *Semantics* (1974, p. 139) Leech distinguishes, via embedded categories, between *embedded noun groups* ('the any-time cereal'), *embedded adjective groups* ('an easy-to-paint picture'), *embedded adverbial groups* ('that all-over, under-the-weather feeling') and *embedded infinitive clauses* ('keep it up energy'). Though seemingly original, such formations can be paralleled by the daring compounds of Shakespeare, such as the '*not-to-be-endured* riots' of which Goneril complains, and the 'ne'er lust-wearied Antony', who is scorned by Caesar.[16] Ambiguities slip in to such modern equivalents as 'the *throwaway* society' and 'the *ready-to-eat* breakfast cereal for *ready-to-eat* people'.

In general it can be claimed that advertising, like journalism, has increased the grammatical flexibility of words, particularly in the extension of nouns into adjectives and verbs, i.e., in a more dynamic direction. (There is, of course, the contrary process, whereby adjectives such as *spectacular*, *special* and *musical* have been 'frozen' into nouns.) Thus, Shield is mobilized into 'the *soap* deodorant', 'Dove *creams* your skin while you wash', Mobil manufactures 'the *confidence* oils', various soaps '*baby* your skin' and, whereas 10 years ago De Beers told us that 'Diamonds are *forever*', we have recently been assured that 'Diamonds are for *now*'. In the first two cases, the grammatical flexibility is being used as something of a weasel to suggest, respectively, that Shield is both a soap and a deodorant, and that Dove soap has the properties of a skin cream.

This flexibility of language suggests, but does not define, the variety of functions of which the products are capable. One consequence is that certain general-purpose terms have undergone such broad generalization that they can now mean almost anything. Examples are *process*, *processor*, *condition*, *conditioner*, *action* and *performance.*

The Glamorization of Outlets

A great deal of advertising involves no more than selling a sow's ear as a silk purse. This can, in part, be done by substitution of 'plain' terms for those which are more attractive or promising. Property developers and estate agents, following the example of Erik the Red, have built up their own vocabulary of 'plus words', such as *charming*, *snug*, *olde-worlde*, *compact*, *characterful*, *unique* and so on. The brazen sentiments of the egregious Squeers are apposite here. He explains the flexible title of Dotheboys Hall:

> 'We call it a Hall up in London, because it sounds better, but they don't know it by that name in these parts. A man may call his house an island if he likes; there's no act of Parliament against that, I believe.
>
> (Dickens, *Nicholas Nickleby*, chapter 7)

Businesses wishing to attract custom by appealing to a sense of sociability (perhaps to counter the sense of alienation and disorientation which urbanization has produced) use various semantic strategies. One is the 'personalized style': the baker becomes *Mr Crusty*, the lawnmower repair chain *Mr Grasshopper*, and so on. Another is to exploit the social associations of *bar*, *inn* and *parlour. Inn*, an Anglo-Saxon word, is now applied to an astonishing range of outlets. *Bar*, a worthy institution recorded as far back as around 1592[O], is now extended to *coffee-bar*, *heel-bar*, *car-bar* and even *corset-bar*. *Parlour* has left its formal ecclesiastical sense far behind. Originally denoting the 'part of a monastery or convent used for conversation', a meaning recorded back to the thirteenth century, it first became secularized as the related part of a mansion or house, and then commercialized as *beauty parlour*, *ice-cream parlour* (from *c.* 1891[O] in the United States) and finally *massage-parlour* (from *c.* 1913[S]), similar in origin, but focusing on what Ian Fleming once called 'an area midway between the solar plexus and the upper thigh'. (Even the first cited quotation, from *Colliers* magazine, remarks that the term is 'an all-too-obvious euphemism'.) Under the designation 'commercial cant', the *OED* also records *misfit parlour*, *oyster parlour* and *tonsorial parlour* (hairdressing salon), which aroused Mencken's irony.

Other terms used to make an establishment sound more professional, more exclusive or more stylish are *clinic*, *boutique* and *studio. Salon*, a typical French borrowing of the early eighteenth century, has also been lured away from its aristocratic social setting to the more mundane *beauty salon*, which may be little more than a hairdresser, and a *relaxation salon*, which may be little better than a massage-parlour in disguise. The deterioration of *parlour*, *salon*, *escort agency* and so on reminds one of the decline of the earlier words *stews* and *bagnio*, which degenerated from Turkish baths to brothels. As Johnson trenchantly observed: 'probably *stews*, like *bagnio* took a bad significance from a bad use'.

THE IMAGE

The cases just discussed illuminate, not so much the use of 'weasel-words', as simply the familiar process of verbal glamorization in order to improve the 'image' of the business establishment in question. The creation or alteration of images has become one of the most important, if not the fundamental, process of modern advertising. In terms of the traditional philosophical distinction between *accident* (external phenomena) and *substance* (essence), the *image* is an artifically created illusion designed to surround a product or institution with certain symbolic associations. Consequently, Rolls-Royce, Cadillac, Omega and Chanel No. 5, artefacts which have absolutely nothing intrinsically distinctive about them whatever, have been made into symbols of status and success.

The 'large promise' which Dr Johnson saw as epitomizing the advertisements of his day are still with us. But the creation of product-images is a more sophisticated, and legally less risky, form of promise-making:

'An Omega does more for you than tell the time'
'Balkan Sobranie is more than a name, it is a philosophy of living'
'Autumn Harvest Pinotage. A dry, fruity, red wine that promises you a new adventure'

As an advertising executive quoted in *The Hidden Persuaders* remarks: 'The cosmetic manufacturers are not selling lanolin, they are selling hope. . . . We no longer buy oranges, we buy vitality. We do not buy just an auto, we buy prestige' (Packard, 1960, p. 15).

Images are created by a variety of techniques, of which the visual is becoming predominant. Colour symbolism, camera angle, design of *logograms* (which date from the 1930s) are carefully programmed. Sound, which may be symbolic, musical or 'muzak', harmonizes with the voice-over, which may be neutral, delicate, scientific, 'macho', 'juvenile precocious' or 'superhuman exhortatory'. Language has in many cases been largely superseded. McLuhan's observations on a particular example have a general application: 'the copy is merely a punning gag to distract the critical faculties while the image of the car goes to work on the hypnotised viewer' (1964, p. 246). Cars are imaged, variously, as shields against accident, reliable companions, virile athletes or purveyors of fun. S. I. Hayakawa noted (1962) how powerful American models were marketed as 'potency symbols', while sports cars were often imaged as 'mistress symbols'. In a *Sunday Times Colour Supplement* advertisement of 1968 we read:

> Trail of dark hair and smell of white heather
> drift of gold day into silver sea night
> sizzle of salt in driftwood fire
> sweet bird of youth sans mortgage sans carrycot
> days of your sports car years
> grab them fast don't let them get away from you
> MG Midget
> road-hugging
> fun-filled
> slung low
> sweet chariot
> at MG dealers

The copy winds its way round a couple embracing alongside the magical automobile, which is parked by the sea shore. In the foreground glow the embers of the fires of passion. . . . This slightly absurd romantic male fantasy is an extreme example of a multitude of such erotic advertisements. *Roget's Thesaurus* has been plundered so that clichés, puns, archaisms and neologisms jostle together, mixing registers for maximum effect: 'sweet bird of youth sans mortgage sans carrycot'.

Even more than popular journalism, advertising seeks to use the erotic impulse as a lure to induce sales. Of course, a great deal of implied or overt sexuality is conveyed by suggestively sensual sounds or by imagery. Usually these advertisements rely on body language rather than words, and so do not form part of this discussion. Cosmetics and all the other paraphernalia of feminine beautification promise, not simply beauty, but youth, attractiveness and seduction. Thus a deodorant is called *Je t'aime* and a brand of underwear is marketed as *Tender Seducers*. Matching male deodorants like *Denim* warn purchasers of overpowering feminine response:

> Denim Musk After Shave.
> You've never had it so wild, warm and exciting.
> Denim. For the man who doesn't have to try too hard.

Virtually any product can be given a sexual 'slant'. A confection called *Jon & Marcia* – 'Cadbury's swinging new chocolate idea' – takes its name from a notorious American record consisting solely of the partners breathing each other's names heavily in (presumably) simulated coitus. The copy cheekily follows the format of the classified 'partner-search' column: '... would like to meet other interesting couples with similar tastes ...'. A chocolate bar sucked in a manner suggesting fellatio is underscored by the imperative: 'Think thick ... To cram more excitement into every bite'. In this area of the market, names must be suggestive, but not too explicit. Hence *Caress* and *Romance* are suitable names for perfumes, but *Orgasm* would be too explicit, just as *Lust in the Dust* would be too explicit for an aphrodisiac deodorant.

Often images have to be changed to reach a different sector of the market. Marlboro cigarettes were originally given a feminine image. When this approach failed, a change described by Vance Packard as one of 'spectacular transvestism' was instituted: 'rugged, virile-looking men' (all tattooed) promised 'man-sized flavour' all in a 'bold red and white' package (1960, pp. 84–5). Contrariwise, Virginia Slims have been successfully converted as part of the accoutrements of the successful career woman. Horlicks was originally sold as a mid-morning drink for genteel ladies; when that market dried up, the product was more successfully turned into a night-cap restorative of the nerves and energy of husbands who were beginning to flag in the rat-race.

Daniel J. Boorstin has observed: 'Now the language of images is everywhere. Everywhere it has displaced the language of ideals. If the right "image" will elect a President or sell an automobile, a religion, a cigarette, or a suit of clothes, why not make America herself – or the American Way of Life – a saleable commodity all over the earth?' (1963, p. 188). As will be seen in the following chapter, the use of 'image-building' techniques in election campaigns is now widespread. 'The image,' Boorstin continues in his penetrating analysis, 'is a pseudo-ideal ... it is synthetic, believable, passive, vivid, simplified and ambiguous' (p. 189).

Large corporations spend fortunes not only on stylized hallmarks or logos, but on slogans which will build their image as responsible members of the community. These slogans perform various functions. Some are simple boosters, such as 'The Ultimate Driving Machine' (BMW), 'Engineered Like No Other Car in the World' (Mercedes-Benz), or the ultimate statement of Teutonic dependability, *Vorsprung durch Technik* (Audi). Others employ an arresting variation in the form of some grammatical irregularity, such as 'Where better really matters' (Buick), 'Everything Keeps Going Right Toyota' (technically an anacolouthon, or break in syntax) or 'Great Features Make Datsun Great' (tautology, verging on nonsense). More significant are those used by the industrially oriented corporations, sensitive to their reputation as potential pollution-makers. They respond with slogans like 'Meeting the Challenge' (Gulf Oil), 'Phillips – Working on Pollution' or 'At U.S. Steel we're involved'. Du Pont's recent contribution is 'There's a world of things we're involved in', while the Diamond Corporation chimes in with campaigns stressing that it is 'responsible' and Total Petroleum claims simply 'We Care'.

These slogans are primarily intended to rebuff the common criticism that corporations are simply heartless capitalist profiteers. Secondly, the key terms used – *involved*, *responsible*, *care* – serve to pre-empt the fashionable radical terminology of liberals and radicals who are critical of 'big business'. No doubt, we shall soon be informed that 'At General Motors, We're Committed'.

A similar development in recent years has been the overt use of advertising media not simply as a vehicle for generalized 'public relations' exercises, but as specific 'opinion-forming' channels. They may take the form of institutional propaganda, like the series 'Join the Army and See the World' or specially-geared justifications by a trade union for a strike or a pay-claim. Boeing, which runs a general 'institutional' series with the slogan 'Getting People Together', used the opinion-forming mode in up-market periodicals to persuade readers of the rightness of the choice of the Boeing AWACS defence system in preference to Nimrod, the British alternative. Several such advertisements verge on political and capitalist propaganda.[17]

CONCLUSION: ADVERTISING AS AN INSTITUTION

It seems true to say that advertising has today established itself as a genre, like science fiction or the horror story, in that it has managed to acquire for itself a conventional rather than a literal response whereby it is read, viewed or listened to with some 'willing suspension of disbelief'. Consequently, its hyperboles, no matter how preposterous they may seem from a literal standpoint, become effective persuaders. 'Legitimate puffery' may have no sanction in law, but makes its encroachments nevertheless.

In part it is the very variety of advertising, ranging from the most sober to the most absurd, which has inculcated this conventional acceptance. (If *all* advertising were absurd, none of it would be taken seriously; if all were sober, there would be no problem.) The verbicidal massacre resulting from advertising has been analysed in some detail, but there is an interesting convention of licence which relates language and commodity. It seems significant that the language of promotion becomes increasingly inflated in direct proportion to the inessentiality of the commodity being marketed. Thus, vegetables are hardly ever advertised, whereas fruit is, as a supposed health food; clothes and cars are promoted in a generally inflated language, the more so if they are expensive; luxuries, such as perfumes, jewellery and furs claim still greater puffery, so that the word *best*, which would not be used of medicines or insurances, is used freely of whisky or watches. But the most strident exaggerations surround the entertainment industry, where copywriters assure us of *classics*, *epics*, *spectaculars* and – when normal words have run out – a steady supply of the *fantabulous*, the *stupendous*, the *stupendiferous* and other Joycean qualities. Once all the emotive words have been drained of their meat, like the weasel's egg, a more desperate style of negative promise is employed: 'This is not just a film,' you are assured portentously, 'but an emotional/harrowing/beautiful experience.'[18] The film-promotion industry has become a capitalist paradigm of the expanding universe, with whole constellations, even galaxies of 'new stars' and 'new worlds' being created annually by an omnivorous publicity machine.

Beyond the convention of inflation (*super* → *hyper* → *mega*) lies the institutionalization of the status-symbol. Here the language of advertising builds, by a kind of tautological magic, upon itself: 'the Rolls-Royce of watches'; 'the champagne of sherries'; 'the Porsche that's better than a Porsche'; 'timeless in styling, Cadillac in craftsmanship'; 'the hand made handmade glass'.

Advertising has even achieved the dubious respectability of art. The work of Pop artists seeks to integrate the artefacts and images of everyday consumerism (Coca-Cola bottles, Campbell soup tins and the like) into artistic compositions and art forms. Generally speaking, however, the relationship of advertising to art is parasitic. Today many 'up-market' advertisements trade on the established cultural associations of major art-works and classical music by the most obvious exploitation and plagiarism, a process akin to the linguistic capitalism which this chapter has analysed.

In brief, the essential displacement of product by image, and of referential language by emotive, has now become an accepted mode in an industry which can reach more than 90 per cent of most populations in the West. Several highly successful campaigns, some among sophisticated readerships, have eliminated language altogether, while others reiterate commercial mantras or mindless slogans. 'The man in the Hathaway shirt', with his captivating eyepatch (a creation of Ogilvy & Mather) proved such a powerful symbol that he eventually appeared without a word of text. A nominalist might argue that, since language can never describe 'the world' accurately, the distortions of advertising merely constitute another form of verbal mystification. It seems, however, that even in the field of vision, which many would think of as strictly referential, advertising claims the right to legitimate illusions. The Independent Television Code of Advertising Standards and Practices allows for the substitution of materials and the use of optical techniques, 'provided that "a fair and reasonable" impression is given':

> Food advertisements pose a particular problem in this respect, especially in colour, where genuine photography of the product may give a quite unappetising impression. It may be necessary, for example, to stuff a soufflé with tissue paper, or spray a sausage with lacquer to make it shine!
>
> (Carter, 1971, p. 94)

This kind of legitimized visual 'weasel' makes one wonder about the genuineness of the claim that advertising is self-policing through agencies such as the Advertising Standards Authority 'the watchdog on British advertising', as Ogilvy calls it (1983, p. 209). So much licence has already been granted that the Authority reminds one of Bacon's apophthegm, 'Laws were like cobwebs; where the small flies were caught, and the great brake through.'

Perhaps the coda to the chapter should be given to Dr Johnson, whose insight into the language of advertising was so clear. We can imagine the bewilderment of the doughty prescriptivist as he ventured into a modern US supermarket intending to purchase viands for his pet cat, Hodge. Promises, large promises, would greet his astonished eyes. Substances claiming to be *nectar* and *ambrosia* would seem to be commonly available, with feline sustenance equally rarefied:

> Every bite-sized clover of Little Friskies is drenched with a digest of real ocean fish by-products for a taste and an aroma your cat will love. All Little Friskies flavors are tested with and approved by a taste test panel of over 500 pampered cats like yours at the Friskies Cat Health Center, Carnation Farms, Washington.

Witnessing the kaleidoscopic cacophony of imperatives, hedonistic, sexual, salutary, dyspeptic and apocalyptic, Dr Johnson would assuredly recall his own pronouncements on advertising. Affronted by some of the more primitive manifestations of articulation, the cave-men grunts, infantile gurgles and juvenile ejaculations, he would surely feel vindicated by the statement he made in the Preface to his *Dictionary*: 'Commerce, however necessary, however lucrative, as it depraves the morals, so it corrupts the language.' On vast hoardings he would see magnified words competing with massive photographic close-ups, the visual equivalent of the exaggerated sounds and doctored voices-over which assailed him, even in the street. He would find it a matter of risibility and indignation that the manufacturers of these monstrous public nuisances should have the further impudence to term themselves 'creative' directors.

As the Doctor made his way around the streets, he would be struck by the final irony that advertisements were being worn as fashion. Whereas a medieval European wore the suit of livery delivered to him by his lord and master as the compulsory badge of servitude and loyalty, here were modern, liberated, democratic Westerners of their own free will wearing the livery of the corporations which dominate their economy and mould their life-style. The heraldic device has been replaced by the commercial logo, the tabard by the T-shirt.[19]

Capitalism is usually thought of, especially in modern times, as being a conservative force opposed to radical revolution. In fact, as was shown in chapter 3, money-power is well able to destabilize and subvert other institutions. In its promotional form as advertising, capitalism is responsible for much institutionalized illiteracy and the subversion of traditional meanings, spellings, grammar and syntax.

NOTES

1 H. L. Mencken, *The American Language*, cited in *OED Supplement*.
2 Paul Johnson, 'The day after that' (*Spectator*, 26 November 1983, p. 18), citing *Forbes* magazine.
3 *Encyclopaedia Britannica Book of the Year*, 1986.
4 This generally used profile (in which 'AB' refers to the professional, managerial class and 'DE' to the unskilled and semi-skilled worker) is described in Carter (1971, p. 89).
5 S. I. Hayakawa, 'Sexual fantasy and the 1957 car', in *The Use and Misuse of Language* (1962).
6 The Ogilvy short-list is: FREE and NEW (pre-eminently), followed by HOW TO, SUDDENLY, NOW, ANNOUNCING, INTRODUCING, IT'S HERE, JUST ARRIVED, IMPORTANT DEVELOPMENT, IMPROVEMENT, AMAZING, SENSATIONAL, REMARKABLE, REVOLUTIONARY, STARTLING, MIRACLE, MAGIC, OFFER, QUICK, EASY, WANTED, CHALLENGE, ADVICE TO, COMPARE, BARGAIN, HURRY, LAST CHANCE and (ironically) THE TRUTH ABOUT.
7 It appears that *Webster* was originally unsympathetic to spelling reform, but was influenced by the earlier initiatives of Benjamin Franklin. (See Baugh, pp. 429–31.)

8 Matoré's valuable distinction is discussed in chapter 1, p. 24.

9 See particularly H. Trevor-Roper, 'The rise of the gentry', in *Historical Essays* (1957).

10 The *OED* notes that 'in the eighteenth century *buck* indicated more the assumption of "spirit" and gaiety of conduct rather than elegance of dress; the latter notion comes forward early in the present [i.e., nineteenth] century.' *Buck*, being descended directly in meaning from the 'male of several animals', combines virility and arrogant stylishness in a way which has since been paralleled by American *stud.*

11 Turner cites the advertisements for 'cephalic tobacco', viper aphrodisiac, Holloway's Pills and the Carbolic Smoke Ball Co. in *The Shocking History of Advertising* (1965).

12 Fielding's campaign against puffery is the subject of a chapter in Blanche B. Elliott (1962). The present quotation is from pp. 117–18. The current publishing sense of *puff* is a pre-publication opinion from a 'name' to be used in advertising.

13 Philip Howard has a collection of essays entitled *Weasel Words* (1978), but they deal more with linguistic vagueness than with deceit, which is the essence of the *weasel.*

14 It is thought that Du Pont did not patent *nylon*, nor put any restrictions on the use of the term, precisely to allow it increased currency and thus greater publicity.

15 From the *New Yorker*, 20 January 1968. (The use of *simulated* is a rather conspicuous weasel.)

16 *King Lear*, I. iv. 226; *Antony and Cleopatra*, II. i. 38.

17 A similar series of advertisements appeared in February 1987 in favour of the Channel Tunnel or *Eurotunnel.*

18 Boorstin (1963) observes on p. 255: 'This is the age of contrivance . . . of the "*un*abridged novel" (abridgement is the norm), of the "*un*cut movie . . .". Fact itself has become "*non*-fiction".'

19 The conversion of modern sport into a capitalist spectacle is most obviously apparent in the changed garb of the players. In Spain, where the bull-fight still retains the quality of a national ritual, there is still resistance to toreadors becoming the visible vehicles of sponsorship.

7
Words and Power: Democracy and Language

Rectification of names is the main business of government.
Confucius

With regard to language, democratic nations prefer obscurity to labour.
de Tocqueville

The political is replacing the metaphysical as the characteristic mode of grasping reality.
Harvey Cox

'L'ÉTAT, c'est moi' ('I *am* the State') was the grand, unequivocal statement of authority attributed to Louis XIV before the Parlement in Paris. In a similar assertion of absolute monarchy, Louis XVI retorted, when one of his judgements was termed illegal: 'It is the law because I wish it.' A. J. P. Taylor has observed: 'In the old days, right up to 1789, a state was simply the property of its owner; Madame de Pompadour called Louis XV "France", even when she was in bed with him.'[1] Though this may seem to us a charmingly intimate Gallicism, not untinged with arrogance, and quite unthinkable of the British Royal Family, we should recall that in Elizabethan English there is the similar semantic assumption, whereby the King is deemed to be the embodiment of the nation. At the beginning of *Macbeth*, the King of Norway is styled 'Norway himself' (I. ii. 51), and when Hamlet leaps into Ophelia's grave he announces himself by means of the royal title, so challenging the murderer-incumbent: 'This is I, Hamlet the Dane!' (*Hamlet*, V. i. 279).[2]

All this was before the Revolution, the revolution the British have never had. Taylor continues: 'And then, suddenly, there appeared the French people who said: "We are France."' The transfer of power, from permanent, oligarchical monarchies to temporary, democratically elected representative governments, is the most significant political change in European history, and forms the theme of this chapter. This is clearly only one aspect of the huge topic of political language, but it is certainly one of the most fruitful and controversial. In related developments, the whole idea of society has changed from one conceived in terms of ranks, orders, degrees and estates, to an amorphous entity referred to as 'the State' or 'society', a power-market comprising many competing interests. With this change the conceptual basis of legitimate power has altered from received hierarchical notions of priority, to those of popularity and communality. These changes have great linguistic implications, since kings customarily command, their rare utterances gaining the force of fiats, whereas democratic politicians are required to persuade and canvass the electorate, their frequent orations, statements, comments and leaks being more in the nature of 'statements of intent', usually of ephemeral duration.

In English history a decisive shift in the balance of power between King and Commons, and a whole ideological change in the notion of authority occurred in the period of the Civil War and the execution of Charles I, by parliamentary authority, in 1649. In the fascinating transcript of his trial we can see the semantic correlative of ideological conflict. The King, understandably, disputes the authority of the court to try him; the court maintains, simply, that it is the authority:

The King	I will answer the same so soone as I know by what authority you do this.
Lord President	If this be all that you will say, then Gentlemen you that brought the Prisoner hither, take charge of him back againe.
The King	I doe require that I may give in my Reasons why I do not answer, and give me time for that.
Lord President	Sir, 'Tis not for prisoners to require.
The King	Prisoners? Sir, I am not an ordinary Prisoner.
Lord President	The Court hath considered of their jurisdiction, and they have already affirm'd their jurisdiction; if you will not answer we shall give order to record your default.
The King	You never heard my Reason yet.
Lord President	Sir, Your Reasons are not to bee heard against the highest Jurisdiction.
The King	Shew me that Jurisdiction where Reason is not to be heard.
Lord President	Sir, We shew it you here, the Commons of England; and the next time you are brought you will know more of the pleasure of the Court; and, it may be, their finall determination.

The King	Shew me where ever the House of Commons was a Court of Judicature of that kind.
Lord President	Sergeant, Take away the Prisoner.[3]

What is profoundly illuminating in this remarkable exchange is that the concepts of 'jurisdiction', 'authority' and even 'reason' are entirely dependent on ideology. The King's ideology is *de jure*, his logic that of the law: authorities and reasons are based on concepts of historical hierarchy, such as priority, seniority and a body of precedent which has crystallized and solidified into a foundation of thought. The Lord President's ideology is *de facto*, the logic of revolutionary power, which overturns the past and is concerned solely with present *realpolitik*. Authority is, simply, 'the will of the people', supposedly embodied in the Commons. The final exchange is the stark expression of these two ideologies. The confrontation expresses in its most naked form the enduring conflict between revolutionary socialism and conservative individualism.

One linguistic consequence is certainly the fragmentation which occurs when an undisputed monarchical authority gives way to temporary representatives, simultaneously 'of' the people, yet symbolically representing them. An undisputed authority speaks, not necessarily in a louder, but in a clearer voice; an ambiguity in the relations between the ruler and the ruled affects even the coherence of the syntax of credential and proclamation. From medieval times, the monarch provides an undisputed syntactical subject:

> John, by the Grace of God, King of England, Lord of Ireland, Duke of Normandy and Aquitaine, and Count of Anjou, sends greetings. . . .

In the Cromwellian Commonwealth the format changes, and an oddly ambiguous format takes over:

> The government of the Commonwealth of England, Scotland and Ireland, and the dominions thereto belonging.
>
> 1. That the supreme legislative authority of the Commonwealth of England [& Co.] . . . shall be and reside in one person, and the people assembled in Parliament: the style of which person shall be the Lord Protector. . . .

The British formula is constitutionally ambiguous: 'Her Majesty's Government . . .'. The Constitution of the United States is headed, with artificial democratic consensus, 'We, the people . . .'. The most common device of 'democratic' style, however, is to resort to pseudo-democratic formulas such as 'the public interest', 'public opinion' or a reified *it. It*, assisted by the grammatical passive, becomes the repository of great power, mysteriously unlocatable, in both democratic and totalitarian regimes. The effectiveness of its disguise is such that one is uncertain whether *it* represents 'the people', 'the government', 'the authorities' or 'Big Brother'.

With the decline of monarchy, authority has had to be fabricated on other bases and out of other words. Since the basic assumptions of monarchical and democratic power are so much at variance, it is not surprising that the word-field of politics has altered greatly. Much of the vocabulary of modern politics, has, in fact, been borrowed from quite diverse fields. The premises of democracy being so revolutionary, it is completely to be expected that several of the crucial terms deal with 'essentially contested concepts' (Gallie, 1964, p. 157), and are abstractions prone to fashion. Prime among these key-terms are *democracy*, *politics* and *politician*, *franchise*, *society* and *revolution.*

'Nothing can be more disorderlie, than the confusion of your Democracie, or popular state', rumbled Bishop Hall in 1614. A contemporary used the term to damn licentiousness of a different kind: 'In wicked men there is a democracy of wild lusts and passions.' (The word had been first used by Elyot in 1531 in a purely descriptive fashion of the Athenian democracy.) These views, which seem now so reactionary, remind us forcibly that democracy was not always the favoured political dispensation or catchword that it is now. It was a most unwelcome innovation (at a time when *innovation* itself was a critical term) to European monarchies, and the word was used in a generally unfavourable fashion until well into the nineteenth century. Byron, three years before he died fighting for Greek independence, indulged in this ironic rhetorical question: 'What is Democracy? . . . an aristocracy of blackguards.' Even Burke remarks in the *Reflections* (1925, p. 102) that a pure democracy is 'the most shameless thing in the world'. *Democrat* appears with an abrupt topicality consequent upon the French Revolution, from *c.* 1790[O]. The quotations in the *OED* are invariably unfavourable; Gibbon remarks (in 1791): 'Even our democrats are more reasonable or more discreet'[O], and recalls in his *Autobiography* (1794) 'the clamour of the triumphing *democrates*'[O].

The hostility evident in these and similar quotations is partly explicable, given the fact that the general notion was that of a 'pure' or literal democracy, namely of power being put directly into the hands of the people *en masse*. As Alexander Hamilton observed in 1777, in these conditions, 'You must expect error, confusion and instability.' Not surprisingly, the polemical variants *mobocracy* and *mobocratical* were to be coined in 1754, *mobocratic* emerged in 1775 and *mobocrat* in 1798.[O] (The classical word for mob rule, *ochlocracy* had been borrowed in 1584.[O]) Hamilton proceeded to advocate the style of democracy which has become dominant in the West, namely, representative democracy, but as Raymond Williams has observed, two basic traditions of *democracy* have emerged since the nineteenth century:

> In the socialist tradition, *democracy* continued to mean *popular power*: a state in which the interests of the majority of the people were paramount and in which these interests were practically exercised and controlled by the majority. In the liberal tradition, *democracy* meant open election of representatives and certain conditions (democratic rights such as free speech) which maintained the openness of election and political argument. These two conceptions, in their extreme forms, now confront each other as enemies.
>
> (1976, p. 85)

Hence the division into 'people's democracies' of the socialist and communist variety, and 'bourgeois' democracy, of the capitalist persuasion. 'Each position,' Williams wryly observes, 'normally is described as "the only true meaning", and the alternative use is seen as propaganda or hypocrisy.' Of whatever brand, *democracy* is now a highly favourable term, having ameliorated more than any other in the field as power was given to, or taken by, the people. The extent to which the term is really valid will be reserved for discussion at the end of this chapter.

Politic and *politician* have always been clouded with suspicion and cynicism, increasingly so as one goes back in time. The earliest senses of *politic*, glossed as 'sagacious, shrewd, expedient', still survive. *Body politic* is, fascinatingly, the propagandist semantic correlative of Henry VIII (Act 24 1532–3), a statement of corporeal political unity designed to assert the indivisible loyalty of his subjects, and to reject any papal claims: 'The Realm of England is an Empire . . . governed by one supreme Head and King . . . unto whom a Body Politick, compact of all sorts and Degrees of people been bounden to bear a natural and humble Obedience.' However, by the late sixteenth century, deterioration is clearly apparent in the sinister senses of 'scheming, crafty, cunning'. Satan is thus termed 'a politick hunter' by Dekker in 1609, while a quotation from 1667 refers to 'the craftiest and politiquest sort of knaves'[O]. References go back to *c.* 1580[O], and it is in this period that *politician* makes its first appearance, in a wholly bad sense: 'A politic person, esp. a crafty plotter or intriguer.' 'The Diuel was . . . so famous a Politician in purchasing,' writes Nashe in 1592, 'that Hel, which at the beginning was but an obscure Village, is now become a huge citie.' Heywood, equally cynical, is more to the point: 'I am a politician, oathes with me Are but the tooles I work with, I may breake An oathe by my profession' (1632).[O] Adam Smith more shrewdly notes the opportunism of 'That insidious and crafty animal, vulgarly called a statesman or politician, whose councils are directed at the momentary fluctuations of affairs' (1776). For Johnson a *politician* was 'A man of artifice; one of deep contrivance.'

With the broadening of the franchise, *politician* starts to ameliorate towards neutrality in the nineteenth century. 'The word "politician" has a bad sense in America', a writer observes in 1879.[O] This neutralization is related to a growing awareness of the power-dynamics, manipulation and role-playing which seem to be part of any social situation. The root of the word in Greek *polis*, 'a city' is revealing here: Greek *politikis* would be literally 'a citizen'.

Today, as a consequence, the term *politics* is greatly generalized, so that one hears of office politics, department politics and even family politics. All manner of decisions and actions, down to the brand of oranges one buys, where one sends one's children to school, have become politicized. One area of focus is that of sexual conflict, especially analysed by writers concerned with women's liberation. Fielding has a rare but nice anticipation of the modern sense in the phrase *matrimonial politics* in *Tom Jones* (1749). *Sexual politics* has become a set phrase, deriving from the title of a book by Kate Millett in 1969. The work produced considerable progeny, including *Vaginal Politics* by Ellen Frankfurter. These radical critiques derive essentially from the generalized Marxist view which 'sees politics everywhere; in biology, in history, in psychology, and even in prehistoric archaeology and linguistics' (Brown, 1969, pp. 116–17). Recent examples of the generalized sense are 'The Politics of Food' (*Newsweek*, 6 July 1987) and 'The politics of nature' (*THES*, 29 May 1987). The plea, 'keep politics out of sport/business/sex', naive as it may be, shows the beginnings of a new emotive use of the word, a sense related to the old 'suspicious' sense. The somewhat infelicitous formation *politicking* (first recorded in 1917[S]), is slowly gaining currency and conveys the same nuance of hostility.

The third *mot-clé* is *franchise*. This has shifted from the sense of 'exclusive privilege' to 'general right', from exceptional individual freedom in conditions of general servitude to a guarantee of power through the vote. The general sense of 'liberty' is the earliest, recorded from *c.* 1290[O] to the mid-seventeenth century. But, for the purposes of this chapter, the most significant development is that of *OED* 6: 'the right to vote', which is first recorded with astonishing topicality in Burke's

Reflections (1790). An archaic sense, 'nobility of mind', shows that the word has developed semantically in exactly the same direction as *free* (A-S *freo*, 'free, noble'), from exclusive nobility to democratic right.

A similar change is to be seen in *society*. In its primary sense, which dates from the sixteenth century, it means 'companionship'. Raymond Williams's statement that it was borrowed in the fourteenth century, and that its meanings 'ranged from active unity in fellowship, as in the Peasants' Revolt of 1381' (1976, pp. 243–4) seems to be an unfounded anachronism, based on a Marxist 'proletarian' etymology, and his attempt to enlist the term in the class-struggle appears to be a striking example of ideological wish-fulfilment. The first recorded instance seems, in fact, to be in Elyot's *Governour* (1531), exactly 150 years later. The general sense then steadily narrows, with various criteria of exclusivity being brought into play, so that by the nineteenth century it denoted not society at large, but virtually a clique, 'the aggregate of leisured, cultured or fashionable persons, regarded as forming a distinct class or body'[O]. Byron, very much an outsider, remarked satirically:

> Society is now one polish'd horde,
> Form'd of two mighty tribes, the *Bores* and *Bored.*
> (*Don Juan*, 1823)

The evolution of the modern, quasi-sociological sense of a mass of undefined individuals is hard to distinguish from other meanings, but seems traceable from the late eighteenth century. Adam Smith writes (1776) of 'every society where the distinction of rank has once been established'. The current near-personification ('Society is changing . . .'; 'One owes something to society') seems to be recorded from 1784, in a quotation from Cowper.[O] The differing attitudes towards society are encapsulated in the variants *socialist* and *socialite.* Generally, one may say that 'society' has ceased to be the 'sociable' notion of earlier times, and has become increasingly abstract and alien.

Revolution shows a basic change in sense from 'turning' to 'overturning', and the focus from a plain fact of nature, such as the revolution of the planets or the Wheel of Fortune, to the overthrow of a tyrant or a regime by collective human action. The physical sense goes back to the late fourteenth century; the political emerges in the early seventeenth. The two English revolutions of that century suggest that *revolution*, if genuinely popular, could have a good sense even then. The Cromwellian revolution was stigmatized as 'The Great Rebellion', though it is possible that Clarendon's brilliant, if polemical, *History of the Rebellion* helped the name to stick. (*Rebellion* was subsequently distinguished in this masterly definition from 1796[O]: 'Rebellion is the subversion of the laws, and Revolution is that of Tyrants.') By contrast, the 'Glorious Revolution' of 1688–9 was so called because of the fact that 'it was bloodless, that there was no civil war, no massacre, no proscription . . .'. Bolingbroke justified it in 1726: 'King James's maladministration rendered a revolution necessary and practicable.'[O]

Of these key words, amelioration is very evident in *democracy*, and marginally so in *politics* and its associates. *Franchise* and *society* have remained basically neutral, though some might say that they have 'lost class'. Naturally, it would be naive to assume, on the basis of the amelioration of *politics* and *politician*, that there has been an ethical improvement in the practice or the practitioners. It is simply that they have become institutionalized. For, quite cynically, expectations of high moral standards from the holders of high democratic office are no more valid nowadays than they were in times of established monarchy. Political chicanery is now hardly the occasion of surprise, let alone outrage, as the Watergate and Irangate scandals have shown.

THE SEMANTIC FIELD

Since democracy is a relatively new dispensation, and (unlike capitalism) has evolved out of a quite different system of power, it is not surprising that only a few of the terms should have originated within the field. Only one word, *husting*, predates the Conquest. Ultimately from Old Norse *husþing* ('house court'), the term originally denoted a meeting of the lord's followers. Even *spokesman*, so Anglo-Saxon in appearance, turns out to be a Renaissance formation. I have not included enduring institutions of power like *parliament* or *court*, since their very stability makes them unrevealing, as opposed to *lobby*, *poll* and *establishment*, all of which have developed new political specializations.

Interestingly, apart from two central words, *democracy* and *ballot*, and a small group of associates made up of *manifesto*, *referendum*, *gerrymander*, *fascist* and *totalitarian*, virtually the whole vocabulary has been borrowed from other activities. Many of the words have undergone extraordinary semantic changes: *canvass* originally meant 'to toss in a sheet of canvas'; *filibuster*, a corruption of *freebooter*, meant originally a 'piratical adventurer' before acquiring the quite different sense of to frustrate legislation by procedural obstacles and delaying tactics; *hierarchy* was originally 'a sacred order' applied to angels; *heckle* in its earliest sense means 'to dress flax', while *gerrymander* is a witty portmanteau of the name of a corrupt US politician and *salamander*.

Such wide shifts of meaning suggest imprecision, which may derive in part from the provisional nature of democratic politics. Many of the words refer to concepts or to roles which are essentially contestable or controversial. The nature of the contract which exists between voter and representative is always a moot point, because of the claims of the constituency, the party, the nation and the individual conscience.[4]

The word-field has been set out in figure 7.1. Nearly all the terms are post-Renaissance, and the growth of the field is fairly slow until the ferment of the seventeenth century. Here the terminological divisions of the Civil War (*cavalier* and *roundhead*) are replaced by the more enduring terms *whig* and *tory* (both originally abusive nicknames deriving from the Exclusion Crisis of 1679–80). But the great excitant of vocabulary is the growth of democratic politics in the nineteenth century, particularly the period of the Reform Bill of 1832. *Constituency*, 'an odious word', according to Macaulay, dates from 1831, the same year in which Peel coined *Conservative*, stigmatized by the same writer as 'the new cant word'. Bryan Magee has pointed out 'the extraordinary fact that the terms "Conservatism", "Socialism" and "trade union" all date their traceable entry into the English language to the same year [1835].'[5] The

FIGURE 7.1 The semantic field of political terms

1500

faction aristocracy democracy vote
ballot canvass
oligarchy spokesman
1600 revolution authority politician
cabal minister
club junta cabinet coalition hierarchy

1700 class constitution slogan whig tory
caucus clique
coterie agitator
public opinion
lobby democrat gerrymander heckle liberal left right
1800 reactionary radical campaign franchise regime terrorism
elite constituency poll Conservative socialism reform
squirearchy civil disobedience demonstration communism
claque Marxist anarchist nihilist filibuster
discrimination referendum nationalism
1900 militant Labour ideology minority pacificism
establishment activist Trotskyite totalitarian fascist
confrontation emergency
Thatcherism/ite

more recent additions show a clear split between 'anaesthetic' words, like *totalitarian*, *activism* and *confrontation*, as opposed to the emotive labels *Trotskyite*, *Thatcherite* and *fascist.*

DETERIORATION OF ELITES

This trend is fairly clearly the obverse of the amelioration of *democracy*, *politician* and its henchmen. As democracy becomes the dominant dispensation, so the previously acceptable notion of oligarchy will assuredly fall into disfavour, and with it the words which describe it. Perhaps the most striking example is *aristocracy*, the first in the field. It makes its first appearance, alongside *democracy*, in Elyot's *Governour* (1531). Elyot, in his usual fashion, gives the etymological meaning, 'The rule of men of beste disposicion', a sense which would hardly be popular now. It is difficult to trace the beginnings of the slightly hostile connotation which the word now commonly carries. Hobbes uses the word literally in his *Rhetoric* (*c.* 1651): 'those that have the best education', but in *The Leviathan* he seems to be the first user of the word with the implication of a privileged oligarchy not based on merit: 'an Assembly of certain persons nominated, or otherwise distinguished from the rest'. Of the various interesting quotations from the nineteenth century, perhaps the most revealing of the rise of a democratic ethos is this from Hallam in 1838: 'The distinguishing characteristic of an aristocracy is the enjoyment of privileges which are not communicable to other citizens simply by anything they can themselves do to obtain them.' *Aristocrat* is 'a popular formation of the French Revolution', and its relation to that event is well shown in the contemporary quotations. Belsham writes in 1789 of 'The genuine spirit of the haughty aristocrate'. The best has clearly become the worst.

Elite is, perhaps ironically, a doublet of *elect*, which has always had a neutral sense. When borrowed in its modern form, in the nineteenth century, meaning 'the choice part or flower' of society, it had become controversial: while Byron could be satirical in *Don Juan* (1823), W. H. Kelly wrote neutrally in 1848 of 'the élite of the Russian nobility'. The *Supplement* adds several quotations referring to 'élite groups', which reveal a generally hostile sense. But no adequate record is given of *elite per se*, in the sense in which the word is widely prevalent in modern sociological studies such as W. Wright Mills's *The Power Elite* (1956). David Riesman uses the term as far back as 1947 in his study of *We happy Few* (1946), a satirical novel about Harvard: 'She [the author, Helen Howe] has not been taken in by the self-deceptions of the élite of culture.' Riesman seems to have been the first user of *élitist*, in 1950.

Hierarchy shows a similar, though more pronounced, deterioration. Originally applied to an order or a host of angels from the fourteenth century, it has steadily moved down the scale of being, referring to 'a collective body of ecclesiastical rulers' from *c.* 1619[O], from whence the similar secular sense develops *c.* 1643 (in Milton's tract on divorce). As with *elite*, the *Supplement* of 1976 gives later examples, but fails to record the quasi-sociological sense in which the word is now commonly used. Today one frequently hears of 'the party hierarchy', 'business hierarchies' and the like, denoting only the top of the hierarchy, not the whole order, and conveying the same nuances of hostility and envy implied in *elite*. An amusingly arch letter to *The Daily Telegraph* alluded to uncritical secular applications of the word. Under the heading 'Hell's Angels', the writer comments: 'In your issue of March 3 you refer to the "Soviet Communist Hierarchy". I eagerly await your publication of a photograph of Mr Brezhnev wearing a cope and chasuble – or even wings.'[6]

Oligarchy reveals in its early history an interesting example of hostility, not so much to elites *per se*, as to elites which lack legitimacy. The earliest quotations are clear 'tactical definitions' (Lewis, 1960, p. 17): 'where men vse euill means to come to authority . . . then is their government not to be called an Aristocracie, but an Oligarchie' (1577).[O] Hobbes chimes in with the cynical observation: 'They that are displeased with Aristocracy, call it Oligarchy', while Burke refers to 'An ignoble oligarchy'. The term has acquired today a quasi-sociological currency, in which irony is often apparent.

Establishment, more generalized and more British, has, particularly as *The Establishment*, come to mean 'the ruling faction' rather than the whole staff, military or ecclesiastical, which was the traditional notion. It is, perhaps, from these callings that the sense of a conservative hierarchy derives. The word is more commonly used by outsiders than insiders, with a veiled criticism of an impenetrable power-group. (Even the most smugly secure would not say 'I'm a member of the Establishment.') The *OED Supplement* (1972) has a masterly definition:

> A social group exercising power generally, or within a given field or institution, by virtue of its traditional superiority, and by the use especially of tacit understandings and often a common mode of speech and having as a general interest the maintenance of the *status quo*.

Quotations, invariably smacking of ironic hostility, date from 1923.

Junta (originally, but erroneously *Junto* down to 1700) is applied, even in the same period, to a bewildering variety of power-groups, namely 'the Cabinet of Charles I, to the Independent and Presbyterian factions of the same period, to the Rump Parliament under Cromwell, and to the Whigs in the reign of William III and Anne.'[O] From its Spanish and Portuguese origins, it refers to a political power-group. Today the word is widely prevalent and has undergone a rather sinister military specialization. The increased currency, and the military associations, are a direct reflection of the way that power has, in the post-colonial era, devolved from the imperial oligarchy to a local democracy, usually temporary, which is then replaced through *coups d'état*, by military dictatorships or juntas. The military specialization of *junta* might be explained by the strong role of the army in South American politics, where *junta* is a general political term. In both monarchic and democratic dispensations, the word has hostile associations, and, given the prevalence of military dictatorships in the world, it seems highly likely that the word's military associations will strengthen. *Juntocracy* may not be a word, but it is a common fact.

More hostility surrounds *plutocracy*, dating from *c.* 1652[O], but not in general use until the nineteenth century. Since the word so accurately alludes to a principal source of power in the West, it is hard to account for its comparative disuse. The journalistic categorizations 'big business' and 'business community', 'business interests' are slightly unsatisfactory, since they imply a false consensus. The word has certainly lost much of its earlier critical sense, exemplified in this quotation from the *Morning Herald* (1839): 'Of all systems of tyranny, a plutocracy is the most cruel, selfish, and grinding.' *Plutocrat*, coined by Charles Kingsley in 1850[O], has the same sense of odium.

Other terms which convey a sense of criticism directed at elites and power-groups are *caucus*, a New England (possibly Algonquin) word, which crossed the Atlantic about a century ago, to be defined damningly by the *OED* as 'a meeting of wire-pullers'; *faction*, from the divisions of the Reformation; and *cabal*, from seventeenth-century English politics, a contemporary with *junta*.

As the democratic dispensation grows, so terms generally referring to exclusive social gatherings fall under suspicion. For instance, *club* was defined by Johnson as 'an assembly of good fellows, meeting under certain conditions'. No modern lexicographers would endorse such wholesome chauvinist joviality, even if it accorded with their own view. In modern times clubs increasingly attract suspicion as insidious remnants of the class-system, or as racist enclaves. Yet it is ironic that in Johnson's own time clubs and coffee houses were far more clearly defined centres of political and business interest than they are nowadays. The main contribution of the twentieth century has been the *nuclear club*, once exclusive, but gaining in numbers. Two French words, *clique* and *coterie*, which crossed the Channel over two centuries ago, have since acquired the sense of a select social 'set'.

The terms just discussed have deteriorated because of the exclusivity of the gatherings they denote. Egalitarianism, the corollary of democratic politics, has highlighted two principal areas of traditional prejudice and discrimination, those of women and race. In both fields, terms have become strongly politicized. *Feminist* (*c.* 1894) and *feminism* (*c.* 1895), which sprang into being in the French Chamber of Deputies as explicit lobbying terms, have since been joined by *sexist* (*c.* 1965), *sexism* (*c.* 1968) and latterly the neutral grammatical and scientific term *gender*. *Race* was also a neutral term for centuries after its absorption into the language *c.* 1600. Its increasing politicization started with the phrases *race-prejudice* (*c.* 1890, in Oscar Wilde), *racial discrimination* (*c.* 1899), *racialism* (*c.* 1907), *racialist* (*c.* 1917), *racist* (*c.* 1932) and *racism* (*c.* 1936)[S]: as the *Supplement* observes under *racial*, these are words 'of considerable frequency in the 20th century'. One notes how *discrimination*, originally a 'good' word, has been tainted by the 'race' association. The emotional tenor of the subject has meant that the pseudo-sociological euphemisms *ethnic*, *group*, *community* and *minority* have been drawn into the field. In both areas there have been dramatic appropriations. *Chauvinist*, which had been in a comparative backwater, was suddenly brought into the front line of the feminist struggle in *male chauvinist pig*, the damning slogan of 1970. Now reduced to plain *chauvinism* it is used more discriminatingly, like *sexism*, of either sex. *Ghetto*, from its Jewish origins in Venice, was first extended to a 'working-class slum' *c.* 1908 and to 'Negro city ghettoes' *c.* 1957[S], which is now its main sense. Both words were strongly rooted in prejudice before their meanings were broadened: this emotional quality perhaps assisted in their transfer.

Those who actively demonstrate their power (or their would-be influence) also attract an emotive response, evident (in ascending order of temperature) in *canvasser*, *lobbyist*, *heckler*, *demonstrator*, *agitator*, *militant* and *activist*. *Agitator* originated in the English Civil War, *heckle*, from its physical origin 'to beat flax', then 'to catechize severely', is borrowed in the nineteenth century from the Scots tradition of the 'public questioning of Parliamentary candidates', contemporary with *demonstrator*, recorded from *c.* 1870[O]. Revealing terms from religious and philosophical origins are *activist*, and *militant*, both politicized in the First World War, the first in association with Germany, the second appropriated by the Suffragette cause. *Lobby* has moved deftly from one establishment to another. Originally a monastic term, 'a cloister, or covered walk' from *c.* 1553[O], it becomes applied to the House of Commons about a century later. The sense of a political pressure-group is chiefly American and dates from the nineteenth century. Early quotations often carry the implication of bribery: 'Lobbying – this is . . . buying votes with money in the lobbies of the Hall of Congress' (1864).[O] Though now an accepted mode of political influence in America, lobbying is still regarded as constitutionally and morally suspect in the United Kingdom. All of these words have nuances which vary according to the different political affiliations of the describer and the reader. One can note, however, that *demonstration* seems to require the adjective 'peaceful' more often than in the past. The differing tones which surround this word-group have a direct relation to the two concepts of democracy outlined earlier, that of direct popular power as opposed to power invested in elected representatives and institutions.

LANGUAGE AND DEMOCRACY

This survey of the evolution of the key terms involved in the democratic process leads us to consider the general effects of democracy on the language itself. A useful starting point is found in some acute observations made by de Tocqueville 150 years ago about the use of the English language in democratic America. He noted 'a love of change for its own sake' in both language and politics; that coinages tended to come from commerce and business rather than metaphysics and theology, and the comic habit (bred of an egalitarian impulse) of seeking 'to dignify a vulgar profession by a Greek or Latin name'.[7] He was particularly scathing about two familiar aspects of American usage. The first, 'a deplorable consequence of democracy' (1863, vol. II, p. 80), was a general lack of precision flowing, in his view, from the assumed equality of all users of the language. The second, 'the great merit and the great imperfection' of democratic language, was 'the continual use of generic terms or abstract expressions' to which 'democratic nations are passionately addicted' (p. 83). He proceeds to give an example which is astonishing in its topicality:

> A democratic writer will be apt to speak of *capacities* in the abstract for *men of capacity*, and without specifying the objects to which their capacity is applied: he will talk about *actualities* to designate in one word the things passing before his eyes at the moment.
>
> (p. 84)

In the ensuing critique, de Tocqueville observes that these abstract terms 'enlarge and obscure the ideas they are intended to convey', and he sums up with magisterial abstraction: 'With regard to language, democratic nations prefer obscurity to labour' (p. 84).

Through these brilliant insights, de Tocqueville has given the basis for positing a causal relationship between the growth of democratic politics and the flexible abstractions so current in democratic society. Had he witnessed a modern US presidential election, de Tocqueville would have made this obvious connection. For a presidential candidate *has* to be all things to all men. The language he employs when campaigning in Idaho must win the votes of the local potato farmers, but it must not alienate the electoral sympathies of the business interests that sell chips, nor the consumer in general. Consequently, it must be generalized, 'prismatic', seeming to 'shine on all deservers', offering promise and promises. Democratic politicians must appear to be authoritative, but must have room to negotiate or manoeuvre. They have to appear to be consistent, jointly and severally, to their own principles, the interests of their constituents, the national interest and the party line. The obvious consequence is that political language is riven with conflicting motives, for it must be apparently clear yet actually ambiguous, apparently dogmatic yet actually flexible.

The most recent development in democratic politics has been the importation of advertising techniques into the political arena. Hitler, the first democratically elected dictator, developed the techniques of acting and voice production in secret. He was able to use the language with alarming effect. Today there is increasing concentration on image-building techniques, the use of symbols, tunes, jingles, variety shows, what is known as *razzmatazz*, all of which has the effect of diminishing the use and impact of language. The 1960 US presidential election (Kennedy v. Nixon) showed the decisive role of the visual media. Since then, all successful candidates have been extremely image-conscious: the dental exposure indulged in by Kennedy, Nixon, Carter and Reagan, the last four elected presidents, attests to an increasing, almost ludicrous concern for contrived photogeneity. Indeed, the smile has become the *sine qua non* of 'success' in the West, a point which becomes very apparent on comparing images of the leaders of Russia and the East. The techniques of advertising would seem, however, to succeed. In his book *The Selling of the President 1968* (1969), Joe McGinniss shows how, with the aid of expert advertising men, Nixon was 'sold', or rather, re-sold to the American people. In Britain the campaign which achieved a landslide Conservative victory in 1983 was managed by a previous marketer of Mars bars, Saatchi & Saatchi, and by a television producer who concentrated on Mrs Thatcher's voice and television appearance.[8] The latest device is the *teleprompter*, or *autocue*, recorded in the United States as far back as 1951. It is more crudely, but more honestly, called the 'head-up device' or 'sincerity machine'.[9]

Few people have understood and exposed the banality of modern political rhetoric with such withering irony as George Orwell. His incisive essay 'Politics and the English Language' contains this memorable image: 'When one watches some tired hack on the platform mechanically repeating the familiar phrases . . . one often has a curious feeling that one is not watching a live human being but some kind of dummy' (1958, p. 84). The problem now is that the 'dummy' is so expertly dressed, groomed, coached and programmed that one can no longer easily draw the line between contrived illusion and genuine reality.

CLASS

The democratization of British society has been dominated by the class factor. Forty years ago Orwell made the blunt observation that 'England is one of the last remaining countries to cling to the outward forms of feudalism.'[10] Be that as it may, it is the evolution of the tenacious vocabulary of class, with its categorization of society, which needs some focus.

Class has steadily taken over the semantic field made up of such traditional terms of hierarchy as *rank*, *order*, *estate* and *degree*. Dating from *c.* 1593, the word was frequently used for the classification of plants and animals, and this scientific association probably gave it greater neutrality when used of people. The *OED* observes that 'Higher and Lower Orders were formerly used', tracing the first instance to Blount's *Glossographia* (1656). The older terms were far more prescriptive, implying that people 'knew their place' in a fixed hierarchy; they thus reinforced the class-structure. The emphasis on economic role (rather than standing) seems first evident in Defoe (1705): ''tis plain [that] the dearness of wages forms our people into more classes than other nations can show'. The tripartite division (upper, middle and working class) has, with the levelling down of democracy, given way to 'a new binary division: in Marxist language, the bourgeoisie and the proletariat' (Raymond Williams, 1976, p. 58). (However, in *Das Kapital*, Marx wrote of 'three great social classes . . . wage-labourers, capitalists and landlords'.)

Although Marx was the great publicist of the notion of class, as he himself conceded, the 'class-struggle' was not really his formulation (as is commonly made out). His theory was much larger and more imposing. As he wrote in a letter to Joseph Weydemeyer (dated 5 March 1852):

> no credit is due to me for discovering the existence of classes in modern society, nor yet the struggle between them. Long before me bourgeois historians had described the historical development of this class-struggle and bourgeois economists the economic anatomy of the classes. What I did was to prove
>
> 1 that the existence of classes is only bound up with particular, historic phases in the development of production;
> 2 that the class-struggle necessarily leads to the dictatorship of the proletariat;
> 3 that this dictatorship itself only constitutes the transition to the abolition of all classes and to a classless society. (cited in Trevor-Roper (1957), p. 291)

The concept of class seems, in the judgement of time, to be, at the least, dubious and provisional: it is an 'essentially contested concept'. Individuals are not necessarily motivated by the predications of class conditions, and two world wars attest to the resounding success of national governments in mobilizing their proletariats to slaughter one another when they should, according to Marxist theory, have been uniting in class-solidarity against their masters. ('A bayonet is a weapon with a worker on each end' was a pacifist slogan of 1940.) But the significance of Marx's theories is not so much whether they are correct, as that they and their terminology have become an accepted currency of mass social explanation. In a real sense, currency is half-achieved conviction. Simply the awareness of a concept like the 'class-struggle' alters one's conception of politics, and as class-terms are given currency by the mass media, so the concept increases in validity.

These class-terms have not been slow in appearing. They have, in journalistic cliché, 'mushroomed' astonishingly from Marx's seminal formulation. A comparison between the original *OED* and the *Supplement* (1972) is most revealing on this point. The relevant fascicle of the *OED* (Cast–Clivy), issued in November 1889, contained some six class-terms: *class-education*, *-grievance*, *-interest*, *-journal*, *-legislation* and *-privilege*. When one turns to the 1972 *Supplement* one is waylaid by nearly three dozen such terms concerned with class antagonism, set out over nearly two columns. They make fascinating reading. *Class antagonism*, one of the first in the field (1850), comes from the translation of the

Communist Manifesto. The publication of this document obviously acted as the major catalyst in the growth of the field, by stimulating class-consciousness in a militant fashion. But Dickens and John Stuart Mill anticipate Marx and Engels with excitingly trenchant quotations. Here are some of the terms, arranged in historical order:

1833 J. S. Mill	That blighting curse of our country, the selfishness of *class morality.*
1839 J. S. Mill	The convictions of the mass of mankind run hand in hand with their interests or with their *class feelings.*
1841 Dickens (*Barnaby Rudge*)	If she were in a more elevated station of society, she would be gouty. Being but a hewer of wood and drawer of water, she is a rheumatic.... These are natural *class distinctions.*
1850 Marx and Engels (*Communist Manifesto*)	As the settlement of the *class struggle* draws near.
1850 Kingsley (*Alton Locke*)	All my *class prejudices* against 'game-preserving' aristocrats'.
1851 T. G. Massey	I shall be accused of sowing *class-hatred.*
1852 Dickens (*Bleak House*)	The turkey always troubled with a *class-grievance.*
1864 Marx (*First International*)	. . . *class privileges and monopolies . . . class rule.*

From this small crop a great field has grown. Most of the terms are, of course, extensions or rewordings of the Marxist concept, and virtually all of them reinforce it. They include *class-barrier*, *-bias*, *-bound*, *-boundaries*, *-conflict*, *-dialect*, *-dictatorship*, *-divisions*, *-enemy*, *-ridden*, *-system* and *class-war.*

This proliferation of class-terms is evidence of increasing class-consciousness.[11] Clearly, more was done in the course of the nineteenth century to remove class-barriers than had been achieved in several centuries before. But the removal of each barrier simply made people more conscious of the inequalities that remained, inequalities which had become ingrained as a system of deference. De Tocqueville wryly observed (in his *Ancien Régime*) the same paradoxical political logic in pre-Revolutionary France: 'the condition of the common people had never improved more rapidly than in the twenty years before the cataclysm . . . [but] . . . the French found their position more intolerable the better it became' (in Brown, 1969, p. 107).

So far as Britain is concerned, some of Marx's prophecies show signs of coming true. The proletariat is certainly more powerful than it was when he wrote *Das Kapital* and *The Communist Manifesto.* On the other hand, respect for the monarchy, belief in representative democracy, and respect for private property remain undiminished. The 'public' schools flourish while state education decays. Attempts at the assumption of direct power by the populace are, outside the economic front, virtually unheard of. Extremists are derisively categorized as 'the loony left' and rapidly isolated. Upward mobility between classes, rather than the abolition of them, seems to be the dominant social fact. As Orwell concluded: 'So it comes that each new wave of parvenus, instead of simply replacing the existing ruling class, has adopted its habits, intermarried with it, and, after a generation or two, become indistinguishable from it' (1958, p. 69).

Nevertheless, *class* has become, through high journalism and low, an indispensable term in all social discourse. The traditional Marxist nomenclature of *bourgeois* and *proletariat* has not, however, really been assimilated into the traditional English vocabulary. Instead, categorizations of a more capitalist character are becoming current. These are the market-research social grades (AB for the managerial and professional class and so on) and the latest American formulation *yuppie* ('young upwardly-mobile professional'). Both of these show that, with increasing social mobility, the notion of class is becoming more fluid and dynamic. *Class* itself is increasingly democratized, in that the colloquial sense of 'distinction' or 'high quality' ('It's got real class') is equated with artefacts or 'status symbols' possessing 'style', which can be purchased.

Finally, although deference towards the aristocracy is still generally prevalent, the Royal Family is increasingly the object of egalitarian familiarity, particularly evident in the first-name 'intimate' style used of 'Di', 'Fergie', 'Randy Andy' and the 'banger-biting Duke', as even *The Times* referred to the Duke of Edinburgh. Marx would have been dismayed to discover that, after the Russian Revolution, the leaders rapidly distanced themselves from the proletariat by assuming superhuman, symbolic or elemental names, like *Stalin*, 'man of steel', *Molotov*, 'a hammer', *Lenin*, from the name of the river near which he had been exiled. This 'titanization' is, of course, the opposite of the classless democratization foretold in Marxist prophecy.

CONCLUSION: THE VALIDITY OF THE TERM 'DEMOCRACY'

The amelioration of the term *democracy* has been so powerful that today virtually all political systems, from the most totalitarian to the genuinely liberal, seek to espouse it. However, this very wide application raises the question as to whether the term might not have become something of a misnomer.

It is not feasible for power to be given to the people in the literal fashion which the word implies, if only for the reasons Kenneth Minogue has advanced: 'In modern life, constant fluctuations of opinion would produce chaos if decisions were daily and immediately responsive to shifting tides of popular opinion.'[12] The system whereby a majority vote gives a mandate to temporarily elected representatives seems a suitable variation, though there is always the unresolvable conflict as to where the ultimate allegiance of a Member of Parliament should lie: with the nation, the constituency, the party or self.

Under the British system there seem to be two inadequacies. The first is that the voters do not elect the Prime Minister, let alone any of the Cabinet. The second is that, without proportional representation, governments frequently represent only a minority of the electorate. In the 1987 General Election, 55 per cent of the electorate were unrepresented. Therefore *democracy* in a strict sense is somewhat diluted.

The United States system is more truly democratic in that the voters elect both President and Vice-President.[13] However, because of the system of loaded state electoral votes, minority governments (in terms of total votes cast) do occur, even in a two-party system. One of the most interesting developments in the United Kingdom has been the 'presidential interpretation' put on what is essentially a party election. The BBC World Service headline for 12 June 1987 was: 'Mrs Thatcher has won the British General Election.' Virtually all the British press took a similar interpretation: 'Thatcher's historic victory' (*The Times*) and 'Maggie's Triumph' (*Daily Mail*) were typical treatments. Only the *Independent* accurately interpreted a 'Tory victory'. It is true that the special status and impact of Mrs Thatcher – evidenced in the terms *Thatcherite* (1977[S]) and *Thatcherism* (1979[S]) – contributed to this view, but the presidential interpretation has been developing for decades. The official titles of the two Germanies ('The German Democratic Republic' and 'The Federal Republic of Germany') have an almost Swiftian precision in their inaccuracy. Behind the Iron Curtain, the so-called 'people's democracies' represent the most distorted and cynically inaccurate interpretation of democracy. Gorbachov, Brezhnev and Stalin were no more 'the people's choice' than was Ivan the Terrible.[14]

Some radicals question whether the publicity given to general elections is not a dishonest manipulation of the populace into believing that power really resides with the democratically elected representatives. On this topic Paul Hoch has caustically denounced 'the role of the media in indoctrinating people in a conception of Democracy which revolves around once-every-four-years election charades' (1974, p. 13). While this is undoubtedly an extreme view, it does serve to remind us that parliaments, congresses and their equivalents form only one segment of a power-market also operated by plutocrats, aristocrats, bureaucrats,[15] military strategists, lobbyists and media interests.

NOTES

1 In *The Listener*, 14 July 1977, p. 44.

2 This 'corporate idiom' does not seem to antedate the Elizabethan era, and may be an aspect of the theory of Divine Right.

3 Quoted in Barber (1976), pp. 48–9.

4 Burke's famous 'ruling' on this contentious point occurred in his Speech to the Electors of Bristol (3 November 1774). In his view, Parliament is 'a *deliberative* assembly of *one* nation, with *one* interest, that of the whole. . . . You choose a member indeed; but when you have chosen him, he is not a member of Bristol, but he is a member of *parliament*.'

5 Bryan Magee, 'The language of politics', in *Encounter*, May 1986, p. 20.

6 Quoted in *Encounter*, October 1976, p. 95.

7 H. L. Mencken also expatiated on this tendency in *The American Language* (1919–48), using examples such as *tonsorial parlor* for 'hairdressing saloon'. It is discussed further in ch. 9.

8 Discussed in 'The marketing of Margaret', in *The Listener*, 16 June 1983, p. 3.

9 *Teleprompter* dates from 1951[S], *autocue* from 1958[S]. *The Times* commented: 'The 1960 election had been televised, teleguided, teleprompted and telephoned as no other had been before.'

10 'The English Class System', in Orwell (1958), p. 68.

11 Compare Angus Wilson's interesting observation, 'I was so class-bound that I was not very class-conscious', in *My Oxford*, ed. Ann Thwaite (London, Robson Books, 1977), p. 103.

12 Kenneth Minogue, 'Two hisses for democracy', in *Encounter*, December 1973, p. 61.

13 The Founding Fathers did not believe, however, that the electorate could be entrusted with the election of a President. They accordingly allocated the decision to the elected representatives. The decision is now an automatic matter of party allegiance.

14 As *The Observer* commented in an article on 'The Grooming of Gorbachov' (14 June 1987, p. 17): 'Inside the Soviet Union few people beyond the Central Committee seemed to have any strong impression of him at all.'

15 *Bureaucracy*, stigmatized by Carlyle as 'the Continental nuisance', is now a series of international burgeoning and self-sustaining establishments. *Bureaucracy* itself is recorded from *c.* 1848, and has built up the semantic correlatives of *bureaucratic* (*c.* 1836) and *bureaucrat* (*c.* 1850)[O]. The deterioration of *officious* (originally meaning 'diligent') and the addition of *officialdom* (from *c.* 1863[O]) are also relevant here.

8
Ideology and Propaganda

When they make a wilderness they call it peace.

Tacitus

'Non-intervention' is a word which means much the same as 'intervention'.

Tallyrand

Force, and fraud, are in war the two cardinal virtues.

Hobbes

In wartime, truth is so precious that she should always be attended by a bodyguard of lies.

Churchill

This agglomeration which was called and which still calls itself the Holy Roman Empire was neither holy, nor Roman, nor an empire.

Voltaire

The atmosphere of accredited mendacity.

Lord Acton

It is untrue that I or anyone else in Germany wanted war in 1939. It was desired and instigated exclusively by those international statesmen who were either of Jewish descent or worked for Jewish interests.

Hitler

THOUGH Herodotus, Plato and Vergil indulged in various forms of propaganda,[1] the genre is usually associated in Western culture with the first appearance of the word, recording 'the foundation in Rome during the Papacy of Gregory XIII [*sic*] of what came to be known a few decades later as the Sacred Congregation concerning the propagation of the faith ("de propaganda fide").'[2] The congregation was entrusted with the care and oversight of foreign missions. Evangelism is an essential aspect of Christian faith, but this particular proselytizing movement was more political in motive, being part of the Counter-Reformation. The word *propaganda* seems to be first recorded in English only about a century later, *c.* 1718°, though there is a reference in 1600 to 'the propagating of the Christian faith'. The main semantic trends have been generalization and deterioration. The word is now used of any kind of overt persuasion. Whereas previously it implied a sincere advancement of sectional interests, it now virtually denotes the dissemination of falsehood or half-truth by specious methods. Brande noted as far back as 1842 that the word was 'a term of reproach'. In this century it has become one of the major methods of mobilizing populations on a mass scale, commonly in the furtherance of some pernicious or evil ideology. What is curious about propaganda is that it is often so open and crude in its methods, and yet frighteningly successful in its achievements.

Propaganda is not, of course, confined to a particular mode or medium; it can be found in virtually any kind of public statement, from 'black radio'[3] to a journalistic feature article. Whereas history should be concerned with interpreting the past, and journalism with interpreting the present, propaganda is primarily involved in moulding attitudes to the future. Yet the ostensible historical observation in *The Communist Manifesto* that 'the history of all hitherto existing society is the history of class struggles' is an obviously propagandist statement. Likewise, the description of President Reagan as 'The Zombie President' in the *Observer* (1 March 1987) is of the same order, building up the belief that the person with the greatest power and responsibility in the West is senile and incompetent.

Ideology, as its origin in *logos* suggests, is inextricably related to words, and it is notable how different world-views or theories of society are embedded in various semantic formulas such as *free enterprise*, *nationalization*, *privatization*, *socialism* and the tautologous *people's democracies*. It seems significant that although *ideology* itself is recorded as far back as *c.* 1796° in various general academic senses relating to ideas, the modern political sense is very recent. The *Supplement* traces the sense to 1909 and defines it as 'A systematic scheme of ideas usually relating to politics or society . . . regarded as justifying actions, *especially one that is held implicitly* . . .' (my italics). It is this implicit quality which gives ideology much of its potency. One is reminded here of Sidney Low's observations on the British constitution: 'We live under a system of tacit understandings. But these understandings themselves are not always understood' (1914, p. 12). It was, however, the intention of the coiner of the French form, *idéologie* (Destutt de Tracy), that the term should reveal the basis of social beliefs and collective notions.

Ideology often becomes verbally impacted into social formulas in the course of time. The key word *free* has, over the centuries, compounded into certain formulas describing the institutions and practices of what we now term the Free World. These formulas, which have grown up spontaneously, include *free speech*, *free association*, *free enterprise*, *free market*, *free elections* and *free society*. Ideology can, alternatively, be reinforced by semantic engineering which masks some specific set of interests. The policy of *apartheid* has been underpinned by a whole semantic structure of factitious statutary definitions. These include the special South African discriminatory sense of *group* (= race) in the Group Areas Act; of *pass* (= permit, recorded from *c.* 1828[S]) in the Pass Laws; of *immorality* (= 'sexual offences between white persons and coloured [i.e., non-white] persons') in the Immorality Act (1957); of *homelands* (= non-white group rural areas, recorded from *c.* 1963[S]) in the Homelands Policy; and of *townships* (= non-white group urban areas, recorded from *c.* 1934[S]). The concept of race, though only referred to via oblique euphemistic classifications, frames these formulations with a mutually exclusive rigour: a citizen belonging to one category cannot, perforce, belong to another. National identity is likewise demarcated: acceptance of the status of a 'homelands' nationality excludes South African nationality. This is the corollary of classification according to colour, using *white* (the prestige category), as against *coloured* (recorded from *c.* 1838[S]), *non-white*, and so on.[4] As with the special Nazi sense of *Aryan* and *non-Aryan*, the semantics of apartheid seeks to isolate the 'master-race' from the others.

Ideologues have often exploited emotive formulas, such as Bismarck's *blood and iron*, the fascist variant *blood and soil*, and Hitler's *final solution* and *Thousand-Year Reich* to mobilize the population. (*Motherland* and *fatherland* had started to take on chauvinist overtones during the nineteenth century, but Charles Morley probably did not realize the prophetic quality of his remark in 1874: 'Every German has his dream of a great Fatherland.') However, under the pressure of opposition, semantic shifts are often engineered. Thus Lincoln avoided the highly contentious term *abolition* in the legislation leading up to the Abolition of Slavery, using the variants *abolishment* and *emancipation*. Similarly, the South African government has reacted to overseas disapproval of *apartheid* by renovating or remodelling the policy at intervals in different semantic outfits: *apartheid* (which was itself a substitute for the older paternalistic term *baaskap*) was replaced by *separate development*, which in turn gave way to *plural democracy*, *vertical differentiation* and *multinationalism.* Similarly, the traditional term *native*, previously pejorative from a Euro-centric point of view, started to acquire pre-emptive political associations, and was replaced by the factitious (and ungrammatical) *bantu.* Thereafter *plural* had a brief career, *black* being finally introduced in legislation only in 1978. Beneath the cover of cosmetic semantics, the ideology of difference has remained intact.

Radical movements use the traditional rhetoric of solidarity: *the struggle*, the *revolution*, *the people*, *the workers.* Conservatives prefer patriotic cyphers like *this great nation*, *blood and soil*, *the fatherland.* In South Africa this division of rhetoric is very apparent; so, too, is the particular intensity of the terms *Uncle Tom*, *collaborator* (both innocent before World War 2) and *sell-out* to designate those who are regarded as traitors to the Black cause. Since 1985 the appropriation of the communist term *comrades* by anti-government activists, the borrowing of *vigilante* to designate their opponents and the horrific new incendiary sense of *necklace* all reflect the polarisation of the struggle within the black community.

We should distinguish, therefore, between overt and subsumed propaganda, between the contrived manufacture of ideological statements and the inherited language of communally received attitudes. Whereas *Aryan*, *Herrenvolk* and *Lebensraum* are part of the factitious ideological vocabulary of Nazism, the terms *barbarian*, *savage* and *nigger* are collective forms of inherited prejudice, subsumed over centuries into the matrices of thought and idiom. Overt propaganda uses lies or myths, disinformation of various kinds, and resorts to violent, emotive language of a highly generalized nature: 'The henchmen of colonial racism and of imperial propaganda have tried to cast a curtain of pretences, fallacies, calumnies, scurrility, adulterations and vile accusations to disguise their machinations, their felonies, their knavery, their infamy, their crime and their irresponsibility.'[5] Here the usual modes of civilized thought and speech are entirely abandoned in favour of a tissue of vituperation as insulting to the intelligence of the audience as to the victim. This could be called a typical example of overt propaganda in both style and mode, since propaganda is most readily identified as supporting or attacking an ideology. Hence 'communist/socialist/left-wing propaganda' constitute familiar set-phrases to the citizens of the West; they would be confused and nonplussed by formulations such as 'capitalist propaganda', 'capitalist indoctrination' and 'capitalist sympathizers' as references to advertisements and businessmen. This endemic and deeply rooted prejudice on the matter of propaganda bears out the point made in the definition of *ideology* in the previous chapter, for the 'home' ideology is implicitly acceptable, while the 'foreign' ideology is implicitly affronting or hostile. There seems to be a revealing bias, for example, in the *Supplement*'s definition of *indoctrination*: 'Add ... *spec.* the "instruction" of prisoners of war, etc., in Communist doctrines, ideas, etc.' Is *indoctrination* specifically 'Communist'?

The more an ideology becomes verbally impacted, the more it becomes subsumed propaganda. For instance, the statement that 'this state action is a violation of human rights' assumes that human beings have some rights which are, or should be, inviolable, an assumption which a totalitarian ideology would not uphold. Similarly, 'your actions are endangering law and order' assumes that 'law and order' should protect the status quo, an assumption unacceptable to some radicals and revolutionaries. In each of these cases, values and terminology are almost inseparable. On the other hand, here is an advertisement placed by General Motors in the *New York Times* of 7 November 1974:

> *A Message to America's car buyers ...*
>
> Inflation-weakened America needs common-sense conservation, not empty austerity. Conservation is insulating the attic and saving fuel; austerity is shivering in your living room.
>
> In a similar way, when new cars replace old, the nation's primary means of transportation gains efficiency. Our new 1975 cars conserve gasoline, even as they emit less pollution, provide more safety features, and cost less to operate and maintain than earlier models.
>
> The purchasing of new cars is the common-sense conservation we need. It keeps the wheels of progress rolling. It means growth and investment. This means more jobs for our people, more revenue for our government, more value for our customers, and more dividends for our stockholders.
>
> No growth makes no sense; not for America, not for anyone. Right now is the time to buy a new car.

Here 'growth' is made to appear the same as 'conservation'. The first quality is one of the 'givens' of capitalism; the second had become, at the time of the advertisement, an important manifestation of social responsibility in the period following the rapid increase in oil prices after 1973. But, underpinning the whole statement, is the unstated near-slogan: 'What's good for General Motors is good for America.' The size of the corporation's labour-force, and the ramifications of its activities, are assumed to give it the privileged position of an institution. In short, buying a car is made to sound like a patriotic duty.

The two examples discussed involve various forms of subsumed propaganda, that is to say, the value-systems underlying the language do not have to be defended, or even seriously thought about. The assumptions may be general, as in *the free world*, *free enterprise*, *the right to self-determination*, *the balance of power*, *interference in internal affairs* or a *threat to world peace*. These stereotypic phrases represent part of the currency of international relations, as well as the rationale on which systems and norms are based.

LINGUISTIC XENOPHOBIA

Embedded in the language, either as idiom or as near-cliché, are a variety of xenophobic formulations, such as *the yellow peril*, *the red threat*, *the communist menace* and so on. These are overt examples, formulated by

FIGURE 8.1 The semantic field of xenophobia

Year	*General Terms*	*Specific Terms*
A-S	Heathen	
1500	Infidel Paynim	
	Primitive	
1550		Bugger Turk Greek
		Coolie
1600	Savage Alien Intruder Interloper	Jew Tartar
	Barbarian Foreigner	
1650		
		Vandal Goth
1700		Macaroni
		Dago
1750		Hottentot
		Yankee
1800	Native	Kaffir Nigger Frog Coon Hun
		Frenchy Wi-wi Sheeny
1850		Jap
		Yid Chink
1900		Kike Limey Fritz
		Wop Bosch Gerry Pom Wog Spic
1950		Paki Honky Gook

Note: The dates given are those of the earliest recorded instance of the critical or hostile sense collective fear or by policy. But there are numerous hostile terms which have been spawned over the centuries, some of them apparent even in Anglo-Saxon. The relevant semantic field is set out in figure 8.1, showing the historical development of both general terms, such as *alien* and *savage*, and the more specific words of insult and race-hatred, such as *frog*, *hun* and *gook*. Historically, as is to be expected, the general terms are older, developing with greatest frequency *c.* 1600[O], with Renaissance exploration and the economic competition consequent upon this mercantile expansion. *Interloper* is originally (*c.* 1590[O]) an unauthorized, trespassing trader, before acquiring the more generalized sense (*c.* 1632) of a profiteering opportunist. Likewise *intruder* carries from *c.* 1534[O] a sense of legal usurpation, the modern sense being clearly recorded from *c.* 1588 (in *Titus Andronicus* II. iii. 65: 'Unmannerly intruder as thou art'). The more specific terms grow most abundantly, it appears, from the nineteenth century, synchronously with the development of imperialism and nationalism. Many are thrown up, predictably, by the great wars of the twentieth century. The terms have interesting phonetic similarities, being short and contemptuous (*pom*, *yid*, *frog*, *wop*, *wog*, *bosch/boche*) or conveying a suggestive dislike through ironic diminutive (*yankee*, *limey*, *sheeny*, *frenchy*, *wi-wi*, *whitey*, *honky*, *gerry* and *limey*).

A broad trend can be seen in the development from terms of religious separation, largely the legacy of the Crusades and the Reformation, to terms of national division, the legacy of political wars and imperialism. Of the former group, *bugger* is very much a key term. Deriving from French *Bougre*, ultimately *Bulgarus*, a Bulgarian, it carries the sense of 'heretic' from the fourteenth century (from *c.* 1340) and 'sodomite' from the sixteenth (from *c.* 1555).[O] The first sense would seem to derive from the group's belonging to the Greek Church, and subscribing to the Albigensian heresy. The second appears to be a malicious extension in physical terms of the idea of spiritual perversion. The attribution of 'filthy' sexual practices to freethinkers and religious 'deviants' is, apparently, an ancient form of propaganda. A writer of 1555 abhors 'rancke bouguers with mankinde, and with beastes, as the saracens are'[O].

Of the general terms, *primitive*, *savage*, *barbarian* and *native*, which flourished in the imperialist and colonial era, have since developed neutral senses where this is possible (as in *native*), or fallen into comparative disuse (as in *savage* or *barbarian*). Other factors have contributed, of course. The increasing awareness and unpopularity of racism has had the effect of censorship, driving the more emotive or critical words underground. Anthropological studies have inculcated respect for the complexity of the cultural, social and linguistic systems which 'primitive', 'savage', 'barbarian', 'natives' have evolved.

Barbarian supplies a link with a different form of linguistic xenophobia, shown in a desire to mock and belittle a foreign language, making it approximate (in colonial ears) to child-language. The term derives from a Greek version of Latin *balbus*, 'stammering', being a derisive imitation of the 'primitive' languages encountered. *Barbarian* turns out to be a classic instance of a word infused with chauvinism. Its use spread with the growth of empires, being applied successively to those who were 'non-Hellene', then 'non-Roman', then 'non-Christian'. In the nineteenth century the Western monopoly of the word ceased, for it was applied by the Chinese contemptuously to foreigners, even in official documents. The earliest quotation, from 1549 and in Scots dialect, sums up the application best: 'Euere nation reputis vthers nations to be barbariens.'

MODERN PROPAGANDA

Without explicating all the sordid details, it becomes clear that xenophobia has such an ancient and diversified semantic field that it appears to be generated by some collective psychological and social impulse, principally to identify an exterior enemy, or to create a scapegoat. The main catalysts are military, religious and mercantile competition, but many other factors come periodically into play. In the past these attitudes and their semantic correlatives seem to have developed spontaneously. In this century they have been propagated with terrifying success.

Trevor-Roper (1967) has pointed out the ironic coincidence that it was during the Renaissance – at precisely the time when European culture was freeing itself of the shibboleths and superstitions of the past, when empirical and scientific modes of thought were becoming dominant – that the Continent became convulsed in the collective lunacy of the witch hunt. The twentieth century can no longer regard itself as superior. Strident, hysterical voices have echoed round the world, attended to by vast, supposedly educated, audiences which have listened as in a state of hypnotic trance, and acted like robots. One is reminded of the disturbing irony in Swift's famous letter to Pope (29 September 1725) on the definition of man: 'I have got Materials Towards a Treatis proving the falsity of that Definition *animal rationale*; and to show it should be only [*animal*] *rationis capax.*' Hitlerian propaganda combined with devastating success stereotypes of chauvinism and xenophobia. *Mein Kampf* planned the reunification of 'the great German Motherland' (1938, p. 17), the resuscitation of 'faith in the unconquerableness of the nation' (p. 162) and the destruction of 'the Jewish machine for conquering the world' (p. 190).

Hitler could not be described as having the appearance of an Aryan *Übermensch*. But he certainly had a remarkably charismatic rhetorical style and devastating vocal properties. It is now known that he took secret lessons in acting and voice training from 1932 onwards. Furthermore, he had an intuitive understanding of crowd-psychology, one of the keys to political developments in this century. 'The age we are about to enter,' Gustave Le Bon had written in 1895, 'will in truth be the era of crowds' (1913, p. 15). 'The divine right of the masses,' he continued epigrammatically, 'is about to replace the divine right of kings' (p. 17). Le Bon noted two seminal points. Firstly, that individuals in a crowd are transformed into a 'sort of collective mind' and, more seriously, that 'the sentiment of responsibility which always controls individuals disappears entirely' (pp. 29, 33). He concluded presciently: 'by the mere fact that he forms part of an organised crowd, a man descends several rungs in the ladder of civilisation. Isolated, he may be a cultivated individual; in a crowd, he is a barbarian' (p. 36).

Hitler's philosophy was overtly savage, openly retrogressive. The *Herrenvolk* were invited to be the lords of the jungle, not effete aristocrats: 'I want a forcible, domineering, unflinching, cruel youth. I want to see the free splendid predatory animal spring from their eyes. Thus I will extinguish thousands of years of human domestication' (Neumann and Koppel, 1962, p. 109). He exploited to the full the dynamics of crowd-psychology: 'Mass assemblies are necessary because whilst attending them the individual . . . submits himself to the magic influence of what we call "mass-suggestion"' (Hitler, 1938, pp. 191–2). The magic worked. More than any other previous ideology, Nazism grew through the mass ritual: individuality was submerged (or expelled) in colossal rallies, just as rationality was engulfed by hysterical logorrhea. Astounding histrionic performances, backed up by Goebbels's propaganda machine, transformed *Lebensraum* from the neutral term it had been since *c.* 1905 to a rallying cry justifying expansionist policies, and the Jews from an alien mercantile cum professional group into a scapegoat and a deadly enemy. In his diary Goebbels interpreted the 'real' struggle in these dualistic, Zoroastrian terms: 'If we did not fight the Jews, they would destroy us. It's a life-and-death struggle between the Aryan race and the Jewish bacillus' (quoted in Sington and Weidenfeld, p. 167).

Not only was Hitler democratically elected; his incitements to barbarism were hideously effective. George Steiner's unflinching juxtaposition of high culture and mindless savagery (1969, p. 15) is as regrettable as it is true: 'We know that a man can read Goethe or Rilke in the evening, that he can play Bach and Schubert, and go to do a day's work at Auschwitz in the morning.' The Nazi obsession with anti-Semitism is itself a grim commentary on the efficacy of propaganda. The source was a document called *The Protocols of the Elders of Zion*, ostensibly a record of secret agreements by which 'world Jewry' planned to dominate the world. Various extraordinary theories surrounding the origin of the *Protocols* were current, but in 1934 a judicial enquiry showed that 'the supposed minutes were highly sophisticated forgeries made in the Paris office of the Russian Political Police (the Okrana) probably for use by the Czarist régime against the Russian liberals' (Maser, 1970, p. 165). It is, therefore, the profoundest irony that Hitler, who believed in the efficacy of 'the big lie' with such cynicism, should have fallen victim to such massive deception, or, as it would now be called, *disinformation*.

THE SEMANTIC DISGUISE OF WAR: ANAESTHETIC AND EMOTIVE STYLES

War, which once frankly occupied a central position in the vocabulary, is slipping out of everyday use, to be replaced by locutions such as *armed aggression*, *intervention*, *military operations* and the like. This form of martial camouflage, semantically speaking, has become highly developed in the course of this century in order to mobilize large civilian armies. Particularly since the Second World War, *armies* have been renamed *defence forces*, *Ministries of War* have become *Ministries of Defence*, only a short step away from the Orwellian *Ministry of Peace* in *Nineteen Eighty-Four*. *Campaigns* are called *operations*, *war zones* are called *operational areas*, *battles* are restyled *military engagements*, *bombs* become *explosive devices* if they are small, *strategic weapons* if they are large. *Soldiers* are called *military advisers*, and the exact nature of their line of command is obscured by such terms as *reservists*, *paramilitary units* and the like. Should, however, a significant victory be scored, then an inflammatory, emotive style is employed: 'gallant armies' achieve 'resounding victories' and 'sweep all before them'. By similar stylistic alternation, so long as the enemy is not a threat, its activities are described in contemptuous understatement, with 'pockets of resistance' being 'stamped out', defences collapsing, raw recruits offering little opposition. Should the enemy score significant successes, these are either subjected to a news blackout if the home state is totalitarian, or made out to be insignificant, temporary gains, or made into 'savage atrocities', 'crimes against humanity' or 'genocide'.

Semantic shifts in time of war are nothing new. It is in Thucydides' classic, *The Peloponnesian War*, in fact, that we find the first clear correlation between social change and semantic change in Western consciousness. In the state of 'war psychosis' or 'war hysteria' which existed among the Corcyreans, the martial compulsion dominated everything:

> To fit in with the change of events, words, too, had to change their usual meanings. What used to be thought of as a thoughtless act of aggression was now regarded as the courage one would expect of a party member; to think of the future and wait was merely another way of saying one was a coward; any idea of moderation was just an attempt to disguise one's unmanly character. (1972, Book III, section 28, p. 242)

As George Steiner has said (1961, p. 6), 'We are still waging Peloponnesian wars.' The fundamental change, however, is that Thucydides is describing changes of meaning symbiotic with shifting values in the speech-community. In our time propaganda machines deliberately manipulate meanings to excite or pacify the populace. In part this derives from the necessity of mobilizing large conscripted civilian armies. George Orwell has shown in various of his works a profound understanding of the rationale and workings of political rhetoric. Forty years after it was written, his essay 'Politics and the English Language' has both classic insight and relevance:

> In our time, political speech and writings are largely the defence of the indefensible. Things like the continuance of British rule in India, the Russian purges and deportations, the dropping of the atom bombs on Japan, can indeed be defended, but only by arguments which are too brutal for most people to face, and which do not square with the professed aims of political parties. Thus political language has to consist largely of euphemism, question-begging and sheer cloudy vagueness. Defenceless villages are bombarded from the air, the inhabitants driven out into the countryside, the cattle machine-gunned, the huts set on fire with incendiary bullets; this is called *pacification*. Millions of peasants are robbed of their farms and sent trudging along the roads with no more than they can carry: this is called *transfer of population* or *rectification of frontiers.* People are imprisoned for years without trial, or shot in the back of the neck or sent to die of scurvy in Arctic lumber camps: this is called *elimination of unreliable elements.* (1958, p. 85)

Orwell has grasped intuitively, as several major writers had done before him, the effectiveness of the literary, abstract, latinized register for the purposes of euphemistic vagueness: 'Such phraseology is needed if one wants to name things without calling up mental pictures of them.' It is a considerable irony that Orwell's use of *pacification* in this passage is the first instance cited in the *Supplement.* Unlike the anaesthetic style, which has a bogus rationality and a deceptive 'air of scientific impartiality', the emotive style is overtly propagandist, trading on the favourable associations of root ideological words, such as *freedom*, *patriotism*, *loyalty*, *blood*, *soil*, *fatherland*, *motherland* and the like. The enemy is vilified as *beasts*, *mad dogs*, *vermin*, *monsters*, *murderers* and *rapists.*

THE VOCABULARY OF DEATH

Killing attracts dysphemisms as well as euphemisms into its word-field. But the euphemisms are surprisingly numerous: *make away with*, *put an end to*, *despatch*, *rub out*, *knock off* do not exhaust the list. But none of these would be used for institutionalized or ideological killing. These operations require, it seems, suitably opaque latinization in which process and responsibility can be disguised. *Execution* took on this sense as far back as *c.* 1430[O]. It has since been joined by the sinister henchmen *extermination*, and *elimination*, both of which have specialized from their Latin root-meaning of 'expel' ('drive beyond the borders' and 'thrust out of doors', respectively). The common modern sense of *exterminate* dates from the mid-seventeenth century, and one senses contemporary sectarian strife behind Hobbes's use of the term in *The Leviathan*: 'A People comming into possession of a Land by warre, do not alwaies exterminate the antient inhabitants.' The grim Nazi addition, *extermination camp*, recorded in the *Supplement*, has quotations only from 1945. *Eliminate* appears to be, lexicographically speaking, a war criminal who has escaped detection. Although *OED* sense 4 ('expel, exclude, remove, get rid of') could include human beings, there are no supporting quotations showing this application, nor are they added in the *Supplement*. The sinister sense of *neutralize* also remains unrecorded. These are serious omissions.

One thing is certain. Just as Attila the Hun left behind him the word for funeral, so the systematic slaughter of civilian populations by totalitarian states in this century has left a large semantic legacy. *Liquidate* (etymologically, to make liquid or clear), was extended to mass-murder as a result of the Russian '*purges*' – in itself a strange euphemism to have originated in penitential purification. (It is first recorded in H. G. Wells's description in *The Shape of Things to Come* (1933) of the 'eternal espionage, censorship and "purges" of the G.P.U. [Russian Secret Police]'.) *Liquidate* is derived, appropriately, from Russian *likvidirovat.* Quotations date from 1924, the best being that of C. S. Lewis in 1943: 'Once we killed bad men, now we liquidate unsocial elements.' Other witness words record (albeit imperfectly) the horrors of the century: one is *genocide*, recorded from 1944[S] in the War Crimes tribunal which brought the Nazi rulers to justice. *Holocaust*, literally a 'whole animal sacrifice', is extended to mean 'a great slaughter or massacre' from *c.* 1833[O]; the term seems to have been applied to the mass-murder of the Jews only from 1965[S]. Gil Elliot reminded us (1973, p. 1): 'The number of man-made deaths so far in the twentieth century is about one hundred million.' The nuclear age adds another dimension of horror and new terms to match. The chillingly insane formation *overkill* was coined in 1946[S], followed by the grotesque hybrids *megadeath* and *megacorpse* (for a million dead), dated from 1953 and 1958 respectively[S]. They are especially bizarre in that, unlike words which are the consequence of conflict, they anticipate the nuclear holocaust.

THE DEFINITION OF THE ENEMY

Since the Second World War, formal declarations of war have virtually ceased. The tactical advantage of surprise attack usually counts for more with the aggressor than any moral advantage which might be gained by statements of warning and intention. Wars are now commonly cloaked in the various euphemisms which have previously been mentioned. This new vocabulary is not entirely attributable to the cynical motive of semantic disguise, but also arises from the verbal accommodation of new, less clearly defined forms of aggression, such as the guerrilla war and urban terrorism. Guerrilla warfare, by its very nature, is difficult to categorize; the sporadic and dispersed forays of independent groups are designed to create confusion. Should attacks be carried out against the civilian population, it becomes hard to distinguish between warfare and terrorism. Consequently, the counter-propaganda that the guerrillas are 'little better than criminals' can easily be deployed. Indeed, the clear identification of guerrillas and terrorists with a single ideology has become increasingly difficult to make in modern times. This point becomes very clear if one makes a comparison between the Boers, the Mau Mau, the Baader Meinhof Gang and the Red Brigade. Though all could be styled 'liberation movements', only the actions of the Boers were directed solely against their enemies, the British. All the other groups have resorted to various degrees of terrorism, or 'coercive intimidation', directed against the civilian population, particularly their own potential supporters.

The irregularity of combat characterizing these and such-like 'armies' has meant that a wide variety of terms is applied to them. The four most favoured terms are: *liberation movements*; *freedom fighters*; *guerrillas* and *terrorists.* Clearly, the word chosen reflects the ideology with which the describer wished to imbue the activity. The first two terms are obviously designed to endorse violent revolution, particularly the overthrow of an oligarchy, in the name of 'democracy'; the stress is on ideology rather than action, more so in the first than in the second. With *guerrilla* and *terrorist* the emphasis is plainly on action, and the terms are commonly used polemically to cast aspersions on the ideological commitment of the fighters, and stress their criminality. The ANC (African National Congress), for example, is labelled differently by those in power in Moscow, Washington, London and Pretoria.

The four terms under discussion reveal two other aspects. They range in tone from favourable euphemism (*liberation movements*) to hostile alarm (*terrorists*). They vary greatly in age. *Terrorist* was a product of the Jacobin Reign of Terror, and Burke, in one of the earliest references (1795) writes of 'Thousands of those Hell-hounds called Terrorists'.[0] The word was later applied to extreme revolutionary societies in Russia, where it is particularly associated with Bakunin and with Nechayev, lesser known but whose writings, according to Walter Lacqueur, were 'greater than that of all other apostles [*sic*] of terrorism'.[6] The same writer has argued that Karl Heinzen (1809–80) advanced the idea of terrorism as a revolutionary philosophy some 20 years before Bakunin, and may therefore be termed the 'godfather' of terrorism.

Guerrilla is first found, interestingly, in a despatch (1809) of Wellington's in the Peninsular War, and almost immediately it is shown as 'passing into adj.' Like *terrorist*, it has generalized widely since then, and has become closely associated with anti-colonial military activity. *Freedom-fighter*, now an established cliché, is much more recent, being dated by the *Supplement* to a poem by John Lehmann in 1942. *Liberation movement* remains unrecorded in the *Supplement*, but there is an interesting addition to *liberate*: 'Add: b. To free (an occupied territory) of the enemy; also *ironically*, to subject to a new tyranny.' G. B. Shaw, the coiner, wrote in 1944: 'All your Italian friends must be starving now that we have "liberated" them.' The sense 'To free from social or male-dominated, etc., conventions' is recorded from 1970. The colloquial abbreviation, *libber*, with its subtly scornful tone, dates from the following year. In part, this derives from the suffix, which can be surprisingly effective in discrediting a group or cause, and it is to this device that we now briefly turn.

-ISMS, -ISTS AND -ITES

These suffixes form a useful cache on which the propagand*ist* can draw in seeking to discredit enemies. However, as one scans the *OED* entries, one is struck by the neutrality of the older references and the polemical quality of many of the more recent. *Baptism*, *mechanism*, *altruist*, *antagonist*, *hoplite* and *sybarite* obviously do not have the same emotive sting found in *feminism*, *Quakerism*, *communist*, *imperialist*, *Jacobite* and *Hitlerite.* This apparent neutrality may be the result of increasing familiarity, but it is more likely to have arisen from the widespread use of the suffix in areas of philosophical, religious and political division. The smaller the division, the stronger the partisan tone. Not surprisingly, the use of the suffix was greatly excited by the ructions of the seventeenth century, when the *isms* broke away from established and orthodox groups to become independent. 'He was the great Hieroglyphick of Jesuitism, Puritanism, Quaqerism [*sic*], and of all the Isms from Schism,' wrote one 'Heraclio Democritus' in 1680[S].

From the late eighteenth century, the *isms* proliferate, being 'chiefly used disparagingly'[O]. Shelley comments ironically, 'He is nothing – no "ist", professes no "-ism" but superbism and irrationalism.'[O] Disraeli's offensive against the Russians in 1878 gave birth to *jingoism* (*jingo* having originated two hundred years earlier as a 'piece of conjuror's gibberish'). *John Bullism* thrived (in disparaging use) through the nineteenth century, having had more wholesome origins in the imagination of Dr John Arbuthnot in 1712. Similar strong feelings of *nationalism* (*c.* 1836[O]) threw up *chauvinism* (borrowed into English *c.* 1870[O], by which time the celebration of Chauvin's excessive patriotism had turned to ridicule). Sometimes the suffix is lengthened for effect, as in *communistic*, *fascistic* and so on.

The *-ite* suffix is the most flexible of the three under discussion, 'denoting a disciple, following or adherent, a person or doctrine', and gives rise to *Wycliffite*, *Brontëite*, *Shelleyite*, *Jacobite*, *Luddite* and *Pre-Raphaelite*, *inter alia.* The *OED* observes: 'These have a tendency to be depreciatory, being mostly given by opponents, and seldom acknowledged by those to whom they are applied.' Conspicuous examples in this century are *Trotskyite*, *Hitlerite* (very much a Russian speciality, though recorded from 1930), *McCarthyite* (1952), *Powellite* (1965) and *Thatcherite* (1977). Sometimes the suffix signifies a deviant from orthodoxy (as in *Trotskyite*), but more commonly it is used polemically to vilify the followers of a leader with right-wing or dictatorial characteristics. In such contexts it becomes something of a riposte to the *-ist* suffix, which, Raymond Williams asserts, tends to be used 'from orthodox and conservative positions' (1976, p. 145).

NEWSPEAK

It seems appropriate to conclude this chapter by saluting the intuitive brilliance of George Orwell through a consideration of the linguistic aspects of the bitter dystopia which he created in *Nineteen Eighty-Four* (first published in 1949). To be sure, the convincing impressiveness with which he depicted the horrific shape of things to come has served to prevent realization of some of his prophecies: that is one of the functions of a dystopia. Newspeak is the product of a totalitarian control over semantics, history and the media more ruthlessly complete than any which has yet emerged in the modern world, though the USSR and China approximate to this state to a certain degree. While some languages may be more pliable in the tyrant's cause, it is only English with which we are here concerned.[7]

> The purpose of Newspeak was not only to provide a medium of expression for the world-view and mental habits proper to the devotees of Ingsoc, but to make all other modes of thought impossible. It was intended that when Newspeak had been adopted once and for all and Oldspeak forgotten, a heretical thought – that is, a thought diverging from the principles of Ingsoc – should be literally unthinkable, at least so far as thought is dependent on words. (Orwell, 1972, p. 241)

Such global control of a mental and semantic kind is unlikely to emerge as long as there is rivalry between Peking and Moscow over the 'proper' interpretation of the tenets of communism. The stage has not yet been reached that 'the word *free* [can] only be used in such statements as "This dog is free from lice"' (1972, p. 241).

In the West, the comparative freedom of the media has not necessarily clarified matters. Whereas totalitarian semantic control may produce an unrealistic dogmatism, free semantic enterprise has resulted in an anarchic tug-of-war in which terms like *democracy*, *socialism* and *revolution* become virtually meaningless because they are appropriated by all sections for legitimation and abuse.

Apart from the organized reduction of the vocabulary, surely the most prescient aspect of Newspeak is that designated by Orwell as 'the B vocabulary', which 'consisted of words which had been deliberately constructed for political purposes'. These 'were in all cases compound words', usually of an abbreviated nature: 'Even in the early decades of the twentieth century, telescoped words and phrases had been one of the characteristic features of political language.' Giving the examples of *Nazi*, *Gestapo*, *Comintern*, Orwell observes that such abbreviations were 'most marked in totalitarian countries and totalitarian organizations'. This is no longer so. On the model of *Gestapo* (*Ge*heime *Sta*ats*po*lizei), the secret agencies of nearly all countries use institutionalized code names: MI5, NKVD, FBI, CIA, Politburo, Boss, Sureté, Ogpu, MVD, Okhrana and KGB. Not only has *Big Brother* passed into the language; his associates have come too. The acronym imparts a legitimacy to the secrecy of the agency, an extension of the abbreviating of a name, whereby, as Orwell shrewdly observes, 'one narrowed and subtly altered its meaning, by cutting out most of the associations that would otherwise cling to it'. He continues with this excellent example:

> The words *Communist International*, for instance, call up a composite picture of universal human brotherhood, red flags, barricades, Karl Marx, and the Paris Commune. The word *Comintern*, on the other hand, suggests merely a tightly-knit organization and a well-defined body of doctrine . . . *Comintern* is a word that can be uttered almost without taking thought, whereas *Communist International* is a phrase over which one is obliged to linger at least momentarily. (1972, pp. 247–8)

Compounds, as was pointed out in chapter 6, tend to produce ambiguity and opaqueness, particularly when they are made up of two general terms, such as *handbook*, or Orwell's *prolefeed* and *bellyfeel.* Furthermore, the possibility of ambiguity increases as the language gains in grammatical flexibility. Modern English has developed substantially in this direction (as is mentioned at the end of chapter 9). In the era of Newspeak there is 'almost complete interchangeability between different parts of speech' (p. 242). In the *Orwellian* dystopia the aim is to make the language a rigorous instrument of orthodoxy (*goodthink*); but this is achieved as much by the powerful central defining authority as through the truncated form of the language itself. (*Goodthink* suggests quite other 'unorthodox' meanings to us, outside the language-prison of the book.) In fact, the absence of such an authority in the West has meant that much ideological language has become very vague, with the flexibility of the language increasing the potential for opacity.

DOUBLETHINK

George Steiner rightly cites Orwell's exposure 'of how the word may lose its humane meanings under the pressure of political bestiality and falsehood. We have scarcely begun, as yet, to apply [his] insights to the actual history of language and feeling' (1969, p. 136). Steiner is particularly incensed at 'the acrobatics of oblivion which followed the fall of Nazism'. Curiously, he does not refer to *doublethink*, Orwell's brilliant diagnosis of the simultaneous accommodation of fact and myth. This seminal insight into the workings of Ingsoc is discovered by Winston Smith as he clandestinely reads the third chapter, 'War is Peace', of Emmanuel Goldstein's *The Theory and Practice of Oligarchical Collectivism*:

> *Doublethink* means the power of holding two contradictory beliefs in one's mind simultaneously, and accepting both of them. . . . The Party intellectual knows in which direction his memories must be altered; he therefore knows that he is playing tricks with reality; but by the exercise of *doublethink* he also satisfies himself that reality is not violated. . . . *Doublethink* lies at the very heart of Ingsoc, since the essential act of the Party is to use conscious deception while retaining the firmness of purpose that goes with complete honesty. (Orwell, 1972, p. 171)

The totally cynical manipulation of history and semantics which *Nineteen Eighty-Four* depicts has not really been achieved in the West. And yet the concept of *doublethink* exactly describes the ambivalence and confusion created in the ordinary citizen by the counter-claims of 'patriotic duty' and 'idealistic commitment' on the one hand, set against *realpolitik*, 'political realities' or 'power politics' on the other. Orwell's stupefying slogan 'WAR IS PEACE' is only an extreme form (writ large) of the much-quoted military axiom 'Attack is the best form of defence.' It illuminates much of the paradoxical logic of the present nuclear debate, of arming for a war in which there will be no survivors, of building deterrents which must never be used, and have doubly failed when they are used. *Doublethink* perfectly describes the ambivalence and duplicity of much foreign policy, especially that of Ministries of 'Defence' maintaining (in a clandestine fashion) 'contained' guerrilla wars in order to keep a strategic hold over a region without allowing the situation to develop into 'real', 'open' war.

Steiner discourses brilliantly in *The Death of Tragedy* on the hypnotic quality of propaganda:

> Words carry us forward toward ideological confrontations from which there is no retreat. This is the root tragedy of politics. Slogans, clichés, rhetorical abstractions, false antitheses come to possess the mind (the 'Thousand Year Reich,' 'Unconditional Surrender,' the 'class war'). Political conduct is no longer spontaneous or responsive to reality. It freezes around a core of dead rhetoric. Instead of making politics dubious and provisional . . . language encloses politicians in the blindness of certainty or the illusion of justice. The life of the mind is narrowed or arrested by the weight of its eloquence. Instead of becoming masters of language, we become its servants. (1961, pp. 56–7)

When Steiner's work was published in 1961, its pessimism seemed unanswerable. The Vietnam War was being fought under the established rhetoric of 'our country right or wrong', 'making the world safe for democracy', 'countering the red threat' and 'ensuring the Vietnamese right to self-determination'. But by the end of the decade, the mood in the United States was distinctly mutinous. Draft cards were being burnt, vast rallies of protest were being organized; even the *New Yorker* commented on the 'credibility gap' which was being exposed in communiqués:

> In the language used in discussing this nation's involvement [*sic*] in Vietnam, there is a growing number of words by which meaning, instead of being underlined and made memorable, is hidden and bypassed.... We march to Vietnam under such bannerets as 'escalate,' 'defoliate,' 'pacification,' 'counterforce concept,' 'controlled responses,' 'damage-limitation forces,' 'benevolent incapacitators,' and 'targeting lists.' (8 May 1965)

A more polemical, indeed subversive, gloss on the situation is to be found in the ironic *Great Society Dictionary*, by Edward S. Herman. In this piece of powerful 'consciousness-raising', *zap* is defined as 'to shoot down in cold blood, especially a Gook'; an *enemy structure* is 'a thatched hut that we destroy'; a *home* is the same, but with 'they' replacing 'we'.

Undoubtedly, the strongest force in resisting the war was not language, but image. Television served to undermine the rhetoric by revealing the reality of human suffering. No abstract latinization could dispel the publicized horrors of *napalm*, which, unleashed from its textbook existence, reduced the skin to a crust like crackling and destroyed the shape of the body. As McLuhan commented in *McLuhan Hot and Cool*: 'TV news coverage of Vietnam has become a disaster as far as Washington is concerned because it has alienated people altogether from that war' (ed. G. E. Stearn (1968), p. 313).

As was seen at the conclusion to the previous chapter, the principal effect of television on American presidential politics (and subsequently in the United Kingdom) has been to devalue language in a way which can only be condemned. In a war situation, television can become the unwitting agent of the truth, exposing the big lie or the unreal claim. It simply depends on what 'the authorities' (whether capitalist media barons, state broadcasting systems or Big Brother) allow the people to see and know.

Propaganda posits in its most acute form the problem of belief in both its psychological and mass mediated aspects. In earlier times of religious extremism such as the Inquisition one could point to the gruesome *auto da fé*, observing that its etymology carried a grim warning, in that the phrase signified an *act of faith.* In this century we have witnessed mass barbarism perpetrated by supposedly civilized and liberated people without the fanatic psychology of projected guilt, dogmatic self-righteousness and superstitious fear which characterized the earlier witch hunt. Psychologically, there is an essential element of wish-fulfilment which lies at the heart of the term *believe*, for the word is fundamentally related to the roots *love* and *lief*, deriving from a Teutonic ancestor **lub*, 'to hold dear, to like'. Given this essentially irrational basis for belief, in that it rests on grounds insufficient for complete demonstration, the attraction of 'the big lie' is merely a logical extension, whereby the preposterous can – paradoxically – lay claim to greater credibility. In addition, there often exists a mediated conspiracy to manipulate the truth, evidenced in the burgeoning practice of *disinformation*. The word is unique in that it is a translation into English of Russian *desinformatsiya*, itself a translation of an Anglicized 'word' which did not originally exist. (This attribution of the word to a foreign source is an effective piece of propaganda in itself.) In Russian the term is the official title of a department of the KGB which plans, co-ordinates and organizes sophisticated political deception on a global scale. To most Westerners, the associations of the term are almost exclusively with ruthless Soviet state-police manipulation. However, the Watergate and Irangate scandals and some of the security leaks in the wake of the Falklands War suggest that disinformation can be used as a weapon in internal power-struggles and not only as a technique of foreign policy.

Perhaps the key term behind much of this chicanery is *security*. This rich and complex word has moved from the spiritual domain into the material and finally into the political. *Security* dates from *c.* 1432°, and though its dominant sense is naturally expressive of the profound human need for 'the condition of being secure', the word was formerly used to convey specifically 'a culpable sense of anxiety, carelessness'. This meaning is recorded from *c.* 1555°, the classic instance being 'Security is mortals' chiefest enemy', a sententia uttered by the witch Hecate in *Macbeth* (III. v. 32–3). This is totally at odds with the modern sense: one cannot imagine it, for example, as a piece of memorabilia in the waiting-room of a psychiatrist, or on the desk of a bank manager or Chief of Staff. Both capitalist enterprise, in the form of banks and insurance companies, and the state, in the form of the *security forces*, the *security police* and so on, have made security into a highly desirable quality.

The amelioration can be seen as a reflection of the increasing secularization of Western society. Hecate's *mot* is essentially a spiritual statement concerning the lack of moral vigilance which is the common consequence of material success. The state of the soul, and the consequent prospect of salvation and damnation being no longer the primary concern of most people in the West, it is inevitable that the more efficient protection of material wealth should become a dominant interest and an achievable good. Today there is an assumption that the individual has a right to security, financial, material and psychological. Only the more sceptical would endorse Germaine Greer's ironic remark: 'The only place that you can achieve security is in a maximum security prison' (1971, p. 255).

Whatever the claims of indivdual security, they cannot compare with the priorities now accorded *national security.* This has acquired the status of ultimate, virtually sacrosanct authority, and so can be invoked to motivate, defend or conceal any stratagem, policy or exploit. It is the ultimate password. Its status became especially apparent in the US Senate sittings in 1986–7 investigating the covert intelligence operations journalistically termed Irangate. The mere utterance of the word seemed to have the force of a spell. The rulers of many modern states exercise their discretionary right to preserve *national security* by any means. They can attribute the practice, after all, to the policy advocated by a respected philosopher: 'It will be for the rulers of our city, then, if anyone, to deceive citizen or enemy for the good of the State; no one else must do so.' The philosopher was not Machiavelli, nor Hobbes, but Plato, in *The Republic* (1955, p. 126).

NOTES

1 These three figures do not, of course, exhaust the list. Herodotus has been called 'the first person to write a patriotic history' (Fraser, 1957, p. 16). Vergil's *Aeneid* is more of a patriotic myth, whereas Plato is quite ruthless in proposing thought-control in lieu of education in *The Republic.*

2 Fraser, 1957, p. 22. The *OED* states that the College of the Propaganda was 'founded in 1622 by Pope Gregory XV'.

3 'Black' radio, one of the techniques of disinformation in political warfare, involves simulating a target radio station in order to feed the listeners propaganda.

4 *Coloured* and *non-white* both have earlier American uses, dating from *c.* 1760 and 1921, respectively.[S] *Apartheid* seems to have been first coined by General Smuts in 1917, but had little currency before the Nationalist Party's electoral campaign in 1948.

5 The Cuban Foreign Minister, addressing the United Nations in 1973 on Chile.

6 Walter Lacqueur, 'Karl Heinzen: the origins of modern terrorism', *Encounter*, August 1977, p. 23.

7 Nietzsche wrote presciently in 1882 in *The Joyful Wisdom*: 'It is certain that the Germans martialise themselves at present in the tone of their language . . . the officer, and in fact the Prussian officer, is the inventor of these tones [which show] something mocking, cold, indifferent in the voice' (1924, pp. 141–3).

9
Conclusion: Verbicide and Semantic Engineering

Everything belongs together in the human understanding; the obscurity of one idea spreads over those that surround it. An error throws shadows over neighbouring truths, and if it happens that there should be men in society interested in forming, as it were, centres of shadow, even the people will find itself plunged into a profound darkness.

Diderot

Words strain,
Crack and sometimes break, under the burden,
Under the tension, slip, slide, perish,
Decay with imprecision, will not stay in place
Will not stay still.

T. S. Eliot

IT EMERGES that a remarkably close relationship exists between social change and semantic change. Indeed, it is not claiming too much to assert that no major social development has been lacking in semantic correlatives. Radical and revealing shifts of meaning can be seen in the terminologies of politics, economics, education, marketing and war. Often, semantic trends such as the moralization of status-words, the secularization of religious terminology, the democratization of class-terms and the moralization of learning, illuminate important and subtle changes which do not fall within the ambit of traditional disciplines. Semantic change is a kind of evidence in itself, one which should play an important role in the discussion of social change.

The influential Saussurean emphasis on the 'arbitrary nature of the sign', that is to say on the unfixed relationship between word and meaning, requires some revision. To be sure, there is no *inherent* relationship between, say, the word *table* and the object table. This situation applies to great numbers of words. But there are several significant areas of English – especially in its Germanic roots – where a mimetic relationship between phonetic form and meaning can be posited: the similarity between the physical activity of enunciation is integral to meaning in, for instance, *spit*, *spew*, *spatter*, *spurt* and many base Germanic words starting with *sp-*. One can see a similar phonetic symbolism in *shudder*, *quiver*, *judder* and *shiver*. The *Oxford Dictionary of Etymology* specifically comments in this respect on the *wr-* consonant combination as 'occurring initially in many words implying twisting or distortion'. Examples would include *wrap*, *wrestle*, *wrest*, *wrinkle*, *wriggle* and a fascinating diversity of words which we would not normally think of under this category, namely *wrist*, *write* and *wrong*. These examples are synchronic, concerned with language as a static system. The study of language in its dynamic or historical evolution (especially the aspect of semantic change) shows clearly that the relationship between words and developing meaning is by no means arbitrary, but directly reflects significant social pressures, changing mores and values.

Technical terms either metamorphose to accommodate new developments, or wither away. (*Dashboard*, an example of the first, was in coaching times a board to stop muck and dung from spattering the driver. *Pen*, originally a feather, is fast becoming obsolete.) Transactional terms, such as *purchase*, *pay* and *vote*, reflect their respectively altered modes. Value-terms, or key words, have an ambivalent or symbiotic relationship to mores and social institutions: they create, they reflect and they reinforce values. Thus, the currency of *freedom*, *self-determination*, *conspicuous consumption* and *affirmative action* is not simply a reflection of these aspirations, but evidence of their continuing value. Significantly, they need not be 'communal coinages', so to speak: *Protestant Work Ethic* was the brilliant formulation of Max Weber, while 'No Taxation without Representation', became a revolutionary slogan based on the words of James Otis. They described the communal aspirations or acceptable behaviour-models of their societies so perfectly that they became ethical slogans or frameworks of understanding. *Freedom*, on the other hand, reflects in its semantic changes the slow evolution of society from a feudal to a democratic basis.

Though verbal 'currency' can be manipulated by those in control of the mass media, it remains an important indicator of value. For example, the limited currency now enjoyed by such terms as *honour*, *virtue*, *temperance*, *modesty*, *chastity* and *virginity*, indicates that they no longer form a central part of a meaningful moral vocabulary. The traditional, rigorous vocabulary of sin and virtue has given way to nebulous, quasi- sociological, concepts of 'normality'. Though *normal* should relate in meaning to *norm* – a scientifically established mean of human behaviour – it tends to oscillate between such scientific restrictions and the tautological notion of 'what the popular conception of normal is'. Behaviourist terms like *pervert*, *deviant* and *delinquent*, reflect a transference of guilt from the individual to environmental factors in an amorphous 'society'. These and the host of Graeco-Latin psychological terms, such as *trauma*, *neurosis*, *psychosis*, *mania*, *projection*, *sublimation* and *rationalization*, were coined or modified to be scientific and non-judgemental, but many are nevertheless increasingly used with hostility and emotive looseness, especially in the adjectival forms *maniac*, *psychotic*, etc. The legacy of behaviourism is also to be found in the mechanistic vocabulary now used of the human personality e.g. 'defence *mechanism*', 'attention-getting *device*', *knee-jerk reaction*, *maladjusted* and many others. (The extension of *stress*, *strain* and *pressure* from physics to human behaviour is also very recent, and only scantily recorded.) The *anomie* or 'normlessness' which Durkheim intuitively analysed to be the distinctive disorientation of modern culture has become evident in the collapse of shared values, ironically highlighted by the scrutiny of statistical methods which reveal the relativity and randomness of human behaviour.[1] Traditional value-terms have, expectedly, shifted in response.

Many terms reflect a culture which is materialistic, superficial and exhibitionist. The essentially mediated and amoral nature of modern 'success' is reflected in the development of the terms *celebrity* (secularized), *personality* (inflated), *prestige* (ameliorated) and *charisma* (trivialized). *Success* (which used to mean simply 'outcome') itself forms part of a revealing word-field reflecting the moralization of value-terms which are imprecise or directionless, such as *progress*, *relevance*, *concern*, *commitment* and *awareness.* Another fashionable word-field reflects the increasing prevalence of the language of 'accidents' (the superficial) as against 'substance' (the essential), especially through theatrical metaphors: *image*, *model*, *scenario*, *game*, *token*, *role*, *drama*, *stance* and *pose* are the more obvious examples. *Model* is especially revealing, having moved from the sense of 'an ideal example' in *model answer*, *model pupil* and so on, to the twentieth-century version of a sexual object displaying clothes, jewellery, accessories, perfume, in fact anything or nothing. Style, rather than content, is the aspect stressed in *cool*, *laid back*, *with it* and *uptight.* Blatant emphasis on physique, to the exclusion of any other attributes, has been the justifiable source of much feminist comment. Even in the male domain there is the symptomatic proliferation of brawn in *he-man*, *muscleman*, *beefcake*, *stud*, *jock* and *hunk*, and their despised antitypes *nerd*, *weed*, *wimp* and *wet*. (Old-fashioned terms like *rotter*, *bounder* and *cad* did at least have a moral base.)

A further field comprises 'active' terms such as *dynamic*, *vibrant*, *energetic*, *action* and *speed. Speed*, we should recall, originally meant 'success', a meaning which is still fossilized in the idiomatic phrase 'more haste, less speed'. *Action*, whether applied to sporting, dramatic or military events, has become a dominating obsession, especially in popular media and culture. Similarly, *modern* (only coined in 1500), *new*, *novel* (adj.) *novelty*, *up-to-date*, *up-to-the-minute* and their numerous associates have shown steady amelioration. (*New-fangled* has had a critical sense ever since it first appeared in the pages of Chaucer.) The ultimate accolade of modernity and excellence is now encoded in the curiously opaque phrase *state of the art.* Contrariwise, one can see the deterioration of the antonymic counterparts *traditional* and *old-fashioned.* The cult of youth has, no doubt, been a major factor in this development, even though the plain descriptive noun *youth* no longer implies innocence and *joie de vivre*; the more modern associations are of hostility or aggression, typified in *hooligans* (1898), *teddy-boys* (1954), *mods* (1960) and *rockers* (1963), *skinheads* (1969) and *punks* (1974). It is notable that *senile*, now often used in a dismissive and impatient fashion, used to be a neutral term, rather as its relation *senior* still is. Respect for one's elders breathes through this description (from 1661) of 'A person in whom Nature, Education and Time have happily Match'd a Senile Maturity of Judgement.' In all these fields, semantic shifts reflect the instability of values in modern civilization in the West.

The influence of the media has been as great on language as on any other aspect of the social fabric. The invention of movable type, initially a stabilizing and unifying influence on language, has since made the language malleable and vulnerable to numerous vested interests. It has become possible for oligarchies commanding access to the media to take advantage of the general state of semantic anarchy by commandeering words and abstracting desired meanings from them. It is no coincidence, therefore, that it should be in those processes where business (money) and government (power) most directly need to manipulate the public that the greatest semantic damage has been done: namely, in advertising, political rhetoric and propaganda. Linguistic capitalism, whereby words are simply appropriated in order that their favourable overtones may benefit a promotion, is now *de rigueur*. It goes without saying that the most important right of government (after self-preservation) is, via the law, to the definition of anything it chooses in the terms it chooses. In totalitarian regimes the terminology does not require even the sanction of an opposition or dissent, so that the greatest 'Orwellian' shifts of meaning can be engineered. However, even in capitalist democracies, the state of linguistic pollution is generally accepted with cynical apathy, punctuated by occasional expressions of outrage. Only vested commercial and political interests protect their corner of the market against intruding competition. The effect of television has been to relegate language to the cause of image-building. This downgrading of language is tacitly admitted in television advertising in the United States, where infantile or comic characterization is increasingly assumed, or varieties of suggestive noises are employed in preference to words, or articulate forms of persuasion.

So far as language variation is concerned, several major developments have occurred. The first is that the separation of registers, a marked feature of the sensitive use of the lexicon since the beginnings of English is becoming less formally observed. This is particularly the case in the United States, for in the democratic ethos it behoves any dignitary, including the President, to use the lower registers in order to persuade his fellow-Americans that he has 'the common touch'. Though one can imagine some earlier presidents castigating oil companies for excessive profiteering, only one of the more recent (President Carter) would use a locution such as 'the greatest rip-off in American history'. In similar vein, President Reagan announced his second term in office with the momentous banality: 'You ain't seen nothing yet!' As is shown in chapter 5, the mixing of registers has become a tradition in American journalism. Even the BBC now regularly uses *row* for 'confrontation' or 'disagreement' and *cash* for 'funds'.

The higher registers are by no means atrophying. But they are increasingly sustained for dubious purposes. They provide caches of rare words useful to those seeking to mystify or impress a gullible public. Shaw's comment in *The Doctor's Dilemma*: 'All professions are conspiracies against the laity' is very apposite linguistically. To a certain extent, a slight language-barrier is inevitable in medicine, since nearly all the adjectives describing parts of the body are latinized: *oral*, *cranial*, *aural*, *dental*, *digital*, etc., have no natural native equivalent, since '*mouthly*', '*skully*', '*early*', '*toothly*' and '*fingerly*' would now seem absurd. The Renaissance saw the borrowing of a whole register of these classically derived medical terms:

Nouns		Adjectives	
fracture	(1541)	*optical*	(1570)
cranium	(1543)	*dental*	(1599)
tibia	(1548)	*visual*	(1603/26)
femur	(1563)	*oral*	(1625)
larynx	(1578)	*vocal*	(1644)
pancreas	(1578)	*nasal*	(1656)
sinus	(1597)	*morbid*	(1656)

The process of *dissociation*, the borrowing of opaque foreign terms, started soon after the Conquest and has been steadily extended, often for motives of pretence and obfuscation. In recent years Latin *doctor*, which supplanted Saxon *leech* centuries ago, is being replaced (particularly in the US) by Greek *physician.* Similarly, *healing* gave way to *treatment*, which in turn is being replaced by *therapy.* It does not seem a coincidence that the most lucrative (if not the most respected) specialisms in the profession are comparatively recent offshoots with Greek titles: *psychiatrist*, *gynaecologist*, *paediatrician*, *orthodontist*, *gerontologist.* (The only branch of medicine with an Anglo-Saxon name is *midwifery.*) The euphemism or inflation of occupational titles is an ancient process, found at least as far back as Chaucer's youth. De Tocqueville observed, and Mencken concurred, that the process is highly developed in the United States, where rat-catchers are styled *rodent operatives* and greengrocers have been termed *vegetable executives.*

The greatest growth-area of latinism has been in the scientific field. Science generates concepts and vocabulary at a great rate; even within a generation the layman falls behind in familiarity, let alone comprehension. The advance of scientific knowledge has required considerable lexical change, whereas in the field of the humanities there has been slower semantic evolution. It is a truism to say that science has become a respected power in a world of crumbling authority. Having largely supplanted religion – as that term is generally understood – it is making considerable inroads into the field of the humanities, with their active connivance or support. The title, the methods and the vocabulary of science are seized upon, with all the avidity of the superstitious, by disciplines anxious about their 'function' and the intellectual coherence of their subject. There is thus a proliferation of imitation sciences: Human Sciences, Communications Science, Social Science, Political Science, Library Science, Health Science. The true sciences, that is those that deal with theorems rather than theories, with precisely verifiable data rather than observations tinged with subjectivity, have started to call themselves the 'exact sciences', a title which *should* be a tautology. In almost any field of the humanities it is now commonplace to come across such terms as *science*, *experiment*, *organic*, *mechanics*, *machinery*, *formula*, *analysis*, *synthesis*, *theory*, *data*, *ratio*, *structure*, *component*, *dynamic* and *apparatus*. Very often the use of such terminology is not matched by the appropriate scientific method, but is a pretentious mask for a traditional, subjective approach. New waves of inkhorn terms, typified by the following sample, appear in the avant-garde journals:

> The literary *sign* is powerfully overdetermined, that is to say, it gathers sense through a wide network of syntactic and semantic relations manifest in the text itself by its very textual situation – a situation that endows it at once with syntagmatic (horizontal) and paradigmatic (vertical) meanings – over and above those values that it assumes through its *macro*textual and *inter*textual allegiances.[2]

Not surprisingly, *semantics* itself has become a suspect word. Nor are the politicians solely to blame. When the ingenuity of scholars is spent constructing grammatical nonsense (or 'un-sense') such as Chomsky's 'Colourless green ideas sleep furiously', then laypeople justifiably feel that they are playing word-games while the language burns.[3] The fascination with theory and the laborious unravelling of pseudo-problems seem to be an abdication of semantic responsibility. A few years ago, in a study which took a sardonic look at the current state of English, Kenneth Hudson introduced this ingenious comment on academic jargon:

> An American Christmas card, produced by one of the wittier members of the academic world, takes the form of three concentric and revolving discs and caricatures the pseudo-scientific style and approach in a masterly fashion. Each disc carries 24 words of this kind and by rotating the discs one can build up a large number of magnificent but totally meaningless phrases, of the kind that stops communication in its tracks. One can have, for instance, 'child-centred procedural dysfunction', or 'innovatory motivational maladjustment', or 'basic theoretical strategy'. The full range of socio-psychological rubbish is here, ready to dope and bemuse the unwary, and to entertain the privileged and dangerous few who have seen through it all. For those who would find it convenient to have this select vocabulary for reference, the words are:
>
> *Outer disc* Activities; communication; resources; synthesis; validation; techniques; consensus; maladjustment; sector; criteria; autonomy; analysis; polarisation; objectivity; strategy; situation; over-involvement; evaluation; components; dysfunction; methodology; quotients; reorganisation; rationalisation.

Middle disc Consultative: empirical; unstructured; implicit; perceptual; psycho-linguistic; co-educational; reactionary; motivational; academic; conceptual; experimental; socio-economic; hypothetical; ideological; theoretical; developmental; compensatory; diagnostic; meaningful; procedural; significant; democratic; sociometric.

Inner disc Disadvantaged; on-going; informal; ultra; inter-disciplinary; cognitive; relevant; correlated; extra; innovatory; viable; supportive; élitist; micro; creative; advanced; basic; divergent; programmed; operational; affective; child-centred; multi; emotive. (Hudson, 1977a, pp. xviii–xix)

These collocations of high-sounding nonsense suggest, through their opaque plausibility, that the aleatory principle evident in the modern and contemporary arts is infiltrating the language of some 'sciences'. Time has certainly vindicated the judgement of George Steiner in 1961: 'Much of present sociology is illiterate. It is conceived in a jargon of vehement obscurity.[4]

When academics in the humanities use language as loosely as this, it is hardly surprising that businessmen appropriate the word 'philosophy', 'research' is debased to dignify virtually any enquiry, and 'discipline' becomes no more than an intellectual vogue-word.

A seminal point concerning the true sciences is that their terminology has to match the elements described and their interrelationship by being extremely flexible. *Aluminium* or *gravity* are thus, like many similar terms, capable of being simple nouns, compounds or adjectives, according to function. This flexibility naturally derives from the shorthand language of the equation, the compound and the formula. The same features are extended, however, to the more general terms of scientific discourse, such as *energy* and *mass*, which have a large general currency. The most marked area of growth is that of opaque adjectives, or nouns used with adjectival function. Thus, the traditional adjective *gravitational* is increasingly ignored, being supplanted in formations such as *gravity anomaly* and *gravity-collapse structure.* Technical uses culled from the *Supplement* show a great proliferation of these opaque uses: 'the limited stock of abiotically-formed energy-rich molecules'; 'positive rather than negative gravity anomalies'; 'the more modern mass spectrographic determinations'.

These uses can be understood, even by lay readers, but understanding is impeded by the tendency towards *agglutination*, through the omission of prepositions and articles, the dominance of noun-forms forced into unnatural contortions of flexibility, particularly as adjective-trains whose sheer weight often exhausts the verb. These developments are strikingly analogous to 'headlinese' (discussed in chapter 5) and to 'adjective-shunting' (discussed in chapter 6). Agglutination is more natural to Greek or Latin, which have a much greater degree of synthesis, or grammatical inflections. Hence, for example, *lecithotrophic*, a typical scientific formation, defined as: 'Of the larvae of certain marine invertebrates, feeding on the yolk of the egg from which they have just emerged.' Twenty words of English are needed to translate fourteen letters in Greek.

The agglutinative idiom, natural to German (which has *Glaubensbekenntnis* for *creed*), partially evident in Old English (which has *staþolfæstlic* for *firm* and *mishealdsumness* for *negligence*), is properly alien to Modern English. It is, nevertheless, increasingly encountered in a great variety of contexts, as in 'fabulous French jet-set mecca' (Nice), 'nature conservation control areas' and 'the United States' inter-continental ballistic missile capability'. Depending on their context and function, such coagulated blocks approximate to jargon, gobbledygook or gibberish. The fact that the units are not technically melded together (as in true agglutination) does not make these ungainly conglomerations readily comprehensible. There are also retrogressive affinities to pidgin: 'I want a take-away super economy double cheeseburger' shows some approximation to Cameroon Pidgin 'You go chop di fain fain swit beef'.

The greatly increased use of *maxi-*, *mini-*, *super-*, *hyper-*, *anti-* and *pro-* generates numerous flexible compounds, such as 'anti-war demonstrations', 'pro-government media campaigns' and so on. In fact, just as *mini* and *maxi* became independent terms of fashion in the 1960s, so *anti* and *pro* can now be used in isolation: 'He's anti the idea.' The increasing assumption is that these forms can be added to words with the ease that plus and minus signs can be added to numbers in an equation. There is also the actual use of *plus* and *minus* in such phrases as 'the plus factor', '*charisma* is a plus word' and 'a minus factor'. (*Plus*, in this era of positive thinking, is the more common.) The developing idiom of arithmetical syntax, particularly prevalent in the United States, allows the use of these words and their contingent phrases on the model of an algebraic formulation such as '$+ (x - y)$': 'He's a friend *plus* he's going to be in the neighbourhood, so I think we should invite him.' This kind of syntax is frequently introduced by the phrase *on account of*: 'I won't go to Miami on account of I don't like planes.' The *Supplement* records this usage from *c.* 1936 as slang, used in Evelyn Waugh and P. G. Wodehouse: 'I was feeling kind of down on account that tooth of mine was giving me the devil.' Particularly in space fiction, the humans speak in a clipped form of *robotese*: *Astronaut X*: 'Shall I lock cabin hatch for security?' *Astronaut Y*: 'Negative.'

Science has brought many other concepts in its wake. *Relativity*, first coined by Coleridge *c.* 1834, was given a new and startling force by Einstein in 1905. His original 'special theory of relativity' has since become a principle. The consequences were perhaps best put by Haldane when he said, 'The world is not only queerer than we imagine, it is queerer than we can imagine.' Relativity has affected, not just the rarefied world of experimental physics, but the value-terms which define a culture. *Value* itself is increasingly made relative, a symptom and a product of *anomie*, so that its old, absolute sense gives way to the plural form *values.* The same process shows *morals* being replaced by *mores*, *liberty* replaced by *freedoms*, *right* by *rights*,[5] *skill* by *skills*, *taste* by *fashion*, *authority* by *authorities. Culture*, not surprisingly, is atomized into *sub-culture*, *pop-culture*, *counter-culture*, *meta-culture* and *high culture.*

The familiar theme of disintegration has many ramifications. Whereas previously the models and the language of politics, the economy, the family and the personality were integrative, they are increasingly becoming divisive. To be sure, previous historians and writers detected the signs of conflict and competitiveness behind the façade of 'the nation', 'the commonwealth', 'society', 'the party', 'the family', 'the individual' and 'the personality'. But now the received ideas and the terminology are themselves fragmentary. No longer can it be asserted as simply as Lawrence did, that the *individual* is, literally, 'indivisible'. Competition and alienation are the dominant themes, found in the class-struggle, 'us and them', the 'haves' and the 'have-nots', in party-politiciking (democracy being an essentially competitive system), in the rat-race, in sibling rivalry, in the Freudian complexes Oedipal and Electral, in the Freudian conflict between Id and Superego, the extension of the warring claims of the Reality Principle and the Pleasure Principle. Psychological terminology has, regrettably, become a byword of imprecision, the root cause of confusion being a conflict of diagnosis between the druggists and the analysts. By contrast, in the political arena, there are such vacuous rhetorical 'labels of solidarity' as 'the workers', 'the people' and 'the struggle'.[6]

Many commentators have written of the inadequacies of the modern political vocabulary in conveying the contemporary realities of power. Bryan Magee, in an excellent article in *Encounter* (May 1986), emphasized the aspect of 'an exhausted terminology', since many of the central terms of the political vocabulary were coined a century and a half ago. They consequently no longer have their pristine clarity and purchase.

(These words include *Socialist*, *Liberal*, *Conservative*, *Communism*, *Capitalism*, *Left*, *Right* and *Centre.*) While acknowledging the signal contribution of Marx, Magee insists that a 'far richer' vocabulary is needed, though – like so many before him – he is unclear how this is to be achieved. In part this vagueness derives from the very generality of democratic politics, which de Tocqueville perceived.

The rarer registers have, because of their dissociative, opaque quality of linguistic obfuscation (of which this is a mild example), become very current in political language. Abstractions such as *liberation*, *progress*, *democracy*, *realism* and the like provide the essential ambiguity which democratic politics requires in the form of room to manoeuvre, and the breadth and flexibility which enables a skilful orator to make plausible, popular claims which will unite divergent interests in time of crisis or war. Most cynically, these terms can be used very effectively to disguise the facts of suffering and death. As George Orwell has so brilliantly demonstrated, it is the latinized abstraction which is invariably chosen to euphemize a horror, or justify it via a species of language which may be labelled *doubletalk.* The earliest recorded use of the phrase 'detention under safe custody' is applied in 1570 to Mary, Queen of Scots. She was kept in this condition for nineteen years before being executed. It is not a new linguistic idiom, but its currency has greatly increased in this century. Indeed, it has been virtually institutionalized, as figure 9.1, 'The semantic field of nonsense', indicates. The problem is that words like *pacification*, *liberation* and *prestige* may change to the virtual opposite of their original meanings and yet still retain their higher register 'status', which endows them with plausibility, if not respectability.

Though the separation of registers is now, as previously remarked, less formally observed, it would be naive to claim that this movement is evidence of a greater integration of the language. On the contrary, there is a strong trend of fragmentation into dialects, sub-codes and idiolects. 'He is very cool' or 'What a neat car!' have different meanings in Cambridge, Massachusetts and Cambridge, England. What is notable about the 'underground' American dialects is that the core vocabulary is ostensibly familiar to a Standard English speaker, but meanings are often entirely different. Examples include *square*, *weird*, *pad*, *soul*, *high*, *acid*, *grass*, *horse*, *camp*, *trip*, *bird*, *cool*, *sweet*, *hit*, *heat*, *fruit*, *bread*, *cat*, *sick* and *gross.* To some extent these dialects are contrived sub-codes, alternative argots which deliberately avoid traditional language, as well as its conventions of public explication. On encountering the unfamiliar word *groovy* from a bohemienne in Greenwich Village, Eugene Landy (compiler of *The Underground Dictionary*, 1971) asked what the word meant. 'With a somewhat surprised look and an astonished voice, she responded, "Groovy means groovy, man"' (p. 14). These dialect uses are consequently of a different order from the traditional British–American sources of confusion, evidenced in *pants*, *pond*, *trailer*, *gas*, *rock*, *dirt*, *pavement*, *public school*, the democratization of *dame* and *lady* in America, and so on.

FIGURE 9.1. The semantic field of nonsense[1]

Date	*Word*
	babble
1400	jargon[2]
1500	jabber
	babel blather (v.)
	prattle gibberish
1600	nonsense fustian gabble
	rubbish
	hocus-pocus
	balderdash
1700	folderol stultiloquence
	rigmarole
	twaddle
1800	catchword
	humbug claptrap[3]
	bunkum
	echolalia officialese[4] poppycock[5]
1900	crap balls logorrhea waffle mumbo-jumbo piffle tripe
	baloney shit blah blab-word hokum
	newspeak pentagonese drivel gobbledygook doubletalk

Notes: 1 The dates given are for the first recorded use in the sense of 'nonsense'

2 *Jargon*, first recorded in Chaucer's 'Merchant's Tale' in the sense of birdsong, has an older sense of 'gibberish'

3 *Claptrap* was originally a ploy to attract applause in the theatre

4 The institutionalization of nonsense was recognized in an edition of *Roget's Thesaurus* (New York, Crowell, 1977), which had a section on 'Official Nonsense', and in *A Dictionary of Euphemisms* (1983), which carried a section on 'The Language of Government: Bureaucratese and Urbababble'

5 The relation between nonsense and excrement, so obvious in many words, is veiled in *poppycock*, derived from Dutch dialect *pappekak*, 'soft shit'.

Authorities and commentators continue to be divided on the extent and significance of the division. In his *Dissertations on the English Language* (1789), Noah Webster, 'Jun. Esquire', argued that 'numerous local causes' and America's being 'placed at a distance from Europe . . . will produce, in a course of time, a language in North America, as different from the future language of England, as the modern Dutch, Danish and Swedish are from the German, or from one another.' Thirty years later, in the Preface to his *Dictionary*, his view was less divisive: '. . . although the body of the language is the same as in England, and it is desirable to perpetuate that sameness, some differences must exist.'

Up to about twenty years ago, most observers agreed with Shaw's celebrated remark that 'England and America are two countries divided by the same language'. Today only some argue, in the words of Thomas Pyles, for 'the essential oneness of all English': 'All too often treatments of the subject have been of what Robert A. Hall, Jr., has somewhere called "The Old Curiosity Shop" variety – even Mencken is in some measure guilty of this – playing up isolated differences in a wholly misleading way' (p. 260). Charles Barber has taken a similar view of the present and future of English: 'One encouraging feature is that the divergent tendencies that have been apparent over the past few centuries now seem to have been slowed down, and perhaps even reversed' (1964, p. 157). Also in 1964 was published under the title of *A Common Language*, conversations between Albert H. Marckwardt and Randolph Quirk. The Foreword contained this observation: 'The two varieties of English, they tell us, have never been so different as people have imagined, and the dominant tendency, for several decades now, has clearly been that of convergence and even greater similarity.'

To a certain extent, the biases and premises of one's discipline are liable to colour one's judgement in this matter: philologists are more likely to concentrate on differences, while linguistic scholars are more likely to focus on the similarities and the enduring structures. Nevertheless, the English language is falling increasingly under the influence of the verbal centres of American culture: these are embodied in the speech-writers of Washington, the advertising copywriters of Madison Avenue, and the script-writers of Hollywood. The principal television export of America is soap-opera (a term recorded from 1938[S]) and 'one-liner' comedy. Since the discourse in those forms is exclusively banal dialogue and not (as in a novel) description and psychological analysis, the popular idiom of American speech tends to become a model of articulateness. Hence the increasingly popular acceptance of *pants* for trousers, *truck* for lorry, *call* for telephone, *mail* for post, *can* for tin, *elevator* for lift, *rookie* for beginner, *vacation* for holiday, *executive* for businessman, *relocate* for move, *medication* for medicine and *automobile* for car. There is increasing acceptance of the American use of otiose prepositions: refer *back*, *forward* planning, win *out* or *through* and listen *up*. British usage has started to adopt the verbal use of *into*, as in American 'He's *into* yoghurt/Bhuddism/skiing.' *OK*, spreading from its obscure origins in New York state politics in 1840, is now the universal word for acceptance, assent or agreement throughout the world. As *okay* it can be stretched into noun, verb or adjective. *Hi!* is rapidly becoming a standard greeting, quite removed from its older English implications of arrest or disapproval.

Though such a development might lead to American English becoming first dominant and then universal, the present effects are disruptive. Not without reason has Robert Burchfield commented on the increasing fragmentation of the core of English: 'I am equally sure that the two main forms of English, American English and English English, separated geographically from the beginning, and severed politically since 1776, are continuing to move apart' (1978, p. 133). This gradual fission must inevitably occur as a result of the dispersal of English to hundreds of millions of speakers throughout the world, just as Sanskrit and the Germanic languages spread and split before it.

Some linguists are accelerating the fission by disputing the validity (let alone the existence) of Standard English by championing traditionally unacceptable forms. For example, studies into American Black English, particularly those of Labov into what he calls Nonstandard Negro English, have sought acceptance for conventions of grammar quite at variance with those of Standard English. Labov (1972) would legitimize the illiteracy 'he don't know nothing' under the somewhat specious category of 'negative concord'.[7] Labov's approach derives from an increasingly descriptive approach in language attitudes; in his case it extends to the attempted legitimation of what has traditionally been regarded as 'bad grammar', 'bad speech' and 'bad language', treated as juvenile aberrations painfully eradicated at school. By contrast, another American academic, Paul Fussell, in his study *Class*, bluntly categorizes the double negative as an absolute class divider: 'Probably the most important, a usage dividing the prole classes from the middles and highers, is the double negative, as in "I can't get no satisfaction"' (1984, p. 153). Burchfield characterizes Black English in a less traditional fashion, as being 'potentially political in its animosity towards the structured patterns of Received American, colourful, animated, fancy, and subversive. If it is possible to see a variety of English as a threat to the acceptability of the language handed down to white Americans from the seventeenth century onwards, this is it' (1985, p. 164).

Varieties of language continue, in short, to represent alternative life-styles and even to symbolize political issues. Dictionaries explicating the various sub-codes have proliferated to the point that 'the dictionary' has become a genre. (For this reason it has its own section in the Bibliography.) The eruption of anger and dismay at the Third Edition of *Webster* (1961) arose from its abandoning the prescriptive policy of its predecessors and from what may fairly be called its oral bias. Journalists and academics, seldom comfortable bed-fellows, took arms against a sea of solecism, demanding greater jurisdiction from a dictionary which they regarded as having abdicated responsibility.[8]

As always, strong claims have been made for individual preference and for accepted convention in matters of usage. In extreme cases, as manifested in an article by Jan Morris, this attitude becomes a defence of idiocy. She uses a familiar starting point, but has a startling twist to her argument:

> 'When I use a word,' said Humpty-Dumpty scornfully to Alice, 'it means just what I choose it to mean – neither more nor less. . . . The question is, which is to be master, that's all.'
>
> Bravo! The Great Egg was right, and I count myself if not among his disciples . . . at least among his grateful admirers.[9]

This was the preamble to a hostile, in fact contemptuous, review of Philip Howard's *New Words for Old* and Kenneth Hudson's *The Dictionary of Diseased English*, both published in 1977. Castigating Howard's criticism of the loose use of *necessarily*, she remarked: 'This is insolent Fowlerism of the most nauseating kind.' (This comment does little justice to Fowler's elegant wit and broad-minded magistracy over English usage.) Overtly importing issues of class, education and ideology, Julian Barnes included Howard in 'the current brand of linguistic prescriptivists – usually of right-wing persuasion and public-school origin – who seem to imagine that whenever a word shifts its meaning nowadays, this is a tiny symbol of the yobs taking over.'[10]

These class-laden comments by Barnes invite a broader discussion of social divisions in language. Although linguistic class-distinctions have existed at least as far back as the Norman Conquest, they have been re-emphasized only comparatively recently. In 1954 Alan S. C. Ross published a paper in a learned Finnish journal, *Neuphilologische Mitteilungen*, on class-indicators in Modern English. Asserting that 'It is only by its language that the upper class is clearly marked off from the others' (manifestly an overstatement), he nevertheless posited a fruitful distinction between usages which are 'U' (upper class) and 'non-U' (other class). They include (U-terms first) *napkin/serviette*, *rich/*

wealthy, *excuse me/ pardon*, *scent/perfume*, *lavatory/toilet*, *lunch/dinner* (for the midday meal) and such U-pronunciations as the drawled 'gawn' for *gone*, 'orf' for *off* and 'gouf' for *golf.* These indicators came to be regarded as generally valid. The distinction became very topical as a result of being popularized in a humorous collection of essays edited by Nancy Mitford under the title *Noblesse Oblige* in 1956. Ross edited a similar symposium called *What Are U?* in 1969. In the Foreword he posed the question 'Are there still linguistic indicators?' He found that while there were comparatively few speech-habits confined to the 'U', the great majority of the 'non-U' indicators still obtained. In the course of a discussion in a subsequent collection, *U and Non-U Revisited* edited by Richard Buckle, he observed that 'the antitheses between U and Non-U have *not* changed' (1980, p. 28).

In the course of an extensive list of non-U words, Ross mentions *champers* for 'champagne'. This shows a broadening of the word, since forms like *soccer* and *rugger* were originally Oxford University slang (1891 and 1893 respectively).[O] Numerous similar formations are mentioned in the *Oxford Dictionary of Etymology*: *bedder*, 'bedroom', *bedsitter*, 'bed-sitting room', *cupper*, 'cup-tie', *fresher*, 'freshman', *Radder*, 'Radcliffe Camera', *Toggers*, 'Torpids', *Adders*, 'Addison's Walk'. The entry concludes 'there have been casual or transitory uses such as *wagger pagger bagger* for waste-paper basket.' There is even a class-distinction between *cupper* (cited above) and *brekker* ('breakfast') as against *cuppa* and *fella*, which are non-U.

As was mentioned in the Introduction, Johnson observed (and condemned) affected usage which he termed 'women's cant', although it seems to have been confined to the upper class ladies of the time. None of the recent commentators on 'U and Non-U' seems to have focused on the extension of the idiom into what may be termed the 'aristocratic oxymoron', heard daily in such arrangements as 'terribly nice', 'awfully sweet' and the like. These exclusively 'U' emotive exaggerations invite a re-examination of certain given notions which have coloured observations about class and usage. It has generally been assumed that 'U' usage is more markedly 'correct' or 'proper', while 'non-U' is more 'common', given to slovenliness and slang. One of the features ignored in these discussions is the prevalence in 'U' usage of baby-language, in forms like *gee-gee*, *wee-wee*, *tummy*, *horsy*, *doggy* and *walkies.* Frequent recourse is also made in 'U' to imprecise but highly suggestive critical words of similar formation, invariably of informal register: *kinky*, *nasty*, *shady*, *ropey*, *lousy*, *sticky*, *stuffy*, *tatty*, *dowdy*, *shabby*, *shaky*, *tawdry* and the reduplicating relatives *hanky-panky*, *namby-pamby*, *hoity-toity* and so on. Often encountered in the formulas *a ***y business* or *a bit ***y*, they are commonly applied to character, quality, clothes or social gatherings. The fact that they may derive from quite heterogeneous roots (*tawdry* from St Audrey and *namby-pamby* from Ambrose Phillips, an eighteenth century fop) has had no bearing on their subsequent register. (*Shabby*, one might note, has survived the stricture of Johnson: 'A word that has crept into conversation and low writing, but ought not to be admitted into the language.'; its verbal origin, *to shab*, meaning broadly to cheat, stigmatized as 'a low barbarous cant word', did not.)

In recent years the lucrative seam of class-consciousness has been adroitly exploited by, notably, Jilly Cooper in *Class* and its sequels. The most overtly exclusive contribution is *The Official Sloane Ranger Handbook* (1982) by Ann Barr and Peter York. This facetious but perceptive study of upper-class mores shows complicated language-games across the traditional boundaries. Not only do 'Sloanes love using non-U words in common accents: "Come into the Leeownge"', they also have a glossary largely composed of words for status-symbols ('Roller' or 'Woler' for *Rolls-Royce*) and hedonistic habits: *chateaued* for 'drunk', *park a custard* or *shoot a cat* for 'vomit', and various terms for sexual intercourse, such as *interior decorating*, *bang* (male, verb) and *cosy* (female, noun). 'Sloane', like 'Punk', is basically an in-group dialect, built round certain dominant focuses of interest. These dialects reveal, if anything, the persistence of class differences.

Although U and non-U usage has become an accepted class-indicator, the division is, perhaps, simplistic. The fact that pronounciation differs so markedly between classes should not obscure the more significant similarity between upper and working classes in areas of word-choice concerning matters which the middle class finds 'embarrassing'. The decent bourgeois prefers euphemism to directness in all things. Upper and working class, on the other hand, both show a far more frank, 'liberated' attitude towards the use of 'four-letter words', towards what are regarded as blasphemous utterances, and in direct reference to traditional areas of euphemism such as money, death, excretion and so on. This is not a new development. The words of the splendid Harry Hotspur are most apposite to the matter of oaths. He scornfully rejects mealy-mouthed, 'decent' delicacy in his wife:

> Swear me, Kate, like a lady as thou art,
> A good mouth-filling oath; and leave 'in sooth',
> And such protest of pepper-gingerbread,
> To velvet guards and Sunday-citizens.
>
> (*Henry IV, Pt. I*, III. i. 257–60)

A modern gloss on these attitudes is provided by Jilly Cooper: 'I once heard my son regaling his friends: "Mummy says *pardon* is a much worse word than *fuck*"' (1981, p. 39).

Yet, lexicographically speaking, in matters of correctness, the past three decades have seen a shift away from the previous linguistic fashion of *laissez-faire*. Robert Burchfield commented in the Preface to Volume III of the *Supplement* (1982):

> During the 1970s the markedly linguistic descriptivism of the post-war years was to some extent brought into question. Infelicities of language, whether in the spoken or the written word, were identified and assailed by a great many people who seemed to believe that the English language itself was in a period of decline. . . . One small legacy of these great debates is that here and there in the present volume I have found myself adding my own opinions about the acceptability of certain words or meanings in educated usage. (pp. v–vi)

The seventh edition of the *Concise Oxford Dictionary* (1982) adopts a subtle prescriptive stance by establishing a standard of educated written usage, conceding that this standard is usually that of a minority. The symbol 'D' is used to signify an area of disputed or controversial usage which 'although widely found, is still the subject of much adverse comment by a significant number of educated writers'. The *Oxford American Dictionary* (1980) takes the policy even further, for 'more than six hundred usage notes indicate the linguistic and social appropriateness of various words and phrases'. The policy adopted is surprisingly conservative, for we are told: 'Careful writers do not use *contact* as a verb, [nor] *aggravate* to mean annoy.' Neither usage is so designated by the *COD*, and *Random House* (1973) even makes a strong historical cum descriptive argument for the process of 'conversion': 'Many verbs have derived from nouns . . . there is no justification for the criticisms commonly heard of using *contact* as a verb.'

Perhaps no word reveals the oscillations of American lexicography as clearly as the word *ain't.* Whereas the Second Edition of *Webster* (1928) had categorized it as 'dialect or illiterate', the Third (1961) attempted a fuller description, but only of the oral usage: 'though disapproved by [*sic*] many and more common in less educated speech, used orally in most parts of the U.S. by many cultivated speakers especially in the phrase *ain't I*'. All this refers to the sense *aren't*; only the sense *have not*, when rendered as, for example 'I ain't seen him', is labelled 'substandard'. This distinction in itself seems dubious. The more significant fact, that the 'many cultivated speakers' would *never* write *ain't*, except for special effect, is ignored. Not without some reason, therefore, was the edition castigated for its oral bias.

Today the tide has turned, at least as far as dictionaries are concerned. 'Ain't,' rules the *Oxford American Dictionary*, 'is avoided in standard speech', a circumstance which is hardly credible in fact. As was mentioned earlier, it is good enough for President Reagan, though he is, admittedly, not a stylist in the line of Jefferson and Lincoln. Perhaps the judicious tact of *Random House* sums up the matter best: 'Ain't is so traditionally and widely regarded as nonstandard that it should be shunned by all who prefer not to be considered illiterate.' The indignation and adrenalin expended over the use of *ain't* are significant, especially since the *meaning* of *ain't* is not in dispute; the problematic questions of propriety, consensus and convention are. Such energy is seldom expended on semantic matters.

Equally important, but generally ignored, is the change in the terminology employed in the discussion of linguistic usage. Broadly speaking, the shift has been from terms of moral absolutism to those of vague sociological relativity. 'Atrocious' was the term used by my English teacher to describe my handwriting when I was about ten. I remember looking the word up and finding that it had something to do with cruelty. It was a term which could then be used of grammar or spelling with equally damning conviction. Without knowing it, this lady formed part of the prescriptive tradition going back to the eighteenth century. Dr Johnson's typical terms of disapproval were 'low', 'ludicrous' and 'cant', but his ultimate category for outer linguistic darkness was 'barbarous', which he defined as 'savage', 'uncivilised' as well as 'unacquainted with the arts'. His younger contemporary, Noah Webster, made some equally condemning remarks in the Preface to his Dictionary (1828) about 'correcting a vicious pronunciation which prevailed extensively among the common people of this country'.

Today, such severely ethical language is eschewed, as it is in many other areas of human behaviour. The short history of critical terms has been *barbarous – vicious – execrable – atrocious – bad – illiterate – incorrect – non-standard.* But perhaps the most revealing semantic shift within the controversial matter of linguistic correctness is the erosion of the meaning of *standard.* What was previously styled unambiguously as *Standard English* had not only the clear status of a majuscule, but a definite qualitative exclusivity. Today, although *standard* is still used, the category does not have the same assured pre-eminence over *non-standard*, nor even over the rarer *sub-standard*, since these terms now imply a legitimate alternative or variety. (The increasing use of *variety* likewise carries egalitarian assumptions.) The ambiguous status of the different categories is evident in these comments (on the acceptability of the double negative) in *The Universal English Grammar* (1985): 'In yet other cases the forms are clearly recognized as unacceptable in the standard variety (such as the multiple negative in *I don't want no money from no one*) though they may be acceptable in some nonstandard varieties' (p. 10). Although the point has not yet been reached at which it could be said that 'All Englishes are equal', it does appear that 'Some Englishes are more English than others.' These changes in terminology reflect the problems of coming to terms with a shift in the centre of gravity in matters of linguistic usage. They were perceived in these prescient remarks by George Steiner over twenty years ago: 'The great energies of the language now enter into play outside England . . . African English, Australian English, the rich speech of West Indian and Anglo-Indian writers, represent a complicated polycentric field of linguistic force, in which the language taught and written on this island is no longer the inevitable authority or focus.' (*Listener*, 21 October 1965). But the problems of a *lingua franca* concern *currency* both in the sense of 'usage' and 'agreed values'.

Generally speaking, it is traditionally conceded that in matters of linguistic usage America tends to follow more of an oral standard and Britain more of a written. These conventions are in many ways extensions of their respective dominant ideologies: the British model focuses on the highest common factor; the American on the lowest common denominator. However, there are curious anomalies in the ruling of the authorities. The inclusion in the *OED Supplement* of 'the more notorious of the four-letter words', as the Editor called them, was as thorough a treatment as such a taboo subject allowed, and occasioned no protests. Yet, eleven years earlier the Third Edition of *Webster* did not feel secure enough to include all, and in 1963 protests and threatened banning faced the *Dictionary of American Slang*, edited by Stuart Berg Flexner and Harold Wentworth.[11] This is still, remarkably, the only American dictionary to include all the four-letter words (or 'big six', as American publishers and broadcasters refer to them). It seems quite astonishing that the *Oxford American Dictionary* (1980), which was claimed to be 'as up to date as *ayatollah* and *gridlock*, an innovative new [*sic*] dictionary bringing lexicography into the 1980s' should actually surpass its predecessors in preciousness by leaving out all the words under discussion, although they form the basic currency of Forty-Second Street.

Awareness that a dictionary has an authoritative format and status has led to works being put out under the title of 'dictionary' which turn out to be glossaries with a clear ideological or 'consciousness-raising' content. Alternatively, pressures put on dictionaries indicate that taboos are moving from sex to race and discrimination. The growth of the descriptive assumption that dictionaries should be 'liberated' from the past constraints of sexual delicacy has developed simultaneously with a dubious dogmatic liberalism which would insist that the dictionary should not appear to foster attitudes of racial prejudice, particularly those that take some verbal form of abuse or opprobrium. Verbally impacted prejudice, in this view, should be doctored or suppressed. As is made clear in chapter 8 in the section titled 'Linguistic Xenophobia', a great deal of racial prejudice has been instilled in opprobrious terms, particularly from *c.* 1700. The awareness of this fact seems more important than its suppression, even in the cause of 'public decency'.

Over the years the *OED*, via the Clarendon Press, has been subjected to considerable pressure and prolonged harassment to suppress the opprobrious senses associated with *Jew* as noun and verb. This resulted in an action in the High Court of Chancery in 1972 (*Shloimovitz* v. *The Clarendon Press*). The case was rejected with costs on 5 July 1973, and the opprobrious senses stand. But the *Supplement* has seen fit to append a sociological explanation of how the prejudicial associations grew up. In fact, the Editor revealed policy on this point some three years before the relevant volume was published by quoting in advance the comment subsequently appended to the entry:

> Sense 2 of the noun will be brought up to date in the following manner: (Further Examples) In medieval England, Jews, though engaged in many pursuits, were particularly familiar as money-lenders, their activities being publicly regulated for them by the Crown, whose protégés they were. In private, Christians also practised money-lending, though forbidden to do so by Canon Law. Thus the name of Jew came to be associated in the popular mind with usury and any extortionate practices that might be supposed to accompany it, and gained an opprobrious sense.

Clearly, it is not – *pace* Burchfield – the *sense* of the word which is being 'brought up to date', since only medieval evidence is being adduced. Rather, one suspects in response to pressures, the *Dictionary* has taken on the role of social interpreter in addition to its usual policy of simply recording semantic evidence for which a variety of sociological explanations may be available. In this particular case what seems significant and anomalous is the tenacity of the 'extortionate' associations centuries after the constraints on money-lending had been removed from Christians.

The case of *Palestinian* is, perhaps, even more revealing. The definition in the *Concise Oxford Dictionary* (6th edn., 1976) originally ran: '(Native or inhabitant) of Palestine; (person) seeking to displace Israelis from Palestine.' Objections to the second part of the definition resulted in its withdrawal. In the Fourth Impression (1977) the definition reads: 'Of, or pertaining to, or belonging to Palestine.' One wonders whether representations from the appropriate quarters would result in explanations of the contentious associations attaching to *French*, *Scots*, *Irish* and *Welsh.*[12]

In this vexatious matter, the policy of the *OED Supplement* is, however, certainly preferable to that of unrealistic expungement adopted by Dr David B. Guralnik, Editor-in-Chief of *Webster's New World Dictionary*, Second College Edition of 1970. He justified the exclusion of words like *dago*, *kike*, *wog* and *wop* in the following way: 'It was decided in the selection process that this dictionary could easily dispense with those true obscenities, the terms of racial or ethnic opprobrium, that are, in any case, encountered with diminishing frequency these days.' Burchfield, rightly, makes a point of specifically rejecting what he calls 'Guralnikism, the racial equivalent of Bowdlerism'. This policy of 'verbal sanitization' is, however, continued in the *Oxford American Dictionary*, and is a revealing influence of social change upon semantic change.

A dictionary has become, from an editor's point of view, an ideological minefield. His liberty, even in supposedly liberal intellectual atmospheres, does not extend to the description of all forms of verbal behaviour, but is constrained by notions of public decency or sectional interests. The pressure is on to 'de-mystify' the dictionary and make it more responsive to a role as a social influence. No longer can it be said that 'The lexicographer is especially protected by the very awe that this work inspires; he is not known as a collector and processor of word-lore; he is just a shadowy phantom behind the overpowering facade of the Dictionary' (Twaddell, 1973).

The notion of authority, almost amounting to caricature, here described is more validly apposite to the idea of the lexicographer in previous centuries than in our own. The image of a Johnson come, like Newton, to impose order on unruly philology, or of a Murray indefatigably teasing out innumerable meanings from rich verbal strands, are both symbolic of periods of semantic conservatism. Ours is becoming a period of semantic destabilization in which authority is generally mocked, or ignored, or fissiparously produces 'authorities'.

As has been mentioned, some of these 'authorities' wish to expose the ideology inherent in language and manipulate it for their own ends, by a process of semantic engineering, using 'tactical definitions' (Lewis, 1960, p. 17), and seeking by their own brand of prescriptivism to impose uncurrent meanings on central words. Consider the following:

> all forms of the word [*fellow*] can be used sex-inclusively [i.e., of either sex].
>
> The disparity in ... the verbs *to mother* (the social act of nurturance) and *to father* (the biological act of insemination) is disappearing. *Fathering*, too, has acquired the meaning 'caring for or looking after someone', previously ascribed only to *mothering*....
>
> ... the seemingly innocuous difference between *blond* and *blonde* becomes in English the difference between the standard (male) and the deviation (female). (Miller and Swift, 1981, pp. 98, 79, 97)

These examples come from *The Handbook of Non-Sexist Writing* by Casey Miller and Kate Swift. Anyone familiar with the history of the language would accept their premise: 'Since English, through most of its history, evolved in a white, Anglo-Saxon, patriarchal society, no one should be surprised that its vocabulary and grammar frequently reflect attitudes that exclude or demean minorities and women' (p. 4). But the fact that the language has evolved through communal use certain forms of linguistic sexism and become an instrument of subtle (and obvious) discrimination is not going to be altered by proffering fictions of wish-fulfilment of the kind quoted. Such obviously imposed meanings make a mockery of the book's sound historical base, and go beyond 'consciousness-raising' into an area of distortion and propaganda. More overtly ideological manipulation of the language is found in *wimmin*, the factitious (and strictly sexist) formation of the Women of Greenham Common: 'We want to spell women in a way that does not spell men' (*Observer*, 13 March 1983) and *s/he*, a common-gender pronoun first recorded in *Gay News* in 1972[S].

The case of *gay* is different. Whatever the merits of the adjective, *gay* has had the sense of 'homosexual' in underground contexts for at least 50 years. (Hugh Rawson, in his *Dictionary of Euphemisms and Other Doubletalk* (1981), cites the much older evidence of John Saul, a male prostitute involved in the Cleveland Street Scandal of 1889, referring in a deposition to the police to his male associates as 'gay'.) Indeed, the new sense has become so powerful that it has driven our the old, established meanings, so that 'having a gay old time' and its relations seem to have vanished, as have the older slang terms for 'homosexual', such as *queer*, *homo*, *fag* and *fairy*.

Though this study has taken 'semantic change' to mean 'change of meaning', 'lexical change' and 'change of register', it is clear that the discussion has to extend beyond the realm of individual word-meanings. The field-approach illuminates trends, brings out unexpected collocations which, arranged in historical format, may then suggest or supply a causal link with social history. However, when one analyses promotional language in general, it becomes clear that whole sections of the lexicon have become atrophied, blighted, or vandalized. *Unique*, *purity*, *marvellous*, *fresh*, *beautiful*, *quality*, these and many more have been afflicted. When one realizes that superlatives are, in terms of linguistic frequency, more common than ordinals, that *very* originally meant 'true', that *really* (adj.) originally meant 'in reality', but that a soft drink can be marketed as 'the real thing', it becomes clear that this whole kind of language has become suspect, as hollow as a weasel's egg from which the meat has been surreptitiously stolen.

Another area of inadequacy lies in the language of catastrophe or disaster. As we saw at the end of chapter 4, *pest*, *plague* and *pox* faded from feared symbols of horrific disease to expressions of bland annoyance. As was mentioned in chapter 8, the vocabulary of death is now grotesquely impoverished. *Outrage* and *obscene* have been similarly trivialized. *Obscene* was originally a word of outrage, with meanings ranging through 'ill-omened', 'inauspicious', 'disgusting' or 'indecent'. The sexual association grew early to be seen in the phrase *obscene parts* for 'genitals', for instance in Pope's *Odyssey* (1725): 'Her parts obscene the raging billows hide.' This sense has steadily dominated the other meanings, and the word is now limited almost entirely to 'obscene language' or 'obscene gestures', not actions. If Dr Guralnik is right in saying that terms of racial opprobrium are 'true obscenities', then what is left to describe Auschwitz? The true horrors of the modern world seem now to be beyond description.

Vico, we recall, distinguished three stages of language, the hieratic or iconic, the heroic or metaphorical, and the conventional or plain; these corresponded to the ages of gods, heroes and men. To these a fourth stage must now be added: the language of mass manipulation, employed to motivate or anaesthetize crowds. Words are utilized solely for effect, and meaning is conceived of as arbitrary, endlessly relative to the point of idiocy.

As the linguistic equivalent of Gresham's Law takes effect, more and more intensifiers are brought into play to achieve verbal impact. Logorrhea becomes psittacism, a parroting repetition. Eventually, the results reach beyond the semantic dimension into the syntactic. As the grammatical and semantic boundaries between words become blurred, so their syntactical arrangement becomes less clear. The brief history of English grammar has been the liberation of forms previously limited by their inflections to a specific function. The point has now been reached where many forms can be, like *up*, not just a preposition, but an adjective (as in *up*-market), an adverb (as in going *up*), a noun (on the *up*) and a verb (to *up* the stakes). While this flexibility is very convenient in everyday speech, it invites abuse for commercial motives. The balance, even the distinction, between nouns and qualifiers becomes disturbed as trains of adjectives are used to shunt nouns with sufficient force to arouse the consumer's interest. As has been shown in chapter 6, the device develops out of technical language into the fashionable: 'diagonal-pivot swing rear axles with four constant-velocity couplings', which is standard technical jargon, insidiously evolves into concatenations such as 'Revlon Realistic Professional Formula Permanent Creme Hair Relaxer', a farrago of market-catching counters.

It is clear that impact is achieved at the cost of clarity. The copywriter is, of course, unconcerned with such costs, and Daniel J. Boorstin has gone so far as to suggest that consumers actually wish to be mystified by the copy (1963, p. 236). Such a view might appear, at first sight, to be super-subtle cynicism, but is, I believe, a suggestive formulation of a 'language conspiracy' in which manipulator, medium and mass connive. I have discussed the general loss of semantic surety and syntactical coherence in terms of the language of advertising chiefly because deception and agglutination features are more apparent there, half-sense is more tolerated, and advertising language is so open in its methods and so clear in its objectives.

The loss of meaning is, I suggest, symptomatic of a general sense of confusion, normlessness, lack of shared values and agreement over the proper forms of government which seems to characterize life in the West, particularly since the Second World War.[13] In short, 'things fall apart' in all senses. Two centuries ago, by contrast, one could point to the semantic ordering of Johnson's *Dictionary*, the splendid architecture of the periodic sentence and the balanced, clockwork ingenuity of the heroic couplet as linguistic symbols of an ordered age.

Though that period is by no means a golden age, a 'well of English undefiled', and though it has its brilliant subversives in Swift and

Sterne, it shows a seriousness in its semantic concerns which is lacking now. It is noteworthy that all the greatest writers of those times, in spite of being staunch believers in liberal independence, in *laissez-faire* economics, and being members of a self-made literary establishment suspicious of academies and academics, nevertheless considered and advocated most seriously some measure of responsible control over the language. Ultimately, what Johnson called 'the spirit of English liberty' prevailed. Nothing was done, formally speaking. Yet Johnson's achievement was far greater than even the range, magisterial intelligence and felicitous exactitude of his definitions makes clear. He instilled a sense of responsibility and concern in the use of the language which ensured a long period of subsequent stability and ordered growth. But his Dictionary was inspired by that profound, clairvoyant pessimism which illuminates his greatest work:

> The tropes of poetry will make hourly encroachments, and the metaphorical will become the current sense; pronunciation will be varied by levity or ignorance, and the pen must at length comply with the tongue; illiterate writers will at one time or another, by publick infatuation, rise into renown, who, not knowing the original import of words, will use them with colloquial licentiousness, confound distinction and forget propriety.

Today the consequence is that English, apparently belonging to everyone, is the responsibility of no one. It has no champion, no guardian, no legal eagles to watch for passing off. Can it really be said that 'the English language is alive and well, in the right hands'?[14]

Rich and subtle words, like *courtesy*, *rhetoric*, *charisma* and *philosophy*, have been impoverished and trivialized; direct and blunt words, like *lie*, *steal*, *kill* and *cheat*, are commonly euphemized, especially when applied to establishments and institutions;[15] key words, encapsulating the concepts and ideals on which society is based, such as *democracy*, *liberation*, *culture*, *liberal*, *image* and *progress*, are largely nebulous. The old words for verbal deception, *gloze*, *palter* and *equivocate*, have politely (and revealingly) disappeared. Today, *caring* and *responsibility* are vogue-words applied vaguely to any endeavour except the language. Yet serious damage is done by the potent combination of the institutionalized verbicide of the market-place and the political double-talk of the authorities. The tower of Babel, a haunting image combining technological progress – absurdly directed – willing slavery and semantic confusion, no longer seems such a remote, desperate symbol.

NOTES

1 Although Durkheim introduced the term in the second (1902) edition of *The Division of Labour in Society*, the first reference to *anomie* in the *Supplement* is for 1933.
2 Alessandro Serpieri, 'Reading the signs: towards a semiotics of Shakespearean drama', in *Alternative Shakespeares*, ed. John Drakakis (Methuen, London, 1985), p. 119. Even *macrotextual* and *intertextual* are glossed as having precisely opposite meanings to what the words apparently signify.
3 The fascination with theory, the exploration of pseudo-problems seem to be an abdication of semantic responsibility.
4 In *Language and Silence*, p. 39.
5 Paul Johnson, in his useful discussion in *Enemies of Society*, analyses the confusion over this term (1977, pp. 109–10).
6 'The Point of Severance: English in 1776 and Beyond', *Encounter*, October, 1978, p. 133. In an interview article by Philip Howard in *The Times* (3 November 1976) Burchfield remarked: 'In the United States the peripheral areas are so numerous that they are forcing their ways into the core, diluting the language, and making American English a progressively more unacceptable model for English speakers at a distance from America.'
7 W. Labov, *Language in the Inner City*, pp. 145–52. (The highly original use of the term *concord* to legitimize what has been traditionally regarded as incorrect grammar is a good example of what Lewis calls a 'tactical definition'.)
8 There is a convenient collection of essays and reviews contributing to the furore in Sledd and Ebbitt (1962).
9 Jan Morris, 'Words are for us, not us for words', *Encounter*, April 1978, p. 75.
10 Julian Barnes, 'Tumble talk', *New Statesman*, 13 October 1978, p. 480.
11 According to Gary Jennings (1965, p. 116), the protests started in the spring of 1963, over two years after the work had been published.
12 It might be necessary to explain, for example, that the 'wild Irish' (so called from *c.* 1547[O]) were originally thus termed since they were not under British rule, and that to *welsh*, i.e., 'to cheat' (from *c.* 1857[O]) is a racing term which casts no aspersions on the Welsh.
13 Mary McCarthy, in a perceptive essay, 'Language Politics', written at the time of the Watergate Scandal, finishes by stressing 'the element of consent in the public. A general will to confusion'. (In *Occasional Prose* (New York, Harcourt, 1985), p. 100.)
14 R. W. Burchfield, Preface to vol. III of the *OED Supplement* (1982), p. v.
15 The growth of euphemisms is reflected in various recent studies, such as Hugh Rawson's *A Dictionary of Euphemisms and Other Doubletalk* (1981), Judith Neaman and Carole Silver's *A Dictionary of Euphemisms* (1983), Jonathon Green's *Newspeak* (1984), and the collection edited by D. J. Enright under the title *Fair of Speech* (1985) which came to my notice too late for discussion in the present work.

Epigraph Sources

Chapter		*Reference*
1	(i)	Barfield, *History in English Words*, p. 14
	(ii)	Steiner, *Extraterritorial*, p. 70
2	(i)	Chaucer, *Prologue*, ll. 43–6
	(ii)	Burke, *Reflections*, p. 83
3	(i)	Pirenne, *A History of Europe*, pp. 217–18
	(ii)	Pope, *Epistle to Bathurst*, ll. 39–42
	(iii)	Though 'Gresham's Law' was attributed to Sir Thomas Gresham, Founder of the Royal Exchange, only in the nineteenth century, the economic phenomenon was understood before his lifetime (1519–79)
4	(i)	Steiner, *Language and Silence*, p. 46
	(ii)	Hooker, cited in Chandos, p. xxi
	(iii)	McLuhan, *The Gutenberg Galaxy*, p. 235
	(iv)	Shakespeare, *The Merry Wives of Windsor*, I. iv. 6
5	(i)	Carlyle, *Heroes and Hero-Worship*, cited in *ODQ*
	(ii)	McLuhan in *McLuhan Hot and Cold*, p. 40
	(iii)	Bacon, *Essays*, 'Of Love'
	(iv)	Defoe, quoted in Williams (1975), p. 183
	(v)	Marx, *Rheinische Zeitung*, 1842, cited in Easton and Guddat (1967), p. 96
6	(i)	Shakespeare, *Romeo and Juliet*, II. ii. 43–4
	(ii)	*The Greenland Saga*, chapter 1
	(iii)	Veblen, *Theory of the Leisure Class*, p. 79
	(iv)	Johnson, *Preface*, p. 25
	(v)	Boorstin, *The Image*, p. 201

7	(i)	Confucius (a traditional attribution)
	(ii)	de Tocqueville, *Democracy in America*, p. 84
	(iii)	Harvey Cox, *The Secular City*, p. 11
8	(i)	Tacitus, *Agricola*, chapter 30
	(ii)	Cited in Fairlie (1975), p. 30
	(iii)	Hobbes, *Leviathan*, chapter 13
	(iv)	Said by Churchill to Stalin, Teheran, November, 1943
	(v)	Voltaire, cited in *OEDQ*
	(vi)	Lord Acton (1973, p. 20). From 'The Study of History', Inaugural Lecture delivered at Cambridge, June 1895
	(vii)	Hitler, quoted in Maser (1970), p. 165
9	(i)	Diderot, *Encyclopédie*, Preface
	(ii)	T. S. Eliot, 'Burnt Norton', Section v
Bibliography		Barfield (1954), p. 216

Bibliography

So many books have appeared since the first edition of *History in English Words* that it would be a mistake to attempt a bibliography.

Owen Barfield

THE Bibliography is arranged in two sections: Dictionaries (arranged chronologically) and Other Works.

1 *Dictionaries*

Harman, Thomas. 1567: *A Caveat or Wareningfor Commen Cursetors vvlgarely called Vagabones.* London: William Gryffeth.

Florio, John. 1578: *First Fruites.* London.

— 1591: *Second Frutes.* London.

Greene, Robert. 1591: *A Notable Discovery of Coosnage. Now daily practised by sundry lewd persons, called Connie-catchers, and Crosse-biters.* London.

Coote, Edmund. 1596: *The English Schoole-Master.* London.

Florio, John. [1598]: *A World of Words, or Most Copious and Exact Dictionarie in Italian and English Collected.* London. Ed. Blount, 1608.

Cawdrey, Robert. 1604: *A Table Alphabeticall, conteyning and teaching the true vvriting, and vnderstanding of hard vsuall English words*. . . . London: Edmund Weaver.

Cotgrave, Randle. [1611]: *A Dictionary of English & French, Compiled for the Commoditie of all such as are desirous of both of the Languages.* London: Octavian Pulleyn, 1650.

Cockeram, Henry. 1623: *The English Dictionarie: or, An Interpreter of hard English Words.* London: Edmund Weaver.

Blount, Thomas. 1656: *Glossographia.* London: Humphrey Moseley and George Sawbridge.

Phillips, Edward. 1658: *The New World of English Words: Or, a General Dictionary.* London: Nath. Brooke.

Phillips, Edward. 1706: *The New World of English Words* [etc.] . . . The Sixth Edition, Revised, Corrected, and Improved . . . by J[ohn] K[ersey] . . . London: J. Phillips.

Bailey, Nathaniel. 1721: *An Universal Etymological Dictionary.* London.
— 1730: *Dictionarium Britannicum: Or a more Complete Universal Etymological English Dictionary than any Extant.* London: T. Cox.
Johnson, Samuel. [1755]: *A Dictionary of the English Language*. London, 1785.
Grose, Francis. [1785]: *A Classical Dictionary of the Vulgar Tongue.* London. Ed. Eric Partridge, London: Routledge, 1931, repr. 1963.
Anonymous. 1841: *The Swell's Night Guide: An Explanation of the Flash Words now in Use in the Metropolis.* London.
Farmer, John S. and William E. Henley. 1890–1904: *Slang and its Analogues, past and present.* New York: Dutton.
Partridge, Eric. 1937: *A Dictionary of Slang and Unconventional English.* London: Routledge; 5th edn repr. 1974.
— 1940: *A Dictionary of Clichés.* London: Routledge.
— 1958: *Origins.* London: Routledge; 4th edn 1977.
Versand, Kenneth (ed.). [1959]: *Polyglot's Lexicon 1943–1966.* New York: Links Books, 1973.
Wentworth, Harold and Stuart B. Flexner. 1960: *A Dictionary of American Slang.* New York: Crowell; 2nd supplemented edn 1975.
Gove, Philip B. (ed.). 1961: *Webster's Third New International Dictionary.* Springfield, Mass.: G. & C. Merriam.
Sperber, Hans and Travis Trittschuh. 1962: *American Political Terms.* Detroit: Wayne State UP.
Finkenstaedt, T., E. Leisi and D. Wolff (eds). 1970: *A Chronological English Dictionary.* Heidelberg: Carl Winter Universitätsverlag.
Major, Clarence. 1970: *Dictionary of Afro-American Slang.* New York: International Publishers.
Landy, Eugene. 1971: *The Underground Dictionary.* New York: Simon & Schuster.
Roberts, G. R. 1971: *A Dictionary of Political Analysis.* London: Longmans.
Rogers, Bruce. 1972: *The Queen's Vernacular.* San Francisco: Straight Arrow Books.
Wilson, Robert. 1972: *Playboy's Book of Forbidden Words.* Chicago: Playboy Press.
Beeton, D. R. and Helen Dorner. 1975: *A Dictionary of English Usage in Southern Africa.* Cape Town: OUP.
[Unspecified]. 1976: *6000 Words: A Supplement to the Third Edition of Webster.* Springfield, Mass.: G. & C. Merriam.
Hudson, Kenneth. 1977a: *The Dictionary of Diseased English.* London: Macmillan.
Dills, Lanie. 1977: *The C.B. Slanguage Dictionary.* New York: Robert M. Silver, Louis J. Martin & Assocs.
Brandford, Jean. 1978: *A Dictionary of South African English.* Cape Town: OUP.
Zettler, Howard. 1978: *-Ologies and Isms: A Thematic Dictionary.* Detroit: Gale Research Co.
Ehrlich, E., Flexner, S. B., Carruth, G. and Hawkins, J. M. 1980: *The Oxford American Dictionary.* Oxford and New York: OUP.
Rawson, Hugh. 1981: *A Dictionary of Euphemisms and Other Doubletalk.* London and Sidney: Macdonald.

Scruton, Roger. 1982: *A Dictionary of Political Thought.* London: Pan/Macmillan.

Neaman, Judith S. and Silver, Carole G. 1983: *A Dictionary of Euphemisms.* London: Hamish Hamilton.

Green, Jonathon. 1984: *Newspeak: A Dictionary of Jargon.* London: Routledge & Kegan Paul.

Kramarae, Cheris and Treichler, Paula A. 1985: *A Feminist Dictionary.* Boston, London and Henley: Pandora Press.

2 *Other Works*

Acton, Lord. 1973: *Lectures in Modern History.* London: Fontana/Collins. [1895]

Alston, R. C. 1965–: *A Bibliography of the English Language from the Invention of Printing to the year 1800.* Printed for the author by E. J. Arnold, Leeds.

Bacon, Francis. 1905: *The Philosophical Works of Francis Bacon.* Ed. J. M. Robertson. London: Routledge.

Bagley, J. J. and P. B. Rowley (eds). 1966: *A Documentary History of England: vol. I (1066–1540).* Harmondsworth: Penguin.

Baker, S. S. 1969: *The Permissible Lie: The Inside Truth About Advertising.* London: Peter Owen.

Barber, Charles L. 1957: *The Idea of Honour in the English Drama 1591–1700.* Göteborg: Elanders Boktryckeri Aktiebolag. (Diss. Gothenburg Univ. 1957.)

— 1964: *The Story of Language.* London: Pan. (Also issued as *The Flux of Language.*)

— 1976: *Early Modern English.* London: Deutsch.

Barfield, Owen. 1954: *History in English Words.* 2nd edn. London: Faber. [London: Methuen, 1926]

Barr, Ann and York, Peter. 1982: *The Official Sloane Ranger Handbook.* London: Ebury Press.

Baugh, Albert C. 1965: *A History of the English Language.* 2nd edn. London: Routledge.

Belson, W. 1967: *The Impact of Television.* London: Crosley Lockwood.

Bennett, H. S. 1952: *English Books and Readers, 1475 to 1557.* Cambridge: CUP.

Blake, N. F. (ed.). 1973: *Caxton's Own Prose.* London: Deutsch.

Bland, A. E., P. A. Brown and R. H. Tawney (eds). 1933: *English Economic History: Select Documents.* London: Bell.

Bloomfield, Morton W. and L. M. Newmark. 1963: *A Linguistic Introduction to the History of English.* New York: Knopf.

Boorstin, Daniel J. 1963: *The Image.* Harmondsworth: Penguin.

— 1973: *The Americans.* Harmondsworth: Penguin.

Bradley, Henry. 1964: *The Making of English.* London: Macmillan. [1904]

Bréal, Michel. 1964: *Semantics: Studies in the Science of Meaning.* Trans. Mrs. Henry Cust. Repr. New York: Dover. [London: Heinemann, 1900]

Brinklow, Henry. 1874: *[The] Complaynt of Roderyck Mors* [*c.* 1542] and *The Lamentacyon of a Christen Agaynst the Cytye of London* [1542]. Ed. J. M. Cooper. London: EETS.

Brook, G. L. 1973: *Varieties of English.* London: Macmillan.
Brown, J. A. C. 1969: *Techniques of Persuasion.* Harmondsworth: Penguin.
Buckle, Richard. 1980: *U and Non-U Revisited.* London: Debrett/Futura.
Burchfield, R. W. 1973: 'The treatment of controversial vocabulary in the *O.E.D.*'. *Transactions of the Philological Society*, pp. 1–28.
— 1976: 'A case of mistaken identity'. *Encounter*, June, pp. 57–64.
— 1978: 'The point of severance: English in 1776 and beyond'. *Encounter*, October, pp. 129–33.
— 1985: *The English Language.* Oxford and New York: OUP.
Burgess, Anthony. 1964: *Language Made Plain.* London: English UP.
Burke, Edmund. 1925: *Reflections on the Revolution in France.* Oxford: OUP. [1790]
Carter, Martin D. 1971: *An Introduction to Mass Communications.* London: Macmillan.
Chandos, John. 1971: *In God's Name.* London: Hutchinson.
Chase, Stuart. 1937: *The Tyranny of Words.* London: Methuen.
Chase, Stuart and Marian Tyler Chase. 1954: *The Power of Words.* New York: Harcourt, Brace.
Chaucer, Geoffrey. 1957: *The Works of Geoffrey Chaucer.* 2nd edn by F. N. Robinson. Boston: Houghton, Mifflin.
Chaytor, H. J. 1945: *From Script to Print.* Cambridge: Heffer.
Cockburn, C. 1967: *I, Claud.* Harmondsworth: Penguin.
Coleman, D. C., K. G. T. McDonnell and S. Pollard. 1957: *A Survey of English Economic History.* London: Blackie.
Cooper, Jilly. 1981: *Class.* New York: Knopf.
Cox, Harvey. 1965: *The Secular City*. London: Methuen.
Denholm-Young, N. 1948: 'The tournament in the thirtenth century', in *Essays in Medieval History Presented to F. M. Powicke.* Oxford: OUP.
Dillard, J. L. 1973: *Black English.* New York: Vintage.
Dobson, R. B. (ed.). 1970: *The Peasants' Revolt of 1381.* London: Macmillan.
Douglas, D. C. and G. W. Greenaway (eds). 1953: *English Historical Documents.* Vol. II. London: Eyre & Spottiswoode.
Easton, Loyd D. and Kurt H. Guddat. 1967: *Writings of the Young Marx on Philosophy and Society.* New York: Anchor.
Elliot, Gil. 1973: *The Twentieth Century Book of the Dead.* Harmondsworth: Penguin.
Elliott, Blanche B. 1962: *A History of English Advertising.* London: Batsford.
Empson, William. 1951: *The Structure of Complex Words.* London: Chatto & Windus.
— 1977: 'Compacted doctrines'. *New York Review of Books*, 27 October, pp. 21–2.
Estrich, Robert M. and Hans Sperber. 1952: *Three Keys to Language.* New York: Holt, Rinehart.
Fairlie, Henry. 1975: 'The language of politics', *Atlantic Monthly*, 29 January.
Flesch, R. 1962: *The Book of Unusual Quotations.* London: Cassell.

Fodor, J. A. and J. J. Katz. 1956: *The Structure of Language.* Englewood Cliffs: Prentice-Hall.
Foster, Brian. 1970: *The Changing English Language.* Harmondsworth: Penguin.
Foxe, John. 1732: *The Book of Martyrs.* London: John Hart.
Fraser, Lindley. 1957: *Propaganda.* Oxford: OUP.
Frayn, Michael, 1966: *The Tin Men.* London: Fontana/Collins.
Freeman, E. A. 1875–9: *The Norman Conquest.* Oxford: OUP.
Fussell, Paul. 1984: *Class.* London: Arrow Books.
Gallie, W. B. 1964: *Philosophy and the Historical Understanding.* London: Chatto & Windus.
Greenhough, J. B. and G. L. Kittredge. 1962: *Words and Their Ways in English Speech.* Repr. Boston: Beacon Press. [New York: Macmillan, 1900]
Greer, Germaine. 1971: *The Female Eunuch.* New York: McGraw-Hill.
Hayakawa, S. I. (ed.). 1962: *The Use and Misuse of Language.* Greenwich, Conn.: Fawcett Publications.
Hayakawa, S. I. et al. 1974: *Language in Thought and Action.* Repr. London: Allen & Unwin. [New York: Harcourt, Brace, 1941]
Higden, Ranulf. [1387]: *Polychronicon.* Trans. John of Trevisa. Rolls Series 1865–6.
Hillerbrand, H. J. 1964: *The Reformation in its Own Words.* London: SCM Press.
Hitler, Adolf. 1938: *My Struggle* [*Mein Kampf*]. Trans. unnamed. London: Hurst & Blackett.
Hobbes, Thomas. 1973: *The Leviathan.* London: Dent. [1651]
Hoch, Paul. 1974: *The Newspaper Game: The Political Sociology of the Press.* London: Calder & Boyars.
Howard, Philip. 1977: *New Words for Old.* London: Hamish Hamilton.
—— 1978: *Weasel Words.* London: Hamish Hamilton.
—— 1980: *Words Fail Me.* London: Hamish Hamilton.
—— 1983: *A Word in Your Ear.* London: Hamish Hamilton.
—— 1984: *The State of the Language: English Observed.* London: Hamish Hamilton.
Hudson, Kenneth. 1977b: *The Jargon of the Professions.* London: Macmillan.
Hughes, D. (ed.). 1918: *Illustrations of Chaucer's England.* London: Longmans.
Hyde, Edward, Earl of Clarendon. 1707: *The History of the Rebellion.* Oxford.
Hymes, Dell (ed.). 1964: *Language in Culture and Society.* New York: Harper & Row.
Jakobson, Roman. 1973: *Main Trends in the Science of Language.* London: Allen & Unwin.
Jennings, Gary. 1965: *Personalities of Language.* New York: Crowell.
Jespersen, Otto. 1962: *Growth and Structure of the English Language.* 9th edn. Oxford: Blackwell. [1905]
—— 1964: *Language: Its Nature, Development and Origin.* London: Allen & Unwin.
Johnson, Paul. 1977: *Enemies of Society.* London: Weidenfeld.
Jones, R. F. 1953: *The Triumph of the English Language.* Stanford: Stanford UP.
Joos, Martin. 1961: *The Five Clocks.* New York: Harcourt, Brace.

Kenyon, John S. 1948: 'Cultural levels and functional varieties of English'. *College English*, X, pp. 31–4.

Koss, Stephen. 1981: *The Rise and Fall of the Political Press in Britain.* Chapel Hill: University of North Carolina Press.

Koziol, Herbert. 1937: *Handbuch der englischen Wortbildungslehre.* Heidelberg: Carl Winter.

Labov, William. 1972: *Language in the Inner City.* Philadelphia: University of Pennsylvania Press.

Lasswell, H., N. Leites and associates. 1949: *Language of Politics.* New York: W. Stewart.

Le Bon, Gustave. 1913: *The Crowd.* Trans. unnamed. London: Fisher & Unwin.

Leech, G. N. 1966: *English in Advertising.* London: Longmans.

— 1974: *Semantics.* Harmondsworth: Penguin.

Leroy, M. 1967: *Main Trends in Modern Linguistics.* Berkeley and Los Angeles: Univ. of California Press.

Lewis, C. S. 1960: *Studies in Words.* Cambridge: CUP.

Low, Sidney. 1914: *The Governance of England.* London: Unwin.

Lynd, Robert and Helen Lynd. 1937: *Middletown in Transition: A Study of Cultural Conflicts.* New York: Harcourt, Brace.

Lyons, John. 1963: *Structural Semantics.* Oxford: Blackwell.

McGinniss, Joe. 1969: *The Selling of the President 1968.* New York: Pocket Books.

McKisack, May. 1959: *The Fourteenth Century.* Oxford: OUP.

McLuhan, Marshall. 1962: *The Gutenberg Galaxy: The Making of Typographic Man.* London: Routledge.

— 1964: *Understanding Media.* London: Sphere.

— and Q. Fiore. 1968: *War and Peace in the Global Village.* New York: Bantam.

Maitland, F. W. 1965: *The Domesday Book and Beyond.* London: Fontana/Collins.

Malory, Sir Thomas. 1947: *The Works of Sir Thomas Malory*, ed. Eugene Vinaver. Oxford: OUP. [1485]

Marcuse, Herbert. 1968: *One Dimensional Man.* London: Sphere.

Marx, Karl and Friedrich Engels. 1959: *Manifesto of the Communist Party.* Trans. Samuel Moore. *Marx: Basic Writings on Politics and Philosophy.* New York: Doubleday.

Maser, Werner. 1970: *Hitler's Mein Kampf: An Analysis.* London: Faber.

Matoré, Georges. 1953: *La Méthode en Lexicologie: Domaine Français.* Paris: Didier.

Mencken, H. L. 1919–48: *The American Language.* New York: Knopf.

Miller, Casey and Kate Swift. 1977: *Words and Women.* London: Gollancz.

— 1981: *The Handbook of Non-Sexist Writing.* London: The Women's Press.

Mott, Frank L. 1967: *American Journalism.* New York: Macmillan.

Mozley, J. F. 1940: *John Foxe and his Book.* London: SPCK.

Murray, K. M. Elisabeth. 1977: *Caught in the Web of Words.* London and New Haven: Yale UP.

Muscatine, Charles. 1972: *Poetry and Crisis in the Age of Chaucer.* Notre Dame: Univ. Notre Dame Press.

Neumann, R. and H. Koppel. 1962: *The Pictorial History of the Third Reich.* Harmondsworth: Penguin.
Nietzsche, F. 1924: *The Joyful Wisdom.* New York: Macmillan. [1882]
Nist, John. 1966: *A Structural History of English.* New York: St Martin's Press.
Ogilvy, David. 1966: *Confessions of an Advertising Man.* London: Mayflower-Dell.
— 1983: *Ogilvy on Advertising.* London and Sydney: Pan.
Ong, Walter. 1958: *Ramus, Method, and the Decay of Logic.* Cambridge, Mass.: Harvard UP.
Orwell, George. 1958: 'Politics and the English language' and 'The English Class System', in *Selected Writings of George Orwell*, ed. G. Bott. London: Heinemann.
— 1972: *Nineteen Eighty-Four.* Harmondsworth: Penguin. [1949]
Packard, Vance. 1960: *The Hidden Persuaders.* Harmondsworth: Penguin.
Palmer, F. R. 1976: *Semantics.* Cambridge: CUP.
Partridge, Eric. 1933: 'Offensive nationality'. In *Words, Words, Words!* London: Methuen, pp. 3–9.
— 1947: *Shakespeare's Bawdy.* London: Routledge.
— 1949: *Name into Word.* London: Secker & Warburg.
Pei, Mario. 1970: *Words in Sheep's Clothing.* London: Allen & Unwin.
Pirenne, Henri. 1939: *A History of Europe.* Trans. B. Miall. London: Allen & Unwin.
Plato. 1955: *The Republic.* Trans. H. D. P. Lee. Harmondsworth: Penguin.
Pool, I. de S., H. Lasswell, J. Lerner et al. 1970: *The Prestige Press: A Comparative Study of Political Symbols.* Cambridge, Mass.: M.I.T. Press.
Postan, M. M. 1972: *The Medieval Economy and Society.* Harmondsworth: Penguin.
Potter, Simeon. 1957: *Modern Linguistics.* London: Deutsch.
— 1960: *Language in the Modern World.* Harmondsworth: Penguin.
— 1963: *Our Language.* Harmondsworth: Penguin.
— 1975: *Changing English.* Rev. edn, London: Deutsch. [1969]
Pyles, Thomas. 1964: *The Origins and Development of the English Language.* New York: Harcourt, Brace.
Quirk, R., Greenbaum, S., Leech, G. and Svartvik, J. 1985: *A Comprehensive English Grammar.* London and New York: Longmans.
Richards, D. and Quick, A. 1961: *Britain 1714–1851.* London: Longmans.
Richards, I. A. 1943: *Basic English and Its Uses.* London: Kegan Paul, Trench, Trubner.
Robertson, D. W., Jr. 1963: *Preface to Chaucer.* Princeton: Princeton UP.
Robinson, Ian. 1973: *The Survival of English.* Cambridge: CUP.
Rose, Richard. 1964: *Politics in England.* Boston: Little, Brown.
Ross, Alan S. C. 1960: 'U and Non-U: an essay in sociological linguistics'. In *Noblesse Oblige*, ed. Nancy Mitford. Harmondsworth: Penguin, pp. 9–32. (Originally 'Linguistic class-indicators in present-day English', *Neuphilologische Mitteilungen*, 1954.)

Ross, Thomas W. 1972: *Chaucer's Bawdy.* New York: Dutton.

Safire, William. 1968: *The New Language of Politics.* New York: Random House.

Samuels, M. L. 1972: *Linguistic Evolution, with Special Reference to English.* Cambridge: CUP.

Santayana, George. 1900: *Interpretations of Poetry and Religion.* London: Black.

Saussure, Ferdinand de. 1966: *Course in General Linguistics.* Ed. Charles Bally and Albert Sechehaye, in collaboration with Albert Reidlinger. Trans. Wade Baskin. New York: McGraw-Hill. [1915]

Schlauch, M. 1960: *The Gift of Tongues.* London: Allen & Unwin.

Schreuder, H. 1929: *Pejorative Sense Development in English*, vol. I. Groningen: P. Noordhoff. (Dissertation Univ. of Amsterdam, 1929. There appears to be no record of subsequent volumes.)

Serjeantson, M. S. 1935: *A History of Foreign Words in English.* London: Routledge.

Serpieri, Alessandro. 1985: 'Reading the signs: towards a semiotics of Shakespearean drama', in *Alternative Shakespeares*, ed. John Drakakis. London: Methuen.

Seymour-Ure, Colin. 1974: *The Political Impact of the Mass Media.* London: Constable; Beverly Hills: Sage.

Shakespeare, William. n.d.: *The Poetical Works of Shakespeare.* Ed. W. J. Craig. Oxford: OUP.

Sington, D. and A. Weidenfeld. 1942: *The Goebbels Experiment.* London: John Murray.

Sledd, James and Wilma Ebbitt (eds). 1962: *Dictionaries and THAT Dictionary: A Casebook on the Aims of Lexicographers and the Targets of Reviewers.* Chicago: Scott, Foresman. (*THAT* refers to *Webster III.*)

Stamp, Gavin. 1986: 'The vanishing church of Bishop Jim', *Spectator*, 8 March.

Starnes, de Witt T. and Gertrude E. Noyes. 1946: *The English Dictionary from Cawdrey to Johnson, 1604–1755.* Chapel Hill: Univ. of North Carolina Press.

Stearn, E. G., ed. 1968: *McLuhan Hot and Cool.* Harmondsworth: Penguin.

Steinberg, S. H. 1966: *Five Hundred Years of Printing.* Harmondsworth: Penguin.

Steiner, George. 1961: *The Death of Tragedy.* London: Faber.

—— 1969: *Language and Silence: Essays 1958–1966.* Harmondsworth: Penguin.

—— 1975: *Extraterritorial: Papers on Literature and the Language Revolution.* Harmondsworth: Penguin.

Stern, Gustav. 1975: *Meaning and Change of Meaning, with Special Reference to the English Language.* Repr. Westport, Conn.: Greenwood Press. [Göteborg: Elanders Boktryckeri Aktiebolag, 1931]

Stoppard, Tom. 1972: *Jumpers.* London: Faber.

Strang, Barbara M. H. 1970: *A History of English.* London: Methuen.

Straumann, Heinrich. 1935: *Newspaper Headlines: A Study in Linguistic Method.* London: Methuen.

Swift, Jonathan. 1957: 'A Proposal for Correcting, Improving and Ascertaining the English Tongue'. Eds Herbert Davis and Louis Landa. Oxford: Blackwell. [1712]

Thucydides. 1972: *The Peloponnesian War.* Trans. Rex Warner. Harmondsworth: Penguin.

Tocqueville, Alexis de. 1863: *Democracy in America.* Trans. Henry Reeve. Rev. Francis Bowen. Cambridge, Mass.

Trevelyan, G. M. 1945: *English Social History.* London: Longmans.

Trevor-Roper, H. R. 1957: *Historical Essays.* London: Macmillan.

— 1967: *The European Witch-Craze of the 16th and 17th Centuries.* Harmondsworth: Penguin.

Trier, Jost. 1931: *Der deutsche Wortschatz im Sinnbezirk des Verstandes: Die Geschichte eines sprachlichen Feldes.* Heidelberg.

Tucker, Susie I. 1972: *Enthusiasm.* Cambridge: CUP.

Turner, E. S. 1965: *The Shocking History of Advertising.* Harmondsworth: Penguin.

Twaddell, W. F. 1973: 'Lexicography and people', in *Lexicography in English*, ed. R. McDavid and A. Duckert. New York.

Ullmann, Stephen. 1951: *Words and Their Use.* London: Muller.

— 1957: *The Principles of Semantics.* 2nd edn. Oxford: Blackwell.

— 1962: *Semantics: An Introduction to the Science of Meaning.* Oxford: Blackwell.

— 1964: *Language and Style.* Oxford: Blackwell.

Veblen, Thorstein B. 1970: *The Theory of the Leisure Class: An Economic Study of Institutions.* London: Unwin. [1899]

Vico, Giambattista. 1948: *The New Science.* Trans. Thomas G. Bergin and M. H. Fish. Ithaca: Cornell UP.

Waldron, R. A. 1967: *Sense and Sense Development.* London: Deutsch.

Weber, Max. 1962: *The Protestant Ethic and the Spirit of Capitalism.* Trans. T. Parsons. New York: Scribners.

White, Lynn, Jr. 1962: *Medieval Technology and Social Change.* Oxford: OUP.

Whitelock, Dorothy (ed.). 1955: *English Historical Documents,* vol. I. London: Eyre & Spottiswoode.

Whorf, Benjamin Lee. 1974: *Language, Thought and Reality: Selected Writings of Benjamin Lee Whorf.* Ed. John B. Carroll. Cambridge, Mass.: M.I.T. Press.

Williams, Francis. 1957: *Dangerous Estate.* London: Longmans.

Williams, Raymond. 1970: *Communications.* Harmondsworth: Penguin.

— 1971: *Culture and Society 1780–1950.* Harmondsworth: Penguin.

— 1975: *The Long Revolution.* Harmondsworth: Penguin.

— 1976: *Keywords.* London: Fontana/Croom Helm.

Wrenn, C. L. 1960: *The English Language.* London: Methuen.

Zandvoort, R. W. and assistants. 1957: *Wartime English.* Groningen: J. B. Walters.

Zeman, Z. A. B. 1966: *Nazi Propaganda.* London: OUP.

Zipf, G. K. 1945: 'The meaning-frequency relationship of words', *Journal of General Psychology*, xxxiii, pp. 251–66.

— 1949: *Human Behavior and the Principle of Least Effort: An Introduction to Human Ecology.* Cambridge, Mass.: Harvard UP.

Subject Index

Word Index